OFFICIAL TOURIST BOARD GUIDE

# Easy Access Britain

# Contents

## Further information



## Useful Indexes

**VisitBritain**

VisitBritain is the organisation created to market Britain to the rest of the world, and England to the British.

Formed by the merger of the British Tourist Authority and the English Tourism Council, its mission is to build the value of tourism by creating world-class destination brands and marketing campaigns.

It will also build partnerships with – and provide insights to – other organisations which have a stake in British and English tourism.

**Tourism for All UK**

TFA UK is the UK's central source of holiday and travel information for people with access requirements.

It is a registered charity which liaises with government and industry bodies.

# How to use this guide

**This is the only official guide for the traveller with access needs, and it's packed with information – from where to stay and how to get there to what to see and do. In fact, everything you need to know to enjoy Britain.**

Choose from a wide range of quality-assessed accommodation to suit all budgets and tastes: from hotels and B&Bs to self-catering properties and camping and caravan parks, all offering accommodation for people with limited mobility or visual and hearing difficulties (see page 10 for a detailed explanation). The access and quality ratings in each entry give a good indication of what you can expect.

For great days out, check out the regional sections where you will find places to visit and popular attractions. You'll also find many more ideas online at visitbritain.com. If you want advice before you travel, get in touch with a regional tourism organisation or a Tourist Information Centre in the area – contact details can be found at the end of each regional section.

National organisations, some specifically for travellers with access needs, offer a wealth of information – from general advice to equipment hire. Turn to the back of the guide for a list of useful contacts and information.

Use this guide to help you plan a short break or holiday – Britain is a great place to discover and it may be more accessible than you think.

Lulworth Cove, Dorset

Accommodation

# Finding accommodation is easy...

## 1. REGIONAL SECTIONS

The guide is divided into regions (see page 3) and accommodation is listed alphabetically by place name within each region.

## 2. COLOUR MAPS

Use the colour maps, starting on page 22, to pinpoint the location of all accommodation featured in the regional sections.

Then refer to the place index at the back of the guide to find the page number.

## 3. INDEXES

The Quick Reference index will help you find the right accommodation if you have a particular requirement, such as a level entry shower, an adapted kitchen, or accommodation with a specific accessible rating.

The place index at the back makes it easy to find accommodation in a particular location – and if you know the name of the establishment, use the property index.

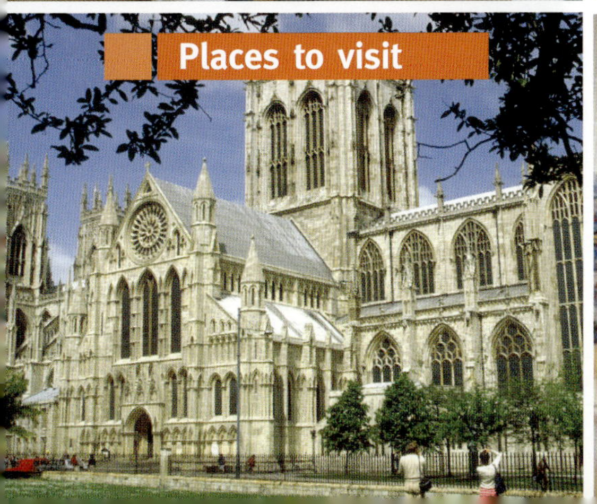


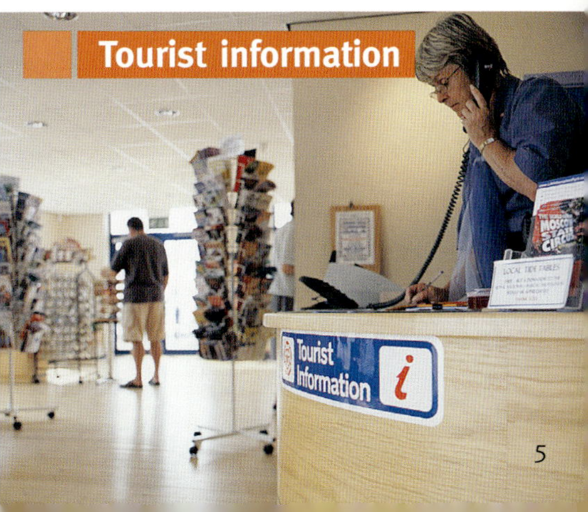

# Accommodation entries explained

Each entry contains detailed information to help you decide if it is right for you. This has been provided by proprietors and our aim is to ensure that it is as objective and factual as possible.

1 Listing under town or village with map reference

2 Quality rating plus Gold and Silver Awards where applicable

3 Prices
**Hotels** – Per room for bed and breakfast (B&B) and per person for half board (HB)
**Guest accommodation** – Per room for bed and breakfast (B&B) and per person for evening meal
**Self-catering** – Per unit per week for low and high season
**Camping and caravan parks** – Per pitch per night for touring pitches; per unit per week for caravan holiday homes

4 National Accessible Scheme rating

5 Establishment name and booking details

6 Indicates when the establishment is open

7 Travel directions

8 Special promotions or facilities

9 Payment accepted

10 At-a-glance facility symbols (see key to symbols overleaf)

1 2 3 4 5

**HUNSTANTON,** Norfolk Map ref 3B1 **HOTEL**

★★

B&B per room per night
**s £45.00–£59.00**
**d £70.00–£99.00**
HB per person per night
**£55.00–£75.00**

## Caley Hall Hotel

Old Hunstanton Road, Old Hunstanton, Hunstanton PE36 6HH
**t** (01485) 533486 **f** (01485) 533348 **e** mail@caleyhallhotel.co.uk
**w** caleyhallhotel.co.uk

General

Rooms

Payment Credit/debit cards, cash/cheques

*2 rooms feature specially adapted bathrooms with level-access shower. The hotel has no steps.*

Caley Hall Hotel and Restaurant is set around a manor-house dating back to 1648. More recently, the old farm outbuildings have been converted to provide the spacious en suite bedrooms, restaurant and bar. Most of the rooms are on the ground floor, and some feature a four-poster bed or whirlpool bath.

**open** All year except Christmas and New Year
**bedrooms** 15 double, 15 twin, 4 single, 5 family, 1 suite
**bathrooms** All en suite

*In Old Hunstanton, on the left-hand side of the A149, just before the turning to the golf course.*

Sample detailed entry

10 9 8 7 6

**A key to symbols can be found overleaf.**

# Key to symbols

Information about many of the accommodation services and facilities is given in the form of symbols.

## Access

- Trained staff
- Staff available to assist by arrangement
- abc Large print information
- Braille information
- Induction loop system at reception
- Facilities for service dogs
- Hoist available

## Leisure

- Clubhouse with bar
- Regular evening entertainment
- Games room
- Outdoor play area
- Swimming pool – indoor
- Swimming pool – outdoor
- Sauna
- Gym
- Tennis court(s)

### Prices

For information on prices see pages 408-410.

### National Accessible Scheme

For information on the National Accessible Scheme see overleaf.

## Hotels and Guest Accommodation

### General

- Children welcome (a number following gives minimum age)
- Designated parking
- Ramped entrance
- Smoking rooms available
- Licensed bar
- Evening meal by arrangement*
- Special diets by arrangement
- Lift
- Garden/patio

### Rooms

- Bedroom(s) on ground floor
- Four-poster bed(s)
- Text phone/inductive coupler
- Typetalk available
- TV listening device
- TV with subtitles
- Tea/coffee facilities in all bedrooms
- Hairdryer in all bedrooms
- Level-entry shower
- Seating in shower
- Toilet seat raiser

* Guest accommodation only

## Self Catering Accommodation

### General

- Children welcome (a number following gives minimum age)
- Cots
- Highchairs
- Parking next to unit
- Smoking units available
- Laundry facilities
- Weekend/midweek bookings

### Unit

- Ramped entrance
- Bedroom(s) on ground floor
- TV listening device
- TV with subtitles
- Text phone/inductive coupler
- Adapted kitchen
- Embossed kitchen equipment
- Microwave
- Dishwasher
- Hairdryer
- Washing machine in all units
- Level-entry shower
- Seating in shower
- Toilet seat raiser
- Linen provided
- Linen available for hire
- Towels provided
- Daily servicing of unit
- Garden/patio

## Camping, Caravan and Holiday Parks

### General

- Overnight holding area
- Motor home pitches reserved for day trips off-site
- Electrical hook-up points for caravans and tents
- Calor Gas/Camping Gaz purchase/exchange service
- Chemical toilet disposal point
- Motor home waste disposal point
- Showers
- Public telephone
- Laundry facilities
- Food shop on site
- Restaurant on site
- Prior booking recommended in summer

### Pitches

- Caravans (number of pitches and rates)
- Motor caravans (number of pitches and rates)
- Tents (number of pitches and rates)
- Caravan holiday homes (number of pitches and rates)
- Log cabins/lodges (number of units and rates)
- Chalets/villas (number of units and rates)

**Note:** web addresses are shown without the prefix www.

# National Accessible Scheme

## England

Accommodation is assessed under VisitBritain's National Accessible Scheme, which includes standards useful for hearing and visually impaired guests in addition to standards useful for guests with mobility impairment.

Accommodation taking part in this scheme will display one or more of the mobility, visual or hearing symbols shown opposite.

When you see one of the symbols, you can be sure that the accommodation and core facilities have been thoroughly assessed against demanding criteria. If you have additional needs or special requirements we strongly recommend that you make sure these can be met by your chosen establishment before you confirm your booking.

## London

This Guide lists hotels in London that have not been assessed under VisitBritain's National Accessible Scheme. These establishments do, however, have bedrooms suitable for wheelchair users and have been audited on behalf of the London Development Agency by Direct Enquiries. For more information go to directenquiries.com/LDAhotels.

## Scotland

All kinds of accommodation are assessed by VisitScotland Quality Advisors, based on criteria drawn up with the co-operation of organisations which deal with wheelchair users. This is part of the VisitScotland grading schemes. Criteria can be found on visitscotland.com/accommodation/accessiblescotland. Accommodation accessibility is checked every three years. Entries show one of three symbols.

**Category 1**
Accessible to a wheelchair user travelling independently.

**Category 2**
Accessible to a wheelchair user travelling with assistance.

**Category 3**
Accessible to a wheelchair user able to walk a few paces and up a maximum of three steps.

## Wales

Owners of all types of accommodation in Wales should have a full Access Statement available to visitors.

## Mobility Impairment Symbols in England

Typically suitable for a person with sufficient mobility to climb a flight of steps but who would benefit from fixtures and fittings to aid balance.

Typically suitable for a person with restricted walking ability and for those who may need to use a wheelchair some of the time and can negotiate a maximum of three steps.

Typically suitable for a person who depends on the use of a wheelchair and transfers unaided to and from the wheelchair in a seated position. This person may be an independent traveller.

Typically suitable for a person who depends on the use of a wheelchair and needs assistance when transferring to and from the wheelchair in a seated position.

Access Exceptional is awarded to establishments that meet the requirements of independent wheelchair users or assisted wheelchair users shown above and also fulfil more demanding requirements with reference to the British Standards BS8300:2001.

## Visual Impairment Symbols in England

Typically provides key additional services and facilities to meet the needs of visually impaired guests.

Typically provides a higher level of additional services and facilities to meet the needs of visually impaired guests.

## Hearing Impairment Symbols in England

Typically provides key additional services and facilities to meet the needs of guests with hearing impairment.

Typically provides a higher level of additional services and facilities to meet the needs of guests with hearing impairment.

## Feedback

For details of how to contact VisitBritain, Visit London, VisitScotland or Visit Wales about the accessibility of a property, please see page 407.

The criteria VisitBritain and national/regional tourism organisations have adopted do not necessarily conform to British Standards or to Building Regulations. They reflect what the organisations understand to be acceptable to meet the practical needs of guests with special mobility or sensory needs and encourage the industry to increase access to all.

# Ratings and awards at a glance

**Reliable, rigorous, easy to use – look out for the following ratings and awards to help you choose with confidence.**

## Star ratings

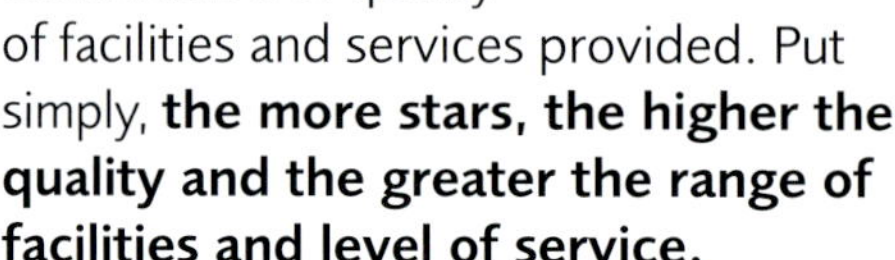

Establishments are awarded a rating of one to five stars based on a combination of quality of facilities and services provided. Put simply, **the more stars, the higher the quality and the greater the range of facilities and level of service.**

The process to arrive at a star rating is very thorough. National tourist board professional assessors visit establishments annually and work to strict criteria to check the available facilities and service. A quality score is awarded for every aspect of the experience.

For **hotels** and **bed and breakfast** accommodation this includes the comfort of the bed, the quality of the breakfast and dinner and, most importantly, the cleanliness. For **self-catering** properties the assessors also take into consideration the layout and design of the accommodation, the ease of use of all appliances, the range and quality of the kitchen equipment, and the variety and presentation of the visitor information provided. **Camping and caravan park** assessments are based on the quality, cleanliness, maintenance and conditions of the facilities provided. They also score the warmth of welcome and the level of care that each establishment offers its guests.

Most national assessing bodies (VisitBritain, VisitScotland, Visit Wales and the AA) operate to a common set of standards, giving a clear guide on exactly what to expect at each level (see page 398).

### Ratings made easy

★
Simple, practical, no frills

★★
Well presented and well run

★★★
Good level of quality and comfort

★★★★
Excellent standard throughout

★★★★★
Exceptional, with a degree of luxury

For full details of the quality assessment schemes, go online at **enjoyengland.com/quality** and **visitscotland.com/quality-assurance**

## Gold and Silver Awards

If you want a superior level of quality guaranteed seek out accommodation in England with a Gold or Silver Award. They are only given to hotels and bed and breakfast properties offering the highest levels of quality within their star rating.

## National Accessible Scheme

Establishments with a National Accessible Scheme rating have been thoroughly assessed to set criteria and provide access to facilities and services for guests with visual, hearing or mobility impairment (see page 10).

## Welcome schemes

VisitBritain runs four special Welcome schemes in England: Cyclists Welcome, Walkers Welcome, Welcome Pets! and Families Welcome. Scheme participants actively encourage these types of visitors and make special provision to ensure a welcoming, comfortable stay.

VisitScotland operates a wide range of Welcome schemes in Scotland.

## Caravan Holiday Home Award Scheme

VisitBritain and VisitScotland run award schemes for individual holiday caravan homes on highly graded caravan parks. In addition to complying with standards for Holiday Parks, these exceptional caravans must have a shower or bath, toilet, mains electricity and water heating (at no extra charge) and a fridge (many also have a colour TV).

Award-winning parks listed in this guide show 'Rose Award' in their entry.

## Visitor Attraction Quality Assurance

Attractions participating in this scheme are visited every year by a professional assessor and must achieve high standards in all aspects of the visitor experience. The assessment focuses on the nature of the welcome, hospitality, services and presentation as well as the standards of toilets, shop and café where provided.

# Classifications explained

**The following classifications will help you decide which type of accommodation is right for you**, whether you are seeking a non-stop, city-buzz holiday; a quiet weekend away; a home-from-home break or camping fun for all the family in England, Scotland and Wales.

## Hotels

| | |
|---|---|
| **Hotel** | A minimum of six bedrooms, but more likely to have over 20. |
| **Small Hotel** | A maximum of 20 bedrooms and likely to be more personally run. |
| **Country House Hotel** | Set in ample grounds or gardens, in a rural or semi-rural location, with the emphasis on peace and quiet. |
| **Town House Hotel** | In a city or town-centre location, high quality with a distinctive and individual style. Maximum of 50 bedrooms, with a high ratio of staff to guests. Possibly no dinner served, but room service available. Might not have a dining room, so breakfast may be served in the bedrooms. |
| **Metro Hotel** | A city or town-centre hotel offering full hotel services, but no dinner. Located within easy walking distance of a range of places to eat. Can be of any size. |
| **Budget Hotel** | Part of a large branded hotel group, offering limited services. A Budget Hotel is not awarded a star rating. |

# Guest Accommodation

| | |
|---|---|
| **Guest Accommodation** | Encompassing a wide range of establishments from one-room bed and breakfasts to larger properties, which may offer dinner and hold an alcohol licence. |
| **Bed and Breakfast** | Accommodating no more than six people, the owners of these establishments welcome you into their home as a special guest. |
| **Guest House** | Generally comprising more than three rooms. Dinner is unlikely to be available (if it is, it will need to be booked in advance). May possibly be licensed. |
| **Farmhouse** | Bed and breakfast, and sometimes dinner, but always on a farm. |
| **Restaurant with Rooms** | A licensed restaurant is the main business but there will be a small number of bedrooms, with all the facilities you would expect, and breakfast the following morning. |
| **Inn** | Pubs with rooms, and many with restaurants as well. |

# Self Catering

| | |
|---|---|
| **Self Catering** | Choose from cosy country cottages, smart town-centre apartments, seaside villas, grand country houses for large family gatherings, and even quirky conversions of windmills, railway carriages and lighthouses. Most take bookings by the week, generally from a Friday or Saturday, but short breaks are increasingly offered, particularly outside the main season. |
| **Serviced Apartments** | City-centre serviced apartments are an excellent alternative to hotel accommodation, offering hotel services such as daily cleaning, concierge and business centre services, but with a kitchen and lounge area that allow you to eat in and relax when you choose. A telephone and Internet access tend to be standard. Prices are generally based on the property, so they often represent excellent value for money for families and larger groups. Serviced apartments tend to accept bookings for any length of period, and many are operated by agencies whose in-depth knowledge and choice of properties makes searching easier at busy times. |
| **Approved Caravan Holiday Homes** | Approved caravan holiday homes are let as individual self-catering units and can be located on farms or holiday parks. All the facilities, including a bathroom and toilet, are contained within the caravan and all main services are provided. There are no star ratings, but all caravans are assessed annually to minimum standards. |
| **Chalets** | Chalets are permanent buildings used as seasonal holiday accommodation, made from timber, part brick or UPVC. They can be single or two storey and are usually situated on a park where common facilities such as refuse disposal are shared. |

# Camping and Caravan Parks

| | |
|---|---|
| **Camping Park** | These sites only have pitches available for tents. |
| **Touring Park** | If you are planning to travel with your own caravan, motor home or tent, then look for a Touring Park. |
| **Holiday Park** | If you want to hire a caravan holiday home for a short break or longer holiday, or are looking to buy your own holiday home, a Holiday Park is the right choice. They range from small, rural sites to larger parks with all the added extras, such as a pool. |

Many parks will offer a combination of these categories.

**Holiday Village***

Holiday villages usually comprise a variety of types of accommodation, with the majority in custom-built rooms, chalets for example. The option to book on a bed and breakfast, or dinner, bed and breakfast basis is normally available. A range of facilities, entertainment and activities are also provided which may, or may not, be included in the tariff.

Holiday villages must meet a minimum entry requirement for both the provision and quality of facilities and services, including fixtures, fittings, furnishings, decor and any other extra facilities. Progressively higher levels of quality and customer care are provided at each star level.

**Forest Holiday Village***

A holiday village which is situated in a forest setting with conservation and sustainable tourism being a key feature. It will usually comprise of a variety of accommodation, often purpose built; and with a range of entertainment, activities and facilities available on site free of charge or at extra cost.

*England only

# Hostel Accommodation

| | |
|---|---|
| **Hostel** | Safe, budget-priced, short-term accommodation for individuals and groups. Visitors usually share a dormitory as well as lounge, bathroom and kitchen facilities, though higher star-rated hostels sometimes have en suite bedrooms and may offer meal services. |
| **Group Hostel** | Hostels that predominantly accept group bookings. |
| **Activity Accommodation** | Caters predominantly for groups and provides fully certified or licensed activities for visitors. May be self catering or fully serviced. |
| **Backpacker** | Similar to hostels, but tend to cater for younger, longer-term independent travellers rather than groups and families. Usually operate on a less rigid basis and offer 24-hour access to guests. |

All of the above are awarded star ratings.

| | |
|---|---|
| **Bunkhouse** | Bunkhouses offer a similar style of accommodation to hostels but usually with more limited services and facilities, often on a self-catering basis. Bunkhouses are not star rated but meet the same minimum requirements as hostels, where applicable. |
| **Camping Barn** | Camping Barns, often referred to as 'stone tents', provide very simple self-catering accommodation, and have the advantage of being roomy and dry. Camping Barns are not star rated and will be assessed as being fit for the purpose, meeting a specific minimum entry requirement. |

# Campus Accommodation

**Campus Accommodation** This includes educational establishments, such as universities and colleges with sleeping accommodation in halls of residence, or student village complexes available for individuals, families and groups.

Availability is mainly throughout the academic vacations (during the summer from June to September, Easter and Christmas), however, some universities provide accommodation all year. There is often a wide choice of recreational facilities, with most venues providing TV rooms, bars and restaurants, and a variety of sporting and special interest holidays.

Establishments meet a minimum requirement for both the provision of facilities and services, including fixtures, fittings, furnishings and decor. Progressively higher levels of quality and customer care are provided for each of the star ratings. Quite simply, the more stars, the higher the overall level of quality you can expect.

# Tourism for All UK

Finding suitable accommodation for holidays or to visit relatives is not always easy, especially if you have to seek out ground floor rooms, a step free entrance and all facilities on one level, or large print menus and colour contrast in the bathroom.

Proprietors can sometimes be unaware of accessible needs resulting in disappointment on arrival when you find numerous steps to encounter and you are unable to seat a wheelchair at the dining room table.

**For those needing accurate advice, help is at hand.**

## All-round service

Tourism for All UK (formerly known as Holiday Care) provides information that helps thousands of people arrange a successful holiday or trip every year. This includes equipment hire, respite care centres, accessible attractions, financial help, activity and children's holidays information as well as advice on accommodation.

Tourism for All is the UK's central source of holiday and travel information for people with access requirements.

## Finding accommodation

For help in finding suitable accommodation or to make a booking call the Tourism For All reservations line. You may also be able to take advantage of special offers at hotels throughout the UK and overseas. (Note, if you use this service all accommodation in the UK will be assessed by the relevant tourist board or Tourism for All. Quality ratings for overseas properties are usually based on self-reporting or member's recommendation.)

## Making friends

Consider joining the Tourism for All UK 'Friends of TFA' scheme. Members share information and experiences and receive a regular newsletter which highlights new accessible accommodation, attractions and places to go. Membership also gives special discounts on publications and accommodation.

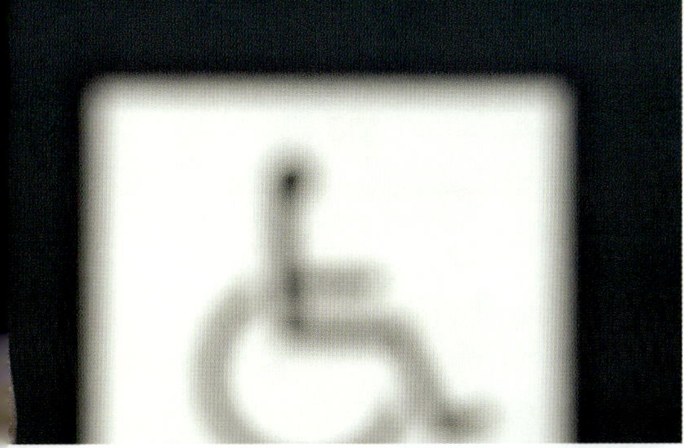

Above: Carrie-Ann Fleming, Tourism For All UK (front right) with members of the Board outside the call centre in Kendal

Tourism for All is the UK's central source of holiday and travel information for people with access requirements.

**information helpline**
0845 124 9971

**reservations** 0845 124 9973
(lines open 9-5 Mon-Fri)

**f** (01539) 735567

**e** info@tourismforall.org.uk

**w** tourismforall.org.uk

or write to
**Tourism for All UK,** c/o Vitalise, Shap Road Industrial Estate, Kendal LA9 6NZ

*TFA UK is a registered charity, No 279169 and Company Limited by Guarantee No 01466822*

Tourism for All UK (TFA) is a charity, formed in 1979. Working with the national tourist boards it has helped to develop the National Accessible Scheme run by VisitBritain, by which accommodation is assessed and rated. The organisation also works with government, speaks at tourism related conferences, promotes good practice and offers consultancy on all kinds of tourism-related access issues.

Improved accessibility throughout the tourism industry is actively encouraged by Tourism for All. Where good practise is established – such as in Chester, and through Cheshire for All, or by Brighton who recently undertook a destination audit, looking at the whole visitor experience from a disabled person's point of view – the charity seeks to celebrate and promote the achievement.

Membership of TFA by local government and industry bodies is an indicator of their commitment to observe their obligations under the Disability Discrimination Act. (Many of these are advertisers in this guide.) Premier Supporters who share the charity's aims include Accor Hotels, InterContinental Hotels, Premier Inns, Thistle Hotels, VisitBritain, VisitScotland, VisitWales, the South West Regional Development Agency, the London Development Agency, Tourism South East, East Midlands Tourism, the MS Society and Vitalise.

## Nominate a property

**Do you have a favourite property that you would like to see in the National Accessible Scheme?**
If so, please email info@tourismforall.org.uk or feedback via the contacts page at tourismforall.org.uk. Nominated properties taking an enhanced entry in the next edition of Easy Access Britain will be offered a free accessibility inspection.

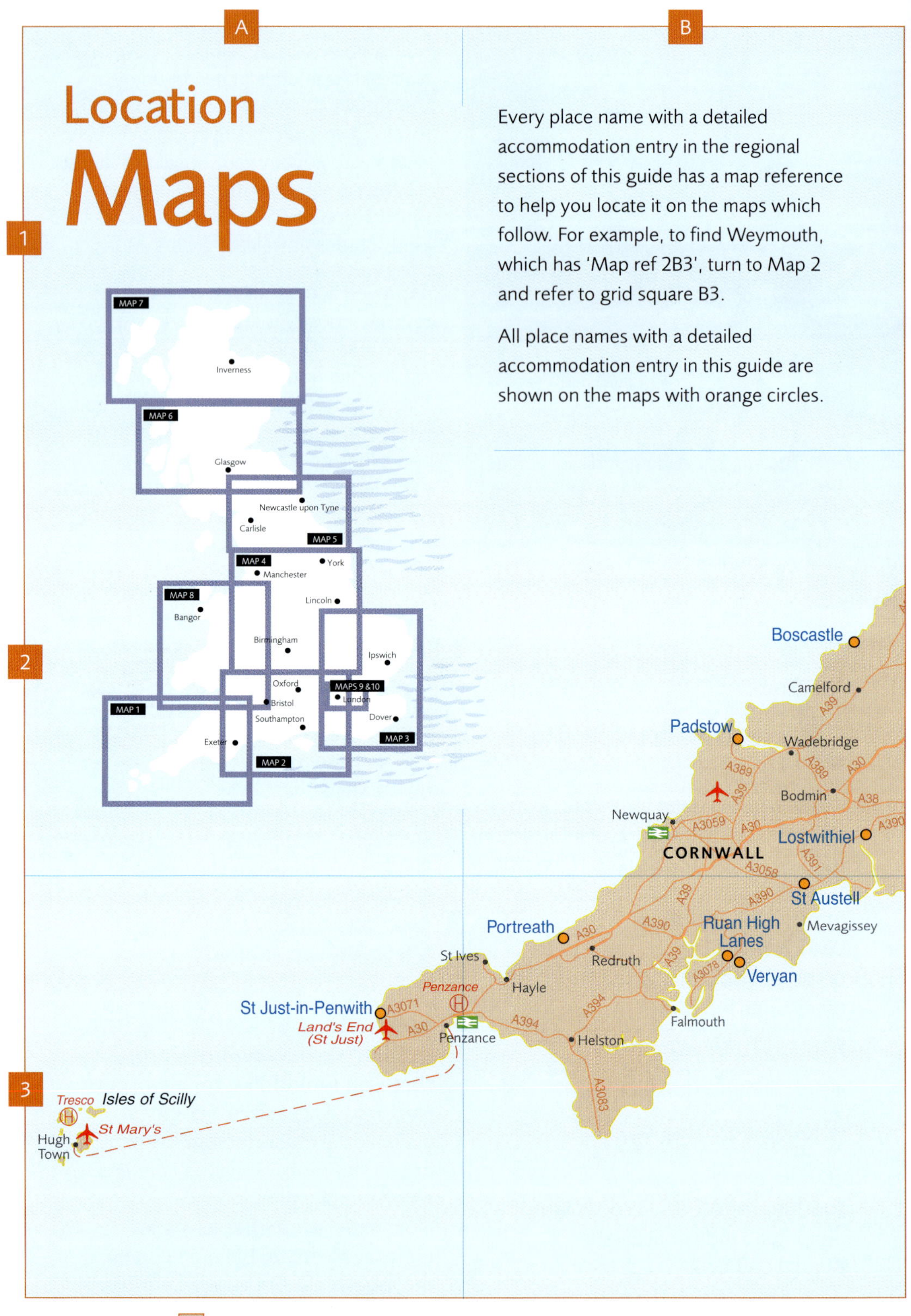


Every place name with a detailed accommodation entry in the regional sections of this guide has a map reference to help you locate it on the maps which follow. For example, to find Weymouth, which has 'Map ref 2B3', turn to Map 2 and refer to grid square B3.

All place names with a detailed accommodation entry in this guide are shown on the maps with orange circles.

Key to regions: South West England

Orange circles indicate a detailed accommodation entry in this guide

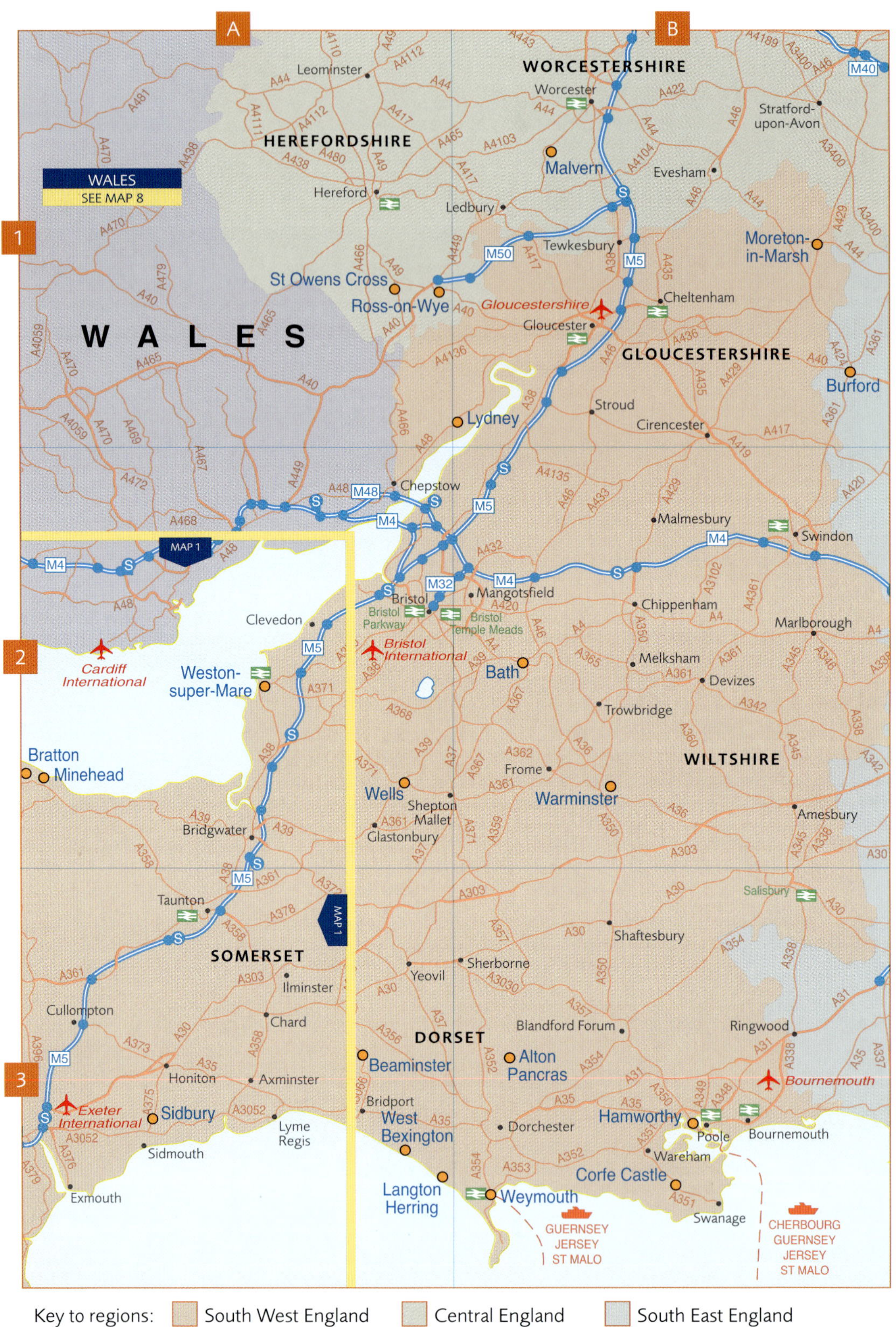


Key to regions: South West England Central England South East England

London

Orange circles indicate a detailed accommodation entry in this guide

Key to regions: Central England South East England London

3
4
25 Miles
40 Km
0
0
N
OSTEND
BOULOGNE
CALAIS
DUNKIRK
Channel Tunnel
ENGLISH CHANNEL
DIEPPE
MAP 2
ESSEX
KENT
GREATER LONDON
SURREY
WEST SUSSEX
EAST SUSSEX
SOUTH DOWNS
Clacton-on-Sea
Witham
Maldon
Chelmsford
Basildon
Southend-on-Sea
London Southend
Sheerness
Whitstable
Herne Bay
Margate
Ramsgate
Kent International
Deal
Dover
Folkestone
Hythe
Lydd
Canterbury
Ashford
Tenterden
Biddenden
Cranbrook
Hastings
Bexhill
Battle
Eastbourne
Chatham
Rochester
Gravesend
Tilbury
Maidstone
Tonbridge
Tunbridge Wells
Hailsham
Uckfield
Seaford
Newhaven
Lewes
Brighton
Hove
Shoreham-by-Sea
Shoreham (Brighton City)
Worthing
Littlehampton
Felpham
Bognor Regis
Haywards Heath
Wych Cross
East Grinstead
Crawley
Horsham
London Gatwick
Redhill
Reigate
Dorking
Guildford
Godalming
Haslemere
Woking
Epsom
Sutton
Croydon
London Biggin Hill
Sevenoaks
Dartford
Bexleyheath
London City
Romford
Brentwood
Harlow
Hertford
Welwyn Garden City
Enfield
London
Heliport
Richmond
Kingston-upon-Thames
Ealing
Barnet
St Albans
Hemel Hempstead
Watford
Uxbridge
Heathrow
Slough
Windsor
Staines
London Luton
M1
M3
M4
M11
M2
M20
M23
M25
M26
A1(M)

## Map 4

Key to regions: Northern England Central England

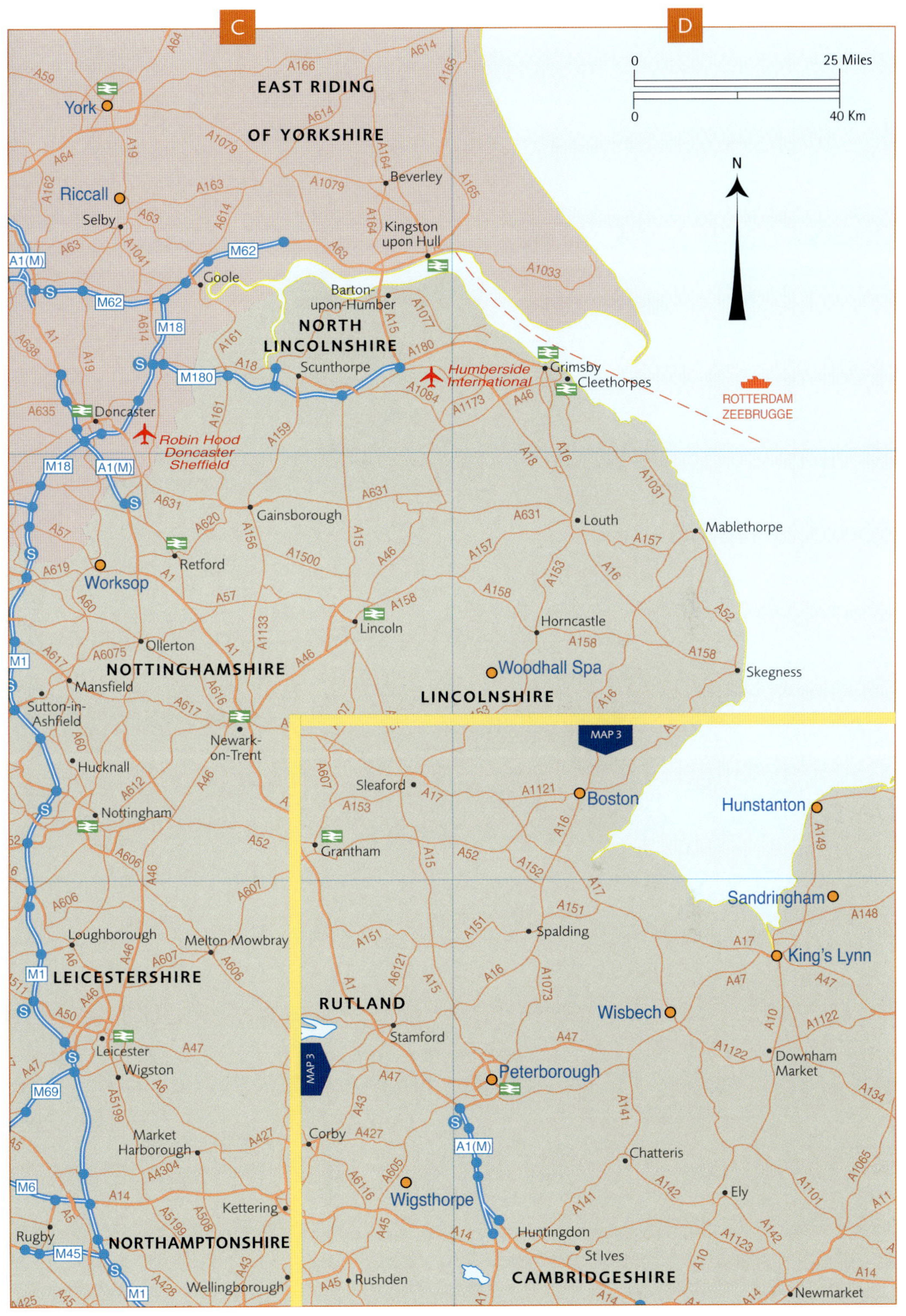


Orange circles indicate a detailed accommodation entry in this guide

# Map 5

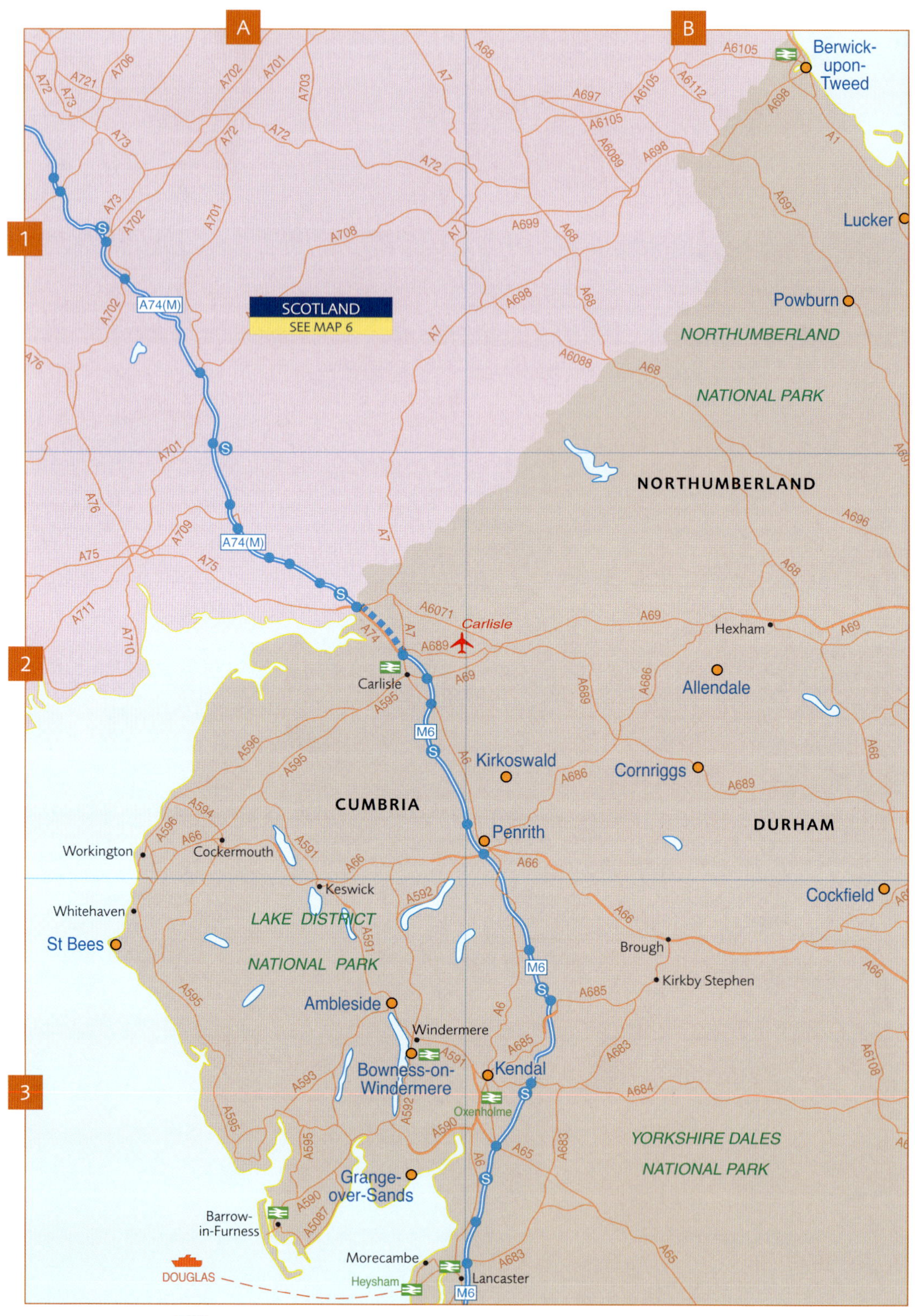


Key to regions: Northern England

Orange circles indicate a detailed accommodation entry in this guide

# Map 6

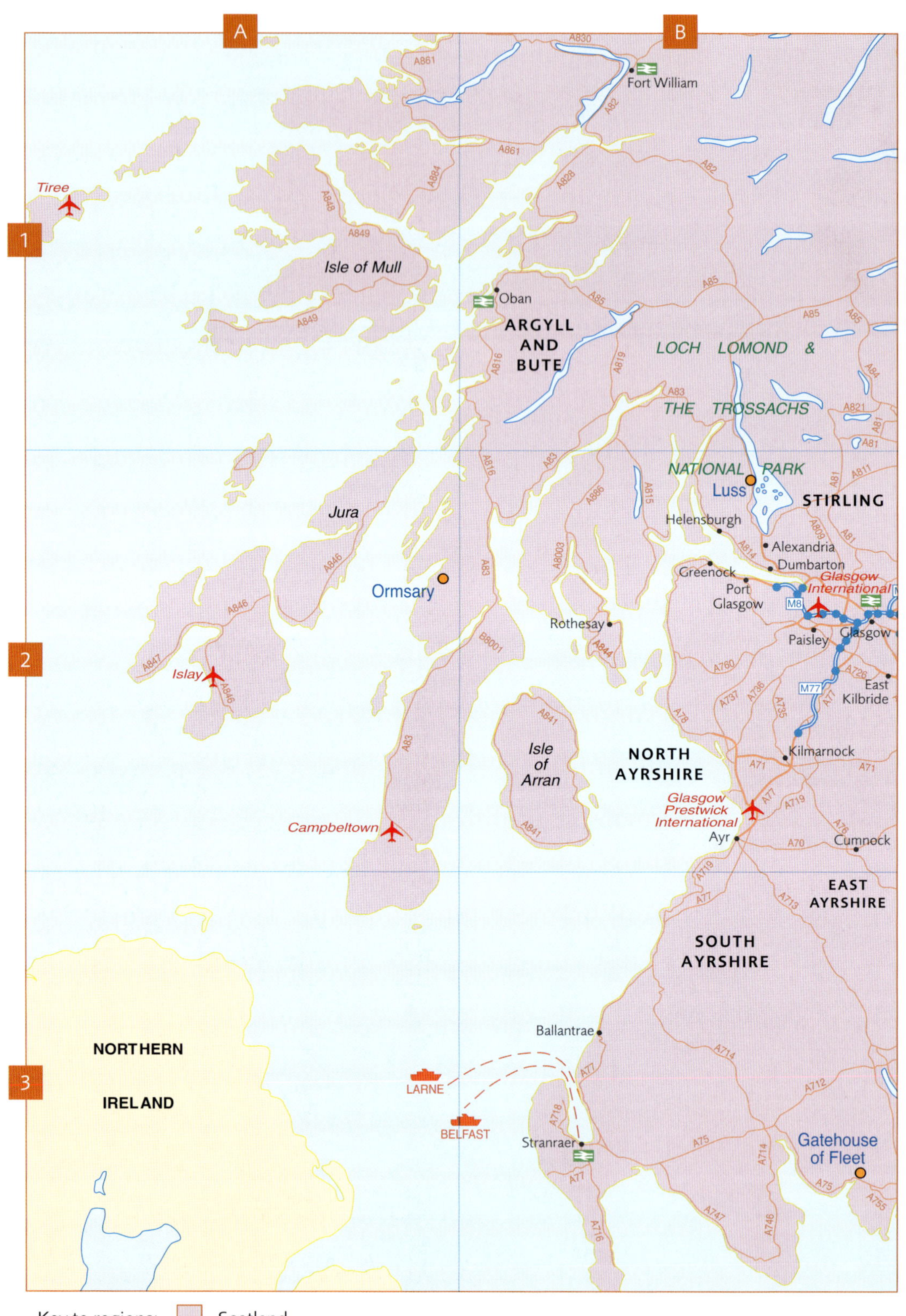

A
B
1
2
3
Fort William
Tiree
Isle of Mull
Oban
ARGYLL AND BUTE
LOCH LOMOND & THE TROSSACHS NATIONAL PARK
Luss
STIRLING
Jura
Helensburgh
Alexandria
Dumbarton
Greenock
Port Glasgow
Glasgow International
Ormsary
Rothesay
Paisley
Glasgow
East Kilbride
Islay
Isle of Arran
NORTH AYRSHIRE
Kilmarnock
Glasgow Prestwick International
Campbeltown
Ayr
Cumnock
EAST AYRSHIRE
SOUTH AYRSHIRE
Ballantrae
NORTHERN IRELAND
LARNE
BELFAST
Stranraer
Gatehouse of Fleet

Key to regions: Scotland

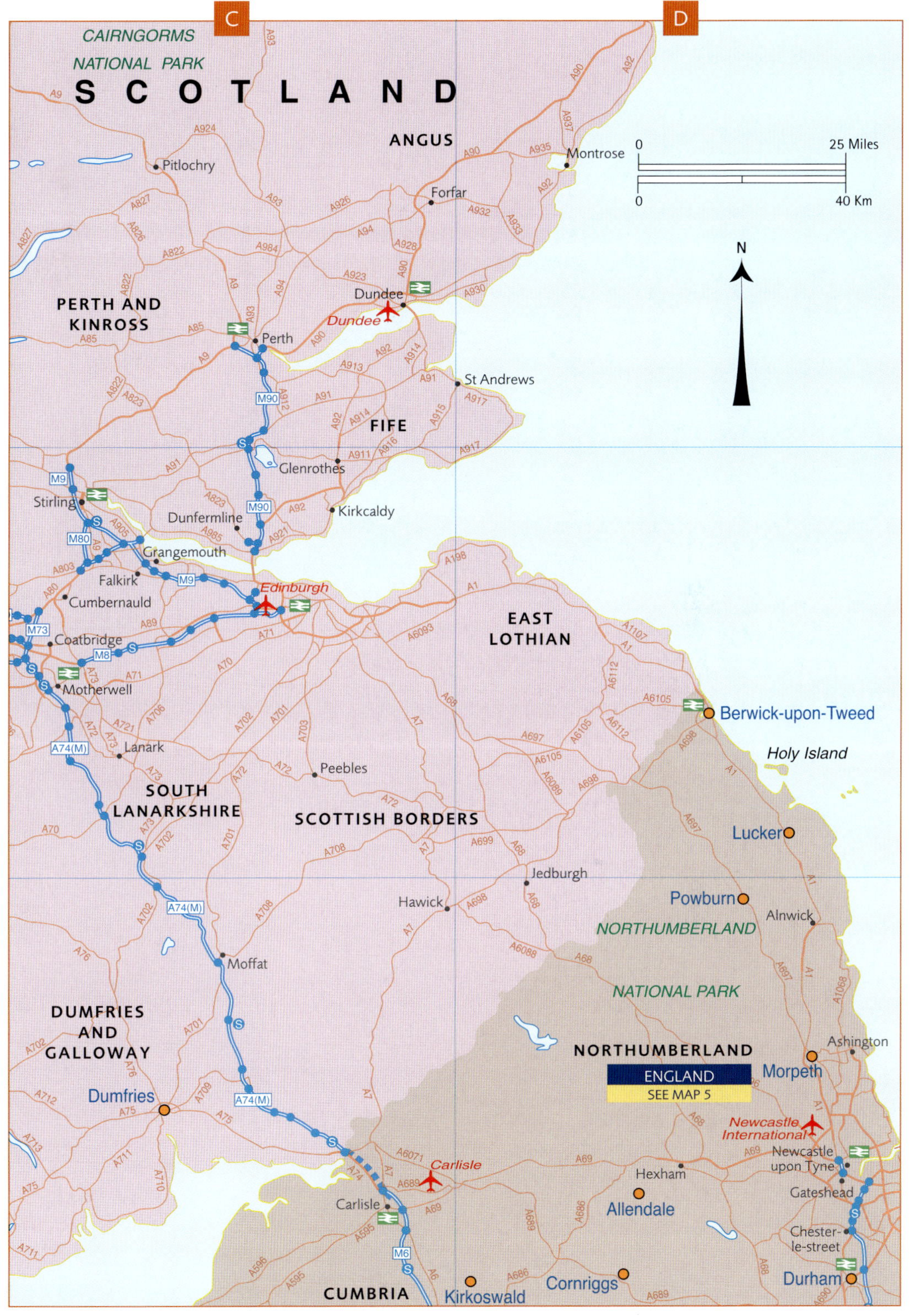


Orange circles indicate a detailed accommodation entry in this guide

# Map 7

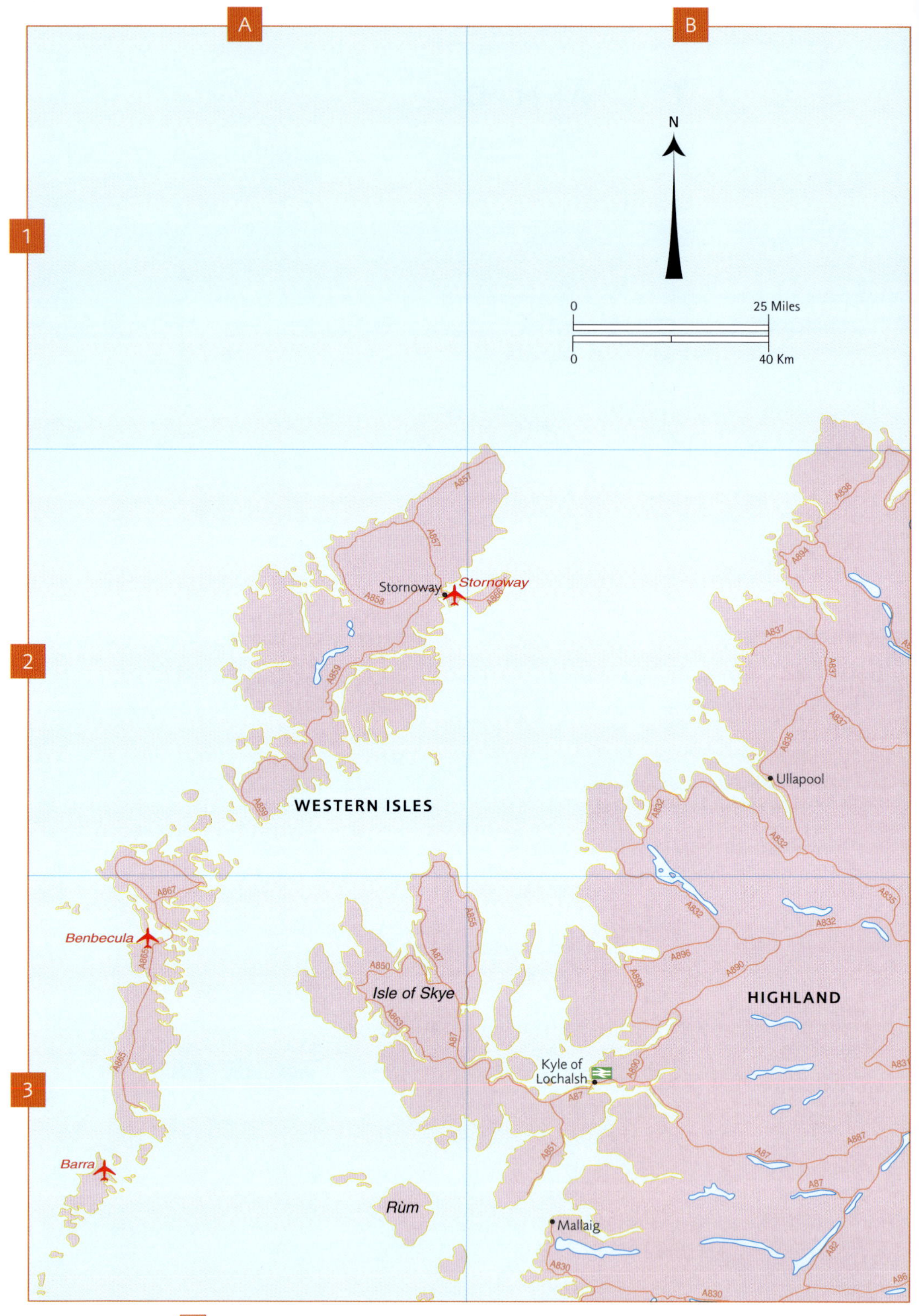


Key to regions: Scotland

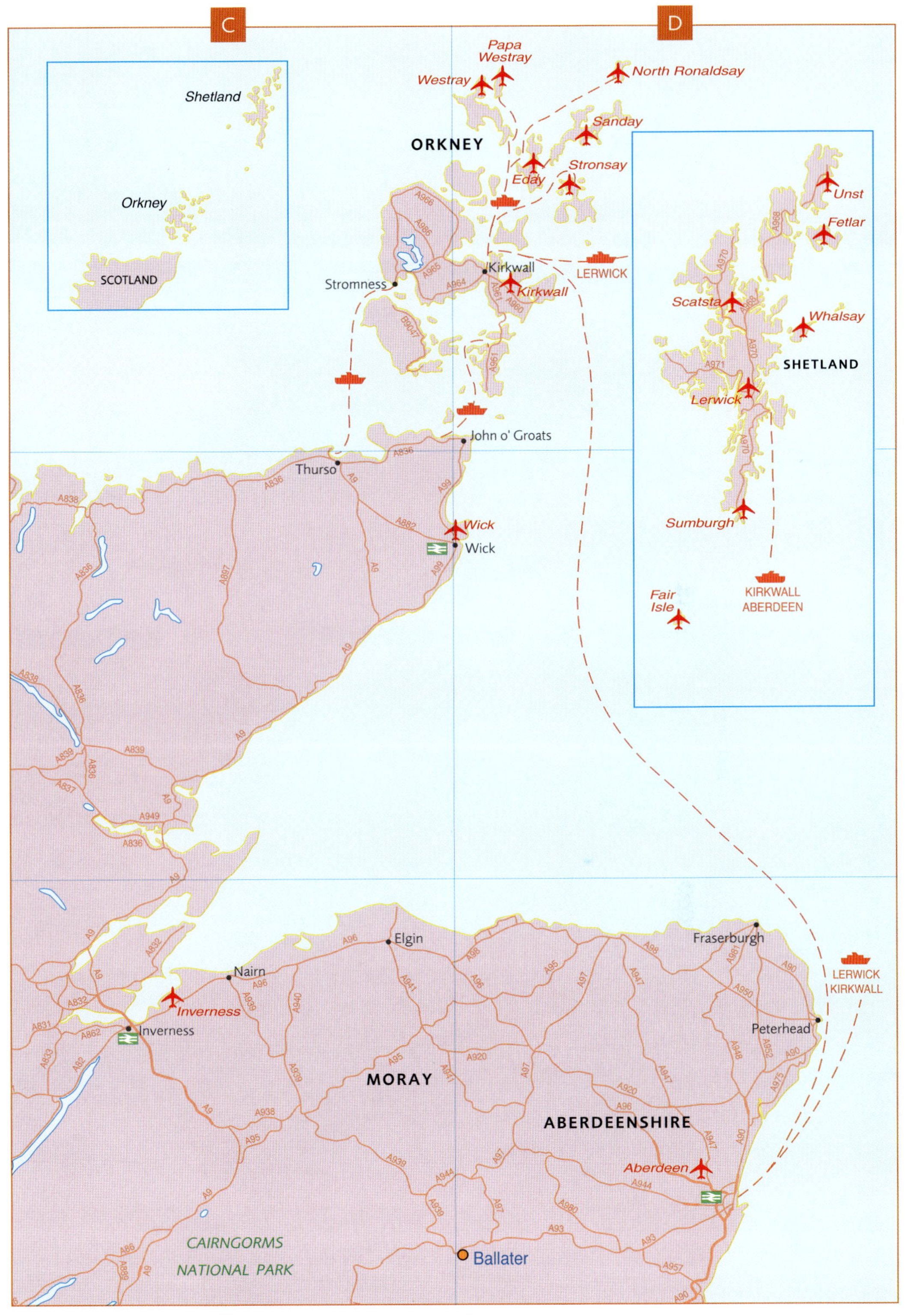


Orange circles indicate a detailed accommodation entry in this guide

Key to regions: Wales

 Orange circles indicate a detailed accommodation entry in this guide

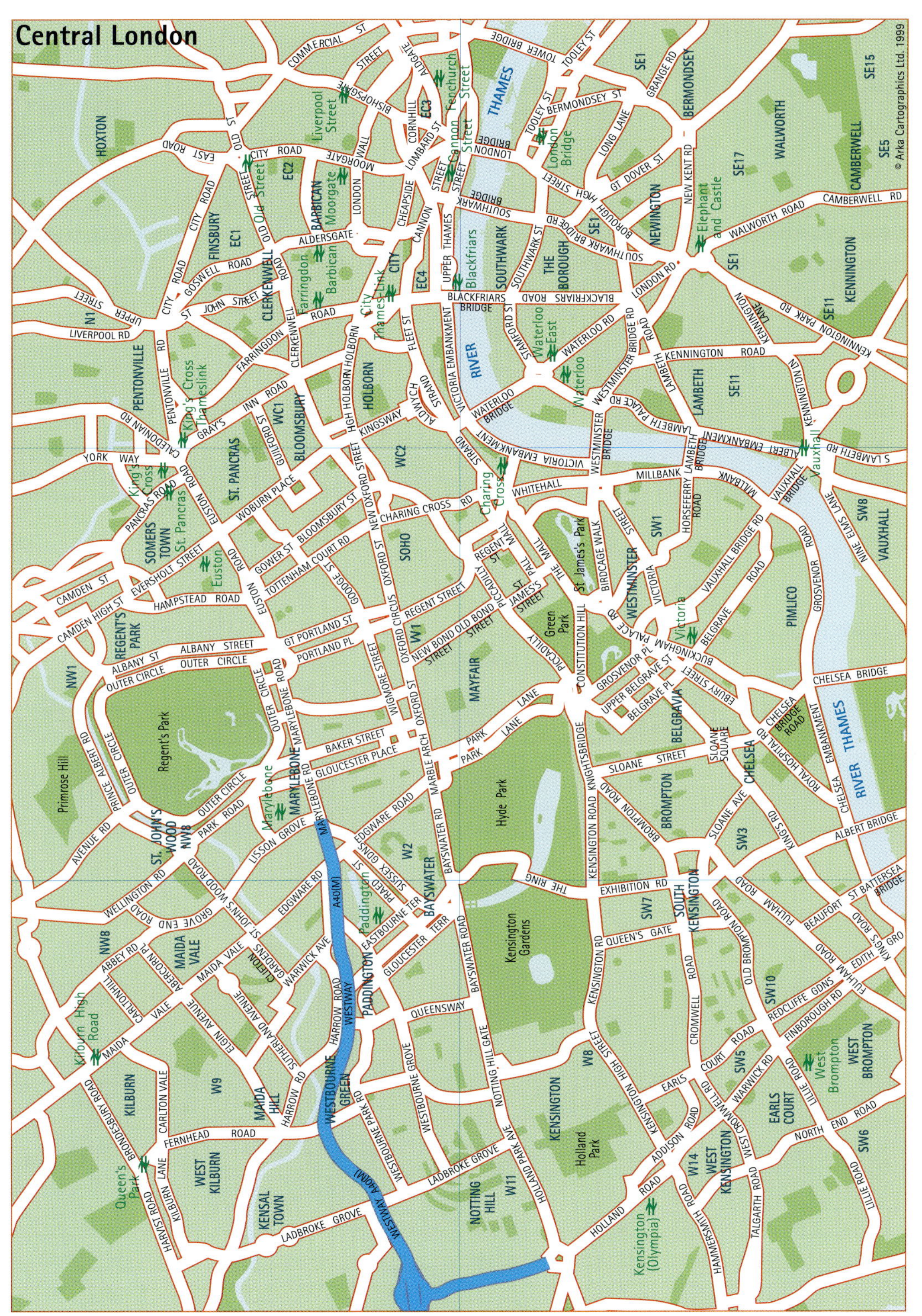
Central London
© Arka Cartographics Ltd. 1999
HOXTON
FINSBURY
EC1
EC2
EC3
EC4
CLERKENWELL
BARBICAN
CITY
PENTONVILLE
N1
ST. PANCRAS
SOMERS TOWN
BLOOMSBURY
WC1
WC2
HOLBORN
SOHO
W1
MAYFAIR
REGENT'S PARK
NW1
NW8
ST. JOHN'S WOOD
MARYLEBONE
W2
BAYSWATER
PADDINGTON
MAIDA VALE
MAIDA HILL
KILBURN
WEST KILBURN
W9
KENSAL TOWN
WESTBOURNE GREEN
NOTTING HILL
W11
KENSINGTON
W8
SOUTH KENSINGTON
SW7
BROMPTON
CHELSEA
SW3
SW10
SW5
EARLS COURT
WEST BROMPTON
SW6
W14
WEST KENSINGTON
BELGRAVIA
WESTMINSTER
SW1
PIMLICO
SW8
VAUXHALL
LAMBETH
SE11
KENNINGTON
SE1
SE17
SE5
SE15
WALWORTH
CAMBERWELL
NEWINGTON
THE BOROUGH
SOUTHWARK
BERMONDSEY
RIVER THAMES
Regent's Park
Primrose Hill
Hyde Park
Kensington Gardens
Green Park
St. James's Park
Holland Park
Liverpool Street
Fenchurch Street
Cannon Street
London Bridge
Moorgate
Barbican
Farringdon
City Thameslink
Blackfriars
Waterloo
Waterloo East
Charing Cross
Elephant and Castle
Vauxhall
Victoria
King's Cross
King's Cross Thameslink
St. Pancras
Euston
Marylebone
Paddington
Kilburn High Road
Queen's Park
Kensington (Olympia)
West Brompton
Old Street
TOWER BRIDGE
LONDON BRIDGE
SOUTHWARK BRIDGE
BLACKFRIARS BRIDGE
WATERLOO BRIDGE
WESTMINSTER BRIDGE
LAMBETH BRIDGE
VAUXHALL BRIDGE
CHELSEA BRIDGE
ALBERT BRIDGE
ST BATTERSEA BRIDGE
WESTWAY
A40(M)
WESTWAY A40(M)

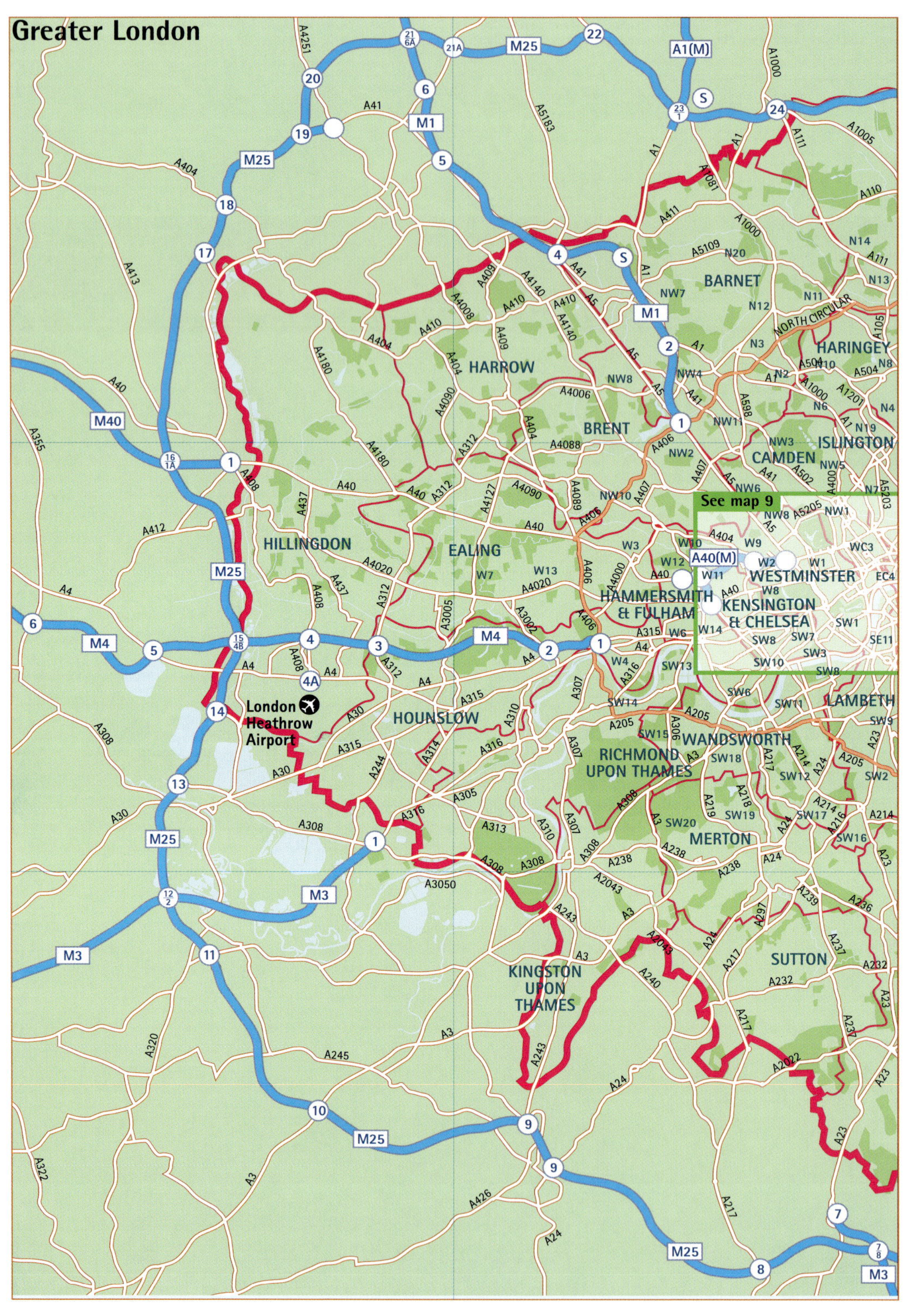
Greater London
See map 9
London Heathrow Airport
BARNET
HARINGEY
HARROW
BRENT
CAMDEN
ISLINGTON
HILLINGDON
EALING
WESTMINSTER
HAMMERSMITH & FULHAM
KENSINGTON & CHELSEA
HOUNSLOW
LAMBETH
WANDSWORTH
RICHMOND UPON THAMES
MERTON
SUTTON
KINGSTON UPON THAMES
NORTH CIRCULAR
M25
M1
M40
M4
M3
A1(M)
A40(M)

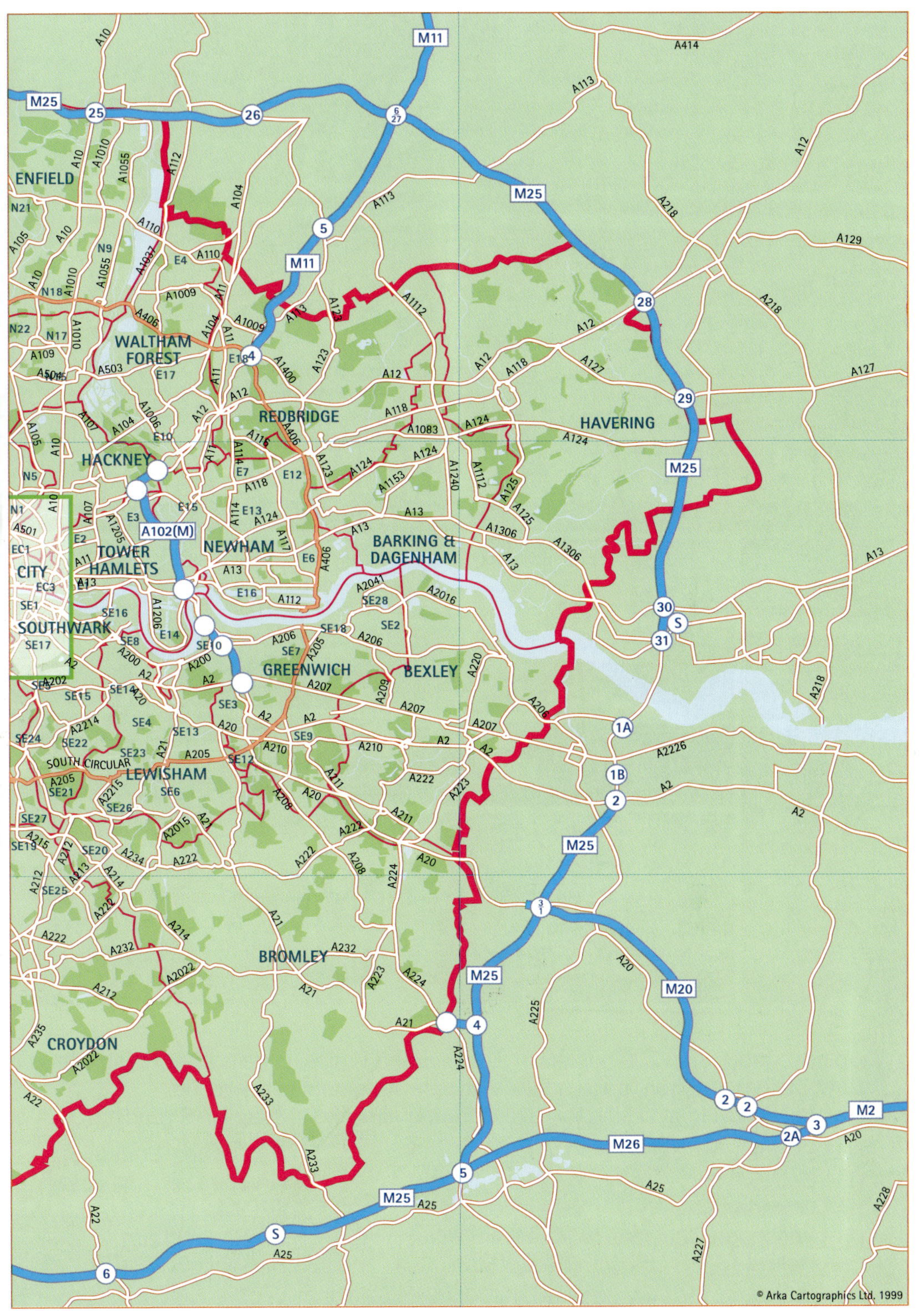
M25
M11
M20
M26
M2
ENFIELD
WALTHAM FOREST
REDBRIDGE
HAVERING
HACKNEY
TOWER HAMLETS
NEWHAM
BARKING & DAGENHAM
CITY
SOUTHWARK
GREENWICH
BEXLEY
LEWISHAM
BROMLEY
CROYDON
SOUTH CIRCULAR
A102(M)
© Arka Cartographics Ltd. 1999

**The following youth hostels offer accommodation suitable for people with accessible needs. If a hostel is participating in the National Accessible Scheme the rating is shown (see page 10). All other youth hostels listed provide at least one wheelchair-accessible bedroom. Please contact the youth hostels directly for more information.**

## England

**YHA Arnside**
★★★ *Hostel*
Redhills Road, Arnside, Cumbria LA5 0AT
**t** 0845 371 9722
**e** arnside@yha.org.uk

**YHA Arundel**
★★★ *Hostel*
Youth Hostel, Warning Camp, Arundel, West Sussex BN18 9QY
**t** 0845 371 9002
**e** arundel@yha.org.uk

**YHA Blaxhall**
★★★ *Hostel*
Heath Walk, Blaxhall, Woodbridge, Suffolk IP12 2EA
**t** 0845 371 9305
**e** blaxhall@yha.org.uk

**YHA Borrowdale**
★★★★ *Hostel*
Longthwaite, Borrowdale, Keswick, Cumbria CA12 5XE
**t** 0845 371 9624
**e** borrowdale@yha.org.uk

**YHA Boscastle**
★★★★ *Hostel*
Palace Stables, Boscastle, Cornwall PL35 0HD
**t** 0845 371 9006
**e** boscastle@yha.org.uk

**YHA Castleton**
★★★ *Hostel*
Castleton, Hope Valley, Derbyshire S33 8WG
**t** 0845 371 9628
**e** castleton@yha.org.uk

**YHA Cheddar**
★★★ *Hostel*
Hillfield, Cheddar, Somerset BS27 3HN
**t** 0845 371 9730
**e** cheddar@yha.org.uk

**YHA Edale**
★★ *Hostel*
Nether Booth, Edale, Derbyshire S33 7ZH
**t** 0845 371 9514
**e** edale@yha.org.uk

**YHA Exford**
★★★ *Hostel*
Exford, Minehead, Somerset TA24 7PU
**t** 0845 371 9634
**e** exford@yha.org.uk

**YHA Hartington**
★★★★ *Hostel*
Hartington, Buxton, Derbyshire SK17 0AT
**t** 0845 371 9740
**e** hartington@yha.org.uk

**YHA Helmsley**
★★★ *Hostel*
Carlton Lane, Helmsley, North Yorkshire YO62 5HB
**t** 0845 371 9638
**e** helmsley@yha.org.uk

**YHA Ilam**
★★★ *Hostel*
Ilam, Ashbourne, Derbyshire DE6 2AZ
**t** 0845 371 9023
**e** ilam@yha.org.uk

**YHA Ironbridge Coalbrookdale**
★★★ *Hostel*
c/o High Street, Coalport, Shropshire TF8 7HT
**t** 0845 371 9325
**e** ironbridge@yha.org.uk

**YHA Ironbridge Coalport**
★★★ *Hostel*
John Rose Building,
High Street, Coalport,
Shropshire TF8 7HT
**t** 0845 371 9325
**e** coalport@yha.org.uk

---

**YHA Kielder**
★★★★ *Hostel*
Kielder Village, Hexham,
Northumberland
NE48 1HQ
**t** 0845 371 9126
**e** kielder@yha.org.uk

---

**YHA Kington**
★★★★ *Hostel*
Victoria Road,
Kington,
Herefordshire HR5 3BX
**t** 0845 371 9053
**e** kington@yha.org.uk

---

**YHA Langdon Beck**
★★★★ *Hostel*
Forest in Teesdale,
Barnard Castle,
Co Durham DL12 0XN
**t** 0845 371 9027
**e** langdonbeck
@yha.org.uk

---

**YHA Lee Valley**
★★★★ *Hostel*
Windmill Lane,
Cheshunt,
Hertfordshire EN8 9AJ
**t** 0845 371 9057
**e** leevalley@yha.org.uk

---

**YHA Leominster**
★★★★ *Hostel*
The Old Priory,
Leominster,
Herefordshire HR6 8EQ
**t** 0845 371 9127
**e** leominster@yha.org.uk

---

**YHA Liverpool**
★★★★ *Hostel*
25 Tabley Street,
off Wapping, Liverpool,
Merseyside L1 8EE
**t** 0845 371 9527
**e** liverpool@yha.org.uk

---

**YHA Lizard Point**
★★★★ *Hostel*
Lizard Point, Helston,
Cornwall TR12 7NT
**t** 0845 371 9550
**e** lizard@yha.org.uk

---

**YHA Lockton**
★★★★ *Hostel*
Old School, Lockton,
Pickering, North Yorkshire
YO18 7PY
**t** 0845 371 9128
**e** lockton@yha.org.uk

---

**YHA London Central**
★★★★ *Hostel*
104-108 Bolsover Street,
London W1W 5LP
**t** 0845 371 9154
**e** londoncentral
@yha.org.uk

---

**YHA London St Pancras**
★★★★ *Hostel*
79-81 Euston Road,
London NW1 2QS
**t** 0845 371 9344
**e** stpancras@yha.org,uk

---

**YHA London Thameside**
★★ *Hostel*
20 Salter Road, London
SE16 5PR
**t** 0845 371 9756
**e** thameside@yha.org.uk

---

**YHA Manchester**
★★★★ *Hostel*
Potato Wharf, Castlefield,
Manchester M3 4NB
**t** 0845 371 9647
**e** manchester@yha.org.uk

---

**YHA Medway**
★★★ *Hostel*
Capstone Road,
Gillingham, Kent ME7 3JE
**t** 0845 371 9649
**e** medway@yha.org.uk

---

**YHA National Forest**
Rating Applied For *Hostel*
48 Bath Lane, Moira,
Derbyshire DE12 6BD
**t** 0845 371 9672
**e** nationalforest
@yha.org.uk

---

**YHA Oxford**
★★★★ *Hostel*
2a Botley Road, Oxford,
Oxfordshire OX2 0AB
**t** 0845 371 9131
**e** oxford@yha.org.uk

---

**YHA Scarborough**
★★★ *Hostel*
Burniston Road, Scarborough, North Yorkshire YO13 0DA
**t** 0845 371 9657
**e** scarborough@yha.org.uk

**YHA Sheringham**
★★ *Hostel*
1 Cremer's Drift, Sheringham, Norfolk NR26 8HX
**t** 0845 371 9040
**e** sheringham@yha.org.uk

**YHA Sherwood Forest**
★★★★ *Hostel*
Forest Corner, Edwinstowe, Nottinghamshire NG21 9RN
**t** 0845 371 9139
**e** sherwood@yha.org.uk

**YHA Treyarnon Bay**
★★★ *Hostel*
Treyarnon, Padstow, Cornwall PL28 8JR
**t** 0845 371 9664
**e** treyarnon@yha.org.uk

**YHA Wells-next-the-Sea**
★★★★ *Hostel*
Church Plain, Wells-next-the-Sea, Norfolk NR23 1EQ
**t** 0845 371 9544
**e** wellsnorfolk@yha.org.uk

**YHA Whitby**
★★★★ *Hostel*
Abbey House, East Cliff, Whitby, North Yorkshire YO22 4JT
t 0845 371 9049
e whitby@yha.org.uk

**YHA Wooler**
★★★ *Hostel*
30 Cheviot Street, Wooler, Northumberland NE71 6LW
**t** 0845 371 9668
**e** wooler@yha.org.uk

**YHA York**
★★★ *Hostel*
Water End, Clifton, York, North Yorkshire YO30 6LP
**t** 0845 371 9051
**e** york@yha.org.uk

## Wales

**YHA Broadhaven**
★★★ *Hostel*
Broadhaven, Haverfordwest, Pembrokeshire SA62 3JH
**t** 0845 371 9008
**e** broadhaven@yha.org.uk

**YHA Cardiff**
★★★ *Hostel*
2 Wedal Road, Roath Park, Cardiff CF14 3QX
**t** 0845 371 9311
**e** cardiff@yha.org.uk

**YHA Conwy**
★★★ *Hostel*
Larkhill, Sychnant Pass Road, Conwy LL32 8AJ
**t** 0845 371 9732
**e** conwy@yha.org.uk

**YHA Danywenallt**
★★★ *Hostel*
Talybont-on-Usk, Brecon, Powys LD3 7YS
**t** 0845 371 9548
**e** danywenallt@yha.org.uk

**YHA Llangattock**
★★★★★ *Bunkhouse*
Wern Watkin Hillside, Llangattock, Crickhowell, Powys NP8 1LG
**t** 0800 019 700
**e** llangattock@yha.org.uk

**YHA Llwyn y Celyn**
★★★ *Hostel*
Libanus, Brecon, Powys LD3 8NH
**t** 0845 371 9029
**e** llwynycelyn@yha.org.uk

**YHA Manorbier**
★★★ *Hostel*
Manorbier, Nr Tenby, Pembrokeshire SA70 7TT
**t** 0845 371 9031
**e** manorbier@yha.org.uk

**YHA Newport**
★★★ *Hostel*
Lower St Mary Street, Newport, Pembrokeshire SA42 0TS
**t** 0845 371 9543
**e** trefdraeth@yha.org.uk

**For more information visit yha.org.uk**

# Relax

Rooms from only

- Clean and comfortable rooms
- Ensuite bathroom
- Universally accessible rooms
- Remote control TV with Freeview
- Family rooms and cots on request
- 24 hour reception, so there's always someone on hand to help
- Great value restaurant at every Premier Inn serving breakfast, lunch and dinner

Lowest Weekend room rate quoted. Price correct at time of print (Sept 08)

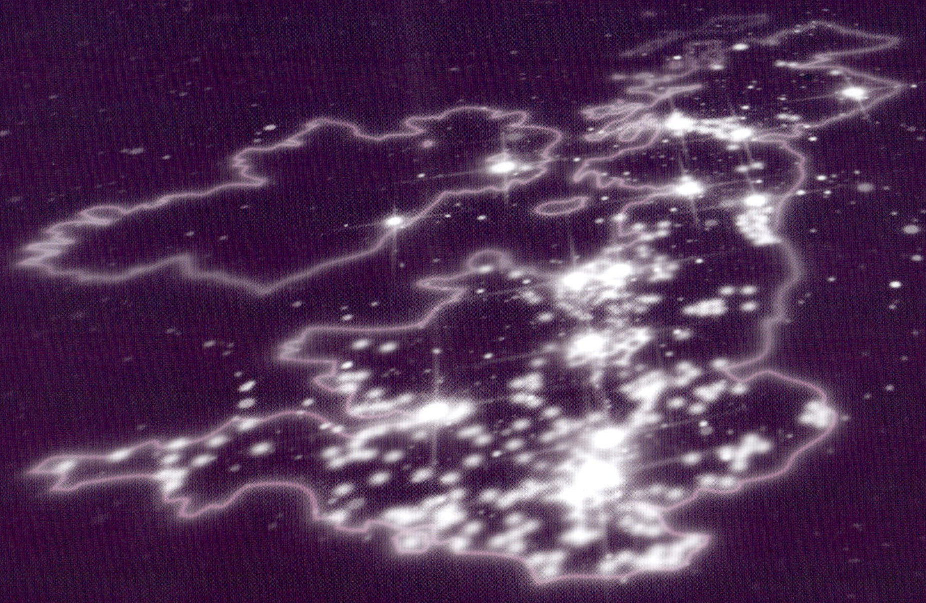

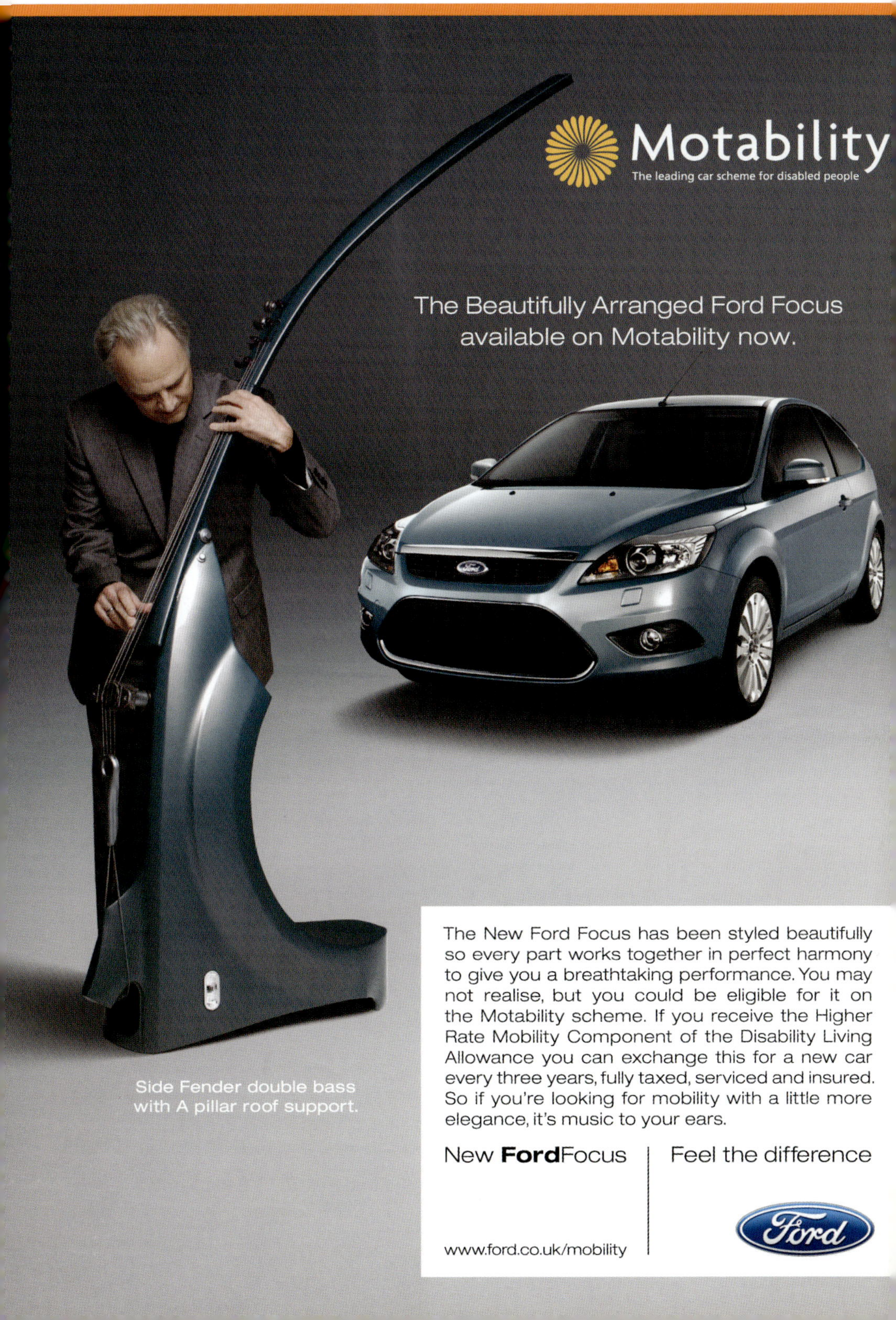
Motability
The leading car scheme for disabled people
The Beautifully Arranged Ford Focus available on Motability now.
Side Fender double bass with A pillar roof support.
The New Ford Focus has been styled beautifully so every part works together in perfect harmony to give you a breathtaking performance. You may not realise, but you could be eligible for it on the Motability scheme. If you receive the Higher Rate Mobility Component of the Disability Living Allowance you can exchange this for a new car every three years, fully taxed, serviced and insured. So if you're looking for mobility with a little more elegance, it's music to your ears.
New FordFocus
Feel the difference
www.ford.co.uk/mobility

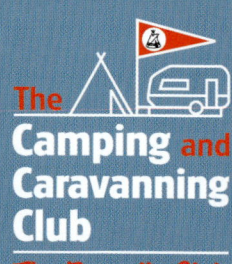

# through our sites...

Lydford Club Site

## Find a site to suit you, on The Club's website with

**SiteSeeker®**

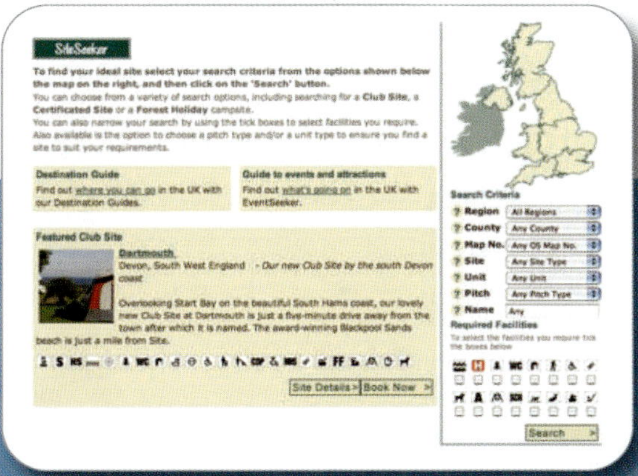

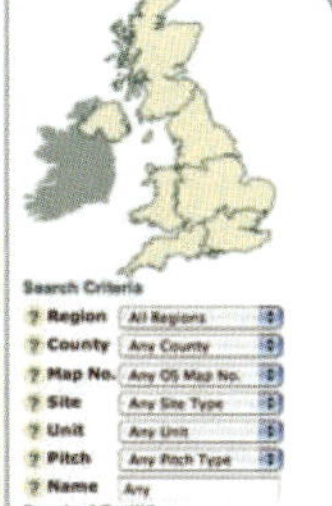

SiteSeeker
To find your ideal site select your search criteria from the options shown below the map on the right, and then click on the 'Search' button.
You can choose from a variety of search options, including searching for a Club Site, a Certificated Site or a Forest Holiday campsite.
You can also narrow your search by using the tick boxes to select facilities you require. Also available is the option to choose a pitch type and/or a unit type to ensure you find a site to suit your requirements.
Destination Guide
Find out where you can go in the UK with our Destination Guides.
Guide to events and attractions
Find out what's going on in the UK with EventSeeker.
Featured Club Site
Dartmouth
Devon, South West England - Our new Club Site by the south Devon coast
Overlooking Start Bay on the beautiful South Hams coast, our lovely new Club Site at Dartmouth is just a five-minute drive away from the town after which it is named. The award-winning Blackpool Sands beach is just a mile from Site.
Site Details >
Book Now >
Search Criteria
Region All Regions
County Any County
Map No. Any OS Map No.
Site Any Site Type
Unit Any Unit
Pitch Any Pitch Type
Name Any
Required Facilities
To select the facilities you require tick the boxes below
Search >

## Join The Club and enjoy the benefits for only £35

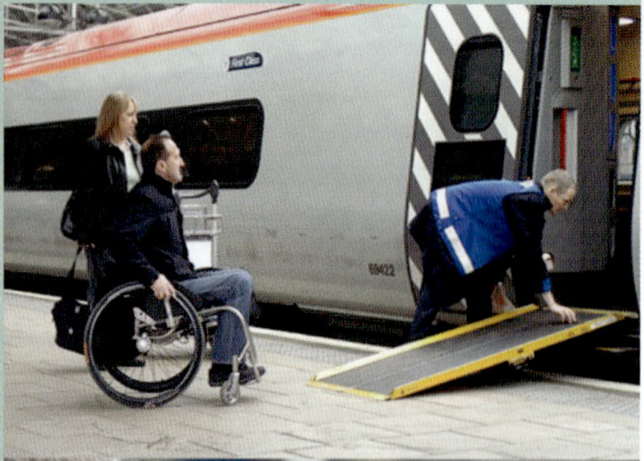

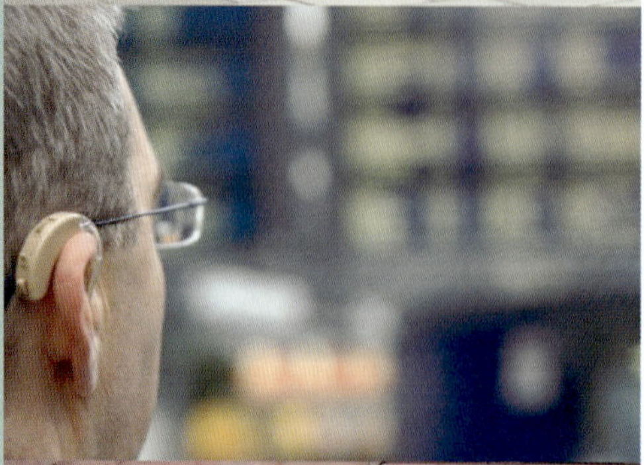

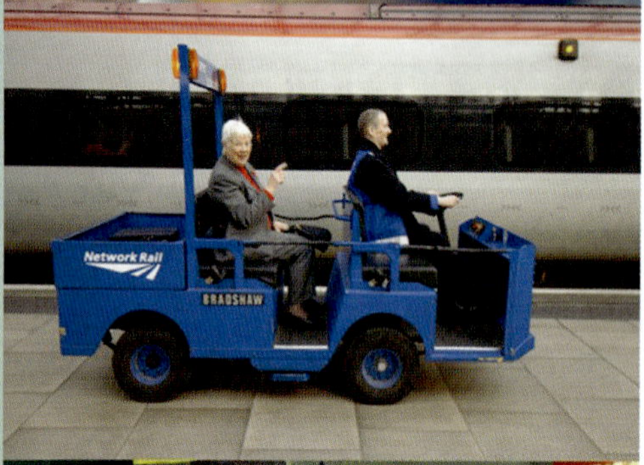
Network Rail
BRADSHAW

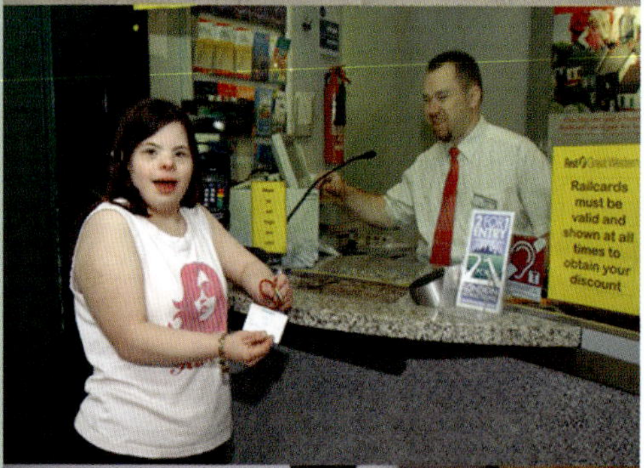
Railcards must be valid and shown at all times to obtain your discount

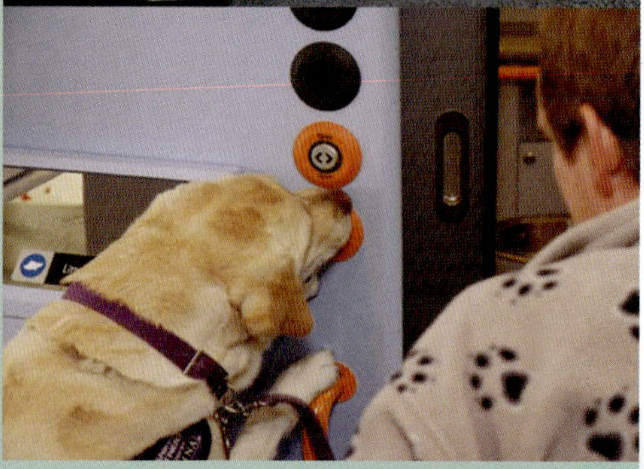

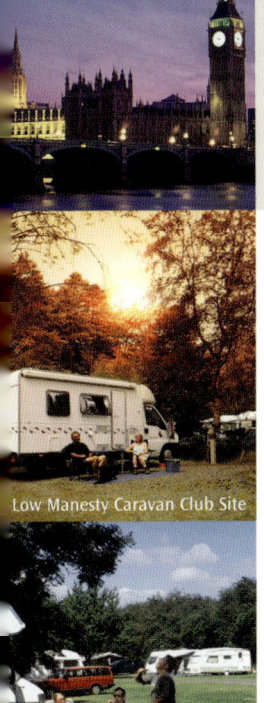

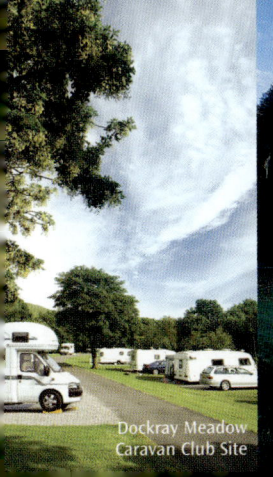

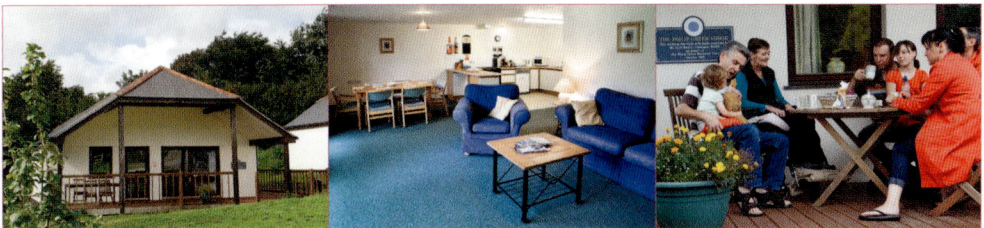

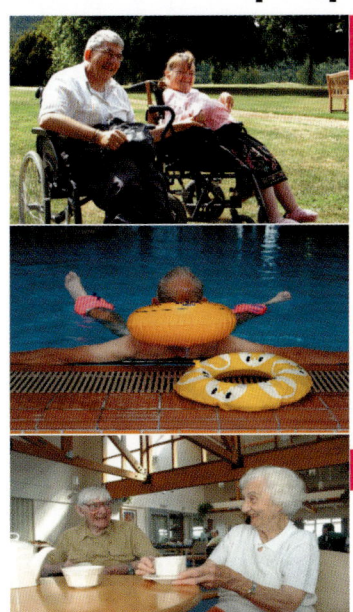

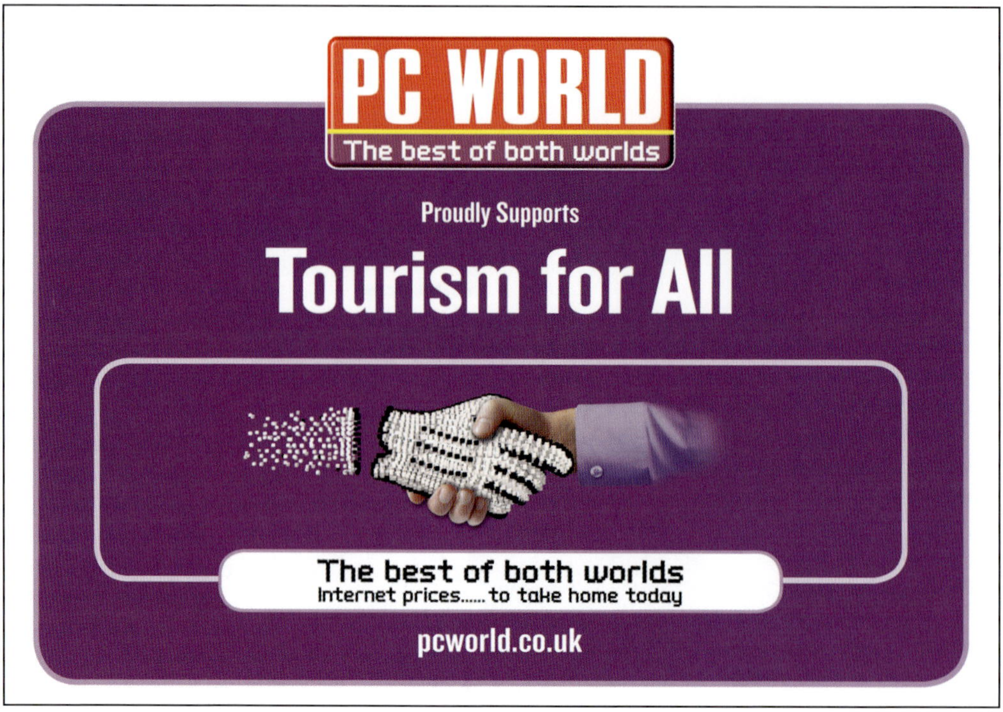
PC WORLD
The best of both worlds
Proudly Supports
Tourism for All
The best of both worlds
Internet prices...... to take home today
pcworld.co.uk

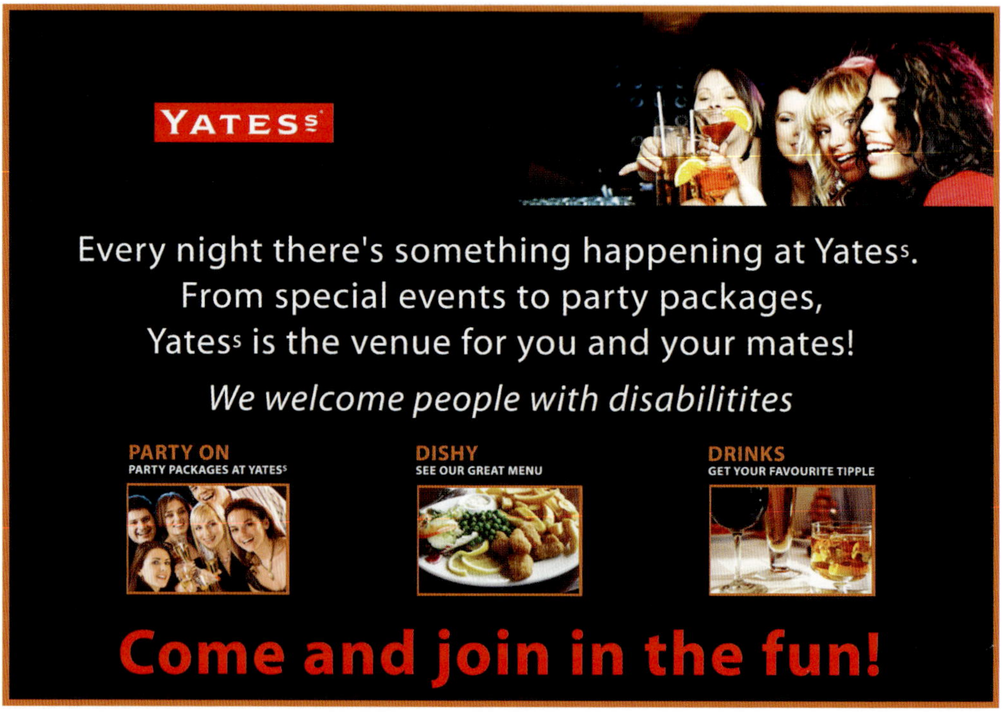
YATES
Every night there's something happening at Yatess.
From special events to party packages,
Yatess is the venue for you and your mates!
We welcome people with disabilitites
PARTY ON
PARTY PACKAGES AT YATESS
DISHY
SEE OUR GREAT MENU
DRINKS
GET YOUR FAVOURITE TIPPLE
Come and join in the fun!

# Northern England

Cheshire, Cumbria, Durham, Greater Manchester, Lancashire, Merseyside, Northumberland, Tees Valley, Tyne and Wear, Yorkshire

Clockwise: Wastwater, Cumbria; Durham Cathedral; North Yorkshire Moors Railway

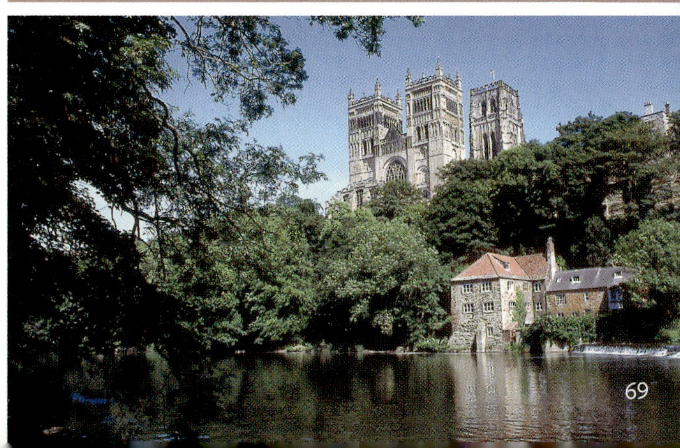

# Great days out

Windswept moors and breathtaking coastlines. Mirrored glass lakes and the magnificent cathedrals of York and Durham. The urban wonders of the Gateshead Millennium Bridge and Urbis in Manchester. Not forgetting all-year-round fun and games at Blackpool... It's all just part of an ordinary day in England's proud and historic North.

## Built to impress

Northern England has more than its fair share of remarkable buildings. **Alnwick Castle**, magically transformed into a location for the renowned Harry Potter films, provides a memorable outing. While in the area, visit **The Alnwick Garden** with its unique water features – the aerial walkways and treehouse restaurant are accessible to everyone, including wheelchair users. Equally impressive is 900-year-old **Durham Cathedral** which perches high above the city and the towering vaulted ceilings of **York Minster**, the largest medieval Gothic cathedral in Northern Europe. Built on simpler scales, the twin Anglo-Saxon monastery of **Wearmouth-Jarrow**, home to the Venerable Bede, is the UK's nomination for World Heritage Status in 2009.

Castle Howard, North Yorkshire

**Fountains Abbey**, Britain's largest monastic ruin, and adjacent **Studley Royal Water Garden** are must-sees. Art-lovers should plan a trip to **Castle Howard** where Canalettos, Holbeins and Gainsboroughs are just some of the art treasures on display. To view the work of William Morris, visit Liverpool's half-timbered **Speke Hall**. And if you're looking for a challenge **The Forbidden Corner**, Leyburn in Yorkshire, will live up to expectations as you get lost in the underground labyrinth of chambers and passages (some parts are only accessible by steps). Or get digging at **Diggerland** – there are adventure parks in Castleford and Durham where children and adults can drive different types of construction machinery.

Left to right: Alnwick Castle, Northumberland; York Minster, Yorkshire

**why not...** learn the fascinating history of Hadrian's Wall at Birdoswald Roman Fort?

## Roman Britain

Venture along **Hadrian's Wall** just as soldiers did nearly two millennia ago. Explore the many forts, milecastles and turrets that dot its length including **Housesteads Fort**, the most complete remaining outpost. The walled city of **Chester** is Britain's best-preserved Roman town – complete with partially excavated amphitheatre. The Dewa fortress – buried beneath the town – now lives on through the **Dewa Roman Experience**.

## Natural wonders

Wide-open spaces abound in the National Parks – Yorkshire alone has over 1,000 square miles to explore. Wander lonely as a cloud in the **Lake District** – home to William Wordsworth and Samuel Taylor Coleridge – and pay a visit to Mr McGregor's garden at the charming **World of Beatrix Potter Attraction**, Windermere. Can you sense mystical goings-on at **Alderley Edge**, Cheshire, linked to the legends of King Arthur? There's an accessible route that offers wonderful views from this Site of Special Scientific Interest. Discover the **Forest of Bowland**, one of Lancashire's Areas of Outstanding Natural Beauty, by Tramper – a four-wheel drive, all-terrain electric buggy.

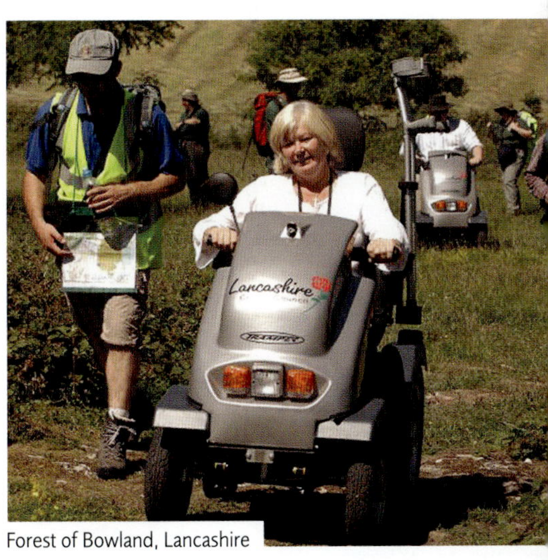


Forest of Bowland, Lancashire

On the north-east coast take a boat to **Holy Island** to behold the treasured Lindisfarne Gospels. Don't forget the binoculars; the **Farne Islands** are home to hundreds of thousands of puffins and dewy-eyed grey seals. Relax under a perfect night sky and take a guided tour of the stars at the **Yorkshire Planetarium**, currently located at **Harewood House**, Leeds.

## Hands-on heritage

Meet people who once worked in cotton mills with a lifetime of stories to share with you at **Quarry Bank Mill** in Cheshire, and learn more about early industrialisation at the **Armley Mills Leeds Industrial Museum**. Get a taste of Victorian times at **Saltaire World Heritage Site**, a 'model' industrial village. Hear vivid tales at the **National Coal Mining Museum** in Wakefield, and let the youngsters try their skills at sweet making at **Beamish**, the award-winning open air museum. Imagine once more the romantic age of steam on the **Settle-Carlisle** or **East Lancashire Railway** or gaze in wonder at the giant locomotives at the **National Railway Museum** in York and **Locomotion** in Shildon.

## City culture

Enjoy the renaissance of **NewcastleGateshead**, highlighted by the stunning architecture of the **Gateshead Millennium Bridge**. Check out new artists at the **Baltic**,

**why not...** join a ghost walk around York, claimed as Europe's most haunted city?

Clockwise: Beamish, Durham; The Deep, Hull; Imperial War Museum North, Manchester

**Centre for Contemporary Art**, or listen to a favourite score at one of **Opera North's** ten theatres. **Seven Stories, the Centre for Children's Books** in Newcastle will touch your imagination and bring back childhood memories. Explore **Liverpool**, famed as the birthplace of The Beatles. You can follow in their footsteps, from the world-famous **Cavern Club**, to John Lennon's childhood home, **Mendips**, now in the care of the National Trust.

In Manchester head for **Salford Quays** and **The Lowry**, an inspirational waterfront centre for the visual arts and entertainment. The gallery scene embraces **Manchester Art Gallery**, the **Cornerhouse** and **The Whitworth**, and there's a choice of 50 free museums, including the **Imperial War Museum North** designed by Daniel Libeskind. In Middlesbrough the newly opened **Middlesbrough Institute of Modern Art** is a gallery of national importance, housing works by Emin, Hockney and Frink among others.

If you're young at heart head for **Blackpool's Pleasure Beach** or book ringside seats at the UK's best circus at the **Blackpool Tower**! Forget Sudoku, stimulate the brain cells at Rotherham's **Magna**, a science adventure centre where fun is unavoidable, or test out a fascinating world of hands-on exploration at **Eureka!** in Halifax.

Above: Baltic, Gateshead
Below: Chester Rows, Chester

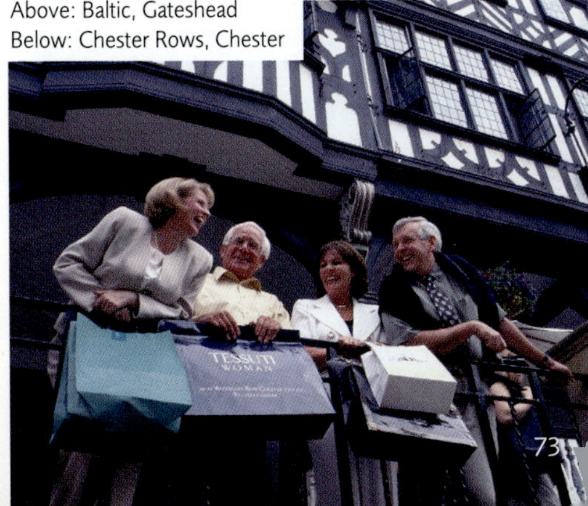

# North East England

**World-famous for our friendliness and hospitality, come and share our passion for this wonderful region of coastline and castles, countryside and culture!**

**Main:** NewcastleGateshead Quayside
**Above:** Beamish Museum, Durham

Want to experience our tranquil countryside and undiscovered coastline? Head for Kielder, where you can take a cruise on Europe's largest man-made lake, wander miles of forest paths and stay in a wheelchair-accessible forest village. Or take a boat trip from Seahouses, on the Northumberland Coast Area of Outstanding Natural Beauty, to see breeding puffins and grey seals on the Farne Islands.

Love your history? Come and marvel at Hadrian's Wall, still marking the northernmost limit of the Roman Empire after almost 2,000 years. You'll find amazing interactive exhibits and events at several of its forts, including Segedunum and Arbeia in North and South Tyneside respectively. You can board HMS Trincomalee, the oldest warship still afloat, at Hartlepool's Maritime Experience in Tees Valley. And at Beamish, an open air museum in Durham, you can travel back in time to 1825 and 1913 via an easy-access bus, to visit the town, farm, manor house and colliery village.

Our cities are alive with world-class culture and fantastic shopping. Visit mima, Middlesbrough's Institute of Modern Art, or BALTIC, Centre for Contemporary Art, on NewcastleGateshead's Quayside, for vibrant and often highly provocative exhibitions. Nearby, The Sage Gateshead, an award-winning centre for music, offers breathtaking waterfront views and access to its café, restaurant and library whether you're attending a concert or not. Or why not treat yourself to some retail therapy at MetroCentre, Europe's largest shopping and leisure complex, or see beautiful glass being hand-made at the National Glass Centre, Sunderland?

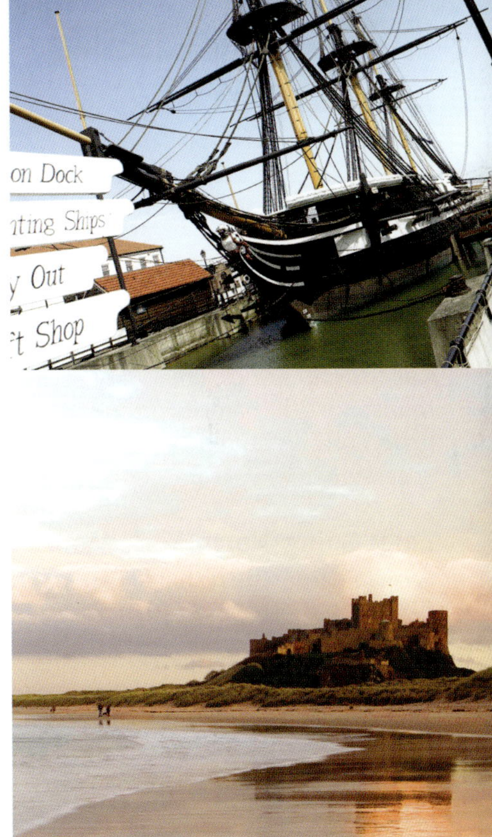

Find out more, and book quality, accessible accommodation at **visitnortheastengland.com/access**
We look forward to welcoming you.

north east
england

**Right:** Bamburgh Castle, Northumberland
**Above right:** Hartlepool's Maritime Experience, Tees Valley

# Useful regional contacts

**England's Northwest**
t (01925) 400100
w visitenglandsnorthwest.com

**North East England**
t 0844 249 5090
w visitnortheastengland.com/access

**Yorkshire Tourist Board**
t (01904) 707961
w yorkshire.com

## Publications

### Access Guide to Blackpool
Available from Visit Blackpool on (01253) 478222 or from visitblackpool.com.

### Durham City Access for All
Available from Durham Tourist Information Centre.
Call (01938) 43720, email touristinfo@durhamcity.gov.uk or go to burrows.co.uk/durhamaccessguide.

### Easy Going North York Moors
Available from the National Park Authority. Call (01845) 597426 or go to visitnorthyorkshiremoors.co.uk.

### Miles without Stiles
An online guide to 21 routes in the Lake District National Park for those with limited mobility. Available from lake-district.gov.uk.

### Welcome to Wyresdale Wheels for All
A leaflet on local trails, accommodation and attractions for people with disabilities in the Scorton area of the Forest of Bowland AONB. Can be downloaded from forestofbowland.com or call (01772) 534709.

## Information

### Disability North
The Dene Centre, Castle Farm Road, Newcastle upon Tyne NE3 1PH
t (0191) 284 0480
e reception@disabilitynorth.org.uk
w disabilitynorth.org.uk
A charity offering advice on holidays in Newcastle-upon-Tyne.

### Visit Chester and Cheshire
w visitchester.com
w visitcheshire.com
The official tourist board websites for the Chester and Cheshire region and a pilot for a European access project.

### Visit Liverpool
w visitliverpool.com
The official tourist board website for Liverpool has an accessibility function on almost all accommodation listed there.

# Tourist Information Centres

Official Partner Tourist Information Centres offer quality assured help with accommodation and information about local attractions and events. To search for attractions and Tourist Information Centres on the move just text INFO to 62233, and a web link will be sent to your mobile phone. To find a Tourist Information Centre by region visit enjoyEngland.com/find-tic.

| | | | |
|---|---|---|---|
| **Accrington** | Town Hall, Blackburn Rd | (01254) 872595 | tourism@hyndburnbc.gov.uk |
| **Alnwick** | 2 The Shambles | (01665) 511333 | alnwicktic@alnwick.gov.uk |
| **Altrincham** | 20 Stamford New Road | (0161) 912 5931 | tourist.information@trafford.gov.uk |
| **Ashton-under-Lyne** | Wellington Road | (0161) 343 4343 | tourist.information@tameside.gov.uk |
| **Aysgarth Falls** | Aysgarth Falls National Park Centre | (01969) 662910 | aysgarth@ytbtic.co.uk |
| **Barnard Castle** | Flatts Road | (01833) 690909 | tourism@teesdale.gov.uk |
| **Barnoldswick** | Fernlea Avenue | (01282) 666704 | tourist.info@pendle.gov.uk |
| **Barrow-in-Furness** | Duke Street | (01229) 876505 | touristinfo@barrowbc.gov.uk |
| **Batley** | Bradford Road | (01924) 426670 | batley@ytbtic.co.uk |
| **Beverley** | 34 Butcher Row | (01482) 391672 | beverley.tic@eastriding .gov.uk |
| **Blackburn** | 50-54 Church Street | (01254) 53277 | visit@blackburn.gov.uk |
| **Blackpool** | 1 Clifton Street | (01253) 478222 | tic@blackpool.gov.uk |
| **Bolton** | Le Mans Crescent | (01204) 334321 | tourist.info@bolton.gov.uk |
| **Bowness** | Glebe Road | (015394) 42895 | bownesstic@lake-district.gov.uk |
| **Bradford** | Centenary Square | (01274) 433678 | tourist.information@bradford.gov.uk |
| **Bridlington** | 25 Prince Street | (01262) 673474 | bridlington.tic@eastriding.gov.uk |
| **Brigg** | Market Place | (01652) 657053 | brigg.tic@northlincs.gov.uk |
| **Burnley** | Croft Street | (01282) 664421 | tic@burnley.gov.uk |
| **Bury** | Market Street | (0161) 253 5111 | touristinformation@bury.gov.uk |
| **Carlisle** | Greenmarket | (01228) 625600 | tourism@carlisle-city.gov.uk |
| **Chester (Town Hall)** | Northgate Street | (01244) 402111 | tis@chester.gov.uk |
| **Cleethorpes** | 42-43 Alexandra Road | (01472) 323111 | cleetic@nelincs.gov.uk |
| **Cleveleys** | Victoria Square | (01253) 853378 | cleveleystic@wyrebc.gov.uk |
| **Clitheroe** | 12-14 Market Place | (01200) 425566 | tourism@ribblevalley.gov.uk |
| **Congleton** | High Street | (01260) 271095 | tourism@congleton.gov.uk |
| **Coniston** | Ruskin Avenue | (015394) 41533 | mail@conistontic.org |
| **Danby** | Lodge Lane | (01439) 772737 | moorscentre@northyorkmoors-npa.gov.uk |
| **Darlington** | 13 Horsemarket | (01325) 388666 | tic@darlington.gov.uk |
| **Doncaster** | 38-40 High Street | (01302) 734309 | tourist.information@doncaster.gov.uk |
| **Durham** | 2 Millennium Place | (0191) 384 3720 | touristinfo@durhamcity.gov.uk |
| **Ellesmere Port** | Kinsey Road | (0151) 356 7879 | cheshireoaks.cc@visitor-centre.net |

| | | | |
|---|---|---|---|
| **Filey*** | The Evron Centre, John Street | (01723) 383637 | fileytic@scarborough.gov.uk |
| **Fleetwood** | The Esplanade | (01253) 773953 | fleetwoodtic@wyrebc.gov.uk |
| **Garstang** | High Street | (01995) 602125 | garstangtic@wyrebc.gov.uk |
| **Grassington** | Colvend, Hebden Road | (01756) 751690 | grassington@ytbtic.co.uk |
| **Guisborough** | Church Street | (01287) 633801 | guisborough_tic@redcar-cleveland.gov.uk |
| **Halifax** | Piece Hall | (01422) 368725 | halifax@ytbtic.co.uk |
| **Harrogate** | Crescent Road | (01423) 537300 | tic@harrogate.gov.uk |
| **Hartlepool** | Church Square | (01429) 869706 | hpooltic@hartlepool.gov.uk |
| **Hawes** | Station Yard | (01969) 666210 | hawes@ytbtic.co.uk |
| **Haworth** | 2/4 West Lane | (01535) 642329 | haworth@ytbtic.co.uk |
| **Hebden Bridge** | New Road | (01422) 843831 | hebdenbridge@ytbtic.co.uk |
| **Helmsley** | Helmsley Castle | (01439) 770173 | helmsley@ytbtic.co.uk |
| **Hexham** | Wentworth Car Park | (01434) 652220 | hexham.tic@tynedale.gov.uk |
| **Holmfirth** | 49-51 Huddersfield Road | (01484) 222444 | holmfirth.tic@kirklees.gov.uk |
| **Hornsea*** | 120 Newbegin | (01964) 536404 | hornsea.tic@eastriding.gov.uk |
| **Huddersfield** | 3 Albion Street | (01484) 223200 | huddersfield.tic@kirklees.gov.uk |
| **Hull** | 1 Paragon Street | (01482) 223559 | tourist.information@hullcc.gov.uk |
| **Humber Bridge** | Ferriby Road | (01482) 640852 | humberbridge.tic@eastriding.gov.uk |
| **Ilkley** | Station Rd | (01943) 602319 | ilkley@ytbtic.co.uk |
| **Kendal** | Highgate | (01539) 725758 | kendaltic@southlakeland.gov.uk |
| **Keswick** | Market Square | (017687) 72645 | keswicktic@lake-district.gov.uk |
| **Knaresborough** | 9 Castle Courtyard | 0845 389 0177 | kntic@harrogate.gov.uk |
| **Knutsford** | Toft Road | (01565) 632611 | ktic@macclesfield.gov.uk |
| **Lancaster** | 29 Castle Hill | (01524) 32878 | lancastertic@lancaster.gov.uk |
| **Leeds** | The Arcade, City Station | (0113) 242 5242 | tourinfo@leeds.gov.uk |
| **Leeming Bar** | The Yorkshire Maid, The Great North Road | (01677) 424262 | leeming@ytbtic.co.uk |

Left to right: Holker Hall and Gardens, Cumbria; Locomotion: The National Railway Museum, Durham

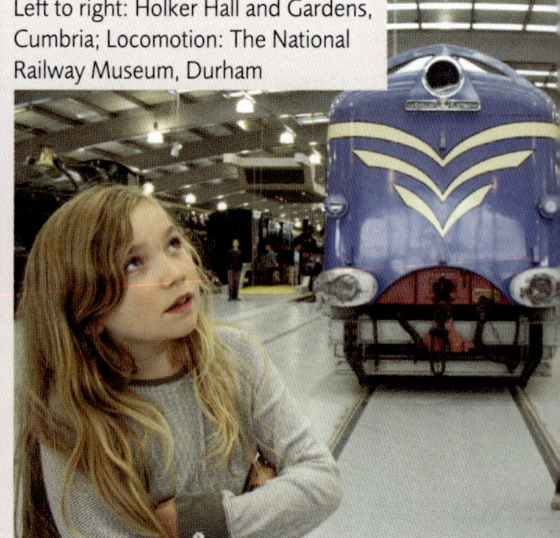

| | | | |
|---|---|---|---|
| **Leyburn** | Railway Street | (01969) 623069 | leyburn@ytbtic.co.uk |
| **Liverpool 08 Place** | Whitechapel | (0151) 233 2459 | contact@liverpool.08.com |
| **Liverpool John Lennon Airport** | Speke Hall Avenue | 0906 680 6886** | info@visitliverpool.com |
| **Lytham St Annes** | 67 St Annes Road West | (01253) 725610 | touristinformation@fylde.gov.uk |
| **Macclesfield** | Town Hall | (01625) 504114 | informationcentre@macclesfield.gov.uk |
| **Malham** | National Park Centre | (01969) 652380 | malham@ytbtic.co.uk |
| **Malton** | 58 Market Place | (01653) 600048 | maltontic@btconnect.com |
| **Manchester Visitor Information Centre** | Lloyd St | 0871 222 8223 | touristinformation@marketing-manchester.co.uk |
| **Morecambe** | Marine Road Central | (01524) 582808 | morecambetic@lancaster.gov.uk |
| **Morpeth** | Bridge Street | (01670) 500700 | tourism@castlemorpeth.gov.uk |
| **Nantwich** | Market Street | (01270) 537359 | touristi@crewe-nantwich.gov.uk |
| **Newcastle-upon-Tyne** | 8-9 Central Arcade | (0191) 277 8000 | tourist.info@newcastle.gov.uk |
| **Northwich** | 1 The Arcade | (01606) 353534 | tourism@valeroyal.gov.uk |
| **Oldham** | 12 Albion Street | (0161) 627 1024 | ecs.tourist@oldham.gov.uk |
| **Otley** | Nelson Street | (01943) 462485 | otleytic@leedslearning.net |
| **Pateley Bridge*** | 18 High Street | 0845 389 0177 | pbtic@harrogate.gov.uk |
| **Pendle Heritage Centre** | Park Hill | (01282) 661701 | heritage.centre@pendle.gov.uk |
| **Penrith** | Middlegate | (01768) 867466 | pen.tic@eden.gov.uk |
| **Pickering** | The Ropery | (01751) 473791 | pickering@ytbtic.co.uk |
| **Preston** | Lancaster Road | (01772) 253731 | tourism@preston.gov.uk |
| **Redcar** | Esplanade | (01642) 471921 | redcar_tic@redcar-cleveland.gov.uk |
| **Reeth** | Hudson House, The Green | (01748) 884059 | reeth@ytbtic.co.uk |
| **Richmond** | Victoria Road | (01748) 828742 | richmond@ytbtic.co.uk |
| **Ripon** | Minster Road | (01765) 604625 | ripontic@harrogate.gov.uk |
| **Rochdale** | The Esplanade | (01706) 924928 | tic@link4life.org |
| **Rotherham** | 40 Bridgegate | (01709) 835904 | tic@rotherham.gov.uk |
| **St Helens** | The World of Glass | (01744) 755150 | info@sthelenstic.com |
| **Salford** | The Lowry, Pier 8 | (0161) 848 8601 | tic@salford.gov.uk |
| **Saltburn-by-the-Sea** | 3 Station Buildings | (01287) 622422 | saltburn_tic@redcar-cleveland.gov.uk |
| **Scarborough** | Brunswick Shopping Centre | (01723) 383636 | tourismbureau@scarborough.gov.uk |
| **Scarborough (Harbourside)** | Sandside | (01723) 383636 | harboursidetic@scarborough.gov.uk |
| **Settle** | Cheapside | (01729) 825192 | settle@ytbtic.co.uk |
| **Sheffield** | 14 Norfolk Row | (0114) 2211900 | visitor@sheffield.gov.uk |
| **Skipton** | 35 Coach Street | (01756) 792809 | skipton@ytbtic.co.uk |
| **Stockport** | 30 Market Place | (0161) 474 4444 | tourist.information@stockport.gov.uk |
| **Sunderland** | 50 Fawcett Street | (0191) 553 2000 | tourist.info@sunderland.gov.uk |
| **Sutton Bank** | Sutton Bank Visitor Centre | (01845) 597426 | suttonbank@ytbtic.co.uk |

| | | | |
|---|---|---|---|
| **Thirsk** | 49 Market Place | (01845) 522755 | thirsktic@hambleton.gov.uk |
| **Todmorden** | 15 Burnley Road | (01706) 818181 | todmorden@ytbtic.co.uk |
| **Wakefield** | 9 The Bull Ring | 0845 601 8353 | tic@wakefield.gov.uk |
| **Warrington** | Academy Way | (01925) 428585 | informationcentre@warrington.gov.uk |
| **Wetherby** | 17 Westgate | (01937) 582151 | wetherbytic@leedslearning.net |
| **Whitby** | Langborne Road | (01723) 383637 | whitbytic@scarborough.gov.uk |
| **Whitehaven** | Market Place | (01946) 598914 | tic@copelandbc.gov.uk |
| **Wigan** | 62 Wallgate | (01942) 825677 | tic@wlct.org |
| **Wilmslow** | Rectory Fields | (01625) 522275 | i.hillaby@macclesfield.gov.uk |
| **Windermere** | Victoria Street | (015394) 46499 | windermeretic@southlakeland.gov.uk |
| **Withernsea*** | 131 Queen Street | (01964) 615683 | withernsea.tic@eastriding.gov.uk |
| **York (De Grey Rooms)** | Exhibition Square | (01904) 550099 | info@visityork.org |
| **York (Railway Station)** | Station Road | (01904) 550099 | info@visityork.org |

*seasonal opening

**calls to this number are charged at premium rate

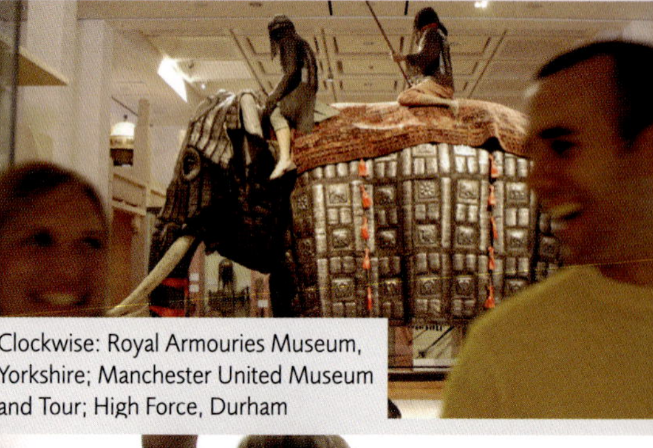

Clockwise: Royal Armouries Museum, Yorkshire; Manchester United Museum and Tour; High Force, Durham

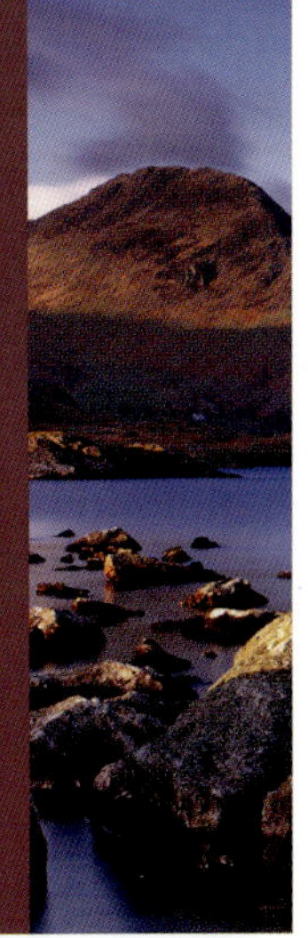

where to stay in

# Northern England

The following establishments participate in VisitBritain's Enjoy England quality assessment scheme and hold a National Accessible Scheme rating. YHA youth hostels in England and Wales are listed in a separate section, see page 40.

Place names in the blue bands with a map reference are shown on the maps at the front of this guide.

## Accommodation symbols

Symbols give useful information about services and facilities. You can find a key to these symbols on page 8.

**ALLENDALE,** Northumberland Map ref 5B2 **SELF CATERING**

SELF CATERING

Units **1**
Sleeps **4**
Low season per wk
**£260.00**
High season per wk
**£290.00–£450.00**

## Station House Flat, Hexham

**contact** Mr & Ms Michael & Verona Woodhouse, Station House Flat, Station House, Hexham NE47 9QF **t** (01434) 683362
**e** info@allendale-holidays.co.uk **w** allendale-holidays.co.uk

Access abc

General

Unit

Payment Cheques

*£25 discount if only one room required. £25 discount for second week.*

Cosy, elegantly decorated, ground-floor holiday flat in waiting rooms and ticket office of terminal station on long-closed Hexham to Allendale railway. Woodburning stove – logs provided. Outstanding quiet countryside location in Area of Outstanding Natural Beauty. Close to Allendale, Village of the Year for all England. One double, one twin or zip-link superking and bed-settee.

**open** All year
**nearest shop** 1.5 miles
**nearest pub** 0.5 miles

*From M6 jct40 or A69 take A686 Penrith – Alston – Haydon Bridge. Follow Allendale. From Allendale, direction Catton 1 mile. Take left (Nenthead, Carrshield), 200yds right-hand side.*

**ALNWICK**, Northumberland — SELF CATERING

★★★★–★★★★★ SELF CATERING

**Bog Mill Farm Holiday Cottages contact** Mrs Ann Mason, Bog Mill Farm Holiday Cottages, Bog Mill Farm, Alnwick NE66 3PA **t** (01665) 604529
**e** stay@bogmill.co.uk **w** bogmill.co.uk

**ALNWICK**, Northumberland — SELF CATERING

★★★–★★★★★ SELF CATERING

**Village Farm contact** Mrs Crissy Stoker, Village Farm, Town Foot Farm, Shilbottle, Alnwick NE66 2HG **t** (01665) 575591
**e** crissy@villagefarmcottages.co.uk **w** villagefarmcottages.co.uk

**ALSTON**, Cumbria — SELF CATERING

★★★★ SELF CATERING

**Proven House**
**t** (01772) 782653
**e** kathleenenglish56@hotmail.com **w** theprovenhouse.co.uk

**AMBLESIDE**, Cumbria Map ref 5A3 — HOTEL

★★★ HOTEL SILVER AWARD

B&B per room per night
**s £95.00–£145.00**
**d £145.00–£220.00**
HB per person per night
**£103.00–£185.00**

## Rothay Manor

Rothay Bridge, Ambleside LA22 0EH **t** (015394) 33605
**e** hotel@rothaymanor.co.uk **w** rothaymanor.co.uk

Access

Rooms

General

Payment Credit/debit cards, cash, cheques

*1 room and 1 suite are adapted for wheelchair users and include roll-in showers, shower chairs, dedicated wheelchair access and disabled parking.*

Regency country-house hotel set in landscaped gardens in the heart of the Lake District, renowned for the warm, comfortable, friendly atmosphere and excellent food and wine. Family owned and run for over 40 years, the hotel makes an excellent base for sightseeing. Special interest holidays and mid-week breaks available.

**open** All year except 3 to 25 January
**bedrooms** 6 double, 4 twin, 1 single, 5 family, 3 suites
**bathrooms** All en suite

*From M6 jct 36 follow A591 to Ambleside. At Ambleside, turn left at traffic lights and left again 0.25 miles further on. Hotel on right.*

**AMBLESIDE**, Cumbria

*See also entry on p108*

**ARMATHWAITE**, Cumbria — CAMPING, CARAVAN & HOLIDAY PARK

★★★★ TOURING PARK

**Englethwaite Hall Caravan Club Site** Armathwaite, Carlisle CA4 9SY
**t** (01228) 560202
**e** enquiries@caravanclub.co.uk **w** caravanclub.co.uk

**BAILIFF BRIDGE,** West Yorkshire Map ref 4B1 — **GUEST ACCOMMODATION**

B&B per room per night
**s £35.00–£45.00**
**d £55.00–£65.00**

## The Lodge at Birkby Hall

Birkby Lane, Brighouse HD6 4JJ **t** (01484) 400321
**e** thelodge@birkbyhall.co.uk **w** birkbyhall.co.uk

Purpose-built B&B with ground-floor bedroom and en suite wetroom. Twin or double bed. Pleasant open farmland surroundings.

**open** All year
**bedrooms** 2 double, 1 twin
**bathrooms** All en suite

Access

Rooms

General

Payment Credit/debit cards, cash, cheques

**BAMBURGH,** Northumberland Map ref 5C1 — **SELF CATERING**

Units **16**
Sleeps **2–6**
Low season per wk
£272.00–£489.00
High season per wk
£441.00–£815.00

## Outchester & Ross Farm Cottages, Belford

**contact** Mrs Shirley McKie, 1 Cragview Road, Belford NE70 7NT
**t** (01668) 213336
**e** enquiry@rosscottages.co.uk **w** rosscottages.co.uk

General

Unit

Payment Credit/debit cards, cash, cheques

Outchester and Ross are both in unique, secluded coastal locations in one of the most beautiful areas of Northumberland between Bamburgh and Holy Island. Our cottages are warm, comfortable and well equipped – each double glazed and with its own private garden. Relax completely and just enjoy being here.

**open** All Year
**nearest shop** 3 miles
**nearest pub** 3 miles

*Maps supplied on booking.*

**BASSENTHWAITE,** Cumbria — **SELF CATERING**

★★★★
SELF CATERING

**Parkergate contact** Ian & Jane Phillips, Parkergate, Bassenthwaite, Keswick CA12 4QG **t** (017687) 76376
**e** info@parkergate.co.uk **w** parkergate.co.uk

**BELFORD,** Northumberland — **SELF CATERING**

**Elwick Farm Cottages contact** Mrs Roslyn Reay, Elwick Farm Cottages, Elwick, Belford NE70 7EL **t** (01668) 213242
**e** w.r.reay@talk21.com **w** elwickcottages.co.uk

At-a-glance symbols are explained on page 8.

**BERWICK-UPON-TWEED,** Northumberland Map ref 5B1 — **GUEST ACCOMMODATION**

GUEST HOUSE

B&B per room per night
**s £30.00–£45.00**
**d £60.00–£80.00**
Evening meal per person
**£10.00**

## Meadow Hill Guest House

Duns Road, Berwick-upon-Tweed TD15 1UB **t** (01289) 306325
**e** christineabart@aol.com **w** meadow-hill.co.uk

A family-run guest house where disabled guests are welcome. Two spacious ground floor rooms, one family and one twin, both with wetroom. Private car park and gardens.

**open** All year
**bedrooms** 2 double, 2 twin, 1 family
**bathrooms** All en suite

Rooms
General

Payment Credit/debit cards, cash, cheques

**BERWICK-UPON-TWEED,** Northumberland — **SELF CATERING**

★★★–★★★★★ SELF CATERING

**West Ord Holiday Cottages contact** Mrs Carol Lang, West Ord Holiday Cottages, West Ord Farm, Berwick-upon-Tweed TD15 2XQ **t** (01289) 386631
**e** stay@westord.co.uk **w** westord.co.uk

**BERWICK-UPON-TWEED,** Northumberland — **CAMPING, CARAVAN & HOLIDAY PARK**

★★★★ TOURING & CAMPING PARK

**Seaview Caravan Club Site** Billendean Road, Berwick-upon-Tweed TD15 1QU
**t** (01289) 305198
**e** enquiries@caravanclub.co.uk
**w** caravanclub.co.uk

**BEVERLEY,** East Yorkshire — **GUEST ACCOMMODATION**

★★★★ GUEST ACCOMMODATION

**Rudstone Walk Country B&B** South Cave, Beverley HU15 2AH
**t** (01430) 422230
**e** office@rudstone-walk.co.uk **w** rudstone-walk.co.uk

**BEVERLEY,** East Yorkshire — **SELF CATERING**

★★–★★★★ SELF CATERING

**Rudstone Walk Country Accommodation contact** Laura Greenwood, Rudstone Walk Country Accommodation, South Cave, Beverley HU15 2AH
**t** (01430) 422230
**e** office@rudstone-walk.co.uk **w** rudstone-walk.co.uk

**BINGFIELD,** Northumberland — **SELF CATERING**

★★★★★ SELF CATERING

**The Hytte contact** Mr & Mrs S R Gregory, The Hytte, Bingfield, Hexham NE46 4HR
**t** (01434) 672321
**e** sgregory001@tiscali.co.uk **w** thehytte.com

**BLACKPOOL,** Lancashire — **HOTEL**

★★★★ HOTEL

**Big Blue Hotel** Pleasure Beach, Ocean Boulevard, Blackpool FY4 1ND
**t** 0845 367 3333
**e** reservations@bigbluehotel.com **w** bigbluehotel.com

**BLACKPOOL,** Lancashire — **GUEST ACCOMMODATION**

★★★ GUEST HOUSE

**Holmsdale** 6-8 Pleasant Street, Blackpool FY1 2JA
**t** (01253) 621008
**e** stay@holmsdalehotel-blackpool.com **w** holmsdalehotel-blackpool.com

**BLACKPOOL,** Lancashire Map ref 4A1 — **GUEST ACCOMMODATION**

★★★
GUEST ACCOMMODATION

B&B per room per night
**s £30.00–£54.50**
**d £37.50–£69.00**
Evening meal per person
**£8.00**

## The Lawton

58-66 Charnley Road, Blackpool FY1 4PF **t** (01253) 753471
**e** lawtonhotel@lycos.co.uk **w** thelawtonhotel.co.uk

1:15 ramped access to keycard entrance into level lobby, bar and dining room. Eight-person lift to all floors. Easy access and ground floor rooms available. Ample parking.

**open** All year
**bedrooms** 24 double, 12 twin, 7 single, 29 family
**bathrooms** All en suite

Access abc
Rooms
General
Payment Credit/debit cards, cash, cheques, euros

**BLACKPOOL,** Lancashire — **SELF CATERING**

★★★★★
SELF CATERING

**The Beach House contact** Mrs Estelle Livesey, The Beach House, 204 Queens Promenade, Blackpool FY2 9JS **t** (01253) 826555
**e** info@thebeachhouseblackpool.co.uk **w** thebeachhouseblackpool.co.uk

**BLACKPOOL,** Lancashire — **SELF CATERING**

★★–★★★★
SELF CATERING

**The Berkeley contact** Lord Lomax-Dwent, The Berkeley, 6 Queens Promenade, Blackpool FY2 9SQ **t** (01253) 623218
**e** info@selfcatering.tv **w** selfcatering.tv

**BLACKPOOL,** Lancashire — **SELF CATERING**

★★★★–★★★★★
SELF CATERING

**Burbage Holiday Lodge contact** Mr & Mrs Crewcock, Burbage Holiday Lodge, 198 Queens Promenade, Blackpool FY2 9JS **t** (01253) 356657
**e** enquires@burbageholidaylodge.co.uk **w** burbageholidaygroup.co.uk

**BLACKPOOL,** Lancashire

*See also entry on p109*

**BLEASDALE,** Lancashire — **SELF CATERING**

★★★★
SELF CATERING

**Bleasdale Cottages contact** Mr Gardner, Bleasdale Cottages, Lower Fairsnape Farm, Bleasdale, Preston PR3 1UY **t** (01995) 61343
**e** robert_gardner1@tiscali.co.uk **w** bleasdalecottages.co.uk

## Accessible Schemes index

If you have specific accessible requirements, the Accessible Schemes index at the back of the guide lists accommodation under different categories for mobility, hearing and visual impairment.

**BOLTON ABBEY,** North Yorkshire Map ref 4B1 — **CAMPING, CARAVAN & HOLIDAY PARK**

TOURING PARK

(57) £14.00–£26.90
(57) £14.00–£26.90
57 touring pitches

## Strid Wood Caravan Club Site

Bolton Abbey, Skipton BD23 6AN **t** (01756) 710433
**w** caravanclub.co.uk

General

Payment Credit/debit cards, cash, cheques

One of the prettiest sites on the network, part of the Bolton Abbey estate, in an open glade surrounded by woodland and the glorious Yorkshire Dales. Within the boundaries of the estate are some 75 miles of footpaths through moors, woods and farmland.

**open** March to January

*Turn off A59 at Bolton Bridge roundabout onto B6160, after 3m turn right into Strid car park. Please note that approach from north on B6160 in unsuitable for caravans.*

**BOSLEY,** Cheshire — **SELF CATERING**

★★
SELF CATERING

**The Old Byre contact** Mrs Dorothy Gilman, The Old Byre, Pye Ash Farm, Leek Road, Macclesfield SK11 0PN **t** (01260) 223293
**e** d.gilman@hotmail.co.uk **w** farmstay.co.uk

**BOSLEY,** Cheshire — **SELF CATERING**

★★★
SELF CATERING

**Strawberry Duck Cottage contact** Mr B Carter, Strawberry Duck Cottage, Bullgate Lane, Bosley, Macclesfield SK11 0PP **t** (01260) 223591
**e** 2007@strawberryduckholidays.co.uk **w** strawberryduckholidays.co.uk

**BOWES,** Durham — **SELF CATERING**

★★★★
SELF CATERING

**Mellwaters Barn contact** Mr Andrew Tavener, East Mellwaters Farm, Stainmore Road, Barnard Castle DL12 9RH **t** (01833) 628181
**e** mellwatersbarn@aol.com **w** mellwatersbarn.co.uk

**BOWNESS-ON-SOLWAY,** Cumbria — **GUEST ACCOMMODATION**

★★★
BED & BREAKFAST

**The Old Chapel** Bowness-on-Solway, Wigton CA7 5BL
**t** (01697) 351126
**e** oldchapelbowness@hotmail.com **w** oldchapelbownessonsolway.com

## Using map references

The map references refer to the colour maps at the front of this guide. The first figure is the map number, the letter and figure that follow indicate the grid reference on the map.

**BOWNESS-ON-WINDERMERE,** Cumbria Map ref 5A3 **SELF CATERING**

★★★★
SELF CATERING

Units **2**
Sleeps **4**
Low season per wk
£350.00–£450.00
High season per wk
£500.00–£530.00

## Lake District Disabled Holidays,

Bowness-on-Windermere

**contact** Stuart & Jane Higham, Lake District Disabled Holidays, Mitchelland Farm, Nr Bowness-on-Windermere, Kendal LA8 8LL
**t** (015394) 47421 **w** lakedistrictdisabledholidays.co.uk

Unique, luxury, log cottages designed for an exceptional level of access. Double bedroom alongside bathroom. Twin bedroom with spacious en suite wetroom, fitted with grab-rails etc. Well-equipped kitchen, part of the worktop at wheelchair height. Panoramic views over our hill-farm.

**open** All year
**nearest shop** 3 miles
**nearest pub** < 0.5 miles

Access abc

General P

Unit

Payment Cash, cheques

**BRIDLINGTON,** East Yorkshire **HOTEL**

★★
HOTEL

**The Bay View Hotel** 52 South Marine Drive, Bridlington YO15 3JJ
**t** (01262) 674225
**e** info@bay-view-hotel.com **w** bay-view-hotel.com

**BRIDLINGTON,** East Yorkshire **GUEST ACCOMMODATION**

★★★★
GUEST HOUSE

**Providence Place** 11 North View Terrace, Bridlington YO15 2QP
**t** (01262) 603840
**e** enquiries@providenceplace.info **w** providenceplace.info

**BUCKDEN,** North Yorkshire **SELF CATERING**

★★★★
SELF CATERING

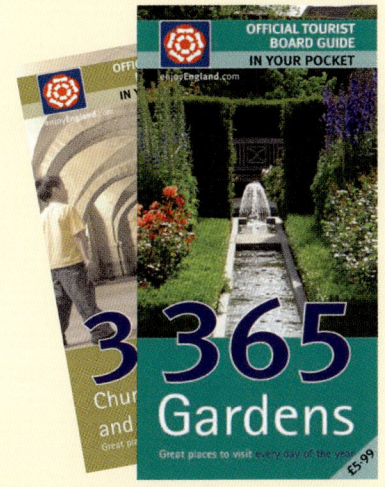

**Dalegarth and The Ghyll Cottages contact** David & Susan Lusted, Dalegarth and The Ghyll Cottages, 11 Dalegarth, Buckden, Skipton BD23 5JU
**t** (01756) 760877
**e** info@dalegarth.co.uk **w** dalegarth.co.uk

**BURY,** Greater Manchester Map ref 4B1 — **CAMPING, CARAVAN & HOLIDAY PARK**

TOURING PARK

(85) £14.00–£26.90
(85) £14.00–£26.90
85 touring pitches

## Burrs Country Park Caravan Club Site

Woodhill Road, Burrs, Bury BL8 1DA **t** (0161) 761 0489
**w** caravanclub.co.uk

General

Payment Credit/debit cards, cash, cheques

*Midweek discount; pitch fees reduced by 50% for stays on Mon, Tue, Wed or Thu night.*

On an historic mill site, Burrs has much to offer with relaxing river and countryside walks, contemporary art, the East Lancashire Steam Railway passing by. The country park is easily accessible, situated just north of Bury town centre and is handy for trips into Manchester.

**open** All year

*From A676 (signposted Ramsbottom), follow signs for Burrs Country Park.*

**CATON,** Lancashire — **SELF CATERING**

SELF CATERING & SERVICED APARTMENTS

**The Croft – Ground Floor Apartment contact** Mrs Sue Brierly-Hampton, 4 The Croft, Caton LA2 9QG
**t** (01524) 770725
**e** suebrierly@hotmail.com

**CHESTER,** Cheshire — **HOTEL**

HOTEL

**Grosvenor Pulford Hotel & Spa** Wrexham Road, Pulford, Chester CH4 9DG
**t** (01244) 570560
**e** reservations@grosvenorpulfordhotel.co.uk **w** grosvenorpulfordhotel.co.uk

**CHIPPING,** Lancashire — **HOTEL**

HOTEL

**The Gibbon Bridge Hotel** Chipping, Forest of Bowland, Preston PR3 2TQ
**t** (01995) 61456
**e** reception@gibbon-bridge.co.uk **w** gibbon-bridge.co.uk

**CLITHEROE,** Lancashire Map ref 4A1 — 

HOTEL

B&B per room per night
**s £57.00–£71.00**
**d £86.00–£102.00**
HB per person per night
**£78.00–£92.00**

## Mytton Fold Hotel and Golf Complex

Whalley Road, Langho, Blackburn BB6 8AB **t** (01254) 240662
**e** info@myttonfold.co.uk **w** myttonfold.co.uk

Family-run hotel. Ground-floor, en suite bedrooms. Level access to bar and restaurant. Stunning gardens and views across Ribble Valley. Service dogs welcome.

**open** All year
**bedrooms** 13 double, 14 twin, 1 family
**bathrooms** All en suite

Rooms

General

Payment Credit/debit cards, cash, cheques

**COCKFIELD,** Durham Map ref 5B3 — **SELF CATERING**

SELF CATERING

Units **2**
Sleeps **4–5**

Low season per wk
**Min £160.00**
High season per wk
**Max £340.00**

## Stonecroft and Swallows Nest, Bishop Auckland

**contact** Mrs Alison Tallentire, Low Lands Farm, Bishop Auckland DL13 5AW **t** (01388) 718251
**e** info@farmholidaysuk.com **w** farmholidaysuk.com

Access

General

Unit

Payment Cash, cheques

*Adapted kitchen, level-entry shower with shower chair, raised toilet seat with handrails, ground-floor bedrooms, turning circles in every room.*

Winners County Durham Accessible Award 2002. Comfortable, cosy, accessible cottage. Level-entry shower, ground-floor bedrooms, all linen and towels provided, log fire, original beams, own garden, gas barbeque. Lots to see and do for everyone. Friendly owner-run farm. A truly relaxing holiday. A warm welcome awaits you.

**open** All Year
**nearest shop** 1 mile
**nearest pub** 1 mile

*Directions on request.*

**CONGLETON,** Cheshire — **GUEST ACCOMMODATION**

★★★★ GUEST ACCOMMODATION

**Sandhole Farm** Manchester Road (A34), Hulme Walfield CW12 2JH
**t** (01260) 224419
**e** veronica@sandholefarm.co.uk **w** sandholefarm.co.uk

**CONISTON,** Cumbria — **CAMPING, CARAVAN & HOLIDAY PARK**

TOURING & CAMPING PARK

**Park Coppice Caravan Club Site** Park Gate, Coniston LA21 8LA
**t** (015394) 41555
**w** caravanclub.co.uk

## What do the star ratings mean?

For a detailed explanation of the quality and facilities represented by the stars, please refer to the information pages at the back of this guide.

**CORNRIGGS,** Durham Map ref 5B2 — **SELF CATERING**

**SELF CATERING**

Units **2**
Sleeps **2–6**
Low season per wk
**£320.00–£380.00**
High season per wk
**£380.00–£560.00**

## Cornriggs Cottages, Cowshill in Weardale, Bishop Auckland

**contact** Mr & Mrs Harry and Janet Elliott, Alice and Nelly's Cottages, c/o Low Cornriggs Farm, Cornriggs, Cowshill DL13 1AQ
**t** (01388) 537600 & 07818 843159
**e** cornriggsfarm@btconnect.com **w** britnett.net/lowcornriggsfarm

Access abc

General

Unit

Payment Credit/debit cards, cash, cheques, euros

*Home baking, Hereford beef and free-range farm eggs all for sale.*

Peacefully located in the heart of Weardale, with spectacular views. Large detached cottages, wheelchair accessible (including accessible WC and shower); fitted to a very high standard. Home baking and breakfast available in the farmhouse. Within easy reach of the Lakes, Hadrian's Wall, Beamish and Durham.

**open** All year
**nearest shop** 4 miles
**nearest pub** 1 mile

**CRASTER,** Northumberland — **SELF CATERING**

★★★★
**SELF CATERING**

**Craster Pine Lodges contact** Mr & Mrs Michael & Fyona Robson, Craster Pine Lodges, 19 Heugh Road, Alnwick NE66 3TJ **t** (01665) 576286
**e** pinelodges@barkpots.co.uk **w** crasterpinelodges.co.uk

**CROW EDGE,** South Yorkshire — **SELF CATERING**

**SELF CATERING**

**Lazy Daisy's contact** Sally Howe, Lazy Daisy's, Daisy Hill Farm, Flouch, Sheffield S36 4HH **t** (01226) 763001
**e** daisyhillfarm@tiscali.co.uk **w** lazydaisys.co.uk

## Don't forget www.

Web addresses throughout this guide are shown without the prefix www. Please include www. in the address line of your browser. If a web address does not follow this style it is shown in full.

## DENSHAW, Greater Manchester — GUEST ACCOMMODATION

FARMHOUSE

**Cherry Clough Farm House Accommodation** Cherry Clough Farm, Denshaw OL3 5UE **t** (01457) 874369

**e** info@cherryclough.co.uk **w** cherryclough.co.uk

## DURHAM, Map ref 5C2 — CAMPING, CARAVAN & HOLIDAY PARK

TOURING & CAMPING PARK

(77) £14.00–£26.90
(77) £14.00–£26.90
77 touring pitches

# Grange Caravan Club Site

Meadow Lane, Durham DH1 1TL **t** (0191) 384 4778

**w** caravanclub.co.uk

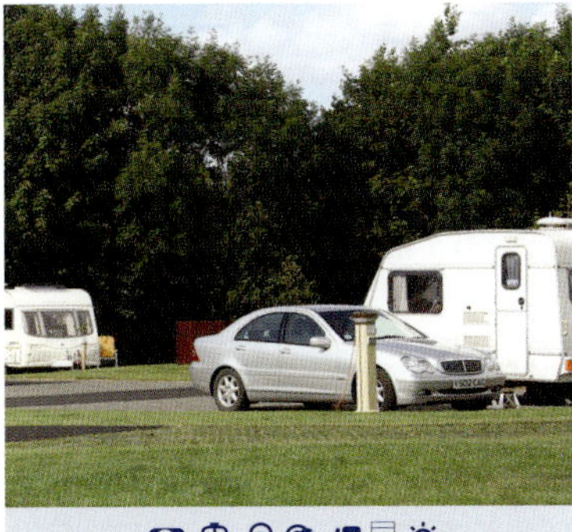

An open and level site, just off the A1(M) and within easy reach of the City of Durham with walks from the site into the city. Durham is only three miles away, dramatically set on its 70-foot rocky semi-island in a hairpin bend of the River Wear.

**open** All year

*A1(M) jct 62, A690 towards Durham. Turn right after 50m. Signposted Maureen Terrace and brown caravan sign.*

General

Leisure

Payment Credit/debit cards, cash, cheques

## EBBERSTON, North Yorkshire — SELF CATERING

SELF CATERING

**Cow Pasture & Swallow-Tail Cottages contact** David & Brenda Green, Cow Pasture & Swallow-Tail Cottages, Studley House Farm, 67 Main Street, Pickering YO13 9NR **t** (01723) 859285
**e** brenda@yorkshireancestors.com **w** studleyhousefarm.co.uk

## ELLESMERE PORT, Cheshire — HOTEL

★★★

HOTEL

**Holiday Inn Ellesmere Port/Cheshire Oaks** Centre Island, Waterways CH65 2AL
**t** (0151) 356 8111
**e** reception@hiellesmereport.com **w** hiellesmereport.com

## FILEY, North Yorkshire — SELF CATERING

SELF CATERING

**5 Leys Holiday Accommodation contact** Mrs Kerry Welsby, 5 Leys Holiday Accommodation, 7-10 The Beach, Filey YO14 9LA **t** 0845 094 5051
**e** info@5leys.co.uk **w** 5leys.co.uk

## Key to symbols

Symbols at the end of each entry help you pick out the services and facilities which are most important for your stay. A key to the symbols can be found on page 8.

## FLAMBOROUGH, East Yorkshire Map ref 5D3 — SELF CATERING

SELF CATERING

Units **2**
Sleeps **1–8**

Low season per wk
£385.00–£430.00
High season per wk
£420.00–£675.00

### Flamborough Rock Cottages, Flamborough, Bridlington

**contact** Mrs J Geraghty, Flamborough Rock Cottages, 13 Dog & Duck Square, Bridlington YO15 1NB **t** (01262) 850996 & 07974 978311
**e** jannicegeraghty@hotmail.co.uk **w** flamboroughrockcottages.co.uk

Clean, comfortable and well-equipped cottage where families with disabled relatives are warmly welcomed. Mobile ramp to lovely patio via double doors. Ground-foor double bedroom with en suite wetroom. Three double bedrooms (two en suite), one room with bunk bed.

**open** All Year
**nearest shop** < 0.5 miles
**nearest pub** < 0.5 miles

Payment Cash, cheques

## GAINFORD, Durham — SELF CATERING

★★★★–★★★★★
SELF CATERING

**East Greystone Farm Cottages contact** Mrs Sue Hodgson, East Greystone Farm Cottages, Main Road, Gainford DL2 3BL **t** (01325) 730236
**e** sue@holidayfarmcottages.co.uk **w** holidayfarmcottages.co.uk

## GARSTANG, Lancashire — SELF CATERING

★★★★★
SELF CATERING

**Barnacre Cottages contact** Mr Terence Sharples, Barnacre Cottages, The Old Shippon, Arkwright Farm, Eidsforth Lane, Garstang PR3 1GN
**t** (01995) 600918
**e** sue@barnacre-cottages.co.uk **w** barnacre-cottages.co.uk

## GATESHEAD, Tyne and Wear — HOTEL

QUALITY-ASSESSED HOTEL

**Hilton Newcastle Gateshead** Bottle Bank, Gateshead NE8 2AR
**t** (0191) 490 9700
**e** reservations.newcastle@hilton.com **w** hilton.co.uk

## GILLING WEST, North Yorkshire — CAMPING, CARAVAN & HOLIDAY PARK

★★★★
TOURING PARK

**Hargill House Caravan Club Site** Gilling West, Richmond DL10 5LJ
**t** (01342) 336732
**e** enquiries@caravanclub.co.uk **w** caravanclub.co.uk

## GRANGE-OVER-SANDS, Cumbria — HOTEL

**Netherwood Hotel** Lindale Road, Grange-over-Sands LA11 6ET
**t** (015395) 32552
**e** enquiries@netherwood-hotel.co.uk
**w** netherwood-hotel.co.uk

## Accessible Schemes index

If you have specific accessible requirements, the Accessible Schemes index at the back of the guide lists accommodation under different categories for mobility, hearing and visual impairment.

**GRANGE-OVER-SANDS,** Cumbria Map ref 5A3 **CAMPING, CARAVAN & HOLIDAY PARK**

TOURING PARK

(131)
£14.00–£26.90
(131)
£14.00–£26.90
131 touring pitches

## Meathop Fell Caravan Club Site

Meathop, Grange-over-Sands LA11 6RB **t** (01539) 532912
**w** caravanclub.co.uk

General

Leisure

Payment Credit/debit cards, cash, cheques

*Midweek discount; pitch fees reduced by 50% for stays on Mon, Tue, Wed or Thu night during saver and low seasons.*

Gentle and peaceful, this thoughtfully laid out site is divided into separate pitching areas which are punctuated by shrubs and grass. This is an ideal base from which to explore north Lancashire and the southern Lake District. Brockhole, the National Park Visitor Centre, is a good place to start your exploration.

**open** All year

*M6 jct 36, A590 to Barrow. After about 3.25 miles take slip road and follow A590 to Barrow. At 1st roundabout follow International Camping signs. Steep approach.*

**GRASMERE,** Cumbria **SELF CATERING**

★★★★
SELF CATERING

**Rothay Lodge & Apartment contact** Lindsay Rogers, Rothay Lodge, c/o 54a Trevor Road, West Bridgford NG2 6FT **t** (015394) 35341
**e** enquiries@rothay-lodge.co.uk **w** rothay-lodge.co.uk

**HARMBY,** North Yorkshire **CAMPING, CARAVAN & HOLIDAY PARK**

★★★
TOURING & CAMPING PARK

**Lower Wensleydale Caravan Club Site** Harmby, Leyburn DL8 5NU
**t** (01969) 623366
**e** enquiries@caravanclub.co.uk
**w** caravanclub.co.uk

**HARROGATE,** North Yorkshire **SELF CATERING**

★★★★
SELF CATERING

**Brimham Rocks Cottages contact** Deborah Gray, Brimham Rocks Cottages, High North Farm, Harrogate HG3 5EY **t** (01765) 620284
**e** brimhamrc@yahoo.co.uk **w** brimham.co.uk

**HARWOOD DALE,** North Yorkshire **GUEST ACCOMMODATION**

★★★★
FARMHOUSE

**The Grainary** Harwood Dale, Scarborough YO13 0DT
**t** (01723) 870026
**e** grainary@btopenworld.com **w** grainary.co.uk

**HAYDON BRIDGE,** Northumberland **GUEST ACCOMMODATION**

★★★★
BED & BREAKFAST

**Grindon Cartshed** Haydon Bridge, Hexham NE47 6NQ
**t** (01434) 684273
**e** cartshed@grindon.force9.co.uk **w** grindon-cartshed.co.uk

At-a-glance symbols are explained on page 8.

## HAYDON BRIDGE, Northumberland — GUEST ACCOMMODATION

★★★★ GUEST HOUSE

**Shaftoe's** 4 Shaftoe Street, Haydon Bridge NE47 6BJ
**t** (01434) 684664
**e** bookings@shaftoes.co.uk **w** shaftoes.co.uk

## HEBDEN BRIDGE, West Yorkshire — CAMPING, CARAVAN & HOLIDAY PARK

★★★★★ TOURING PARK

**Lower Clough Foot Caravan Club Site** Cragg Vale, Hebden Bridge HX7 5RU
**t** (01422) 882531
**w** caravanclub.co.uk

## HESLEDEN, Durham — GUEST ACCOMMODATION

★★★★ INN SILVER AWARD

**The Ship Inn** Main Street, High Hesleden TS27 4QD
**t** (01429) 836453
**e** sheila@theshipinn.net
**w** theshipinn.net

## HEXHAM, Northumberland — SELF CATERING

★★★★ SELF CATERING

**Old Byre contact** Mrs Elizabeth Courage, Old Byre, Rye Hill Farm, Slaley, Hexham NE47 0AH **t** (01434) 673259
**e** info@ryehillfarm.co.uk **w** ryehillfarm.co.uk

## HIGH CATTON, East Yorkshire — SELF CATERING

★★★★–★★★★★ SELF CATERING

**The Courtyard contact** Sheila Foster, The Courtyard, High Catton, Stamford Bridge, York YO41 1EP **t** (01759) 371374
**e** foster-s@sky.com **w** highcattongrange.co.uk

## ILKLEY, West Yorkshire — SELF CATERING

★★★★–★★★★★ SELF CATERING

**Westwood Lodge contact** Tim Edwards, Westwood Lodge, Westwood Drive, Ilkley LS29 9JF **t** (01943) 433430
**e** welcome@westwoodlodge.co.uk **w** westwoodlodge.co.uk

## INGLETON, Durham — SELF CATERING

★★★★★ SELF CATERING

**Mill Granary Cottages contact** Mr & Mrs Richard & Kate Hodgson, Mill Granary Cottages, Middleton House, Ingleton DL2 3HG **t** (01325) 730339
**e** info@millgranary.co.uk **w** millgranary.co.uk

## INGLETON, North Yorkshire — GUEST ACCOMMODATION

★★★★ GUEST HOUSE

**Riverside Lodge** 24 Main Street, Ingleton LA6 3HJ
**t** (01524) 241359
**e** info@riversideingleton.co.uk **w** riversideingleton.co.uk

**KENDAL,** Cumbria Map ref 5B3 — **SELF CATERING**

★★★
SELF CATERING

Units 1
Sleeps 2–4
Low season per wk
£270.00–£320.00
High season per wk
£320.00–£370.00

## Barkinbeck Cottage, Kendal

**contact** Mrs Ann Hamilton, Barkinbeck Cottage, Barkin House Barn, Gatebeck, Kendal LA8 0HX **t** (015395) 67122 **e** barkinhouse@yahoo.co.uk
**w** barkinbeck.co.uk

Converted barn in peaceful, rural location. Ideal for visiting the Lakes and Yorkshire Dales. Level access throughout. Adapted bathroom. One double, one twin bedroom, open fire, panoramic views. Owner maintained.

**open** All year
**nearest shop** 5 miles
**nearest pub** 5 miles

General 12 P

Unit

Payment Cash, cheques

**KENDAL,** Cumbria Map ref 5B3 — **CAMPING, CARAVAN & HOLIDAY PARK**

★★★★
TOURING PARK

(141)
£14.00–£26.90
(141)
£14.00–£26.90
141 touring pitches

## Low Park Wood Caravan Club Site

Sedgwick, Kendal LA8 0JZ **t** (01539) 560186
**e** enquiries@caravanclub.co.uk **w** caravanclub.co.uk

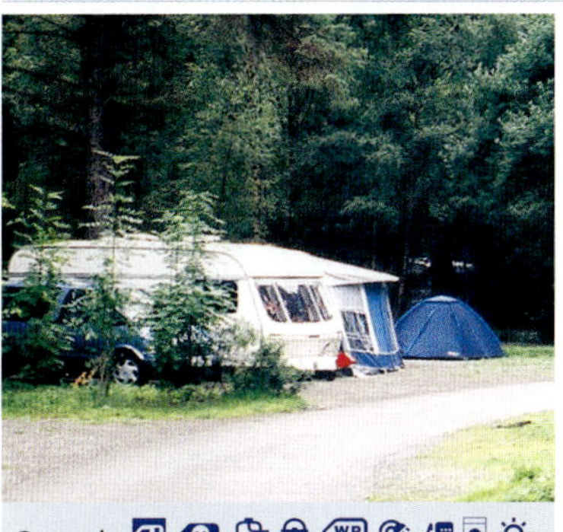

General

Leisure

Payment Credit/debit cards, cash, cheques

*Midweek discount; pitch fees reduced by 50% for stays on Mon, Tue, Wed or Thu night outside peak and value season.*

From the country lane approach running beside a tumbling river, to the glades where you pitch amidst the wild flowers. This site is heaven – so peaceful you'll not want to leave. Take your binoculars, as the bird life is varied and colourful, and if you're a wild flower enthusiast you'll find plenty to note.

**open** March to November

*Leave M6 at jct 36 and go onto A590 signed South Lakes. After approximately 3.25 miles leave via slip road (signed Milnthorpe, Barrow) at roundabout and follow caravan signs.*

**KIELDER WATER,** Northumberland — **SELF CATERING**

SELF CATERING

Awaiting NAS rating

**Calvert Trust Kielder** Falstone, Kielder NE48 1BS
**t** (01434) 250232
**e** enquiries@calvert-kielder.com **w** calvert-trust.org.uk

At-a-glance symbols are explained on page 8.

## KIELDER WATER, Northumberland — SELF CATERING

SELF CATERING

**Falstone Barns** **contact** Mrs Nicolette Forster, Falstone Barns, Falstone Farm, Falstone, Hexham NE48 1AA **t** (01434) 240251
**e** info@falstonebarns.com **w** falstonebarns.com

## KIRKBYMOORSIDE, North Yorkshire — GUEST ACCOMMODATION

**The Cornmill** Kirby Mills, Kirkbymoorside, York YO62 6NP
**t** (01751) 432000
**e** cornmill@kirbymills.demon.co.uk
**w** kirbymills.demon.co.uk

## KIRKBYMOORSIDE, North Yorkshire — SELF CATERING

★★★★
SELF CATERING

**Low Hagg Holidays** **contact** Mr J Lee, Low Hagg Holidays, Low Hagg, Starfitts Lane, York YO62 7JF **t** (01751) 430500
**w** longhaggfarm.com

## KIRKOSWALD, Cumbria Map ref 5B2 — SELF CATERING

★★★★
SELF CATERING

Units **5**
Sleeps **2–4**
Low season per wk
£270.00
High season per wk
£380.00

### Howscales, Penrith

**contact** Liz Webster, Howscales, Kirkoswald, Penrith CA10 1JG
**t** (01768) 898666 **e** liz@howscales.co.uk **w** howscales.co.uk

Hazelrigg, a single-storey cottage, has one large double, or twin by arrangement, with an en suite bathroom. Stunning garden and views. Ample parking. Service dogs welcome. Four other properties available for carers/family.

**open** All year
**nearest shop** 1.5 miles
**nearest pub** 1.5 miles

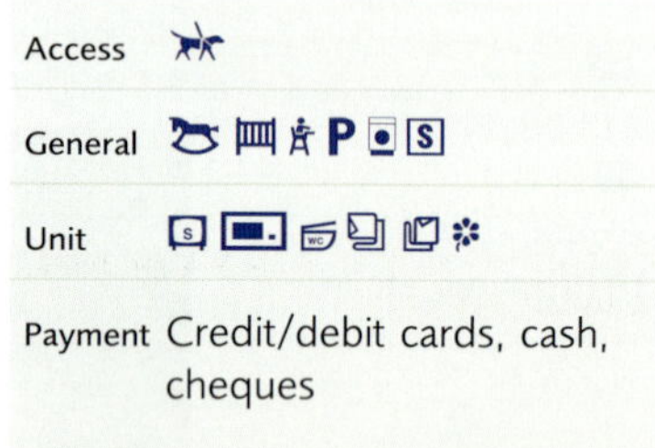

Access
General
Unit
Payment Credit/debit cards, cash, cheques

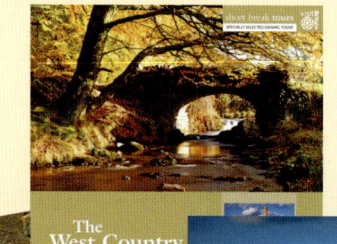

**KNARESBOROUGH,** North Yorkshire Map ref 4B1 — **CAMPING, CARAVAN & HOLIDAY PARK**

TOURING PARK

(72) £14.00–£26.90
(72) £14.00–£26.90
72 touring pitches

## Knaresborough Caravan Club Site

New Road, Scotton, Knaresborough HG5 9HH **t** (01423) 866196
**w** caravanclub.co.uk

General

Leisure

Payment Credit/debit cards, cash, cheques

This site offers a gateway to the Yorkshire Dales and the many attractions of the north of England. The site is surrounded by mature trees and hedges and on fine days it is sunny yet well sheltered. Knaresborough is an historic market town with a town crier, ancient walkways, castle ruins and cobbled alleys.

**open** March 2009 to January 2010

*Turn right off A59 onto B6165. After approximately 1.5 miles turn right immediately after petrol station into New Road. Site is on right-hand side after 50yds.*

**LAMPLUGH,** Cumbria — **CAMPING, CARAVAN & HOLIDAY PARK**

★★★★
TOURING PARK

**Dockray Meadow Caravan Club Site** Lamplugh CA14 4SH
**t** (01946) 861357
**w** caravanclub.co.uk

**LONGHORSLEY,** Northumberland — **SELF CATERING**

★★★★–★★★★★
SELF CATERING

**Beacon Hill Farm Holidays contact** Mr Alun Moore, Beacon Hill Farm, Beacon Hill, Longhorsley, Morpeth NE65 8QW **t** (01670) 780900 & 07802 517121
**e** alun@beaconhill.co.uk **w** beaconhill.co.uk

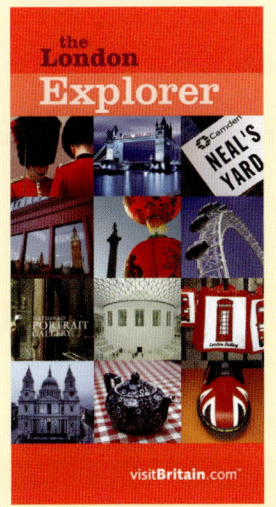



At-a-glance symbols are explained on page 8.

## LUCKER, Northumberland Map ref 5B1 — SELF CATERING

★★★★-★★★★★
SELF CATERING

Units 1
Sleeps 2
Low season per wk
Min £343.00
High season per wk
Max £532.00

### Lucker Hall Steading, Lucker

Alnwick Castle Cottages, Belford NE70 7JQ **t** (01668) 219941
**e** jane@nehc.co.uk **w** alnwickcastlecottages.co.uk

General

Unit

Payment Credit/debit cards, cash, cheques, euros

*3-night breaks available Nov-Mar. Similar, larger cottages available for 3-4 guests.*

A deceptively spacious property for two at Lucker Hall Steading, in the heart of the delightfully peaceful village; and yet just a short drive to Bamburgh beach or Alnwick Castle and Gardens. The contemporary design includes superking or twin beds, spacious wetroom, superbly equipped kitchen and comfortable leather sofas. Service dog welcome.

**open** All year
**nearest shop** 2 miles
**nearest pub** < 0.5 miles

*1.5 miles off A1 turning at Warenford for Lucker. 10 minutes from Alnwick. 4 miles to Bamburgh. 18 miles to Berwick.*

## LYTHAM ST ANNES, Lancashire — HOTEL

★★★
HOTEL

**The Chadwick Hotel** South Promenade, Lytham St Annes FY8 1NP
**t** (01253) 720061
**e** sales@thechadwickhotel.com **w** thechadwickhotel.com

## MANCHESTER, Greater Manchester — HOTEL

QUALITY-ASSESSED HOTEL

**Hilton Manchester Deansgate** 303 Deansgate, Manchester M3 4LQ
**t** (0161) 870 1600
**e** reservations.manchesterdeansgate@hilton.com **w** hilton.co.uk

## MANCHESTER, Greater Manchester — HOTEL

★★★★
HOTEL
SILVER AWARD

**The Midland Hotel** Peter Street, Manchester M60 2DS
**t** (0161) 236 3333
**e** midlandreservations@qhotels.co.uk
**w** themidland.co.uk

## MANCHESTER, Greater Manchester — GUEST ACCOMMODATION

GUEST ACCOMMODATION

**Luther King House** Brighton Grove, Wilmslow Road, Manchester M14 5JP
**t** (0161) 224 6404
**e** reception@lkh.co.uk **w** lkh.co.uk

## MANCHESTER, Greater Manchester

*See also entries on p110*

## MORECAMBE, Lancashire — SELF CATERING

★★★
SELF CATERING

**Eden Vale Luxury Holiday Flats** **contact** Mr Jason Coombs, Eden Vale Luxury Holiday Flats, 338 Marine Road Central, Morecambe LA4 5AB
**t** 07739 008301
**e** jicoombs@onetel.com **w** edenvalemorecambe.co.uk

## MORPETH, Northumberland Map ref 5C2 — HOTEL

# Longhirst Hall

Longhirst, Morpeth NE61 3LL **t** (01670) 791348 **e** enquiries@longhirst.co.uk
**w** longhirst.co.uk

B&B per room per night
**s £70.00–£112.00**
**d £75.00–£125.00**
HB per person per night
**£70.00–£90.00**

Longhirst, the perfect base to explore the castles and coastlines of Northumberland. Located outside the market town of Morpeth, less than one hour from Alnwick Gardens and Bamburgh Castle.

**open** All year
**bedrooms** 56 double, 21 twin
**bathrooms** All en suite

Access
Rooms
General
Leisure
Payment Credit/debit cards, cash, cheques

## MORPETH, Northumberland — HOTEL

**Macdonald Linden Hall Hotel** Longhorsley NE65 8XF
**t** 0870 194 2123
**e** lindenhall@macdonald-hotels.co.uk
**w** lindenhall-hotel.co.uk

## NEWBROUGH, Northumberland — GUEST ACCOMMODATION

★★★★
FARMHOUSE

**Carr Edge Farm** Newbrough NE47 5EA
**t** (01434) 674788
**e** stay@carredge.co.uk **w** carredge.co.uk

## NEWLANDS, Cumbria — CAMPING, CARAVAN & HOLIDAY PARK

★★★★
TOURING PARK

**Low Manesty Caravan Club Site** Manesty, Keswick CA12 5UG
**t** (017687) 77275
**e** enquiries@caravanclub.co.uk **w** caravanclub.co.uk

## NEWTON-IN-BOWLAND, Lancashire — SELF CATERING

★★★★
SELF CATERING

**Stonefold Holiday Cottage** **contact** Ms Helen Blanc, Stonefold Holiday Cottage, Slaidburn Road, Newton-in-Bowland, Clitheroe BB7 3DL **t** 07966 582834
**w** stonefoldholidaycottage.co.uk

## NEWTON-ON-RAWCLIFFE, North Yorkshire — SELF CATERING

★★★★
SELF CATERING

**Sunset Cottage** **contact** Pat Anderson, Sunset Cottage, Newton-on-Rawcliffe, Pickering YO18 8QF **t** (01751) 472172
**e** bookings@boonhill.co.uk **w** boonhill.co.uk/sunset.htm

## NORTHALLERTON, North Yorkshire — GUEST ACCOMMODATION

**Lovesome Hill Farm** Northallerton DL6 2PB
**t** (01609) 772311
**e** pearsonlhf@care4free.net
**w** lovesomehillfarm.co.uk

At-a-glance symbols are explained on page 8.

**PATELEY BRIDGE,** North Yorkshire — **SELF CATERING**

SELF CATERING & SERVICED APARTMENTS

**Helme Pasture, Old Spring Wood contact** Mrs Rosemary Helme, Hartwith Bank, Summerbridge, Harrogate HG3 4DR
**t** (01423) 780279
**e** helmepasture@btinternet.com **w** helmepasture.co.uk

**PENRITH,** Cumbria Map ref 5B2 — **CAMPING, CARAVAN & HOLIDAY PARK**

HOLIDAY, TOURING & CAMPING PARK

(151) £14.90–£28.30
(151) £14.90–£28.30
151 touring pitches

## Troutbeck Head Caravan Club Site

Troutbeck, Penrith CA11 0SS **t** (017684) 83521
**e** enquiries@caravanclub.co.uk **w** caravanclub.co.uk

General

Leisure

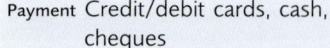

Payment Credit/debit cards, cash, cheques

This site is set in classical north Lakeland countryside, near Ullswater and surrounded by the great outdoors. Fabulous for nature lovers and walkers alike, the site nestles in a valley alongside a babbling brook, below Great Mell Fell and with spectacular views of Blencathra to the west.

**open** March 2009 to January 2010

*Leave M6 at jct 40 onto A66 signposted Keswick. In about 7.25 miles turn left onto A5091, signposted Dockray/Ullswater, site on right after 1.5 miles.*

**PICKERING,** North Yorkshire — **SELF CATERING**

★★★★–★★★★★

SELF CATERING

**Beech Farm Cottages contact** Rooney Massara, Beech Farm Cottages, Main Street, Wrelton, Pickering YO18 8PG **t** (01751) 476612
**e** holiday@beechfarm.com **w** beechfarm.com

**PICKERING,** North Yorkshire — **SELF CATERING**

★★★★

SELF CATERING

**Easthill Farm House and Gardens contact** Mrs Diane Stenton, Easthill Farm House and Gardens, Wilton Road, Thornton Dale, Pickering YO18 7QP
**t** (01751) 474561
**e** info@easthill-farm-holidays.co.uk **w** easthill-farm-holidays.co.uk

## What if I need to cancel?

It is advisable to check the proprietor's cancellation policy in case you have to change your plans at a later date.

**PICKERING,** North Yorkshire Map ref 5D3 **SELF CATERING**

★★★★
SELF CATERING

Units **9**
Sleeps **2–8**
Low season per wk
£196.00–£440.00
High season per wk
£456.00–£1,036.00

## Keld Head Farm Cottages, Pickering

**contact** Julian & Penny Fearn, Keld Head Farm Cottages, Keld Head, Pickering YO18 8LL **t** (01751) 473974
**e** julian@keldheadcottages.com **w** keldheadcottages.com

Access abc

General

Unit

Payment Credit/debit cards, cash, cheques, euros

*Six single-storey easy-access cottages. Senior citizen and two-person discounts. Short breaks. See virtual tour on website.*

On the edge of Pickering, in open countryside overlooking fields where sheep and cows graze, sit nine beautiful, spacious, character stone cottages, tastefully furnished with the emphasis on comfort and relaxation. Award-winning level access gardens with garden house. Local shops, York, moors and coast easily accessible. Ample parking.

**open** All Year
**nearest shop** < 0.5 miles
**nearest pub** 0.5 miles

*Cottages are on western periphery of Pickering, at corner of A170 and road signposted Marton. Turn into this road and the entrance is on the left.*

**PICKERING,** North Yorkshire **SELF CATERING**

★★★★
SELF CATERING

**Mel House Cottages contact** John Wicks, Let's Holiday, Mel House, Newton-on-Rawcliffe, Pickering YO18 8QA **t** (01751) 475396
**e** holiday@letsholiday.com **w** letsholiday.com

**PICKERING,** North Yorkshire **SELF CATERING**

★★★★
SELF CATERING

**North Yorkshire Cottages contact** Kevin and Elaine Bedford, North Yorkshire Cottages, 117 Eastgate, Pickering YO18 7DW **t** (01751) 476653
**e** vbenq@northyorkshirecottages.co.uk **w** northyorkshirecottages.co.uk

**PICKERING,** North Yorkshire **SELF CATERING**

★★★★
SELF CATERING

**Rawcliffe House Farm contact** Duncan & Jan Allsopp, Rawcliffe House Farm, Stape, Pickering YO18 8JA **t** (01751) 473292
**e** stay@rawcliffehousefarm.co.uk **w** rawcliffehousefarm.co.uk

**POULTON-LE-FYLDE,** Lancashire **SELF CATERING**

★★★★
SELF CATERING

**Hardhorn Breaks contact** Mr Pawson, Hardhorn Breaks, High Bank Farm, Fairfireld Road, Poulton-le-Fylde FY6 8DN **t** (01253) 890422
**e** blackpoolnick@btinternet.com **w** highbank-farm.com

At-a-glance symbols are explained on page 8.

**POWBURN,** Northumberland Map ref 5B1 **CAMPING, CARAVAN & HOLIDAY PARK**

(76) £12.20–£25.10
(76) £12.20–£25.10
76 touring pitches

## River Breamish Caravan Club Site

Powburn, Alnwick NE66 4HY **t** (01665) 578320
**w** caravanclub.co.uk

General

Leisure

Payment Credit/debit cards, cash, cheques

The site is set amid the Cheviot Hills, with excellent walking and cycling in the immediate area. A footbridge in Branton (one mile away) takes you over the river to the delightful Breamish Valley. At the National Park Centre at Ingram, staff will help you plan your stay.

**open** March to November

*Turn off A1 onto A697; in about 20 miles (0.25 miles past Powburn) turn left immediately past service station on right. Site on right.*

**PRESTON,** East Yorkshire **GUEST ACCOMMODATION**

**Little Weghill Farm** Weghill Road, Preston, Hull HU12 8SX
**t** (01482) 897650
**e** info@littleweghillfarm.co.uk
**w** littleweghillfarm.co.uk

**QUEBEC,** Durham **SELF CATERING**

**Hamsteels Cottages contact** Mrs June Whitfield, Hamsteels Cottages, Hamsteels Hall, Hamsteels Lane, Quebec DH7 9RS **t** (01207) 520388
**e** june@hamsteelshall.co.uk **w** hamsteelshall.co.uk

**RAINOW,** Cheshire **SELF CATERING**

**Coach House contact** Mr Ivor Williams, Coach House, Kerridge End House, Kerridge End, Macclesfield SK10 5TF **t** (01625) 424220
**e** info@kerridgeendholidaycottages.co.uk **w** kerridgeendholidaycottages.co.uk

**RIBCHESTER,** Lancashire **GUEST ACCOMMODATION**

**Riverside Barn** Riverside, Ribchester PR3 3XS
**t** (01254) 878095
**e** relax@riversidebarn.co.uk
**w** riversidebarn.co.uk

**RIBCHESTER,** Lancashire **SELF CATERING**

**Pinfold Farm contact** Mr Davies, Pinfold Farm, Preston Road, Ribchester PR3 3YD
**t** (01254) 820740
**e** davies-pinfold@yahoo.co.uk **w** pinfoldfarm.co.uk

**RICCALL,** North Yorkshire Map ref 4C1 — **SELF CATERING**

Units **2**
Sleeps **6**
Low season per wk
**£275.00–£395.00**
High season per wk
**£500.00–£600.00**

## South Newlands Farm Self Catering, Selby

**contact** Mrs Peggy Swann, South Newlands Farm Self Catering, Selby Road, Riccall, York YO19 6QR **t** (01757) 248203 **e** southnewlandsfarm@yahoo.co.uk **w** southnewlands.co.uk

Family-friendly accommodation for all levels of ability. Three bathrooms, en suite wetroom, family bathroom. Light and spacious bungalows. Well located; eight miles from York with easy access to the dales, moors and coast. Highly recommended.

**open** All year
**nearest shop** 1 mile
**nearest pub** 1 mile

Payment Cash, cheques

**ROTHBURY,** Northumberland — **CAMPING, CARAVAN & HOLIDAY PARK**

★★★★
TOURING PARK

**Nunnykirk Caravan Club Site** Nunnykirk Caravan Park, Nunnykirk NE61 4PZ
**t** (01669) 620762
**e** enquiries@caravanclub.co.uk **w** caravanclub.co.uk

**RUNSWICK BAY,** North Yorkshire — **GUEST ACCOMMODATION**

★★★★
INN
SILVER AWARD

**Ellerby** Ryeland Lane, Ellerby, Saltburn-by-the-Sea TS13 5LP
**t** (01947) 840342
**e** david@ellerbyhotel.co.uk
**w** ellerbyhotel.co.uk

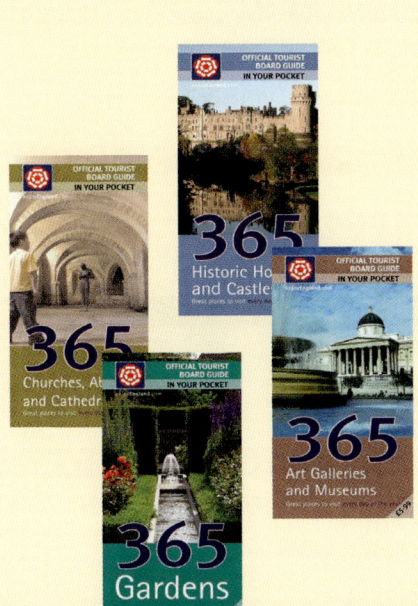



At-a-glance symbols are explained on page 8.

## ST BEES, Cumbria Map ref 5A3 — SELF CATERING

SELF CATERING

Units **2**
Sleeps **4–5**
Low season per wk
£300.00–£350.00
High season per wk
£400.00–£600.00

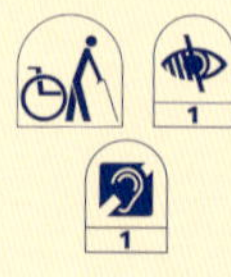

### Springbank Farm Lodges, St Bees

**contact** Carole Woodman, Springbank Farm, High Walton, St Bees CA22 2TY **t** (01946) 822375
**e** stevewoodman@talk21.com **w** springbanklodges.co.uk

Access abc

General

Unit

Payment Credit/debit cards, cash, cheques

*Short breaks available.*

Relax in our spacious two-bedroomed lodges. Enjoy the panoramic views and spectacular sunsets. One double room with en suite, one twin room. Family wetroom. Wide balcony and veranda. Designed for accessibility. Quiet location on our rare-breed farm. Close to amenities, the beach and the western Lakes.

**open** All year
**nearest shop** 1 mile
**nearest pub** 1 mile

*M6 jct40 (Penrith). A66 (Workington), A595 Whitehaven. Continue A595 bypass Whitehaven. Take 1st right after West lakes Science Park (St Bees). On right after 1 mile.*

## SCARBOROUGH, North Yorkshire — GUEST ACCOMMODATION

★★★ GUEST ACCOMMODATION

**The Scarborough Travel and Holiday Lodge** 33 Valley Road, Scarborough YO11 2LX **t** (01723) 363537
**e** enquiries@scarborough-lodge.co.uk **w** scarborough-lodge.co.uk

## SELBY, North Yorkshire — SELF CATERING

★★★★ SELF CATERING

**Lund Farm Cottages contact** Mr Chris Middleton, Lund Farm Cottages, Lund Farm, Gateforth, Selby YO8 9LE **t** (01757) 228775
**e** lundfarm@talktalk.net **w** lundfarm.co.uk

## SETTLE, North Yorkshire — HOTEL

★★ SMALL HOTEL

**New Inn Hotel** Clapham, Near Settle LA2 8HH
**t** (01524) 251203
**e** info@newinn-clapham.co.uk **w** newinn-clapham.co.uk

## SEWERBY, East Yorkshire — SELF CATERING

★★★★–★★★★★ SELF CATERING

**Field House Farm Cottages contact** Mr & Mrs Foster, Field House Farm Cottages, Jewison Lane, Sewerby, Bridlington YO16 6YG **t** (01262) 674932
**e** john.foster@farmline.com **w** fieldhousefarmcottages.co.uk

## SKELWITH FOLD, Cumbria

*See entry on p110*

## SLEIGHTS, North Yorkshire — SELF CATERING

★★★ SELF CATERING

**Groves Dyke Holiday Cottage** **contact** Niall Carson, Groves Dyke Holiday Cottage, Woodlands Drive, Sleights, Whitby YO21 1RY **t** (01947) 810220
**e** relax@grovesdyke.co.uk **w** grovesdyke.co.uk

## SNEATON, North Yorkshire — CAMPING, CARAVAN & HOLIDAY PARK

★★★★ TOURING PARK

**Low Moor Caravan Club Site** Sneaton, Whitby YO22 5JE
**t** (01947) 810505
**e** enquiries@caravanclub.co.uk **w** caravanclub.co.uk

## SOUTHPORT, Merseyside — GUEST ACCOMMODATION

★★★ FARMHOUSE

**Sandy Brook Farm** 52 Wyke Cop Road, Scarisbrick, Southport PR8 5LR
**t** (01704) 880337
**e** sandybrookfarm@lycos.co.uk **w** sandybrookfarm.co.uk

## SOUTHPORT, Merseyside — SELF CATERING

★★★ SELF CATERING

**Sandy Brook Farm** **contact** Mr Core, Sandy Brook Farm, 52 Wyke Cop Road, Scarisbrick, Southport PR8 5LR **t** (01704) 880337 & 07719 468712
**e** sandybrookfarm@lycos.co.uk **w** sandybrookfarm.co.uk

## STAVELEY, Cumbria — SELF CATERING

★★★ SELF CATERING

**Avondale** **contact** Helen Hughes, Avondale, 2 Lynstead, Thornbarrow Road, Windermere LA23 2DG **t** 07811 670260
**e** enquiries@avondale.uk.net **w** avondale.uk.net

## STOCKTON-ON-TEES, Tees Valley — CAMPING, CARAVAN & HOLIDAY PARK

★★★★★ TOURING & CAMPING PARK

**White Water Caravan Club Park** Tees Barrage, Stockton-on-Tees TS18 2QW
**t** (01642) 634880
**w** caravanclub.co.uk

## THORPE BASSETT, North Yorkshire — SELF CATERING

★★★★ SELF CATERING

**The Old Post Office** **contact** Sandra Simpson, The Old Post Office, Thorpe Bassett, Malton YO17 8LU **t** (01944) 758047
**e** ssimpsoncottages@aol.com **w** ssimpsoncottages.co.uk

## THRELKELD, Cumbria — GUEST ACCOMMODATION

★★★★ GUEST HOUSE SILVER AWARD

**Scales Farm Country Guest House** Scales, Threlkeld, Penrith CA12 4SY
**t** (017687) 79660
**e** scales@scalesfarm.com
**w** scalesfarm.com

## THURSTASTON, Merseyside — CAMPING, CARAVAN & HOLIDAY PARK

★★★★ TOURING & CAMPING PARK

**Wirral Country Park Caravan Club Site** Station Road, Thurstaston CH61 0HN
**t** (0151) 648 5228
**e** enquiries@caravanclub.co.uk
**w** caravanclub.co.uk

## TURTON, Greater Manchester — SELF CATERING

★★★★ SELF CATERING

**Clough Head Farm** **contact** Mrs Ethel Houghton, Clough Head Farm, Broadhead Road, Turton BL7 0JN **t** (01254) 704758
**e** ethelhoughton@hotmail.co.uk **w** cloughheadfarm.co.uk

At-a-glance symbols are explained on page 8.

**WARRINGTON,** Cheshire — **GUEST ACCOMMODATION**

★★★ GUEST ACCOMMODATION

**Tall Trees Lodge** Tarporley Road, Lower Whitley, Warrington WA4 4EZ
**t** (01928) 790824 & (01928) 715117
**e** booking@talltreeslodge.co.uk **w** talltreeslodge.co.uk

**WHINFELL,** Cumbria — **SELF CATERING**

★★★ SELF CATERING

**Topthorn Holiday Cottages contact** Diane Barnes, Topthorn Holiday Cottages, Topthorn Farm, Whinfell, Nr Kendal LA8 9EG **t** (01539) 824252
**e** info.barnes@btconnect.com **w** topthorn.com

**WINDERMERE,** Cumbria — **HOTEL**

★★★ COUNTRY HOUSE HOTEL GOLD AWARD

**Linthwaite House Hotel** Crook Road, Bowness-on-Windermere, Windermere LA23 3JA
**t** (015394) 88600
**e** stay@linthwaite.com **w** linthwaite.com

**WINDERMERE,** Cumbria — **CAMPING, CARAVAN & HOLIDAY PARK**

★★★★ TOURING PARK

**Braithwaite Fold Caravan Club Site** Glebe Road, Bowness-on-Windermere, Windermere LA23 3HB **t** (015394) 42177
**e** enquiries@caravanclub.co.uk **w** caravanclub.co.uk

**WINSTON,** Durham — **SELF CATERING**

★★★★ SELF CATERING

**Alwent Mill Cottage contact** Mrs Libby Hampson, Alwent Mill Cottage, Alwent Mill, Alwent Mill Lane, Winston DL2 3QH **t** (01325) 730479
**e** libby@alwentmill.co.uk

**WOOLER,** Northumberland — **SELF CATERING**

★★★★ SELF CATERING

**Crookhouse contact** Mrs Lynne Holden, Crookhouse, Kirknewton, Wooler NE71 6TN **t** (01668) 216113
**e** stay@crookhousecottages.co.uk **w** crookhouse.co.uk

**WOOLER,** Northumberland — **SELF CATERING**

★★★★ SELF CATERING

**Fenton Hill Farm Cottages contact** Mrs Margaret Logan, Fenton Hill Farm Cottages, Fenton Hill Farm, Wooler NE71 6JJ **t** (01668) 216228
**e** stay@fentonhillfarm.co.uk **w** fentonhillfarm.co.uk

**YAPHAM,** East Yorkshire — **SELF CATERING**

★★★★–★★★★★ SELF CATERING

**Wolds View Holiday Cottages contact** Margaret Woodliffe, Wolds View Holiday Cottages, Mill Farm, Yapham, Driffield YO42 1PH
**t** (01759) 302172
**e** info@woldsview.co.uk

**YORK,** North Yorkshire — **HOTEL**

★★★ HOTEL

**Best Western Monkbar Hotel** St Maurice's Road, York YO31 7JA
**t** (01904) 638086
**e** sales@monkbarhotel.co.uk **w** bestwestern.co.uk

**YORK,** North Yorkshire — **HOTEL**

★★★ HOTEL GOLD AWARD

**The Grange Hotel** 1 Clifton, York YO30 6AA
**t** (01904) 644744
**e** info@grangehotel.co.uk
**w** grangehotel.co.uk

**YORK,** North Yorkshire — **GUEST ACCOMMODATION**

★★★
GUEST ACCOMMODATION

**The Groves** St Peters Grove, York YO30 6AQ
**t** (01904) 559777
**e** info@thegroveshotelyork.co.uk **w** thegroveshotelyork.co.uk

**YORK,** North Yorkshire — **SELF CATERING**

★★★
SELF CATERING

**Classique Select Holiday Accommodation contact** Mr Rodney Inns, Classique Select Holiday Accommodation, 21 Larchfield, Stockton Lane, York YO31 1JS **t** (01904) 421339
**w** classique-york.co.uk

**YORK,** North Yorkshire — **SELF CATERING**

★★★–★★★★★
SELF CATERING

**Stakesby Holiday Flats contact** Mr Anthony Bryce, Stakesby Holiday Flats, 4 Saint George's Place, York YO24 1DR **t** (01904) 611634
**e** ant@stakesby.co.uk **w** stakesby.co.uk

**YORK,** North Yorkshire — **CAMPING, CARAVAN & HOLIDAY PARK**

★★★★★
TOURING PARK

**Beechwood Grange Caravan Club Site** Malton Road, York YO32 9TH
**t** (01904) 424637
**w** caravanclub.co.uk

**YORK,** North Yorkshire Map ref 4C1 — **CAMPING, CARAVAN & HOLIDAY PARK**

TOURING & CAMPING PARK

(102)
£14.90–£28.90
(102)
£14.90–£28.90
102 touring pitches

## Rowntree Park Caravan Club Site

Terry Avenue, York YO23 1JQ **t** (01904) 658997
**w** caravanclub.co.uk

General

Payment Credit/debit cards, cash, cheques

A very popular site, level and on the banks of the Ouse, within easy walking distance of the beautiful and historic city of York, and a good base to explore Yorkshire. York is a feast – there's so much to see you'll find the days slipping past before you go anywhere else.

**open** All year

*A64 onto A19 signposted York centre. After 2 miles join one-way system. Keep left over bridge. Left at International Caravan Club site. Right onto Terry Avenue. Site on right in 0.25 miles.*

## Place index

If you know where you want to stay, the index by place name at the back of the guide will give you the page number listing accommodation in your chosen town, city or village. Check out the other useful indexes too.

At-a-glance symbols are explained on page 8.

# National Accessible Scheme ratings only

The following establishments hold a National Accessible Scheme rating as shown in their entry, but do not participate in a quality assessment scheme. However, to participate in the National Accessible Scheme accommodation must meet a minimum level of quality.

**AMBLESIDE,** Cumbria Map ref 5A3 **SELF CATERING**

Units **1**
Sleeps **1–7**
Low season per wk
**Min £240.00**
High season per wk
**Max £540.00**

**Awaiting NAS rating**

## Nationwide Bungalow, Ambleside

**contact** Gail Lewis, Livability, PO Box 36, Cowbridge CF71 7GB
**t** 08456 584478 **e** selfcatering@livability.org.uk or glewis@livability.org.uk
**w** livabilityholidays.org.uk

Holiday bungalow, specially adapted for disabled people, close to Lake Windermere. Accommodation for up to seven people in three bedrooms. Level throughout. Roll-in shower. Mobile hoist, shower-chair and profiling bed available.

**open** All year
**nearest shop** 1 mile
**nearest pub** 1 mile

Access
General
Unit

Payment Credit/debit cards, cash, cheques, euros

**BLACKPOOL,** Lancashire Map ref 4A1 **HOTEL**

B&B per room per night
**s £25.00–£85.00**
**d £40.00–£130.00**

## Norbreck Castle Hotel

Queens Promenade, Blackpool FY2 9AA **t** (01253) 352341
**w** britanniahotels.com

Access

Rooms

General

Leisure

Payment Credit/debit cards, cash, cheques

*23 specially adapted rooms. Two, three and four-night packages available throughout the year.*

With 480 en suite bedrooms, nightly live entertainment, a fun and sports bar, cinema and full leisure facilities, this complex is the complete holiday experience all under one roof. The perfect holiday venue for the whole family.

**open** All year
**bedrooms** 160 double, 112 twin, 71 single, 132 family, 5 suites
**bathrooms** All en suite

*From the M55 follow the signs for North Shore. The hotel is located 3 miles north of Blackpool Tower.*

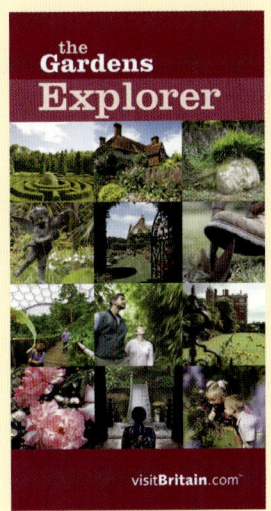

**MANCHESTER,** Greater Manchester Map ref 4B1 **HOTEL**

B&B per room per night
**s £77.95–£143.95**
**d £86.90–£152.90**

## Bewleys Hotel – Manchester Airport

Outwood Lane, Manchester Airport, Manchester M90 4HL
**t** (0161) 498 1390
**e** manchesterairport@bewleyshotels.com **w** bewleyshotels.com

Rooms

General

Payment Credit/debit cards, cash, cheques

*Holiday car parking is available on request. Up to 8 days £35 and up to 15 days £45. We offer free Wi-Fi and airport shuttle.*

Contemporary, relaxed and informal: the ethos behind Bewleys Hotels. Situated adjacent to the airport terminals. Free Wi-Fi and a complimentary shuttle service to the airport is included in your stay. Famlies are welcome and we offer a superb menu in our Brasserie to suit all tastes and budgets.

**open** All year
**bedrooms** 254 double, 22 twin, 89 family
**bathrooms** All en suite

*M56 jct5. Follow signs for Terminal 3 and we are situated on the left.*

**MANCHESTER,** Greater Manchester **HOTEL**

**The Lowry Hotel** 50 Dearmans Place, Chapel Wharf M3 5LH **t** (0161) 827 4000
**e** enquiries@thelowryhotel.com **w** roccofortehotels.com

**SKELWITH FOLD,** Cumbria **SELF CATERING**

**Crop Howe contact** Mrs Susan Jackson, Heart of the Lakes, Old Lake Road, Ambleside LA22 0DH
**t** (01539) 433251

## Remember to check when booking

Please remember that all information in this guide has been supplied by the proprietors well in advance of publication. Since changes do sometimes occur it's a good idea to check details at the time of booking.

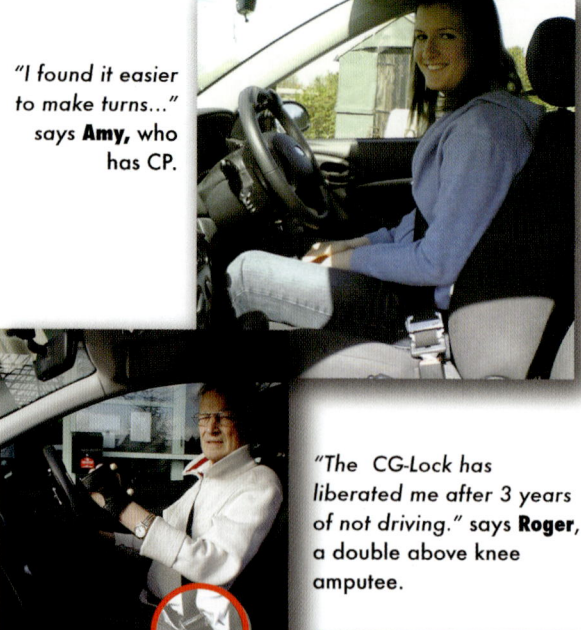

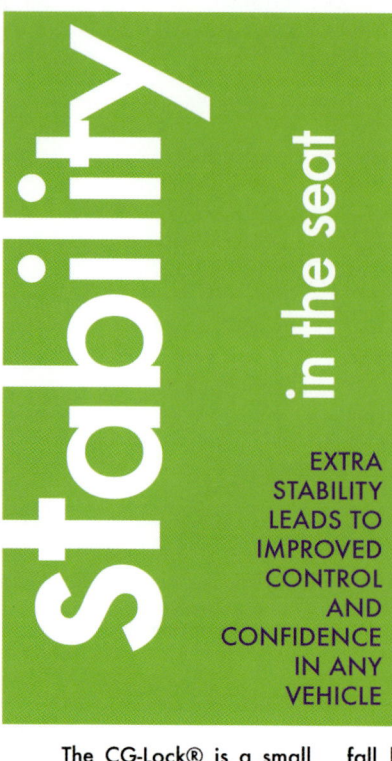

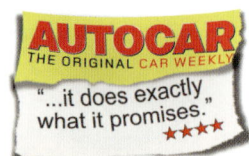

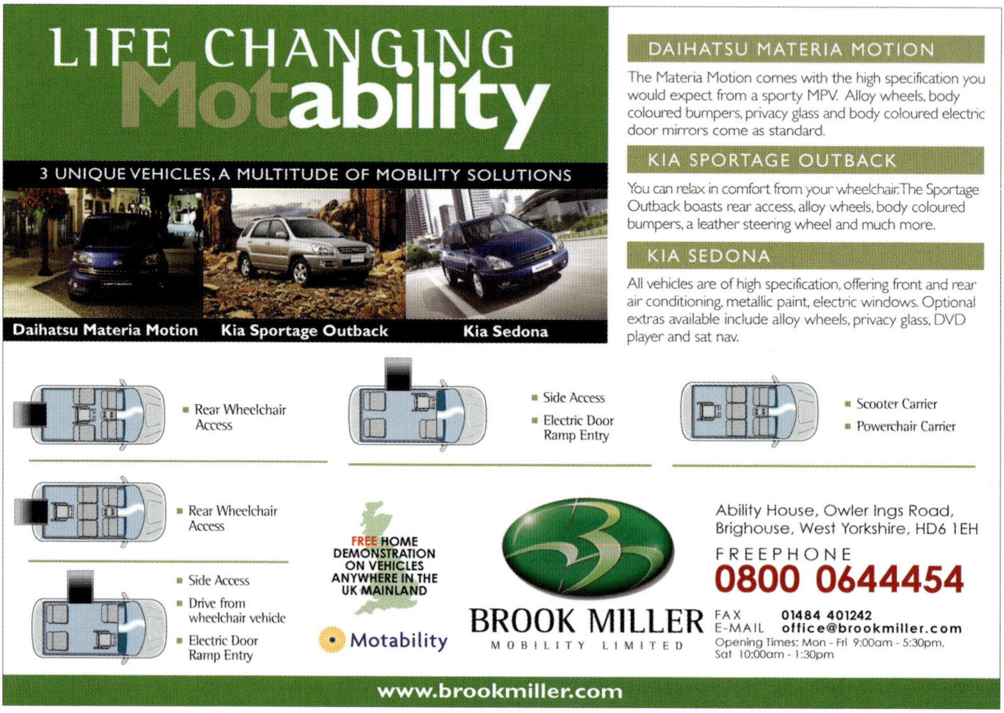

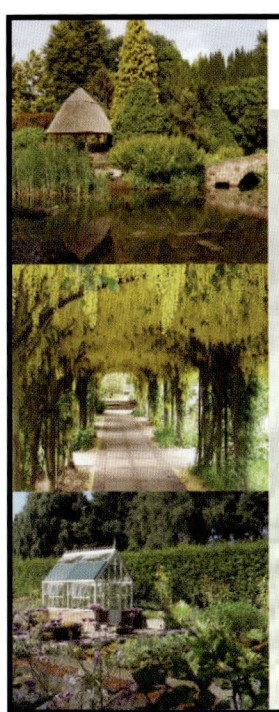

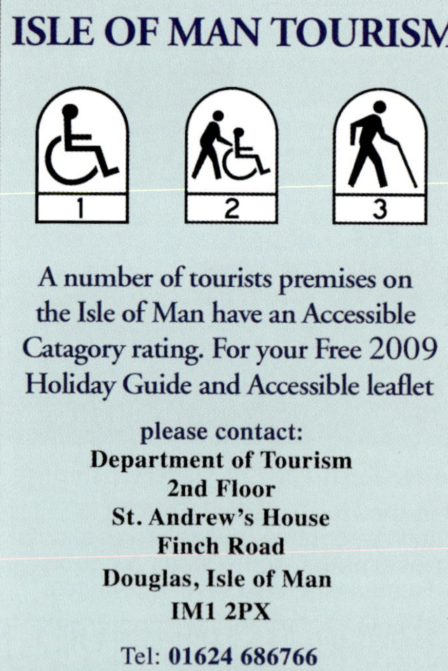
ISLE OF MAN TOURISM
1
2
3
A number of tourists premises on the Isle of Man have an Accessible Catagory rating. For your Free 2009 Holiday Guide and Accessible leaflet
please contact:
Department of Tourism
2nd Floor
St. Andrew's House
Finch Road
Douglas, Isle of Man
IM1 2PX
Tel: 01624 686766
Brochure Enquiries Tel: 08457 686868 (24 hours)

take a closer look!
BLACKPOOL ZOO
Full disabled access
East Park Drive, FY3 8PP. Tel: (01253) 830830
www.blackpoolzoo.org.uk

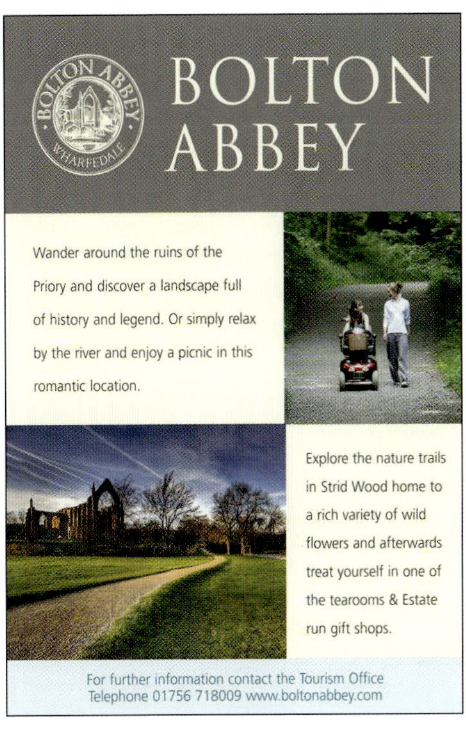
BOLTON ABBEY
BOLTON ABBEY WHARFEDALE
Wander around the ruins of the Priory and discover a landscape full of history and legend. Or simply relax by the river and enjoy a picnic in this romantic location.
Explore the nature trails in Strid Wood home to a rich variety of wild flowers and afterwards treat yourself in one of the tearooms & Estate run gift shops.
For further information contact the Tourism Office
Telephone 01756 718009 www.boltonabbey.com

the Quay to a great day out!
lowryoutletmall.com
LOWRY OUTLET MALL
FAMOUS BRANDS DISCOUNT SHOPPING
SALFORD QUAYS
Upto 50% discount off high street prices
Great group discounts and incentives available
Easy disabled access
For more information, contact
Terry Douglas
tel: 0161 848 1850
email: terry.douglas@emerson.co.uk

Blackpool Sandcastle WATER PARK
THE UK'S LARGEST INDOOR WATERPARK
18 Fantastic slides and attractions
Open all year round
A great day out for all the family
Sandcastle Waterpark is Accessible Friendly.
If you require any further information please call our Safety Hotline on 01253 340721 where our staff will be happy to discuss your individual requirements.
www.sandcastle-waterpark.co.uk
01253 340700 / 340709
Located opposite the Pleasure Beach, Blackpool

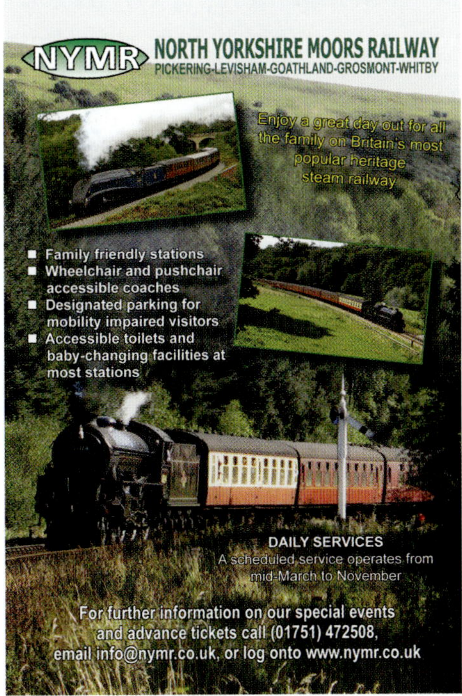
NYMR NORTH YORKSHIRE MOORS RAILWAY
PICKERING-LEVISHAM-GOATHLAND-GROSMONT-WHITBY
Enjoy a great day out for all the family on Britain's most popular heritage steam railway
Family friendly stations
Wheelchair and pushchair accessible coaches
Designated parking for mobility impaired visitors
Accessible toilets and baby-changing facilities at most stations
DAILY SERVICES
A scheduled service operates from mid-March to November
For further information on our special events and advance tickets call (01751) 472508, email info@nymr.co.uk, or log onto www.nymr.co.uk

WYRE ESTUARY COUNTRY PARK
The Wyre Estuary...
a Special Place for People and Wildlife
On the banks of the River Wyre, Lancashire, the Country Park provides a visitor centre linked to a network of paths and country lanes enabling you to explore the area on foot, bicycle, and horseback or in a wheelchair. Main paths are surfaced and flat and there is also a 3/4 of a mile circular route for the partially sighted.
Wyreside Visitor Centre
Wyre Estuary Country Park, River Road, Stanah, Thornton Cleveleys, Lancashire FY5 5LR
Telephone: 01253 857890 email: mailroom@wyrebc.gov.uk
Wyre Borough Council
LIVE WYRE LOVE WYRE
Walkin' Wyre
Better Health One Step at a Time
For a copy of the Health Walks Calendar please contact 01253 863100
Wheels for all – Specially adapted cycles for a range of abilities are available to hire with prior notice from the Visitor Centre.
Tramper Buggy now available to hire.
WHEELS FOR ALL

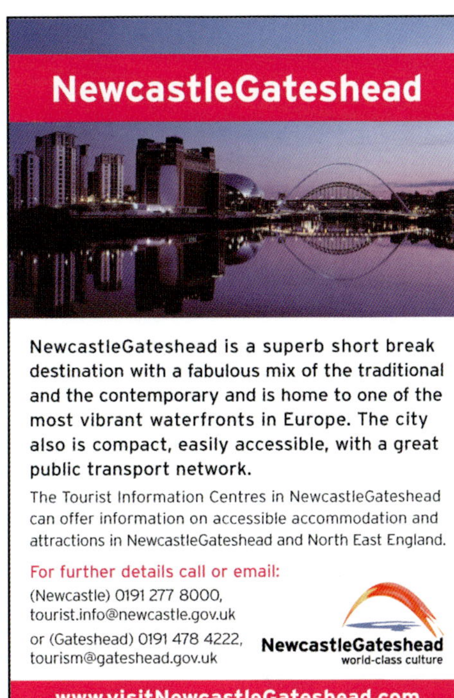
NewcastleGateshead
NewcastleGateshead is a superb short break destination with a fabulous mix of the traditional and the contemporary and is home to one of the most vibrant waterfronts in Europe. The city also is compact, easily accessible, with a great public transport network.
The Tourist Information Centres in NewcastleGateshead can offer information on accessible accommodation and attractions in NewcastleGateshead and North East England.
For further details call or email:
(Newcastle) 0191 277 8000, tourist.info@newcastle.gov.uk
or (Gateshead) 0191 478 4222, tourism@gateshead.gov.uk
NewcastleGateshead
world-class culture
www.visitNewcastleGateshead.com

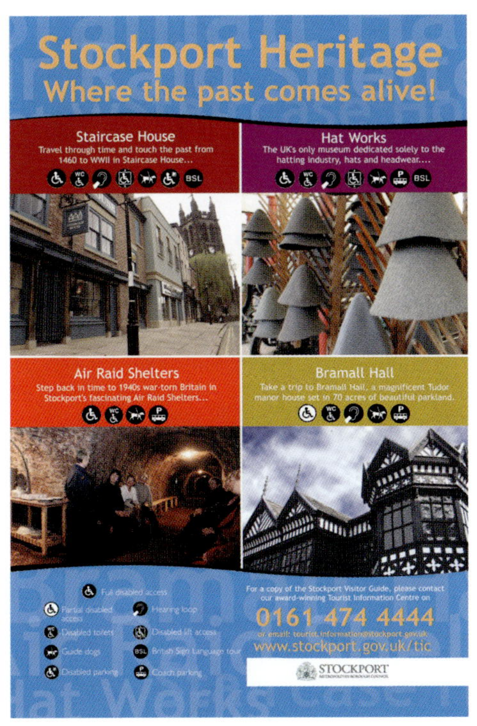
Stockport Heritage
Where the past comes alive!
Staircase House
Travel through time and touch the past from 1460 to WWII in Staircase House...
Hat Works
The UK's only museum dedicated solely to the hatting industry, hats and headwear....
Air Raid Shelters
Step back in time to 1940s war-torn Britain in Stockport's fascinating Air Raid Shelters...
Bramall Hall
Take a trip to Bramall Hall, a magnificent Tudor manor house set in 70 acres of beautiful parkland.
Full disabled access
Partial disabled access
Hearing loop
Disabled toilets
Disabled lift access
Guide dogs
British Sign Language tour
Disabled parking
Coach parking
For a copy of the Stockport Visitor Guide, please contact our award-winning Tourist Information Centre on
0161 474 4444
or email: tourist.information@stockport.gov.uk
www.stockport.gov.uk/tic
STOCKPORT
METROPOLITAN BOROUGH COUNCIL

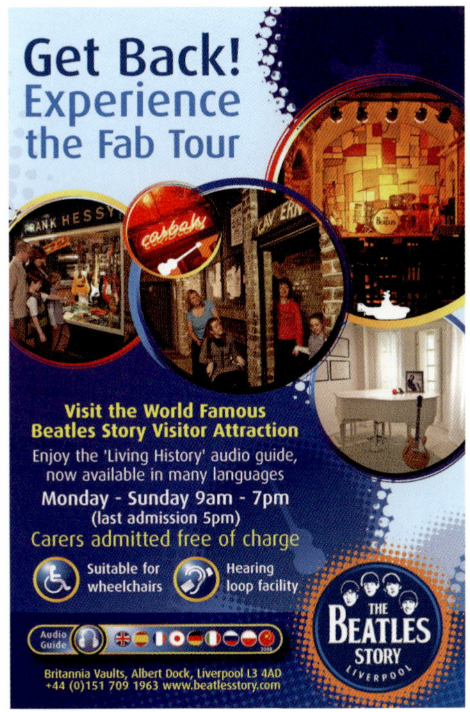
Get Back!
Experience the Fab Tour
Visit the World Famous Beatles Story Visitor Attraction
Enjoy the 'Living History' audio guide, now available in many languages
Monday - Sunday 9am - 7pm
(last admission 5pm)
Carers admitted free of charge
Suitable for wheelchairs
Hearing loop facility
Audio Guide
THE BEATLES STORY LIVERPOOL
Britannia Vaults, Albert Dock, Liverpool L3 4AD
+44 (0)151 709 1963 www.beatlesstory.com

10th ANNIVERSARY
BLUE PLANET AQUARIUM
1998-2008
BLUE PLANET AQUARIUM
Experience the magic up close!
0151 357 8804
www.blueplanetaquarium.com
M56 JUNCTION 15

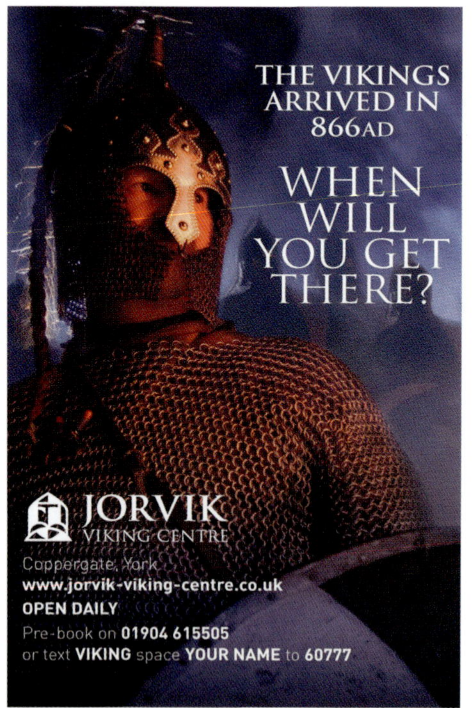
THE VIKINGS ARRIVED IN 866AD
WHEN WILL YOU GET THERE?
JORVIK VIKING CENTRE
Coppergate, York
www.jorvik-viking-centre.co.uk
OPEN DAILY
Pre-book on 01904 615505
or text VIKING space YOUR NAME to 60777

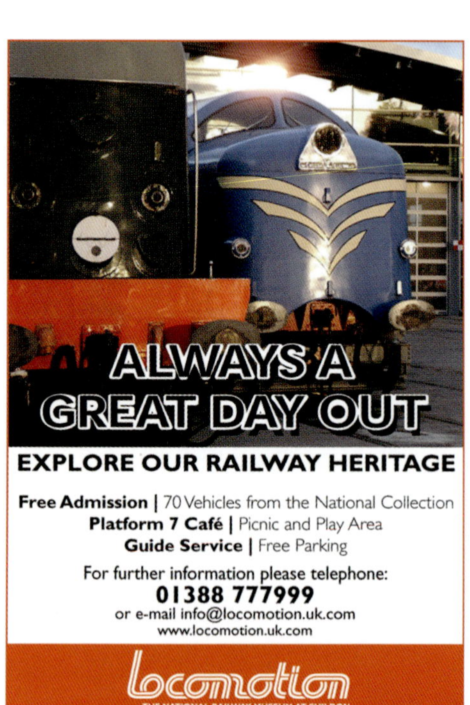
ALWAYS A GREAT DAY OUT
EXPLORE OUR RAILWAY HERITAGE
Free Admission | 70 Vehicles from the National Collection
Platform 7 Café | Picnic and Play Area
Guide Service | Free Parking
For further information please telephone:
01388 777999
or e-mail info@locomotion.uk.com
www.locomotion.uk.com
locomotion
THE NATIONAL RAILWAY MUSEUM AT SHILDON
Shildon, Co. Durham DL4 1PQ

Liverpool Cathedral
Britain's largest Cathedral with access for all
An inspired, great value day out
• New BSL tour on portable DVD
• Film theatre with induction loop
• Interactive computer Stations
• Tactile displays with Braille included
• Café bar with internet access
• Full programme of events
www.liverpoolcathedral.org.uk
For further details and group bookings call:
Jenny Moran
0151 702 7284

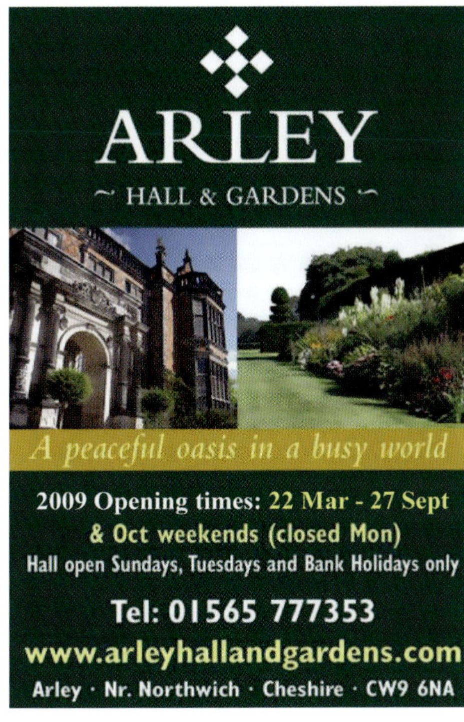
ARLEY
~ HALL & GARDENS ~
A peaceful oasis in a busy world
2009 Opening times: 22 Mar - 27 Sept
& Oct weekends (closed Mon)
Hall open Sundays, Tuesdays and Bank Holidays only
Tel: 01565 777353
www.arleyhallandgardens.com
Arley · Nr. Northwich · Cheshire · CW9 6NA

WEST LANCASHIRE
DISTRICT COUNCIL

RAVENGLASS AND ESKDALE
RAILWAY
AN ADVENTURE FOR ALL
With easy level access to the trains at both our main stations, carriages specifically designed to cater for wheelchairs, with staff at your service, there's no reason why anyone should miss out on a steamy journey on Lakeland's oldest, longest and most scenic railway, not to mention a visit to our cafés and shops. Visit our website or for a pre-booked party trip chat it through by 'phone.
www.ravenglass-railway.co.uk
Tel: 01229 717171

LOTTERY FUNDED

COUNCIL FOR THE DISABLED

1-2 Bodlewell house, High street east, Sunderland, SR1-2AS
Tel; 0191 5678107 - 0191 5143346
Fax: 0191-5678107

WHEELCHAIR HIRE

Short term loans for holidays, shopping or injuries. Hire from as little as £5.00
Telephone to ensure advance bookings.

PEOPLES PEDAL POWER

Healthy cycling on specially adapt tricycles for Disabled People in park surroundings.

WELFARE & BENEFITS ADVISOR

Help and advice on all welfare & benefit issues Telephone to book an appointment.

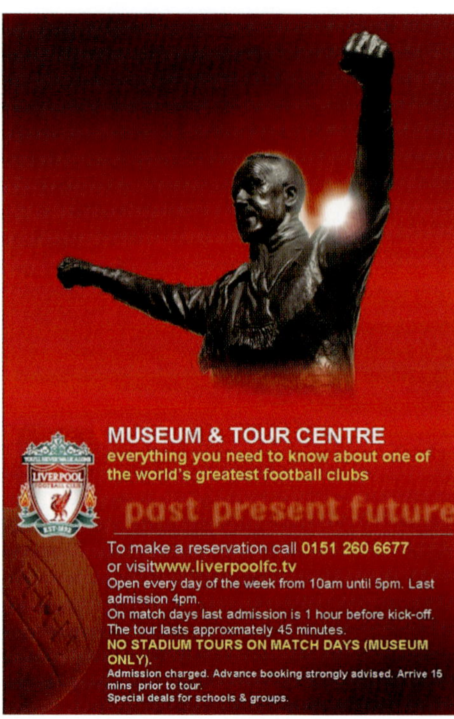

THE BOWES MUSEUM

## A Collection of Treasures

Get close to some of Europe's most wonderful fine and decorative arts and enjoy the acclaimed exhibition programme.

**The Bowes Museum**
Barnard Castle, County Durham, DL12 8NP
t: 01833 690606
e: info@thebowesmuseum.org.uk
**www.thebowesmuseum.org.uk**
Open daily from 10.00

Call for your free programme

the art of having a great day out
At Tate Liverpool you can enjoy the very best modern and contemporary art in a stunning dock side location; the Albert Dock.
Go to www.tate.org.uk/liverpool or call 0151 702 7400 for more information.
LIVERPOOL
TATE
Auguste Rodin, The Kiss (le Baiser), 1901-4 © Tate
At Tate Liverpool until April 2009

The Royal Exchange Theatre is a 7-sided module suspended from four pillars in Manchester's historic Cotton Exchange that presents a huge variety of plays.
Royal Exchange Theatre
ACCESS FACILITIES INCLUDE:
• Wheelchair spaces and a lift
• BSL interpreted and Audio Described performances with Touch Tour
• Infra-red assisted hearing facilities, Guide Dogs welcome
• Large print, Braille and Audio versions of the season brochure
If you have particular access requirements, or would like to receive one of our brochures, please contact the Box Office.
Box Office 0161 833 9833
Fax 0161 615 6696
Email box.office@royalexchange.co.uk
Minicom 0161 615 6699
Royal Exchange Theatre, St Ann's Square, Manchester M2 7DH

PLAY TIME!
SHOW TIME!
BLACKPOOL TOWER AND CIRCUS®
YOU CAN'T MISS IT!
www.blackpooltower.co.uk
For further information on the attractions shows and events you can enjoy as part of
THE NORTH WEST'S BIGGEST DAY OUT!

ANDERTON BOAT LIFT
The first of its kind
Winner of Access for All 2008 in the Visit Chester & Cheshire Awards
Group rates available for 12 or more
Open now till October
For bookings, prices, opening times and trip times call 01606 786777 or visit www.andertonboatlift.co.uk
Anderton Boat Lift Lift Lane Anderton Northwich Cheshire CW9 6FW

Salford Heritage Service is your ticket to the past...
Stroll down Lark Hill Place, our authentic Victorian Street at Salford Museum and Art Gallery. Step in to the world of Tudors at Ordsall Hall. Trace your family tree at Salford Local History Library.
Exhibitions • Activities • Workshops • Events
Salford Museum and Art Gallery/Local History
Peel Park, Crescent, Salford M5 4WU
0161 778 0800.
Mon-Fri 10am-4.45pm. Sat/Sun 1-5pm
Ordsall Hall Ordsall Lane, Salford M5 3AN.
0161 872 0251
Mon-Fri 10am-4pm. Sun 1-5pm
www.salford.gov.uk/museums

Silver Award - Large Visitor Attraction 2008
Tullie House Museum & Art Gallery
Open daily, all year around
except: 25th/26th Dec & 1st Jan
Tullie House, Castle Street
Carlisle CA3 8TP
www.tulliehouse.co.uk
Tel: 01228 618 718
A great day out for everyone.
Fully accessible
TULLIE HOUSE
MUSEUM AND ARTS SERVICES CARLISLE
CARLISLE CITY COUNCIL
www.carlisle.gov.uk

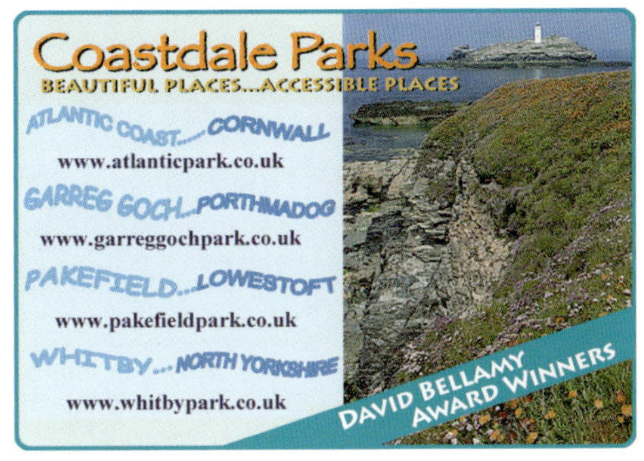
Coastdale Parks
BEAUTIFUL PLACES...ACCESSIBLE PLACES
ATLANTIC COAST...CORNWALL
www.atlanticpark.co.uk
GARREG GOCH...PORTHMADOG
www.garreggochpark.co.uk
PAKEFIELD...LOWESTOFT
www.pakefieldpark.co.uk
WHITBY...NORTH YORKSHIRE
www.whitbypark.co.uk
DAVID BELLAMY AWARD WINNERS

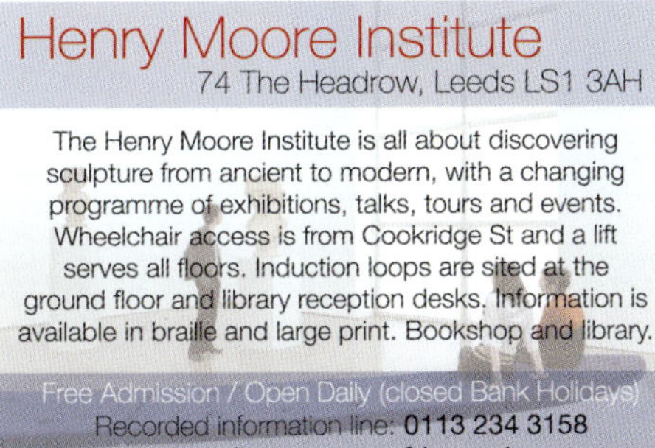
Henry Moore Institute
74 The Headrow, Leeds LS1 3AH
The Henry Moore Institute is all about discovering sculpture from ancient to modern, with a changing programme of exhibitions, talks, tours and events. Wheelchair access is from Cookridge St and a lift serves all floors. Induction loops are sited at the ground floor and library reception desks. Information is available in braille and large print. Bookshop and library.
Free Admission / Open Daily (closed Bank Holidays)
Recorded information line: 0113 234 3158
www.henry-moore-fdn.co.uk

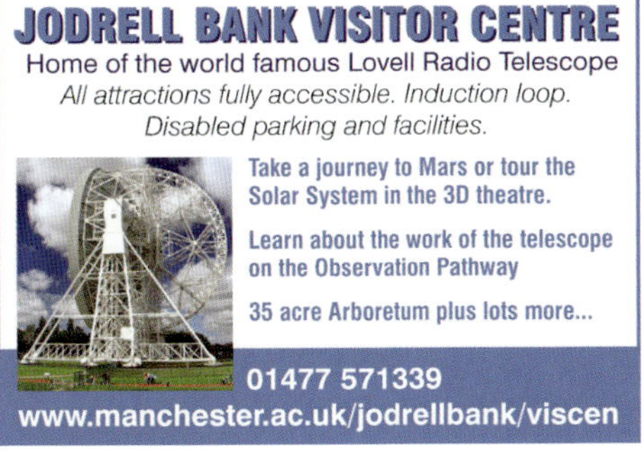
JODRELL BANK VISITOR CENTRE
Home of the world famous Lovell Radio Telescope
All attractions fully accessible. Induction loop.
Disabled parking and facilities.
Take a journey to Mars or tour the Solar System in the 3D theatre.
Learn about the work of the telescope on the Observation Pathway
35 acre Arboretum plus lots more...
01477 571339
www.manchester.ac.uk/jodrellbank/viscen

DISCOVER
THE NATIONAL COAL MINING MUSEUM
Underground tours
Pit ponies
Adventure playground
Nature trail
Train rides
Interactive galleries
Exhibitions
Historic buildings
And much, much more!
FREE ADMISSION FOR EVERYONE
On the A642 halfway between Wakefield and Huddersfield
www.ncm.org.uk tel 01924 848806
NCM
NATIONAL COAL MINING MUSEUM for England

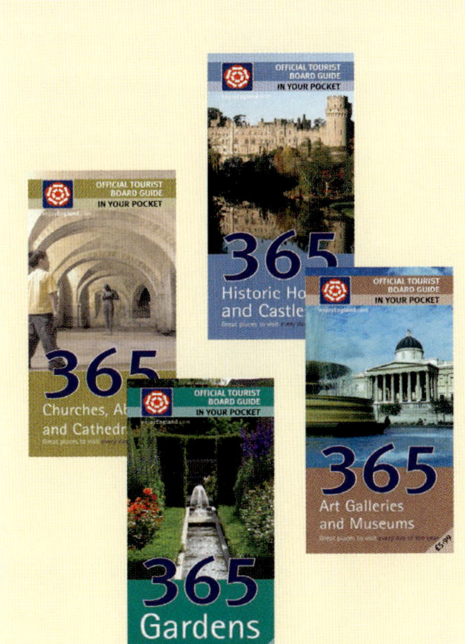


# Great days out in your pocket

- 365 Museums and Galleries
- 365 Historic Houses & Castles
- 365 Churches, Abbeys & Cathedrals
- 365 Gardens

These essential VisitBritain themed guides give you great ideas for places to visit every day of the year! Ideal for your pocket or the glove box.

Clearly presented, each entry provides location and contact details, opening times, description and facilities. *In Your Pocket* guides are available in good bookshops and online at visitbritaindirect.com for just £5.99 each.

# Central England

Bedfordshire, Cambridgeshire, Derbyshire, Essex, Herefordshire, Hertfordshire, Leicestershire, Lincolnshire, Norfolk, Northamptonshire, Nottinghamshire, Rutland, Shropshire, Staffordshire, Suffolk, Warwickshire, West Midlands, Worcestershire

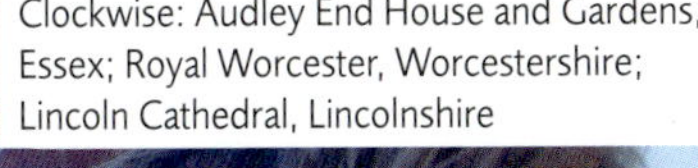

Clockwise: Audley End House and Gardens, Essex; Royal Worcester, Worcestershire; Lincoln Cathedral, Lincolnshire

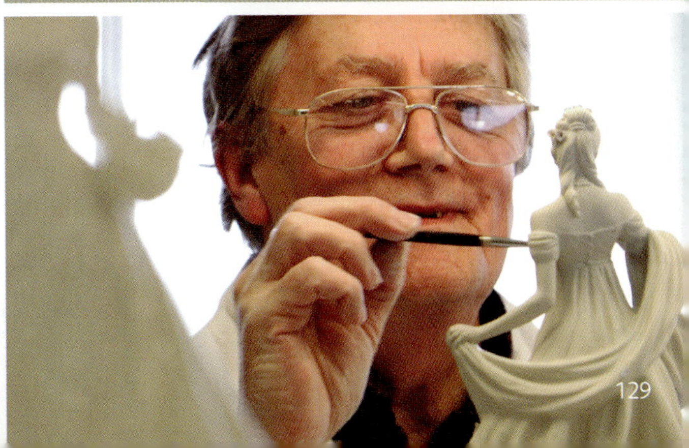

# Great days out

**Artistic connections and inspiring landscapes, industrial heritage brought to life, thrilling spectator sports – it's all on a plate in Central England. Pack a picnic and explore the Pennines or the Malvern Hills, drift along one of the many canals that criss-cross the region or spot oyster catchers in one of the coastal nature reserves.**

## Creative masterpieces

With such a rich mix of industry, history, culture and raw natural beauty it's not surprising Central England sparked so much creative energy.

Royal Shakespeare Company, Warwickshire

Spot the landscapes in the **Stour Valley**, that inspired local boy John Constable. On the streets of **Stratford-upon-Avon**, you just can't avoid references to the town's greatest son, William Shakespeare – book a seat at the **Royal Shakespeare Company**.

Take a factory tour at **Wedgwood Visitor Centre,** Stoke-on-Trent – it can be accessed by wheelchair and there is dedicated disabled parking. Or visit the **Wedgwood Museum**.

Find out what shaped DH Lawrence's early life at his birthplace in **Eastwood**, near Nottingham. See at first hand the decadence of Lord Byron in gothic **Newstead Abbey** and, on a musical note, Benjamin Britten's **Aldeburgh Festival** at Snape Maltings, Suffolk, is the place for classical concerts in a rural setting. On Aldeburgh's beach, you can't miss a huge sculpture, **The Scallop**, dedicated to the composer. For more music, visit **Audley End House and Garden**, Essex, to enjoy a summer evening concert.

## Action and adventure

Head for the **National Space Centre**, Leicester, where you can test your ability to survive a little more with a voyage on the interactive Human Spaceflight. Pick up a Thrill Hopper ticket that gives you great value access to top theme park attractions: **Drayton Manor Theme Park**, **Alton Towers**, **Snowdome** and **Waterworld**. Take a

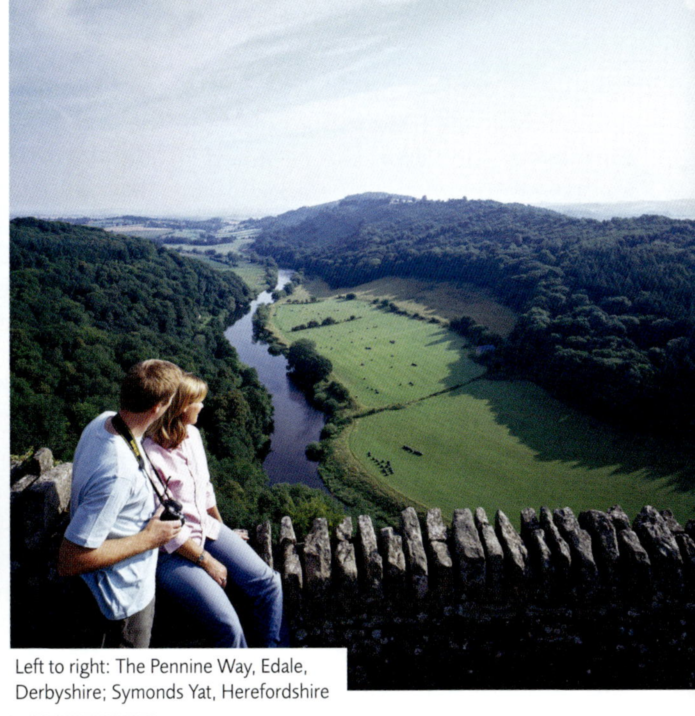

Left to right: The Pennine Way, Edale, Derbyshire; Symonds Yat, Herefordshire

**did you know...** Derbyshire's Dovedale was formed from ancient coral reefs? Enjoy the stunning scenery.

walk on the wild side in **Woburn Safari Park**, hunt for the Lost World Tribe in the Lost World Maze at the **Dinosaur Adventure Park** near Norwich or let the kids hit the assault course at **Conkers**, Swadlincote, in the heart of the National Forest. More of a spectator? Thrill to the sight of high-octane drag racing at **Santa Pod Raceway** or book early for the British Grand Prix at **Silverstone**. Hold on to your horse and back a winner at **Newmarket**, the historic home of British horseracing.

Create your own adventures crossing in and out of Wales on **Offa's Dyke Path** or tackle part of the **Heart of England Way**. There's 270 miles of the **Pennine Way**, stretching from the Peak District all the way to the Scottish Borders, to dip into or explore the long-distance paths that reach East Anglia's numerous sandy beaches. In the west of the region follow the **Wye Valley** through breaktaking scenery, including outstanding views from **Symonds Yat**.

Woburn Safari Park, Bedfordshire

## Spotlight on the past

Spend time in the historic cities of **Shrewsbury** and **Worcester** – noted for uneven Tudor half-timbered architecture. Reach for your camera as you pass through **Much Wenlock**, one of the beautiful black and white villages of Shropshire. See the multi-million pound restoration of one of Britain's most important historic gardens at **The Trentham Estate** – there is a large number of fully accessible gardens, each telling a magical story of its own. Castles and grand homes dot the landscape – **Kenilworth Castle** and **Warwick Castle** are favourites.

**did you know...** Lincoln Cathedral doubled as Westminster Abbey in The Da Vinci Code film?

For Elizabethan architecture at its most impressive, **Hardwick Hall** and **Chatsworth** are hard to beat. Step back into the area's proud industrial past at the **Ironbridge Gorge Museums**. Of the ten museums, the majority have good access, with lifts, ramps, tactile handling objects and welcoming staff on hand to help. Have a chat with the working craftsmen at **The Black Country Living Museum**. Relive a turning point in history at **Bosworth Battlefield**, Sutton Cheney. Trace the history of fighter planes at the **Imperial War Museum Duxford** in Cambridgeshire, Europe's premier aviation museum, or visit the National Cold War Exhibition at **RAF Museum Cosford**. There are wide aisles throughout the museum, and

Clockwise: Chatsworth House, Derbyshire; The Trentham Estate, Staffordshire; Warwick Castle, Warwickshire

wheelchairs and electric scooters are available free of charge, on a first come first served basis.

## Time and tides

Picnic, flask and binoculars at the ready for mile upon mile of sandy and shingle beaches running from Essex to Lincolnshire. Undeniably beautiful is the **National Nature Reserve at Holkham**, Norfolk, where creeks, sand dunes, pinewoods, pastures and marshes have merged. Down along the coast at **RSPB Minsmere**, Suffolk, peer from a hide to see just a few of the wading birds and waterfowl. Learn about seal rescue at **Natureland Seal Sanctuary**, Skegness. Seek out the havens of **Frinton-on-Sea**, **Covehithe** and **Anderby Creek** and the coast's numerous quaint fishing villages. For bustling seaside resorts, try **Felixstowe**, **Southend-on-Sea** and **Great Yarmouth**. Try out a hammock, avoid the rats and beware of the cannon fire in Below Decks, an interactive recreation of HMS Victory, at the **Norfolk Nelson Museum** in Great Yarmouth.

Moving inland, explore the rivers and dykes in the **Fens** – spread over Cambridgeshire, Lincolnshire, Norfolk and Rutland. At **Fenscape**, the interactive Fens discovery centre in Spalding, learn about the unique past of the inhospitable marshland.
For lazy days spent with friends and family, what could be more calming than the reed-fringed waterways of the **Norfolk Broads**?

Above: RAF Cosford, Shropshire
Below: RSPB Minsmere Nature Reserve, Suffolk

# Useful regional contacts

**East Midlands Tourism**
**w** discovereastmidlands.com

**East of England Tourism**
**t** (01284) 727470
**w** visiteastofengland.com

**The Heart of England – the West Midlands Region**
**w** visittheheart.com

**Marketing Birmingham**
**t** 0844 888 3883
**w** visitbirmingham.com

**Black Country Tourism**
**t** 0845 815 1516
**w** blackcountrytourism.co.uk

**Coventry & Warwickshire Visitor Information**
**t** 0844 499 8409
**w** visitcoventryand warwickshire.co.uk

**Visit Herefordshire**
**t** (01432) 260621
**w** visitherefordshire.co.uk

**Shakespeare Country**
**t** 0870 160 7930
**w** shakespeare-country.co.uk

**Shropshire Visitor Information**
**t** (01743) 281200
**w** shropshiretourism.info

**Destination Staffordshire**
**t** (01889) 880151
**w** enjoystaffordshire.com

**Destination Worcestershire**
**t** (01905) 728787
**w** visitworcestershire.org

## Publications

**Disability Access Bedford**
A range of leaflets from Bedford Council and Access Group. Call (01234) 221762 or visit bedford.gov.uk.

**You're Welcome**
A free guide to the Peak District produced by the National Park Authority. Call (01629) 816200.

## Information

**Disabled Holiday Information**
PO Box 186, Oswestry SY10 1AF
**e** info@disabledholidayinfo.org.uk
**w** disabledholidayinfo.org.uk
Provides holiday information for people with disabilities and produces a range of wheelchair user's guides on attractions, accessible sites and trails, and activities in Shropshire. The publications are available by post or may be downloaded from the website.

**Good Access East of England**
**w** goodaccesseastofengland.co.uk
An online directory of accessible accommodation, amenities and disability services in the East of England.

# Tourist Information Centres

Official Partner Tourist Information Centres offer quality assured help with accommodation and information about local attractions and events. To search for attractions and Tourist Information Centres on the move just text INFO to 62233, and a web link will be sent to your mobile phone. To find a Tourist Information Centre by region visit enjoyEngland.com/find-tic.

| | | | |
|---|---|---|---|
| **Aldeburgh** | 152 High Street | (01728) 453637 | atic@suffolkcoastal.gov.uk |
| **Ashbourne** | 13 Market Place | (01335) 343666 | ashbourneinfo@derbyshiredales.gov.uk |
| **Ashby-de-la-Zouch** | North Street | (01530) 411767 | ashby.tic@nwleices.gov.uk |
| **Bakewell** | Bridge Street | (01629) 813227 | bakewell@peakdistrict-npa.gov.uk |
| **Bewdley** | Load Street | (01299) 404740 | bewdleytic@wyreforestdc.gov.uk |
| **Birmingham Rotunda** | 150 New Street | 0844 888 3883 | callcentre@marketingbirmingham.com |
| **Bishop's Stortford** | The Old Monastery | (01279) 655831 | tic@bishopsstortford.org |
| **Brackley** | 2 Bridge Street | (01280) 700111 | tic@southnorthants.gov.uk |
| **Braintree** | Market Square | (01376) 550066 | tic@braintree.gov.uk |
| **Bridgnorth** | Listley Street | (01746) 763257 | bridgnorth.tourism@shropshire.gov.uk |
| **Burton upon Trent** | Horninglow Street | (01283) 508111 | tic@eaststaffsbc.gov.uk |
| **Bury St Edmunds** | 6 Angel Hill | (01284) 764667 | tic@stedsbc.gov.uk |
| **Buxton** | The Crescent | (01298) 25106 | tourism@highpeak.gov.uk |
| **Castleton** | Buxton Road | (01433) 620679 | castleton@peakdistrict-npa.gov.uk |
| **Chesterfield** | Rykneld Square | (01246) 345777 | tourism@chesterfield.gov.uk |
| **Church Stretton** | Church Street | (01694) 723133 | churchstretton.scf@shropshire.gov.uk |
| **Colchester** | Trinity Street | (01206) 282920 | vic@colchester.gov.uk |
| **Coventry Cathedral** | Cathedral Ruins, 1 Hill Top | (024) 7623 4297 | tic@cvone.co.uk |
| **Coventry Ricoh** | Phoenix Way | 0844 873 6397 | richoh@cvone.co.uk |
| **Coventry Transport Museum** | Hales Street | (024) 7622 7264 | tic@cvone.co.uk |
| **Derby** | Market Place | (01332) 255802 | tourism@derby.gov.uk |
| **Felixstowe** | 91 Undercliff Road West | (01394) 276770 | ftic@suffolkcoastal.gov.uk |
| **Flatford** | Flatford Lane | (01206) 299460 | flatfordvic@babergh.gov.uk |
| **Harwich** | Iconfield Park | (01255) 506139 | harwichtic@btconnect.com |
| **Hereford** | 1 King Street | (01432) 268430 | tic-hereford@herefordshire.gov.uk |
| **Hunstanton** | The Green | (01485) 532610 | hunstanton.tic@west-norfolk.gov.uk |
| **Ipswich** | St Stephens Lane | (01473) 258070 | tourist@ipswich.gov.uk |
| **Ironbridge** | Coalbrookdale | (01952) 884391 | tic@ironbridge.org.uk |
| **King's Lynn** | Purfleet Quay | (01553) 763044 | kings-lynn.tic@west-norfolk.gov.uk |
| **Lavenham** | Lady Street | (01787) 248207 | lavenhamtic@babergh.gov.uk |

| | | | |
|---|---|---|---|
| **Leamington Spa** | The Parade | (01926) 742762 | leamington@shakespeare-country.co.uk |
| **Leek** | Stockwell Street | (01538) 483741 | tourism.services@staffsmoorlands.gov.uk |
| **Leicester** | 7/9 Every Street | 0906 294 1113** | info@goleicestershire.com |
| **Lichfield** | Castle Dyke | (01543) 412112 | info@visitlichfield.com |
| **Lincoln** | 9 Castle Hill | (01522) 873213 | tourism@lincoln.gov.uk |
| **Lowestoft** | Royal Plain | (01502) 533600 | touristinfo@waveney.gov.uk |
| **Ludlow** | Castle Street | (01584) 875053 | ludlow.tourism@shropshire.gov.uk |
| **Maldon** | Coach Lane | (01621) 856503 | tic@maldon.gov.uk |
| **Malvern** | 21 Church Street | (01684) 892289 | malvern.tic@malvernhills.gov.uk |
| **Matlock** | Crown Square | (01629) 583388 | matlockinfo@derbyshiredales.gov.uk |
| **Matlock Bath** | The Pavillion | (01629) 55082 | matlockbathinfo@derbyshiredales.gov.uk |
| **Newmarket** | Palace Street | (01638) 667200 | tic.newmarket@forest-heath.gov.uk |
| **Northampton** | The Royal & Dernage Theatre | (01604) 838800 | northampton.tic@northamptonshire enterprise.ltd.uk |
| **Oswestry** | Mile End | (01691) 662488 | tic@oswestry-bc.gov.uk |
| **Oundle** | 14 West Street | (01832) 274333 | oundletic@east-northamptonshire.gov.uk |
| **Peterborough** | 3-5 Minster Precincts | (01733) 452336 | tic@peterborough.gov.uk |
| **Ripley** | Market Place | (01773) 841488 | touristinformation@ambervalley.gov.uk |
| **Ross-on-Wye** | Edde Cross Street | (01989) 562768 | tic-ross@herefordshire.gov.uk |
| **Rugby** | Rugby Art Gallery Museum & Library | (01788) 533217 | visitor.centre@rugby.gov.uk |
| **Saffron Walden** | Market Square | (01799) 510444 | tourism@uttleford.gov.uk |
| **Shrewsbury** | The Square | (01743) 281200 | visitorinfo@shrewsbury.gov.uk |
| **Sleaford** | Carre Street | (01529) 414294 | tic@n-kesteven.gov.uk |
| **Solihull** | Homer Road | (0121) 704 6130 | artscomplex@solihull.gov.uk |
| **Southwold** | 69 High Street | (01502) 724729 | southwold.tic@waveney.gov.uk |
| **Stafford** | Market Street | (01785) 619619 | tic@staffordbc.gov.uk |
| **Stoke-on-Trent** | Victoria Hall, Bagnall Street | (01782) 236000 | stoke.tic@stoke.gov.uk |
| **Stowmarket** | The Museum of East Anglian Life | (01449) 676800 | tic@midsuffolk.gov.uk |
| **Stratford-upon-Avon** | Bridgefoot | 0870 160 7930 | stratfordtic@shakespeare-country.co.uk |
| **Sudbury** | Market Hill | (01787) 881320 | sudburytic@babergh.gov.uk |
| **Swadlincote** | West Street | (01283) 222848 | Jo@sharpespotterymuseum.org.uk |
| **Tamworth** | 29 Market Street | (01827) 709581 | tic@tamworth.gov.uk |
| **Warwick** | Jury Street | (01926) 492212 | touristinfo@warwick-uk.co.uk |
| **Witham** | 61 Newland Street | (01376) 502674 | ticwitham@braintree.gov.uk |
| **Woodbridge** | Station Buildings | (01394) 382240 | wtic@suffolkcoastal.gov.uk |
| **Worcester** | High Street | (01905) 728787 | touristinfo@cityofworcester.gov.uk |

*seasonal opening

**calls to this number are charged at premium rate

where to stay in
# Central England

The following establishments participate in VisitBritain's Enjoy England quality assessment scheme and hold a National Accessible Scheme rating. YHA youth hostels in England and Wales are listed in a separate section, see page 40.

Place names in the blue bands with a map reference are shown on the maps at the front of this guide.

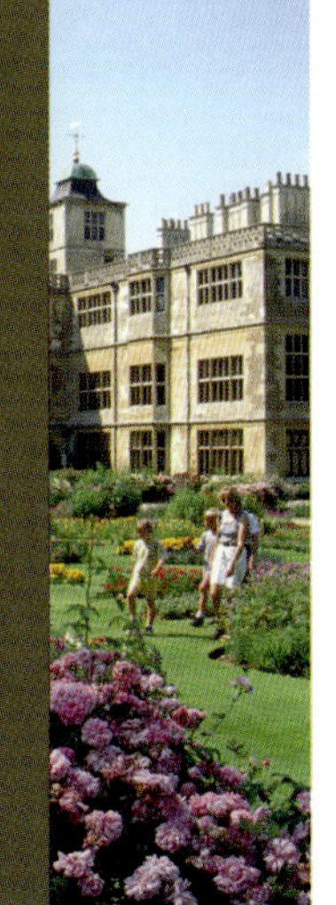

### Accommodation symbols

Symbols give useful information about services and facilities. You can find a key to these symbols on page 8.

## ALDEBURGH, Suffolk — HOTEL

**Brudenell Hotel** The Parade, Aldeburgh IP15 5BU
**t** (01728) 452071
**e** info@brudenellhotel.co.uk
**w** brudenellhotel.co.uk

## ALFORD, Lincolnshire — HOTEL

**Half Moon Hotel and Restaurant** 25-28 West Street, Alford LN13 9DG
**t** (01507) 463477
**e** halfmoonalford25@aol.com **w** thehalfmoonalford.com



At-a-glance symbols are explained on page 8.

## ASHBOURNE, Derbyshire Map ref 4B2 — SELF CATERING

★★★★–★★★★★
SELF CATERING

Units **3**
Sleeps **2–16**
Low season per wk
£342.00–£498.00
High season per wk
£509.00–£895.00

### Ancestral Barn, Ashbourne

**contact** Mrs Sue Fowler, Ancestral Barn, Church Farm, Stanshope, Nr Alstonefield, Ashbourne DE6 2AD **t** (01335) 310243
**e** sue@fowler89.fsnet.co.uk **w** dovedalecottages.co.uk

General

Unit

Payment Cash, cheques

*Fabulous canopy bed downstairs in king-size bedroom with walk-in shower and seat for the ambulant disabled. A real touch of luxury.*

Ancestral Barn sleeps six (two king-size, one twin); splendid canopy beds, all rooms en suite. Downstairs bedroom (king-size bed) is fully accessible. Two further cottages also available. Church Cottage is cosy and warm, whilst Dale Bottom Cottage boasts fabulous gardens. All cottages nestled on organic farm near Dovedale and full of old-world charm.

**open** All year
**nearest shop** 3 miles
**nearest pub** 1 mile

*M1 junction 25, A515 Ashbourne/Buxton road. Left opposite Newton Chalets, left at river through Milldale to Watt Russell pub. Left, then 1st left to Stanshope, immediately after hall turn left.*

## ASHBOURNE, Derbyshire — CAMPING, CARAVAN & HOLIDAY PARK

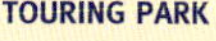

★★★★
TOURING PARK

**Blackwall Plantation Caravan Club Site** Kirk Ireton, Ashbourne DE6 3JL
**t** (01335) 370903
**e** enquiries@caravanclub.co.uk **w** caravanclub.co.uk

## ASHDON, Essex — SELF CATERING

★★★
SELF CATERING

**Hill Farm Holiday Cottages contact** Mrs Annette Bel, Hill Farm Holiday Cottages, Radwinter Road, Ashdon, Saffron Walden CB10 2ET **t** (01799) 584881
**e** hillfarm-holiday-cottages@hotmail.co.uk **w** hillfarm-holiday-cottages.co.uk

## Awaiting a rating

If you are considering accommodation that is awaiting a National Accessible Scheme rating, please confirm with the proprietor what facilities you can expect before booking.

## AYLMERTON, Norfolk Map ref 3B1 — HOTEL

★★★
SMALL HOTEL

B&B per room per night
**s £58.00–£74.00**
**d £96.00–£128.00**

### Roman Camp Inn

Holt Road, Aylmerton NR11 8QD **t** (01263) 838291
**e** enquiries@romancampinn.co.uk **w** romancampinn.co.uk

Attractive traditional inn with two superior ground floor rooms adapted for disabled guests with large wet rooms. Full access throughout the inn and garden. Large car park adjacent to entrance.
**open** All year except Christmas
**bedrooms** 10 double, 4 twin, 1 single
**bathrooms** All en suite

Access abc
Rooms
General
Payment Credit/debit cards, cash, cheques

## BACTON, Norfolk — SELF CATERING

★★★
SELF CATERING

**Primrose Cottage contact** Mr & Mrs Allan Epton, Cable Gap Holiday Park, Coast Road, Norwich NR12 0EW **t** (01692) 650667
**e** holiday@cablegap.co.uk **w** cablegap.co.uk

## BAKEWELL, Derbyshire — CAMPING, CARAVAN & HOLIDAY PARK

★★★★★
TOURING PARK

**Chatsworth Park Caravan Club Site** Chatsworth, Bakewell DE45 1PN
**t** (01246) 582226
**w** caravanclub.co.uk

## BARTON TURF, Norfolk — SELF CATERING

★★★★
SELF CATERING

**The Piggeries contact** Mrs Joyce Leach, Chestnut View, 8–10 High Street, Spaldwick, Huntingdon PE28 0TD **t** (01480) 890216
**e** info@norfolkcottages.co.uk **w** norfolkcottages.co.uk

## BEESTON, Norfolk Map ref 3B1 — SELF CATERING

★★★
SELF CATERING

Units **1**
Sleeps **6**
Low season per wk
**Min £275.00**
High season per wk
**Max £550.00**

### Holmdene Farm, King's Lynn

**contact** Mrs Gaye Davidson, Holmdene Farm, Syers Lane, Beeston, King's Lynn PE32 2NJ **t** (01328) 701284 **w** holmdenefarm.co.uk

Beeston is a quiet village in the middle of rural Norfolk – voted Village of the Year in 2005. The Stables enable the less mobile visitor to enjoy a family holiday.
**open** All Year
**nearest shop** 0.5 miles
**nearest pub** 0.5 miles

General
Unit
Payment Cash, cheques

## BELCHFORD, Lincolnshire — SELF CATERING

★★★★–★★★★★
SELF CATERING

**Poachers Hideaway contact** Jacki Harris, Poachers Hideaway, Flintwood Farm, Belchford LN9 5QN **t** (01507) 533555
**e** info@poachershideaway.com **w** poachershideaway.com

At-a-glance symbols are explained on page 8.

**BIRMINGHAM,** West Midlands Map ref 4B3 **CAMPING, CARAVAN & HOLIDAY PARK**

★★★★★
TOURING PARK

(99) £14.00–£26.90
(99) £14.00–£26.90
99 touring pitches

## Chapel Lane Caravan Club Site

Chapel Lane, Wythall, Birmingham B47 6JX **t** (01564) 826483
**w** caravanclub.co.uk

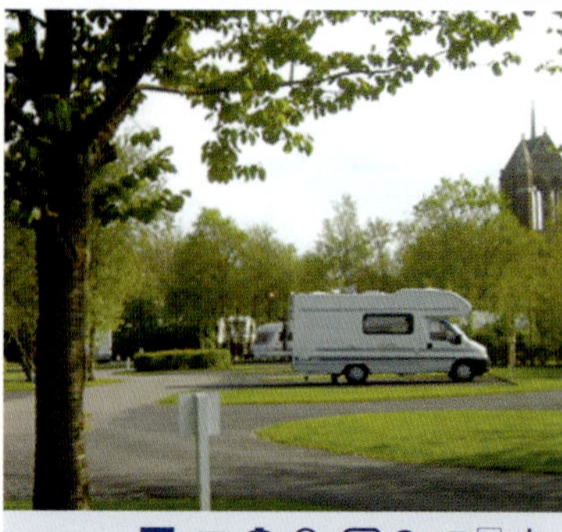

General

Leisure

Payment Credit/debit cards, cash, cheques

*Midweek discount; pitch fees reduced by 50% for stays on Mon, Tue, Wed or Thu.*

Surprisingly rural, in the shadow of an old chapel and with a pleasant open aspect, yet convenient for the motorways (M1, M6 and M42), Birmingham and the National Exhibition Centre. The Transport Museum is adjacent to the site and Becketts Farm Shop with restaurant is just a ten-minute walk away.

**open** All year

*From M1 jct 23a, jct 3 off M42 then A435 to Birmingham. After 1 mile at roundabout take 1st exit, Middle Lane. Turn right at church then immediately right into site.*

**BLACKSHAW MOOR,** Staffordshire **CAMPING, CARAVAN & HOLIDAY PARK**

★★★★★
TOURING PARK

**Blackshaw Moor Caravan Club Site** Blackshaw Moor, Leek ST13 8TW
**t** (01538) 300203
**w** caravanclub.co.uk

**BLAKENEY,** Norfolk **HOTEL**

★★
HOTEL

**The Pheasant Hotel** Coast Road, Kelling, Holt NR25 7EG
**t** (01263) 588382
**e** enquiries@pheasanthotelnorfolk.co.uk **w** pheasanthotelnorfolk.co.uk

**BOSTON,** Lincolnshire **SELF CATERING**

★★★★
SELF CATERING

**Crewyard Cottages contact** Colin Ash, Crewyard Cottages, Everards, Highgate, Leverton, Boston PE22 0AW **t** (01205) 871389
**e** gina@gina31.wanadoo.co.uk **w** crewyardholidaycottages-boston.co.uk

## Place index

If you know where you want to stay, the index by place name at the back of the guide will give you the page number listing accommodation in your chosen town, city or village. Check out the other useful indexes too.

## BOSTON, Lincolnshire Map ref 3A1 — SELF CATERING

★★★★–★★★★★
SELF CATERING

Units **8**
Sleeps **1–5**
Low season per wk
£320.00–£350.00
High season per wk
£440.00–£490.00

### Elms Farm Cottages, Boston

**contact** Carol Emerson, Elms Farm Cottages, The Elms, Hubberts Bridge, Boston PE20 3QP **t** (01205) 290840 & 07887 652021
**e** carol@elmsfarmcottages.co.uk **w** elmsfarmcottages.co.uk

Access abc
General
Unit
Payment Credit/debit cards, cash, cheques

East Midlands Tourism Self-Catering Holiday of the Year 2007/08, Lincolnshire Tourism Accommodation of the Year 2007/08. Eight cottages all with level access, four with wet rooms suitable for wheelchairs. All furnished to a high standard. Large grass field with wildflower meadow, rare breed chickens and tourist information room. The ideal place to relax and enjoy the Lincolnshire countryside.

**open** All Year
**nearest shop** 2 miles
**nearest pub** < 0.5 miles

*On A1121, 250m from Hubberts Bridge crossroads.*

## BRASSINGTON, Derbyshire — SELF CATERING

★★★★
SELF CATERING

**Hoe Grange Holidays** Hoe Grange Holidays, Hoe Grange, Brassington, Matlock DE4 4HP **t** (01629) 540262
**e** info@hoegrangeholidays.co.uk **w** hoegrangeholidays.co.uk

## BRIDGNORTH, Shropshire

*See entry on p163*

## BROMYARD, Herefordshire — CAMPING, CARAVAN & HOLIDAY PARK

★★★★
TOURING PARK

**Bromyard Downs Caravan Club Site** Brockhampton, Bringsty, Bromyard WR6 5TE
**t** (01885) 482607
**w** caravanclub.co.uk

## BURGH ON BAIN, Lincolnshire — SELF CATERING

★★★★
SELF CATERING

**Bainfield Lodge** **contact** Marian Walker, Bainfield Lodge, Bainfield House, Main Road, Market Rasen LN8 6JY **t** (01507) 313540
**e** dennis.walker1@btinternet.com **w** bainfieldholidaylodge.co.uk

## BUXTON, Derbyshire — SELF CATERING

★★★★
SELF CATERING

**Wheeldon Trees Farm** **contact** Deborah & Martin Hofman, Wheeldon Trees Farm, Earl Sterndale, Buxton SK17 0AA **t** (01298) 83219
**e** stay@wheeldontreesfarm.co.uk **w** wheeldontreesfarm.co.uk

**BUXTON,** Derbyshire Map ref 4B2 — **CAMPING, CARAVAN & HOLIDAY PARK**

TOURING & CAMPING PARK

(117) £12.20–£25.10
(117) £12.00–£25.10
117 touring pitches

## Grin Low Caravan Club Site

Grin Low Road, Ladmanlow, Buxton SK17 6UJ **t** (01298) 77735
**w** caravanclub.co.uk

General

Leisure

Payment Credit/debit cards, cash, cheques

*Midweek discount; pitch fees reduced by up to 50% for stays on Mon, Tue, Wed or Thu night outside peak and value season.*

Hidden away on the valley floor, Grin Low is conveniently placed for just about everything going on in and around the Peak District, but particularly for the civilised little town of Buxton with its colourful Pavilion Gardens and the Opera House which offers a wide range of events.

**open** March to November

*From Buxton left off A53 Buxton to Leek road. Within 1.5 miles at Grin Low signpost, in 300yds turn left into site approach road; site entrance 0.25 miles.*

**CAMBRIDGE,** Cambridgeshire Map ref 2D1 — **CAMPING, CARAVAN & HOLIDAY PARK**

TOURING & CAMPING PARK

(60) £12.20–£25.10
(60) £12.20–£25.10
60 touring pitches

## Cherry Hinton Caravan Club Site

Lime Kiln Road, Cherry Hinton, Cambridge CB1 8NQ **t** (01223) 244088
**w** caravanclub.co.uk

General

Payment Credit/debit cards, cash, cheques

Set in old quarry workings and within a site of special scientific interest, this site has been imaginatively landscaped to create the impression of being in the heart of the countryside while only a ten-minute bus journey on the 'park & ride' (0.5 miles from site) to the city centre.

**open** All year

*M11 jct 9 onto A11. After 7 miles slip road signposted Fulbourn and Tevisham. In Fulbourn continue to roundabout signposted Cambridge. At traffic lights turn left. Left again into Lime Kiln Road.*

## CHADDESLEY CORBETT, Worcestershire — HOTEL

★★★ HOTEL GOLD AWARD

**Brockencote Hall** Chaddesley Corbett, Nr Kidderminster DY10 4PY
**t** (01562) 777876
**e** info@brockencotehall.com
**w** brockencotehall.com

## CHELMSFORD, Essex — HOTEL

★★ SMALL HOTEL

**Boswell House Hotel** 118-120 Springfield Road, Chelmsford CM2 6LF
**t** (01245) 287587
**e** boswell118@aol.com **w** boswellhousehotel.co.uk

## CHESTERFIELD, Derbyshire — HOTEL

★★ SMALL HOTEL SILVER AWARD

**Abbeydale Hotel** Cross Street, Chesterfield S40 4TD
**t** (01246) 277849
**e** abbeydale1ef@aol.com
**w** abbeydalehotel.co.uk

## CHURCH STRETTON, Shropshire — SELF CATERING

★★★★ SELF CATERING

**Botvyle Farm Holiday Cottages**
**t** (01694) 722869
**e** enquiries@botvylefarm.co.uk **w** botvylefarm.co.uk

## CLACTON-ON-SEA, Essex

*See entry on p163*

## CLEETHORPES, North East Lincolnshire — GUEST ACCOMMODATION

★★★★ GUEST HOUSE

**Tudor Terrace Guest House** 11 Bradford Avenue, Cleethorpes DN35 0BB
**t** (01472) 600800
**e** tudor.terrace@ntlworld.com **w** tudorterrace.co.uk

## COTTON, Suffolk — SELF CATERING

★★★★ SELF CATERING

**Coda Cottages contact** Mrs Kate Sida-Nicholls, Coda Cottages, 2 Park Farm, Dandy Corner, Cotton, Stowmarket IP14 4QX **t** (01449) 780076
**w** codacottages.co.uk

## COVENHAM ST BARTHOLOMEW, Lincolnshire — SELF CATERING

★★★★–★★★★★ SELF CATERING

**Westfield Mews & Lodges contact** Mrs J Cream, Westfield Mews & Lodges, Westfield House, Louth LN11 0PB
**t** (01507) 363217

## CRATFIELD, Suffolk — SELF CATERING

★★★★ SELF CATERING

**Holly Tree Farm Barns contact** Rachel Boddy, Holly Tree Farm, Bell Green, Cratfield, Halesworth IP19 0DN **t** (01986) 798062
**e** hollytreebarns@lycos.co.uk **w** hollytreebarns.co.uk

## CRATFIELD, Suffolk — SELF CATERING

★★★★ SELF CATERING

**School Farm Cottages contact** Mrs Claire Sillett, School Farm, Church Road, Cratfield, Halesworth IP19 0BU **t** (01986) 798844
**e** schoolfarmcotts@aol.com **w** schoolfarmcottages.com

## CRAVEN ARMS, Shropshire — SELF CATERING

★★★★ SELF CATERING

**Strefford Hall Self Catering – Robins & Swallows Nest**
**contact** Mrs Caroline Morgan, Strefford Hall, Strefford, Craven Arms SY7 8DE
**t** (01588) 672383
**w** streffordhall.co.uk

At-a-glance symbols are explained on page 8.

## CROMER, Norfolk — GUEST ACCOMMODATION

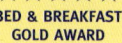

**Incleborough House Luxury Bed and Breakfast** Lower Common, East Runton, Cromer NR27 9PG
**t** (01263) 515939
**e** enquiries@incleboroughhouse.co.uk **w** incleboroughhouse.co.uk

## DERBY, Derbyshire — CAMPING, CARAVAN & HOLIDAY PARK

★★★
TOURING PARK

**Elvaston Castle Caravan Club Site** Borrowash Road, Elvaston, Derby DE72 3EP
**t** (01332) 571342
**e** enquiries@caravanclub.co.uk **w** caravanclub.co.uk

## DEREHAM, Norfolk — GUEST ACCOMMODATION

**Greenbanks** Wendling, Dereham NR19 2AB
**t** (01362) 687742
**e** jenny@greenbankshotel.co.uk **w** greenbankshotel.co.uk

## DISS, Norfolk Map ref 3B2 — SELF CATERING

Units **4**
Sleeps **4–8**
Low season per wk
**£425.00–£755.00**
High season per wk
**£767.00–£1,346.00**

### Norfolk Cottages – Malthouse Farm, Gissing

**contact** Mrs Cathy Smith, Norfolk Cottages Booking Office, 17 Owen Road, Diss IP22 4ER **t** (01379) 658021 **e** bookings@norfolkcottages.net
**w** norfolkcottages.net

Small complex of rural courtyard cottages sleeping four (smallest) to eight (largest). Indoor pool and spa with hoist. Ground-floor bedrooms with wetrooms. Service dogs welcome. Short breaks available – see website.

**open** All Year
**nearest shop** 4 miles
**nearest pub** < 0.5 miles

Payment Credit/debit cards, cash, cheques

## DONINGTON, Lincolnshire — GUEST ACCOMMODATION

**Browntoft House** Browntoft Lane, Donington PE11 4TQ
**t** (01775) 822091
**e** finchedward@hotmail.com
**w** browntofthouse.co.uk

## EAST HARLING, Norfolk — SELF CATERING

**Berwick Cottage contact** Mrs Miriam Toosey, Berwick Cottage, The Lin Berwick Trust, Upper East Street, Sudbury CO10 1UB **t** (01787) 372343
**w** thelinberwicktrust.org.uk

## EDWARDSTONE, Suffolk Map ref 3B2 — SELF CATERING

★★★★
SELF CATERING

Units **2**
Sleeps **2–6**
Low season per wk
Min £300.00
High season per wk
Max £675.00

### Sherbourne Farm Lodge Cottages, Sudbury

**contact** Mrs Anne Suckling, Sherbourne House Farm, Edwardstone, Sudbury CO10 5PD **t** (01787) 210885
**e** enquiries@sherbournelodgecottages.co.uk **w** sherbournelodgecottages.co.uk

Family farm location. Stunning barn conversions in idyllic setting. Two-bedroomed twin/double, kitchen/living area, wet room. Village shops, pubs nearby. Enjoy our special Wildlife-Watch evening – an unforgettable experience!

**open** All year
**nearest shop** < 0.5 miles
**nearest pub** < 0.5 miles

Payment Cash, cheques

## ELY, Cambridgeshire — GUEST ACCOMMODATION

★★★
GUEST HOUSE

**Wood Fen Lodge** 6 Black Bank Road, Little Downham, Ely CB6 2UA
**t** (01353) 862495
**e** info@woodfenlodge.co.uk **w** woodfenlodge.co.uk

## EWYAS HAROLD, Herefordshire — SELF CATERING

★★★★
SELF CATERING

**Old King Street Farm contact** Robert Dewar, Old King Street Farm, Ewyas Harold, Golden Valley HR2 0HB **t** (01981) 240208
**e** info@oldkingstreetfarm.co.uk **w** oldkingstreetfarm.co.uk

## FINESHADE, Northamptonshire — CAMPING, CARAVAN & HOLIDAY PARK

★★★★
TOURING PARK

**Top Lodge Caravan Club Site** Fineshade, Duddington, Corby NN17 3BB
**t** (01780) 444617
**w** caravanclub.co.uk

## FLASH, Staffordshire — SELF CATERING

★★★
SELF CATERING

**Northfield Farm contact** Mrs Elizabeth Andrews, Northfield Farm, Flash, Buxton SK17 0SW **t** (01298) 22543
**e** northfield@btinternet.com **w** northfieldfarm.co.uk

## FOXLEY, Norfolk — SELF CATERING

★★★–★★★★
SELF CATERING

**Moor Farm Stable Cottages contact** Mr Paul Davis, Moor Farm, Foxley, Dereham NR20 4QP **t** (01362) 688523
**e** mail@moorfarmstablecottages.co.uk **w** moorfarmstablecottages.co.uk

## FRITTON, Norfolk — SELF CATERING

★★★★
SELF CATERING

**Fritton Lake Country World contact** Mr Brian Humphrey, Fritton Lake Country World, Beccles Road, Fritton, Great Yarmouth NR31 9HA
**t** (01493) 488208
**w** great-yarmouth.angle.uk.com/attractions/frittonlake.cgi

## GAINSBOROUGH, Lincolnshire — GUEST ACCOMMODATION

★★★
BED & BREAKFAST

**Blyton (Sunnyside) Ponds** Sunnyside Farm, Station Road, Blyton, Gainsborough DN21 3LE **t** (01427) 628240
**e** blytonponds@msn.com **w** blytonponds.co.uk

At-a-glance symbols are explained on page 8.

## GOULCEBY, Lincolnshire — SELF CATERING

★★★★ SELF CATERING

**Bay Tree Cottage contact** Gordon Reid, Bay Tree Cottage, Goulceby Post, Ford Way, Goulceby, Louth LN11 9WD **t** (01507) 343230
**e** info@goulcebypost.co.uk **w** goulcebypost.co.uk

## GREAT SNORING, Norfolk — GUEST ACCOMMODATION

★★★★ FARMHOUSE SILVER AWARD

**Vine Park Cottage B&B** Thursford Road, Fakenham NR21 0PF
**t** (01328) 821016
**e** rita@vineparkcottagebandb.co.uk **w** vineparkcottagebandb.co.uk

## GREAT YARMOUTH, Norfolk — CAMPING, CARAVAN & HOLIDAY PARK

★★★★★ HOLIDAY PARK

**Great Yarmouth Caravan Club Site** Great Yarmouth Racecourse, Jellicoe Road, Great Yarmouth NR30 4AU **t** (01493) 855223
**w** caravanclub.co.uk

## HAGWORTHINGHAM, Lincolnshire — SELF CATERING

★★★★ SELF CATERING

**Kingfisher Lodge contact** Nick Bowser, Kingfisher Lodge, The Estate Office, Leverton, Boston PE22 0AA **t** (01205) 870210 & 07970 128531
**e** office@ewbowser.com **w** meridianretreats.co.uk

## HALSTEAD, Essex — GUEST ACCOMMODATION

★★★ INN

**The White Hart** 15 High Street, Halstead CO9 2AA
**t** (01787) 475657
**w** innpubs.co.uk

## HAPPISBURGH, Norfolk — SELF CATERING

★★★★ SELF CATERING

**Boundary Stables contact** Mr & Mrs Julian and Elizabeth Burns, Boundary Stables, Grub Street, Happisburgh NR12 0RX **t** (01692) 650171
**e** bookings@boundarystables.co.uk **w** boundarystables.co.uk

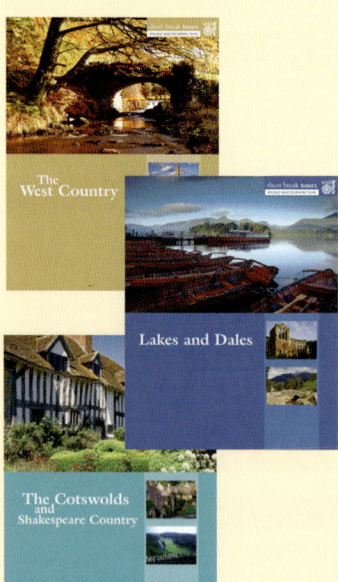

**HAPPISBURGH,** Norfolk Map ref 3C1 **SELF CATERING**

Units **4**
Sleeps **4–6**
Low season per wk
**£310.00–£543.00**
High season per wk
**£434.00–£798.00**

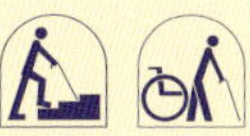

## Church Farm Barns, Happisburgh

Church Farm Barns **t** (01692) 650137
**e** churchfarmbarns@hotmail.co.uk
**w** norfolkholidayaccommodation.com

Access

General

Unit

Payment Cash, cheques

*Cottages can be booked in any combination for family/group holidays, to provide accommodation for 8, 10, 12, 14, 16 or 20 people respectively.*

Sympathetic conversion of barn and stables into four holiday cottages and a recreation room, all of exceptional quality, offering guests the opportunity to relax in a rural idyll less than fifteen minutes' drive from the Norfolk Broads. Hepworth Cottage is level-entry with wider doorways, ground-floor bedroom and a walk-in en suite shower room. Moore, Hitchens and Nicholson Cottages are entered via a step and have ground-floor bedrooms with bathroom or shower room.

**open** All year
**nearest shop** < 0.5 miles
**nearest pub** < 0.5 miles

**HARTINGTON,** Derbyshire **SELF CATERING**

★★★★ SELF CATERING

**Ash Tree Cottage contact** Mrs Clare Morson, Nettletor Farm, Mill Lane, Buxton SK17 0AN **t** (01298) 84247
**e** nettletorfarm@btconnect.com

**HARTINGTON,** Derbyshire **SELF CATERING**

**Old House Farm Cottages contact** Mrs Sue Flower, Old House Farm Cottages, Old House Farm, Newhaven, Buxton SK17 0DY **t** (01629) 636268
**e** s.flower1@virgin.net **w** oldhousefarm.com

## Remember to check when booking

Please remember that all information in this guide has been supplied by the proprietors well in advance of publication. Since changes do sometimes occur it's a good idea to check details at the time of booking.

At-a-glance symbols are explained on page 8.

## HAUGHLEY, Suffolk Map ref 3B2 — SELF CATERING

SELF CATERING

Units **3**
Sleeps **2–5**
Low season per wk
£240.00–£320.00
High season per wk
£300.00–£440.00

### Red House Farm Cottages, Haughley, Stowmarket

**contact** Mrs Mary Noy, Red House Farm, Haughley, Stowmarket IP14 3QP
**t** (01449) 673323 **e** mary@redhousefarmhaughley.co.uk

Enjoy the peace and tranquility of Suffolk, staying in Stable Cottage. It provides ground-floor accommodation with easy access and sleeps four people in two rooms, plus an additional single bed.

**open** All Year
**nearest shop** 1 mile
**nearest pub** 1 mile

General 

Unit

Payment Credit/debit cards, cash, cheques

## HENLEY, Suffolk Map ref 3B2 — SELF CATERING

★★★★
SELF CATERING

Units **5**
Sleeps **1–6**
Low season per wk
£260.00–£390.00
High season per wk
£400.00–£650.00

### Damerons Farm Holidays, Ipswich

**contact** Mr & Mrs Wayne & Sue Leggett, Damerons Farm Holidays, Main Road, Henley, Ipswich IP6 0RU
**t** (01473) 832454 & 07881 824083
**e** info@dameronsfarmholidays.co.uk **w** dameronsfarmholidays.co.uk

Three cottages (Level 1 access) sleeping between one and six people, and The Old Dairy (Level 3 access) sleeping two, plus sofa bed. Beautiful countryside setting.

**open** All year
**nearest shop** 2.5 miles
**nearest pub** 1 mile

Access

General

Unit

Payment Credit/debit cards, cash, cheques

## HEREFORD, Herefordshire — SELF CATERING

★★★★
SELF CATERING

**Grafton Villa Farm Cottages** **contact** Mrs Jennie Layton, Grafton Villa Farm Cottages, Grafton Villa, Grafton, Hereford HR2 8ED
**t** (01432) 268689
**e** jennielayton@ereal.net **w** graftonvilla.co.uk

## HOLBECK, Nottinghamshire — GUEST ACCOMMODATION

★★★★★
BED & BREAKFAST GOLD AWARD

**Browns** The Old Orchard Cottage, Holbeck, Worksop S80 3NF
**t** (01909) 720659
**e** browns@holbeck.fsnet.co.uk
**w** brownsholbeck.co.uk

## HOLT, Norfolk — SELF CATERING

★★★–★★★★★ SELF CATERING

**Wood Farm Cottages contact** Mrs Diana Jacob, Wood Farm Cottages, Plumstead Road, Holt NR24 2AQ **t** (01263) 587347
**e** info@wood-farm.com **w** wood-farm.com

## HORNCASTLE, Lincolnshire — HOTEL

★★★ HOTEL

**Best Western Admiral Rodney Hotel** North Street, Horncastle, Lincoln LN9 5DX
**t** (01507) 523131
**e** reception@admiralrodney.com **w** admiralrodney.com

## HORNING, Norfolk — SELF CATERING

★★★–★★★★★ SELF CATERING

**King Line Cottages contact** Mr Robert King, King Line Cottages, 4 Pinewood Drive, Horning NR12 8LZ **t** (01692) 630297
**e** kingline@norfolk-broads.co.uk **w** norfolk-broads.co.uk

## HORSINGTON, Lincolnshire — SELF CATERING

★★★ SELF CATERING

**Wayside Cottage contact** Ian Williamson, Mill Lane Holiday Cottages, 72 Mill Lane, Woodhall Spa LN10 6QZ **t** (01526) 353101
**w** skegness.net/woodhallspa.htm

## HOVETON, Norfolk

*See entries on p163*

## HUNSTANTON, Norfolk Map ref 3B1 — HOTEL

★★★ HOTEL

B&B per room per night
**s £49.00–£99.00**
**d £70.00–£150.00**
HB per person per night
**£55.00–£95.00**

# Caley Hall Hotel

Old Hunstanton Road, Old Hunstanton, Hunstanton PE36 6HH
**t** (01485) 533486
**e** mail@caleyhallhotel.co.uk **w** caleyhallhotel.co.uk

Rooms

General

Payment Credit/debit cards, cash, cheques

*2 rooms feature specially adapted bathrooms with level-access shower. The hotel has no steps.*

Caley Hall Hotel and Restaurant is set around a manor-house dating back to 1648. More recently, the old farm outbuildings have been converted to provide the spacious en suite bedrooms, restaurant and bar. Most of the rooms are on the ground floor, and some feature a four-poster bed or whirlpool bath.

**open** All year except Christmas and New Year
**bedrooms** 15 double, 15 twin, 4 single, 5 family, 1 suite
**bathrooms** All en suite

*In Old Hunstanton, on the left-hand side of the A149, just before the turning to the golf course.*

## HUNSTANTON, Norfolk — SELF CATERING

★★★★ SELF CATERING

**Foxgloves Cottage contact** Terry & Lesley Heade, Foxgloves Cottage, 29 Avenue Road, Hunstanton PE36 5BW **t** (01485) 532460
**e** deepdenehouse@btopenworld.com **w** smoothhound.co.uk/hotels/deepdene.html

## HUNTINGDON, Cambridgeshire — CAMPING, CARAVAN & HOLIDAY PARK

★★★★ TOURING PARK

**Houghton Mill Caravan Club Site** Mill Street, Huntingdon PE28 2AZ
**t** (01480) 466716
**e** enquiries@caravanclub.co.uk **w** caravanclub.co.uk

## ILAM, Staffordshire — SELF CATERING

★★★★ SELF CATERING

**Beechenhill Farm Cottages contact** Mrs Sue Prince, Beechenhill Farm Cottages, Beechenhill Farm, Ilam, Ashbourne DE6 2BD **t** (01335) 310274
**e** beechenhill@btinternet.com **w** beechenhill.co.uk

## KILPECK, Herefordshire — SELF CATERING

★★★★ SELF CATERING

**Sizecroft Farm contact** Ms V Stockley, Sizecroft Farm, c/o Gosmore Farm, Clehonger HR2 9SN
**t** (01432) 277122

## KING'S LYNN, Norfolk Map ref 3B1 — HOTEL

★★ HOTEL SILVER AWARD

B&B per room per night
**s £107.00–£168.00**
**d £280.00–£310.00**
HB per person per night
**£122.00–£168.00**

# Park House Hotel

King's Lynn PE35 6EH **t** (01485) 543000
**e** parkinfo@lcdisability.org **w** parkhousehotel.org.uk

Access

Rooms

General

Leisure

Payment Credit/debit cards, cash, cheques

*Short breaks and themed weeks available.*

A country-house hotel with a difference. Located on the Royal Sandringham Estate, the hotel is adapted for people with mobility difficulties and is fully wheelchair accessible. Care is on hand if required and charged for accordingly. Optional entertainment and excursions are always available.

**open** All year
**bedrooms** 8 twin, 8 single
**bathrooms** All en suite

*From King's Lynn A149 following signs to Hunstanton. Approx 3 miles turn right signed Sandringham Country Park. Continue forward for approx 1 mile, hotel on right.*

## KNIGHTCOTE, Warwickshire — SELF CATERING

★★★★★ SELF CATERING

**Arbor Holiday & Knightcote Farm Cottages** contact Craig & Fiona Walker, Arbor Holiday & Knightcote Farm Cottages, The Bake House, Knightcote, Southam, Warwick CV47 2EF **t** (01295) 770637
**e** fionawalker@farmcottages.com **w** farmcottages.com

## LEDBURY, Herefordshire — SELF CATERING

★★★-★★★★ SELF CATERING

**Old Kennels Farm** contact Mrs Jeanette Wilce, Old Kennels Farm, Bromyard Road, Ledbury HR8 1LG **t** (01531) 635024
**e** wilceoldkennelsfarm@btinternet.com **w** oldkennelsfarm.co.uk

## LIGHTHORNE, Warwickshire — GUEST ACCOMMODATION

★★★★ FARMHOUSE SILVER AWARD

**Church Hill Farm B & B** Lighthorne, Warwick CV35 0AR
**t** (01926) 651251
**e** sue@churchillfarm.co.uk
**w** churchhillfarm.co.uk

## LINCOLN, Lincolnshire — SELF CATERING

★★★★ SELF CATERING

**Cliff Farm Cottage** contact Rae Marris, Cliff Farm Cottage, Cliff Farm, North Carlton LN1 2RP **t** (01522) 730475
**e** rae.marris@farming.co.uk **w** cliff-farm-cottage.co.uk

## LITTLE SNORING, Norfolk — SELF CATERING

★★★★ SELF CATERING

**Jex Farm Barns** contact Mr Stephen & Lynne Harvey, Jex Farm Barns, Thursford Road, Little Snoring, Fakenham NR21 0JJ
**t** (01328) 878257 & 07979 495760
**e** farmerstephen@jexfarm.wanadoo.co.uk **w** jexfarm.co.uk

## LITTLE TARRINGTON, Herefordshire — CAMPING, CARAVAN & HOLIDAY PARK

★★★★★ TOURING & CAMPING PARK

**Hereford Camping & Caravanning Club Site** The Millpond, Little Tarrington HR1 4JA
**t** (01432) 890243
**e** enquiries@millpond.co.uk **w** campingandcaravanningclub.co.uk

## LOUGHBOROUGH, Leicestershire — HOTEL

★★★★ HOTEL

**Burleigh Court** Loughborough University, Loughborough LE11 3TD
**t** (01509) 211515
**e** info@welcometoimago.com **w** welcometoimago.com

## LOWESTOFT, Suffolk — HOTEL

★★★ HOTEL

**Hotel Victoria** Kirkley Cliff, Lowestoft NR33 0BZ
**t** (01502) 574433
**e** info@thehotelvictoria.co.uk **w** thehotelvictoria.co.uk

## LUDLOW, Shropshire — SELF CATERING

★★★★ SELF CATERING

**Goosefoot Barn Cottages** contact Mrs Sally Loft, Goosefoot Barn Cottages, Pinstones, Diddlebury, Craven Arms SY7 9LB **t** (01584) 861326
**e** sally@goosefoot.freeserve.co.uk **w** goosefootbarn.co.uk

## LUDLOW, Shropshire — SELF CATERING

★★★ SELF CATERING

**Mocktree Barns Holiday Cottages** contact Clive & Cynthia Prior, Mocktree Barns Holiday Cottages, Leintwardine, Ludlow SY7 0LY **t** (01547) 540441
**e** mocktreebarns@care4free.net **w** mocktreeholidays.co.uk

At-a-glance symbols are explained on page 8.

**LUDLOW,** Shropshire Map ref 4A3 — **SELF CATERING**

SELF CATERING

Units **6**
Sleeps **2–6**
Low season per wk
Min £220.00
High season per wk
Max £360.00

## Sutton Court Farm Cottages, Ludlow

**contact** Mrs Jane Cronin, Sutton Court Farm, Little Sutton, Stanton Lacy, Ludlow SY8 2AJ **t** (01584) 861305 **e** enquiries@suttoncourtfarm.co.uk
**w** suttoncourtfarm.co.uk

Holly Cottage is a ground floor cottage sleeping two and has a private patio garden. Cream teas and evening meals available to order. Five other cottages on site. Short breaks always available.

**open** All Year
**nearest shop** 6 miles
**nearest pub** 6 miles

Access
General
Unit
Payment Cash, cheques

**MABLETHORPE,** Lincolnshire — **SELF CATERING**

★★★★
SELF CATERING

**Grange Cottages contact** Ann Graves, Grange Cottages, Main Road, Alford LN13 0JP **t** (01507) 450267
**w** grange-cottages.co.uk

# Country ways

The Countryside Rights of Way Act gives people new rights to walk on areas of open countryside and registered common land.

To find out where you can go and what you can do, as well as information about taking your dog to the countryside, go online at countrysideaccess.gov.uk.

And when you're out and about...

**Always follow the Country Code**

- Be safe – plan ahead and follow any signs
- Leave gates and property as you find them
- Protect plants and animals, and take your litter home
- Keep dogs under close control
- Consider other people

**MALVERN,** Worcestershire Map ref 2B1 **SELF CATERING**

★★★★–★★★★★
SELF CATERING

Units **7**
Sleeps **2–12**
Low season per wk
£267.00–£1,248.00
High season per wk
£589.00–£2,800.00

## Hidelow House Cottages, Acton Beauchamp, Worcester

**contact** Mrs Pauline Diplock, Hidelow House Cottages, Acton Green, Acton Beauchamp, Bromyard WR6 5AH **t** (01886) 884547
**e** easyaccess@hidelow.co.uk **w** hidelow.co.uk

Access

General

Unit

Payment Credit/debit cards, cash, cheques, euros

*Rangle of aids-to-living available including: profiling bed, hoist, mattress, shower chairs and more. Qualified carers; profile of local accessible places to visit; and home-cooked frozen meals all available.*

Worry-free, award-winning holiday accommodation offering second-to-none care, service and specialist facilities for disabled guests, carers and pets. Homely, level-access, spacious, single-storey cottages. Roll-in shower rooms; wheelchair-friendly kitchens; accessible, landscaped gardens and stunning views across rural Herefordshire. Fully accessible shop; visitors' information room with free broadband and payphone; laundry and drying room.

**open** All year
**nearest shop** < 0.5 miles
**nearest pub** 3 miles

*M5 jct 7. A4103 Worcester to Hereford. Turn right at B4220, signposted Bromyard. Hidelow House is 2 miles from this junction on left.*

## Where can I get help and advice?

Tourist Information Centres offer friendly help with accommodation and holiday ideas as well as suggestions of places to visit and things to do. You'll find contact details at the beginning of each regional section.

At-a-glance symbols are explained on page 8.

**MANNINGTREE,** Essex Map ref 3B2 **GUEST ACCOMMODATION**

B&B per room per night
**s £50.00–£60.00**
**d £60.00–£80.00**

## Curlews

Station Road, Bradfield, Manningtree CO11 2UP **t** (01255) 870890
**e** margherita@curlewsaccommodation.co.uk
**w** curlewsacccommodation.co.uk

Rooms

General 8

Payment Credit/debit cards, cash, cheques

*Favourable discounted rates for the autumn and winter seasons. Gas and electricity included.*

Luxury self catering and B&B accommodation offering outstanding, elevated, panoramic views over the River Stour Estuary. This recently renovated property has been finished to the highest standard and provides spacious en suite wetroom, carers' room, sitting room and custom-built kitchen for wheelchair users. Seasonal rates apply.

**open** All year
**bedrooms** 3 double, 4 twin, 1 single, 1 family, 1 suite
**bathrooms** All en suite

*Turn off A120 onto Clacton Road. After 1.5 miles, turn right at TV mast and continue for a further 1.5 miles.*

**MARTIN,** Lincolnshire **SELF CATERING**

**The Manor House Stables contact** Sherry Forbes, The Manor House Stables, Timberland Road, Martin LN4 3QS **t** (01526) 378717
**e** sherryforbes@hotmail.com **w** manorhousestables.co.uk

**MICHAELCHURCH ESCLEY,** Herefordshire **SELF CATERING**

★★★★
SELF CATERING

**Holt Farm contact** Nick Pash, Hideaways
**t** (01747) 828170
**e** enq@hideaways.co.uk **w** hideaways.co.uk

**MIDDLEWOOD GREEN,** Suffolk Map ref 3B2 **SELF CATERING**

★★★
SELF CATERING

Units **1**
Sleeps **2–4**
Low season per wk
£200.00–£300.00
High season per wk
£300.00–£380.00

## Leys Farmhouse Annexe, Stowmarket

**contact** Mrs Heather Trevorrow, Leys Farmhouse Annexe, Blacksmith's Lane, Middlewood Green, Earl Stonham, Stowmarket IP14 5EU **t** (01449) 711750
**e** leysfarmhouse@btinternet.com **w** leysfarmhouseannexe.co.uk

Double bed in bedroom, double sofa bed in lounge. Very peaceful, rural situation. Well equipped. Outdoor swimming pool by arrangement.
**open** All year except Christmas
**nearest shop** 3 miles
**nearest pub** 1 mile

## MILDENHALL, Suffolk — CAMPING, CARAVAN & HOLIDAY PARK

★★★★
TOURING PARK

**Round Plantation Caravan Club Site** Brandon Road, Bury St Edmunds IP28 7JE
**t** (01638) 713089
**e** enquiries@caravanclub.co.uk **w** caravanclub.co.uk

## MUNDESLEY, Norfolk — GUEST ACCOMMODATION

★★★★
GUEST HOUSE

**Overcliff Lodge** 46 Cromer Road, Mundesley NR11 8DB
**t** (01263) 720016
**e** overcliffodge@btinternet.com **w** overclifflodge.co.uk

## NAYLAND, Suffolk Map ref 3B2 — SELF CATERING

SELF CATERING

Units **2**
Sleeps **6–8**
Low season per wk
**£755.00–£995.00**
High season per wk
**£1,500.00–£1,955.00**

### Gladwins Farm, Nayland

**contact** Mrs P Dossor, Gladwins Farm, Harpers Hill, Colchester CO6 4NU **t** (01206) 262261
**e** gladwinsfarm@aol.com **w** gladwinsfarm.co.uk

General
Leisure
Unit
Payment Credit/debit cards, cash, cheques, euros

Two luxury, accessible cottages sleeping six or eight people in wooded grounds with marvellous views over Suffolk's rolling Constable Country. Charming villages and gardens to explore – not far from the sea. Adapted bathrooms, level gardens, private hot tubs. East of England Holiday of the Year 2003, 2006. Suffolk Self-Catering Holiday of the Year 2007.

**open** All Year
**nearest shop** 0.5 miles
**nearest pub** < 0.5 miles

*From A12 take A133 to Colchester. Follow signs to A134 Sudbury. Nayland is 6 miles out. Entrance to farm approximately 800m past village.*

## OLD BRAMPTON, Derbyshire — SELF CATERING

SELF CATERING

**Chestnut and Willow Cottages contact** Mr & Mrs Jeffrey & Patricia Green, Chestnut and Willow Cottages, Priestfield Grange, Old Brampton, Chesterfield S42 7JH **t** (01246) 566159
**e** patricia_green@btconnect.com

## OUNDLE, Northamptonshire — SELF CATERING

SELF CATERING

**Oundle Cottage Breaks contact** Mr & Mrs Simmonds, Oundle Cottage Breaks, Market Place, Oundle, Peterborough PE8 4BE **t** (01832) 275508
**e** richard@simmondsatoundle.co.uk **w** oundlecottagebreaks.co.uk

At-a-glance symbols are explained on page 8.

**PETERBOROUGH,** Cambridgeshire Map ref 3A1 **CAMPING, CARAVAN & HOLIDAY PARK**

★★★★★
HOLIDAY PARK

(252)
£14.00–£26.90
(252)
£14.00–£26.90
252 touring pitches

## Ferry Meadows Caravan Club Site

Ham Lane, Peterborough PE2 5UU **t** (01733) 233526
**w** caravanclub.co.uk

General

Leisure

Payment Credit/debit cards, cash, cheques

*Midweek discount; pitch fees reduced by up to 50% for stays on Mon, Tue, Wed or Thu night.*

Probably the perfect family holiday site. Level and open, and ideally located in a country park with steam trains, lake, cycle and walking trails and every kind of sporting facility laid on. There's a super watersports centre for sailing and windsurfing, and coarse fishing may be had in the lakes.

**open** All year

*From any direction, on approaching Peterborough, follow the brown signs to Nene Park and Ferry Meadows.*

**PRESTHOPE,** Shropshire **CAMPING, CARAVAN & HOLIDAY PARK**

★★★
TOURING PARK

**Presthope Caravan Club Site** Stretton Road, Much Wenlock TF13 6DQ
**t** (01746) 785234
**w** caravanclub.co.uk

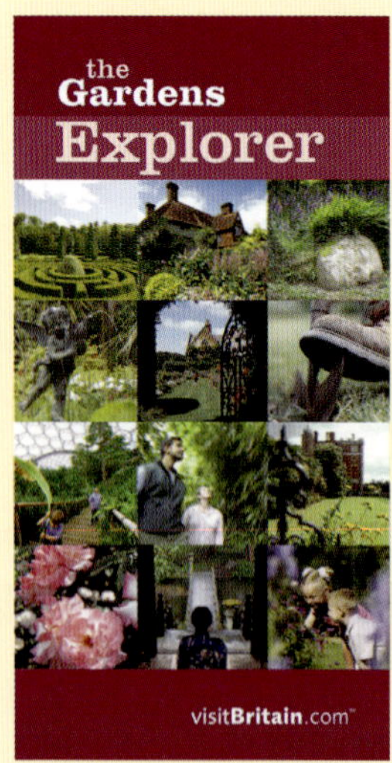


## Do you like visiting gardens?

Discover Britain's green heart with this easy-to-use guide. Featuring a selection of the most stunning gardens in the country, The Gardens Explorer is complete with a handy fold-out map and illustrated guide. You can purchase the Explorer series from good bookshops and online at visitbritaindirect.com.

**REDDITCH,** Worcestershire Map ref 4B3 **GUEST ACCOMMODATION**

**INN**

B&B per room per night
**s £45.00–£55.00**
**d £50.00–£55.00**
Evening meal per person
**£5.00–£8.00**

## White Hart Inn

157 Evesham Road, Redditch B97 5EJ **t** (01527) 545442
**e** enquiries@whitehartredditch.co.uk

Rooms

General

Payment Credit/debit cards, cash, cheques

Ten en suite bedrooms, disabled facilities, conference and wedding facilities. Local to NEC, Birmingham, Worcester and Stratford. Large, free car park.

**open** All year
**bedrooms** 3 double, 6 twin, 1 family
**bathrooms** All en suite

**ROSS-ON-WYE,** Herefordshire Map ref 2A1 **GUEST ACCOMMODATION**

★★★★

**GUEST ACCOMMODATION**

B&B per room per night
**s £48.00–£50.00**
**d £65.00–£95.00**
Evening meal per person
**£19.50–£24.50**

## Portland House Guest House

Whitchurch, Ross-on-Wye HR9 6DB **t** (01600) 890757
**e** info@portlandguesthouse.co.uk **w** portlandguesthouse.co.uk

Access abc

Rooms

General

Payment Credit/debit cards, cash, cheques, euros

*Shop, restaurant and pub within 60 yds.*

Uniquely placed in the Wye Valley between Monmouth and Ross-on-Wye. Portland House has wide and open areas for wheelchair users. The gorgeous Lloyd Suite has a double bed and a single bed, plus easy chairs, and a small conservatory overlooks the garden. A special place to relax.

**open** February to December
**bedrooms** 2 double, 1 twin, 2 family, 1 suite
**bathrooms** All en suite

*Leave Monmouth on A40 towards Ross-on-Wye. Approx 3 miles sign on left Whitchurch/ Symonds Yat West. Pass BP garage. Turn in at Crown Hotel. Portland House faces you.*

At-a-glance symbols are explained on page 8.

## ST OSYTH, Essex — SELF CATERING

★★★★
SELF CATERING

**The Cartlodge at Lee Wick Farm contact** Mr Robert Clarke, The Cartlodge at Lee Wick Farm, The Barn, Lee Wick Lane, St Osyth, Clacton-on-Sea CO16 8ES **t** (01255) 823031
**e** info@leewickfarm.co.uk **w** leewickfarm.co.uk

## ST OWENS CROSS, Herefordshire Map ref 2A1 — SELF CATERING

Units **1**
Sleeps **16**
Low season per wk
**£1,800.00–£2,000.00**
High season per wk
**£2,000.00–£3,500.00**

### Trevase Granary, Ross-on-Wye

**contact** Mrs Liz Pursey, Trevase Granary, Trevase Farm, St Owens Cross, Hereford HR2 8ND **t** (01989) 730210 **e** stay@trevasecottages.co.uk
**w** trevasecottages.co.uk

A traditional stone barn converted with disabled guests' requirements covered. Equipped with stairlift for large family reunions and group holidays. Luxury, comfort and stunning surroundings.
**open** All Year
**nearest shop** 2 miles
**nearest pub** 2 miles

Access
General P
Unit
Payment Credit/debit cards, cash, cheques

## SANDRINGHAM, Norfolk Map ref 3B1 — GUEST ACCOMMODATION

B&B per room per night
**s £40.00–£64.00**
**d £64.00–£75.00**

### Oyster House

Lynn Road, West Rudham, King's Lynn PE31 8RW **t** (01485) 528327
**e** oyster-house@tiscali.co.uk **w** oysterhouse.co.uk

A 17thC farmhouse with large country garden. Ground-floor, en suite rooms in a quiet courtyard with facilities for the less mobile. Ideal base for the North Norfolk coast, Sandringham and the Burnhams.
**open** All year except Christmas and New Year
**bedrooms** 1 double, 1 twin
**bathrooms** All en suite

Access
Rooms
General P
Payment Cash, cheques, euros

## SANDRINGHAM, Norfolk — CAMPING, CARAVAN & HOLIDAY PARK

★★★★★
TOURING PARK

**The Sandringham Estate Caravan Club Site** Glucksburgh Woods, Sandringham PE35 6EZ **t** (01553) 631614
**e** enquiries@caravanclub.co.uk **w** caravanclub.co.uk

## SANDY, Bedfordshire — SELF CATERING

★★★★
SELF CATERING

**Acorn Cottage contact** Mrs Margaret Codd, Acorn Cottage, Tempsford Road, Great North Road, Sandy SG19 2AQ **t** (01767) 682332
**e** margaret@highfield-farm.co.uk **w** highfield-farm.co.uk

## SHREWSBURY, Shropshire — GUEST ACCOMMODATION

★★★★
BED & BREAKFAST
GOLD AWARD

**Lyth Hill House** 28 Old Coppice, Lyth Hill, Shrewsbury SY3 0BP
**t** (01743) 874660
**e** bnb@lythhillhouse.com
**w** lythhillhouse.com

**SIBTON,** Suffolk — SELF CATERING

★★★★ SELF CATERING

**Bluebell, Bonny, Buttercup & Bertie contact** Mrs Margaret Gray, Bluebell, Bonny, Buttercup & Bertie, Park Farm, Saxmundham IP17 2LZ
**t** (01728) 668324
**e** mail@sibtonparkfarm.co.uk **w** sibtonparkfarm.co.uk

**SKEGNESS,** Lincolnshire — GUEST ACCOMMODATION

★★★ GUEST ACCOMMODATION

**Chatsworth** 16 North Parade, Skegness PE25 2UB
**t** (01754) 764177
**e** info@chatsworthhotel.co.uk **w** chatsworthskegness.co.uk

**SKEGNESS,** Lincolnshire — SELF CATERING

★★★★ SELF CATERING

**Ingoldale Park contact** Cathryn Whitehead, Ingoldale Park, Roman Bank, Ingoldmells PE25 1LL **t** (01754) 872335
**e** ingoldalepark@btopenworld.com **w** ingoldmells.net

**SOUTHWOLD,** Suffolk — GUEST ACCOMMODATION

★★★★ GUEST ACCOMMODATION SILVER AWARD

**Newlands Country House** 72 Halesworth Road, Southwold IP18 6NS
**t** (01502) 722164
**e** info@newlandsofsouthwold.co.uk
**w** tiscover.co.uk

**SOUTHWOLD,** Suffolk — SELF CATERING

★★★ SELF CATERING

**Hightide contact** Rebecca Meo, Acanthus Property Letting Services
**t** (01502) 724033
**e** websales@southwold-holidays.co.uk **w** southwold-holidays.co.uk

**STRATFORD-UPON-AVON,** Warwickshire — HOTEL

★★★★ HOTEL SILVER AWARD

**Stratford Victoria** Arden Street, Stratford-upon-Avon CV37 6QQ
**t** (01789) 271000
**e** stay@qhotels.co.uk
**w** qhotels.co.uk

**SWAFFHAM,** Norfolk — CAMPING, CARAVAN & HOLIDAY PARK

★★★★ TOURING PARK

**The Covert Caravan Club Site** High Ash, Thetford IP26 5BZ
**t** (01842) 878356
**e** enquiries@caravanclub.co.uk **w** caravanclub.co.uk

**TITCHWELL,** Norfolk — HOTEL

★★★ HOTEL GOLD AWARD

**Titchwell Manor Hotel** Titchwell Manor, Nr Brancaster, Titchwell PE31 8BB
**t** (01485) 210221
**e** margaret@titchwellmanor.com
**w** titchwellmanor.com

**TUGFORD,** Shropshire — GUEST ACCOMMODATION

★★★★ FARMHOUSE

**Tugford Farm B&B** Tugford Farm, Craven Arms SY7 9HS
**t** (01584) 841259
**e** tugfordfarm@yahoo.co.uk **w** tugford.com

**WALTON-ON-THE-NAZE,** Essex — GUEST ACCOMMODATION

★★★★ GUEST ACCOMMODATION

**Bufo Villae Guest House** 31 Beatrice Road, Walton-on-the-Naze CO14 8HJ
**t** (01255) 672644
**e** bufovillae@btinternet.com **w** bufovillae.co.uk

At-a-glance symbols are explained on page 8.

## WANGFORD, Suffolk — GUEST ACCOMMODATION

★★★★ GUEST ACCOMMODATION

**The Plough Inn** London Road, Wangford, Southwold, Beccles NR34 8AZ
**t** (01353) 698000
**e** wangfordplough@talktalkbusiness.net **w** the-plough.biz

## WATTISFIELD, Suffolk — SELF CATERING

★★★ SELF CATERING

**Jayes Holiday Cottages contact** Mrs Denise Williams, Jayes Holiday Cottages, Walsham Road, Wattisfield, Diss IP22 1NZ **t** (01359) 251255
**w** jayesholidaycottages.co.uk

## WATTISHAM, Suffolk — SELF CATERING

★★★★ SELF CATERING

**Wattisham Hall Holiday Cottages contact** Jeremy and Jo Squirrell, Wattisham Hall, Wattisham, Ipswich IP7 7JX **t** (01449) 740240
**e** enquiries@wattishamhall.co.uk **w** wattishamhall.co.uk

## WHITCHURCH, Herefordshire — SELF CATERING

★★★ SELF CATERING

**Tump Farm Holiday Cottage contact** Mrs Debbie Williams, Tump Farm Holiday Cottage, Tump Farm, Whitchurch, Ross-on-Wye HR9 6DQ
**t** (01600) 891029
**e** clinwilcharmaine@hotmail.com

## WICKHAM SKEITH, Suffolk — SELF CATERING

★★★ SELF CATERING

**Netus Barn contact** Mrs Joy Homan, Street Farm, Eye IP23 8LP
**t** (01449) 766275
**e** joygeoff@homansf.freeserve.co.uk **w** netusbarn.co.uk

## WIGSTHORPE, Northamptonshire Map ref 3A2 — SELF CATERING

★★★★★ SELF CATERING

Units **3**
Sleeps **2–4**
Low season per wk
**£250.00–£350.00**
High season per wk
**£350.00–£600.00**

### Nene Valley Cottages, Wigsthorpe

**contact** Heather Ball, The Cottage, Glapthorn, Northamptonshire PE8 5BQ **t** (01832) 273601 & 07962 085720
**e** stay@nenevalleycottages.co.uk **w** nenevalleycottages.co.uk

Idyllic rural setting with commanding views over the Nene Valley. All home comforts and more in two of the units, each with two twin bedrooms and one with a single twin bedroom that interconnects with a larger unit. The third, smaller cottage is adapted for those with impaired mobility and has a sofa bed for a carer.

**open** All Year
**nearest shop** 4 miles
**nearest pub** 2 miles

General P S

Unit

Payment Cash, cheques

*The single bedroom cottage is a luxury M31 property that has been created with all the needs of the less mobile in mind.*

**WISBECH,** Cambridgeshire Map ref 3A1 — **SELF CATERING**

SELF CATERING

Units **3**
Sleeps **2–4**
Low season per wk
**£150.00–£200.00**
High season per wk
**£200.00–£400.00**

## Common Right Barns, Wisbech

**contact** Mrs Teresa Fowler, Common Right Barns, Plash Drove, Tholomas Drove, Wisbech PE13 4SP **t** (01945) 410424
**e** teresa@commonrightbarns.co.uk **w** commonrightbarns.co.uk

Self-catering, accessible properties in beamed barn buildings featuring level access throughout, including shower rooms. Ample parking, accessible paths and delightful gardens. Some additional mobility aids loaned on site. Situated in a small Fenland hamlet, five miles from the Georgian port of Wisbech. Central for many towns and attractions.

**open** All year
**nearest shop** 2 miles
**nearest pub** 0.5 miles

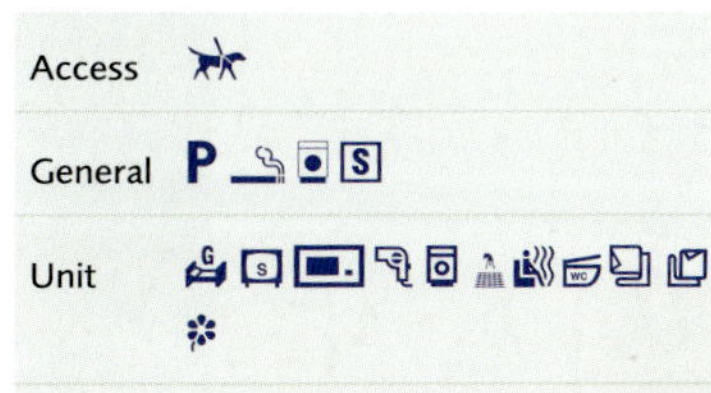


Payment Cash, cheques

**WISSETT,** Suffolk — **SELF CATERING**

★★★★
SELF CATERING

**Wissett Lodge contact** Mrs Claire Kiddy, Wissett Lodge, Lodge Lane, Wissett, Halesworth IP19 0JQ **t** (01986) 873173
**e** geoffrey.kiddy@farmersweekly.net **w** wissettlodge.co.uk

**WOODHALL SPA,** Lincolnshire Map ref 4D2 — **HOTEL**

HOTEL

B&B per room per night
**s £99.00**
**d £148.00**
HB per person per night
**£97.00–£134.00**

## Petwood Hotel

Stixwould Road, Woodhall Spa LN10 6QG **t** (01526) 352411
**e** reception@petwood.co.uk **w** petwood.co.uk

Originally built in the early 1900s, the Petwood Hotel stands in a 30-acre estate and is famous for its magnificent gardens. Individually designed bedrooms. Short holidays available.

**open** All year
**bedrooms** 21 double, 13 twin, 6 single, 8 family, 5 suites
**bathrooms** All en suite

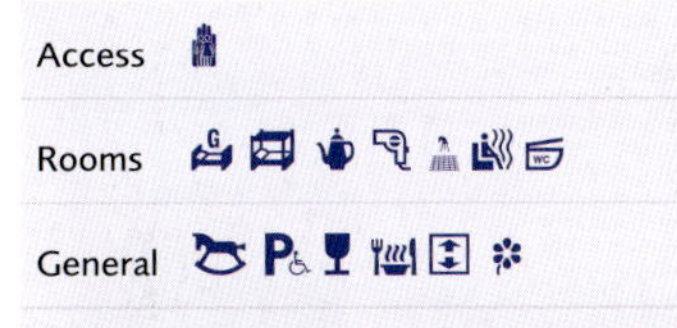


Payment Credit/debit cards, cash, cheques, euros

**WOODHALL SPA,** Lincolnshire — **GUEST ACCOMMODATION**

**Kirkstead Old Mill Cottage** Tattershall Road, Woodhall Spa LN10 6UQ
**t** (01526) 353637
**e** barbara@woodhallspa.com
**w** woodhallspa.com

**WOODHALL SPA,** Lincolnshire — **SELF CATERING**

SELF CATERING

**Mill Lane Holiday Cottage contact** Ian Williamson, Mill Lane Holiday Cottage, 72 Mill Lane, Woodhall Spa LN10 6QZ **t** (01526) 353101
**w** skegness.net/woodhallspa.htm

At-a-glance symbols are explained on page 8.

**WORKSOP,** Nottinghamshire Map ref 4C2 **CAMPING, CARAVAN & HOLIDAY PARK**

(183)
£14.90–£28.90
(183)
£14.90–£28.90
183 touring pitches

## Clumber Park Caravan Club Site

Lime Tree Avenue, Clumber Park, Worksop S80 3AE **t** (01909) 484758
**w** caravanclub.co.uk

There's a great feeling of spaciousness here, the site is on 20 acres within 4,000 acres of parkland where you can walk, cycle or ride. Children will enjoy Clumber Park as it is part of what was once Sherwood Forest, and there are plenty of reminders of the Forest's most famous resident, Robin Hood.

**open** All year

*From the junction of the A1 and A57, take the A614 signposted to Nottingham for 0.5 miles. Turn right into Clumber Park site. The club is signposted thereafter.*

General

Leisure

Payment Credit/debit cards, cash, cheques

*Midweek discount; pitch fees reduced by up to 50% for stays on Mon, Tue, Wed or Thu night.*

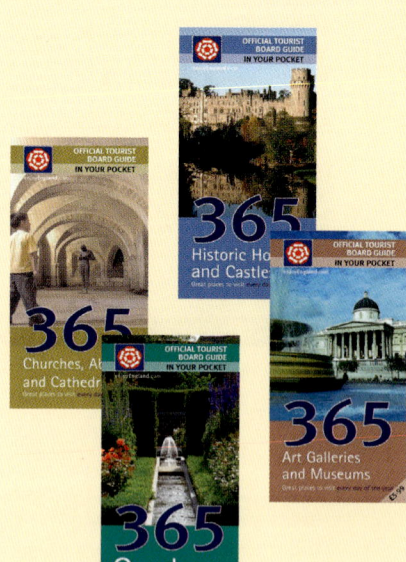

# National Accessible Scheme ratings only

The following establishments hold a National Accessible Scheme rating as shown in their entry, but do not participate in a quality assessment scheme. However, to participate in the National Accessible Scheme accommodation must meet a minimum level of quality.

## BRIDGNORTH, Shropshire — SELF CATERING

**The Malthouse contact** Mr & Mrs Brian & Janet Russell, The Malthouse, Bridgnorth WV16 6QT **t** (01244) 356666
**e** info@sykescottages.co.uk **w** shropshire.sykescottages.co.uk

## CLACTON-ON-SEA, Essex Map ref 3B3 — SELF CATERING

Units **1**
Sleeps **1–7**
Low season per wk
Min £240.00
High season per wk
Max £520.00

Awaiting NAS rating

### Groomhill

**contact** Gail Lewis, Livability, PO Box 36, Cowbridge CF71 7GB
**t** 08456 584478 **e** selfcatering@livability.org.uk or glewis@livability.org.uk
**w** livabilityholidays.org.uk

Holiday bungalow specially adapted for disabled people, near town centre and seafront. Three twin bedrooms and sofa bed. Roll-in shower, hoist, shower-chair and profiling bed available.
**open** All year
**nearest shop** 2 miles
**nearest pub** 2 miles

## HOVETON, Norfolk Map ref 3C1 — SELF CATERING

Units **2**
Sleeps **2–7**
Low season per wk
Min £240.00
High season per wk
Max £520.00

Awaiting NAS rating

### Broomhill, Hoveton

**contact** Gail Lewis, Livability, PO Box 36, Cowbridge CF71 7GB
**t** 08456 584478 **e** selfcatering@livability.org.uk or glewis@livability.org.uk
**w** livabilityholidays.org.uk

Two self-contained flats by Wroxham Broad, owned by Grooms Holidays, Designed for wheelchair users. One on ground floor, other has lift access to first floor. Each has double twin and bunk bedrooms, sofa bed, roll-in shower, shower-chair, hoist and profiling bed available. Can be booked separately.
**open** All year
**nearest shop** 1 mile
**nearest pub** 1 mile

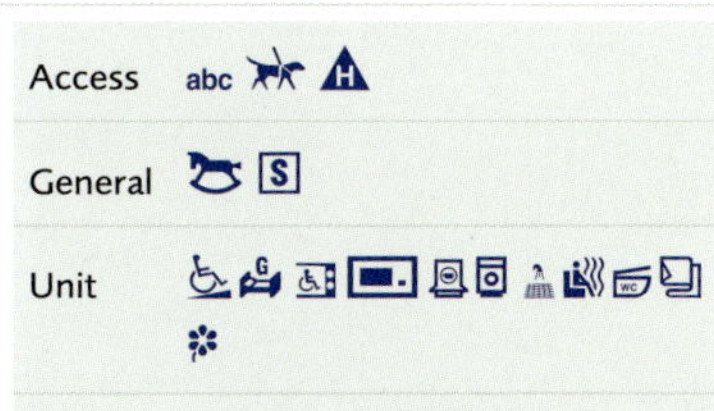


## HOVETON, Norfolk — SELF CATERING

Awaiting NAS rating

**Wroxham (Flat 2 Ground Floor) contact** Ms Gail Lewis, Livability, PO Box 36, Cowbridge CF71 7GB **t** 08456 584478
**e** selfcatering@livability.org.uk **w** livability.org.uk

At-a-glance symbols are explained on page 8.

# Local bus information

## Online

Visit **www.traveline.info**

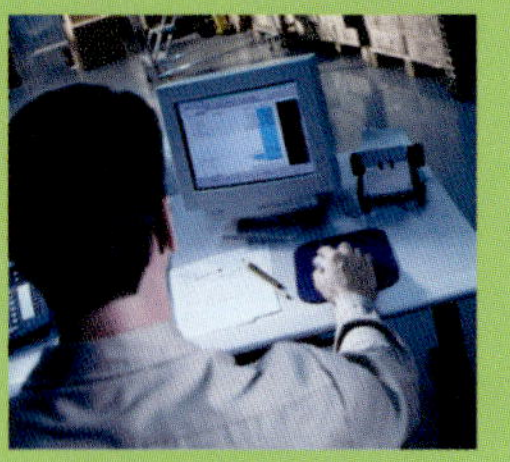

## By phone

Phone **0871 200 22 33**

## To read

Timetables available from:

Council Information Centres,
Tourist Information Centres,
Libraries,
Norwich Bus Station,
King's Lynn Bus Station

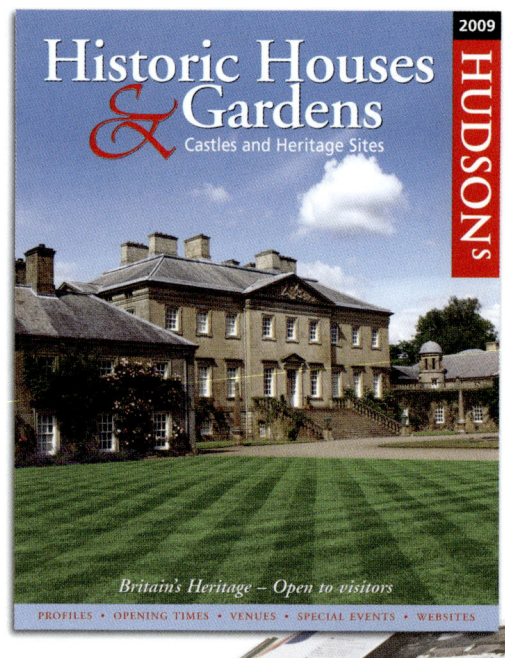

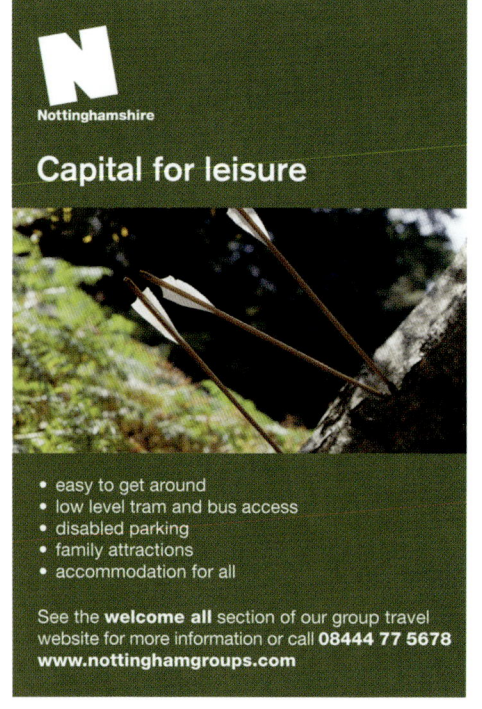

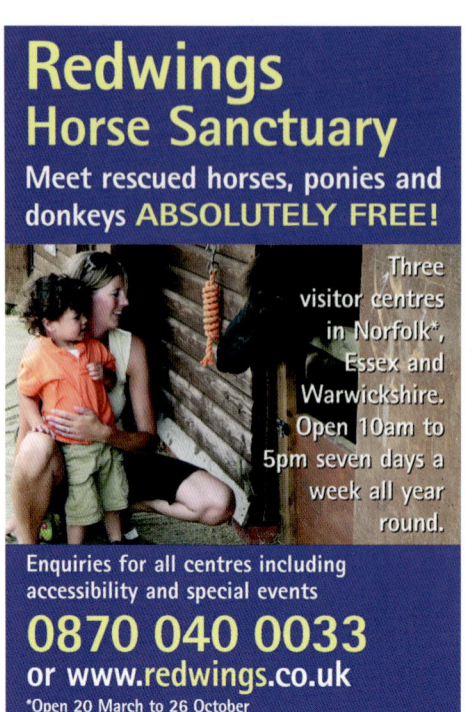

SHREWSBURY
Goodness Gracious Great Days Out!
For information on visiting historic Shrewsbury, events, accessible accommodation, Shopmobility, and audio version of our brochure:
Tel: Visitor Information on 01743 281200
Email: visitorinfo.gov.uk
Visit www.visitshrewsbury.com

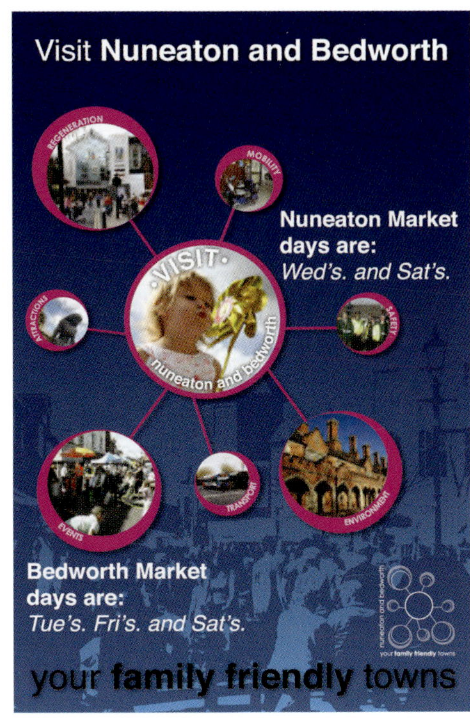
Visit Nuneaton and Bedworth
REGENERATION
MOBILITY
ATTRACTIONS
VISIT
nuneaton and bedworth
SAFETY
EVENTS
TRANSPORT
ENVIRONMENT
Nuneaton Market days are:
Wed's. and Sat's.
Bedworth Market days are:
Tue's. Fri's. and Sat's.
your family friendly towns

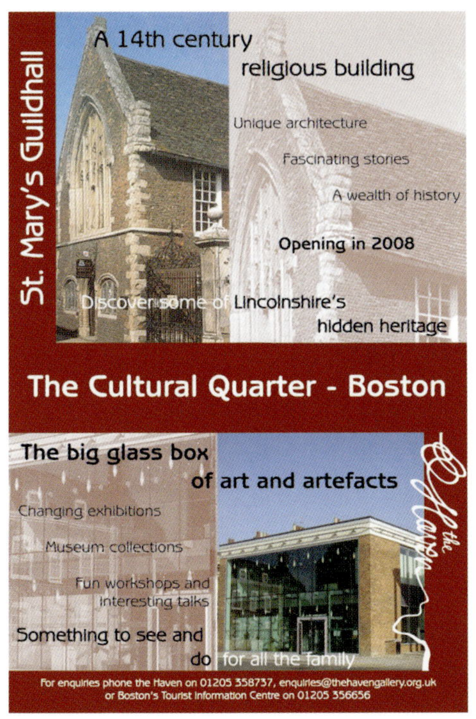
St. Mary's Guildhall
A 14th century religious building
Unique architecture
Fascinating stories
A wealth of history
Opening in 2008
Discover some of Lincolnshire's hidden heritage
The Cultural Quarter - Boston
The big glass box of art and artefacts
Changing exhibitions
Museum collections
Fun workshops and interesting talks
Something to see and do for all the family
the Haven
For enquiries phone the Haven on 01205 358737, enquiries@thehavengallery.org.uk
or Boston's Tourist Information Centre on 01205 356656

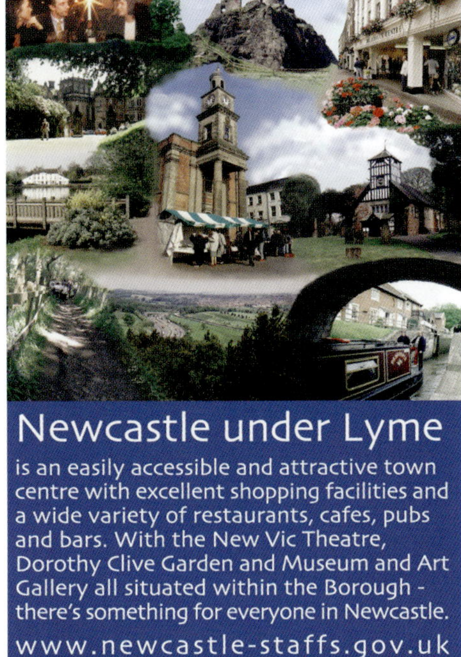
Newcastle under Lyme
is an easily accessible and attractive town centre with excellent shopping facilities and a wide variety of restaurants, cafes, pubs and bars. With the New Vic Theatre, Dorothy Clive Garden and Museum and Art Gallery all situated within the Borough - there's something for everyone in Newcastle.
www.newcastle-staffs.gov.uk

© 2008 Gullane (Thomas) Limited
A HIT Entertainment Company
total family entertainment
Voted "BEST UK VALUE DESTINATION" 2007 Group Leisure
Over 100 rides & attractions, spectacular live shows, Zoo & Thomas Land™ too!
Drayton Manor THEME PARK home of THOMAS LAND
Call 24hr Infoline: 0844 472 1950
SAVE MONEY & BUY TICKETS ONLINE:
www.draytonmanor.co.uk
DRAYTON MANOR THEME PARK, TAMWORTH, STAFFS B78 3TW
ON THE A4091, JUNCTIONS 9 & 10 OF THE M42 & EXIT T2 OF THE M6 TOLL

175 Years of Plants & People
THE BIRMINGHAM BOTANICAL GARDENS & GLASSHOUSES
Westbourne Road, Edgbaston, Birmingham
PEACE AND TRANQUILITY at THE BIRMINGHAM BOTANICAL GARDENS & GLASSHOUSES
Take tea on the Terrace or just stroll around the 15 acre 'Oasis of Delight'
OPEN DAILY Tel: 0121 454 1860
www.birminghambotanicalgardens.org.uk
Group Bookings by prior appointment

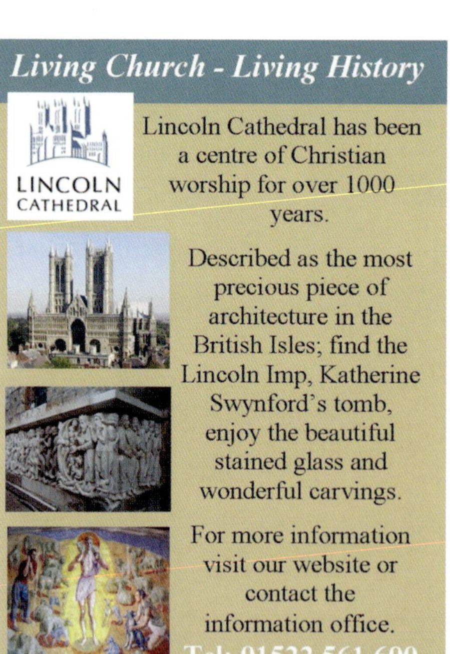
Living Church - Living History
LINCOLN CATHEDRAL
Lincoln Cathedral has been a centre of Christian worship for over 1000 years.
Described as the most precious piece of architecture in the British Isles; find the Lincoln Imp, Katherine Swynford's tomb, enjoy the beautiful stained glass and wonderful carvings.
For more information visit our website or contact the information office.
Tel: 01522 561 600
www.lincolncathedral.com

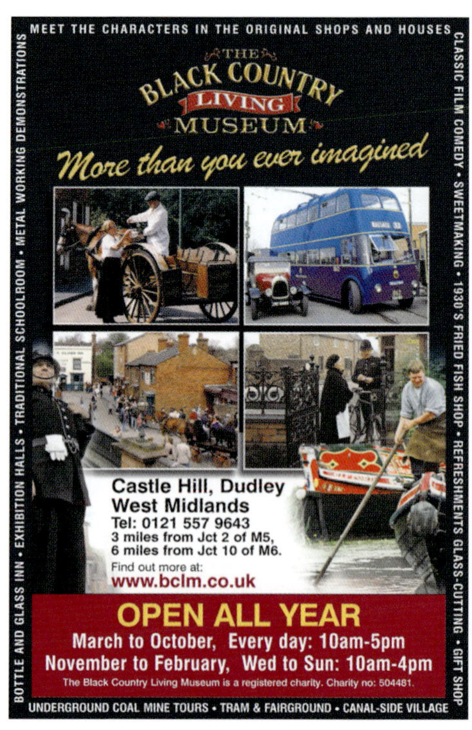
MEET THE CHARACTERS IN THE ORIGINAL SHOPS AND HOUSES
THE BLACK COUNTRY LIVING MUSEUM
More than you ever imagined
Castle Hill, Dudley
West Midlands
Tel: 0121 557 9643
3 miles from Jct 2 of M5,
6 miles from Jct 10 of M6.
Find out more at:
www.bclm.co.uk
OPEN ALL YEAR
March to October, Every day: 10am-5pm
November to February, Wed to Sun: 10am-4pm
The Black Country Living Museum is a registered charity. Charity no: 504481.
UNDERGROUND COAL MINE TOURS • TRAM & FAIRGROUND • CANAL-SIDE VILLAGE
BOTTLE AND GLASS INN • EXHIBITION HALLS • TRADITIONAL SCHOOLROOM • METAL WORKING DEMONSTRATIONS
CLASSIC FILM COMEDY • SWEETMAKING • 1930'S FRIED FISH SHOP • REFRESHMENTS GLASS-CUTTING • GIFT SHOP

## Colchester Museums

Colchester Museums is committed to providing access to its museums, collections, and services to as wide an audience as possible.

**Colchester Castle**

Offers handling sessions, films and touch tours for the blind and visually impaired. There is ramped access to the ground floor, a lift to the first floor and an accessible toilet on the ground floor.

**Hollytrees Museum**

Provides access to all public areas of the museum for wheelchair users. Display cases are at wheelchair height, mixed with other sensory interpretations. There are tactile RNIB Maps.

**Natural History Museum**

Has level access. It provides hands-on interactive and sensory experiences throughout the displays. There is an accessible nature trail and the museum has an accessible toilet.

Colchester Museums work with an advisory group called PORTAL, which is made up of people with a variety of disabilities. Colchester Museums strives to remove barriers which prohibit access to the museum collections through this collaboration.

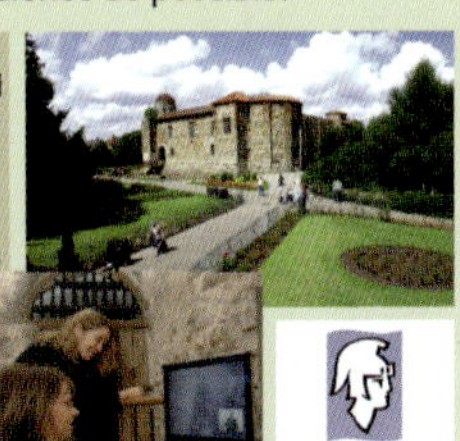

Visit **www.colchestermuseums.org.uk** for more information

For advice and booking, or to receive an access information leaflet, please contact:
**bookings.information@colchester.gov.uk** or call **01206 282937**, minicom **01206 507803**.

Colchester

DERBY CITY COUNCIL

## Derby Markets

Telephone 01332 255519 or
Minicom 01332 256666
for further assistance.

Easy access for all

The Eagle Market
Monday to Saturday – 9am to 5.30pm

Market Hall
Monday to Saturday – 9am to 5.30pm

Allenton Market
Friday – 9am to 4.30pm Saturday – 9am to 5pm

Allenton Flea/Craft Market
Tuesday – 4pm to 7.30pm

Cattle Market Car Boot Sales
Every Sunday – 7.30am to 2pm

Farmers' Market
Every third Thursday of the month

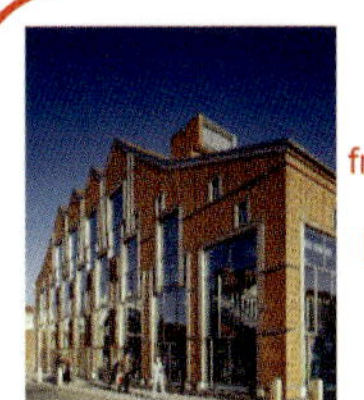

Situated in the centre of Lichfield, the Garrick makes theatre available to everyone. The theatre boasts two separate venues; the main auditorium, and the more intimate studio space. The Green Room Café is the perfect place for a relaxing coffee and light lunch with friends, a pre-show dinner, or just evening drinks. The Green Room Wine Bar has a selection of cocktails to tempt every palette, as well as a selection of real ales and wines. The Café, bar, and all areas of the main house and studio are easily reached by both stairs and lifts to every floor, making them easy to access for all abilities.

Past performers at the Garrick include Jane McDonald, Honour Blackman, Todd Carty, Anthony Costa, Kevin Kennedy, and Olivier Award Winner Matthew Kelly. We have also played host to stars such as Nick Owen, Phil Cool, Frank Carson, and Ricky Tomlinson.

LICHFIELD**GARRICK**
*Theatre & Studio*

**To receive our new season brochure, call the Box Office on 01543 412121, go to www.lichfieldgarrick.com , or visit us in Castle Dyke, Lichfield City centre.**

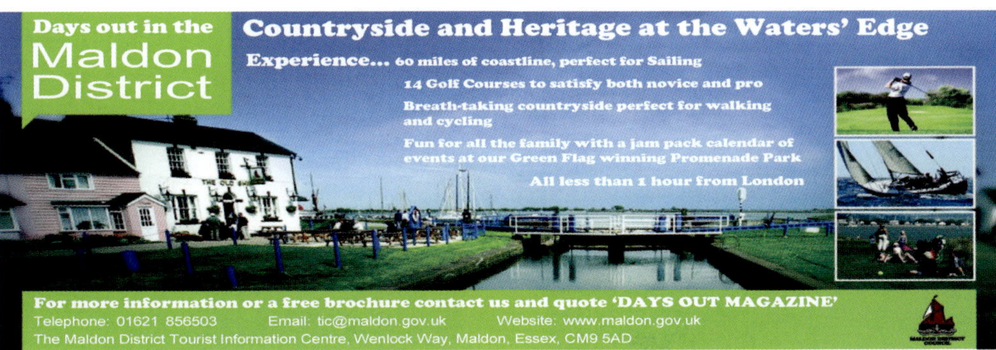
Days out in the
Maldon
District
Countryside and Heritage at the Waters' Edge
Experience... 60 miles of coastline, perfect for Sailing
14 Golf Courses to satisfy both novice and pro
Breath-taking countryside perfect for walking and cycling
Fun for all the family with a jam pack calendar of events at our Green Flag winning Promenade Park
All less than 1 hour from London
For more information or a free brochure contact us and quote 'DAYS OUT MAGAZINE'
Telephone: 01621 856503
Email: tic@maldon.gov.uk
Website: www.maldon.gov.uk
The Maldon District Tourist Information Centre, Wenlock Way, Maldon, Essex, CM9 5AD

CITY OF NOTTINGHAM

## Shopmobility

We offer a complete award-winning mobility service

- The **Free** loan of self propelled, powered wheelchairs and scooters for use about the city centre for anyone who has a disability requiring them to use a wheelchair to get around
- A **Free** guide service for the visually impaired
- Operating from two central bases within the city centre

**For further information please call 0115 915 3888**

**Welcome To Oswestry**

**Oswestry** is a traditional market town set in North West Shropshire on the borders of England and Wales. There is a shopmobility scheme and an excellent access guide produced by the local access group which is downloadable from **www.access-oswestry.org.uk**.

Amongst the excellent accessible attractions and activities on offer in the area are The Llanymynech Industrial Heritage Site with wheelchair access inside the Hoffman Kiln, Whittington Castle with a new accessible path on to the battlements, Paintballing at Rednall Aerodrome and Llangollen Canalboat Trust's Dayboat hire.

For details of accessible accommodation and attractions visit **www.disabledholidayinfo.org.uk/oswestry** or send for copies of the 4 'Wheelchair User's Guides' on accessible attractions, activities, countryside trails and transport for Shropshire to :-

**Disabled Holiday Information, P.O.Box 186, Oswestry, SY10 1AF.**

Alternatively contact Oswestry's Visitor Information Centres

Phone: **01691 662488 / 662753** or visit **www.oswestrybc.gov.uk**

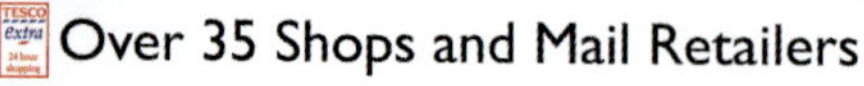


**Serpentine Green Shopping Centre, Hampton, Peterborough**
**Tel: 01733 896479 www.serpentinegreen.net**

## Peter Le Marchant Trust

For over thirty years the Trust has provided day outings and holidays on waterways for people of all ages with any kind of disability or serious illness

Canalside Moorings,
Beeches Road,
Loughborough,
Leicestershire LE11 2NS
phone/fax: 01509 265590
Email: lynnsmith@peterlemarchanttrust.co.uk

Come and Discover the wonderful county of Herefordshire where you can be assured of a warm welcome, good quality accommodation and excellent food and drink.

To receive a copy of our guide including accessible accommodation contact:

**Herefordshire Tourism on 01432 260621**

## Hartsholme Country Park & Swanholme Lakes Local Nature Reserve

Hartsholme Country Park and Swanholme Lakes Local Nature Reserve an oasis of countryside just three miles from the centre of the City of Lincoln. Featuring woodland, heathland, meadows and lakes, these wildlife havens are the perfect choice for the whole family to relax and unwind.

For those who find a day visit just isn't enough camping facilities are available from March to October in our English Tourism Council 3 star rated Touring Park.

Tel 01522 873577
Camp site 01522 873578
email hartsholmecp@lincoln.gov.uk
www.lincoln.gov.uk

## The Royal Family's country retreat in Norfolk

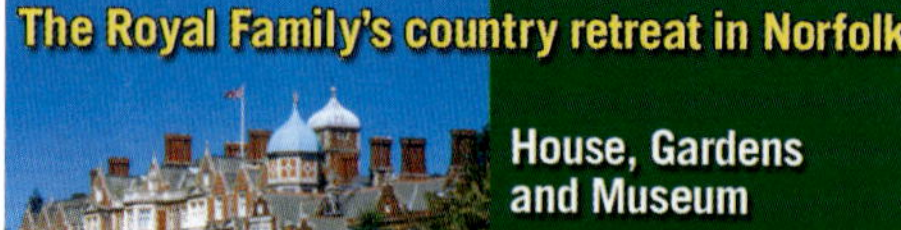

**House, Gardens and Museum**

open Easter to October

Fully accessible throughout

Full catering facilities & gift shop

**For information call 01553 612908 or www.sandringhamestate.co.uk**

You are welcome to visit the grounds and magnificent Chapel, but are reminded that this is a College where tutors, students and staff live, work and study.

Opening Times throughout the year:

*During Term:*

| | |
|---|---|
| Monday to Friday | 9:30am – 4:30pm |
| Saturday | 9:30am – 3:15pm |
| Sunday | 1:15pm – 2:15pm |
| (and during BST) | 5:00pm – 5:30pm |

*Out of Term:*

| | |
|---|---|
| Monday to Saturday | 9:30am – 4:30pm |
| Sunday | 10:00am – 5:00pm |

Admission Prices:
Adults £5.00 Senior Citizens, Children (12–17 years) and Students £3.50
*Children under 12 are free – only as part of a family unit (not groups)*

The Chapel is sometimes closed to the public, due to recordings, broadcasts etc. and you should contact the Tourist Liaison Officer, Tel: (01223) 331212 when planning a visit.

*the line for all seasons*

The best way to see the beauty of the River Severn is from a steam-hauled train on the Severn Valley Railway.

**Kidderminster – Bewdley – Bridgnorth**

Specially adapted carriges in certain trains.
Access to toilets and buffet at each terminus.

THE RAILWAY STATION, BEWDLEY, WORCESTERSHIRE, DY12 1BG

TEL: 01299 403816 www.svr.co.uk

Clacton • Frinton • Walton • Jaywick • St Osyth
Harwich • Dovercourt • Mistley • Manningtree • Brightlingsea

For information or brochure requests contact one of our Tourist Information Centres on:

**Clacton** 01255 686633
**Harwich** 01255 506139
**Walton** 01255 675542
*(Open Easter & Spring Bank Holiday to Mid Sept)*

www.essex-sunshine-coast.org.uk

## Visit the disability compliant play area at East Carlton Country Park

- Exhibition
- Restaurant & Shop
- Free Electric Buggy Hire

**Tel. 01394 389700**

THE NATIONAL TRUST Charity No. 205846

Don't worry, he's just a big pussycat.

Set in 50 acres of parkland, Twycross Zoo is alive with rare animals, exotic birds and strange reptiles. Pop in and meet them all in the flesh. For full prices and opening times call 01827 880250 or visit twycrosszoo.org

Atherstone, Warwickshire CV9 3PX

**A haven of peace and tranquillity**

Over three miles of woodland walks, with superb views of our private broad. Summer events, bird watching, boat trips & new Sensory Garden.

**90% disabled access. Scooters and wheelchairs available to hire – please book in advance.**

School Road, Sth Walsham, Norwich, NR13 6DZ
01603 270449
www.fairhavengarden.co.uk

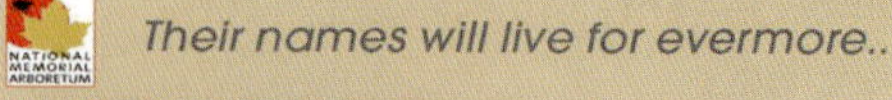

Site of the Armed Forces Memorial – the nation's memorial to those lost in conflict since the end of WWII.

**National Memorial Arboretum**
Croxall Road, Alrewas
Staffordshire. DE13 7AR

Phone: 01283 792333
Fax: 01283 792034
Email: info@thenma.org.uk
Web: www.thenma.org.uk

Charity No. 1043992
The National Memorial Arboretum Company Limited is part of the Royal British Legion

Discover 250,000 years of local history!

Archaeological artifacts, pictures, paintings and costumes relating to Thurrock's industrial and community development.

Find out about our 16 parishes that make up modern day Thurrock

Walks, talks, education and other heritage events undertaken.

Museum Enquiries on 01375 413965
www.thurrock.gov.uk/heritage/museum

Thurrock Museum & Heritage Services is part of Communities, Libraries and Cultural Services, Community Well-being, Thurrock Council.

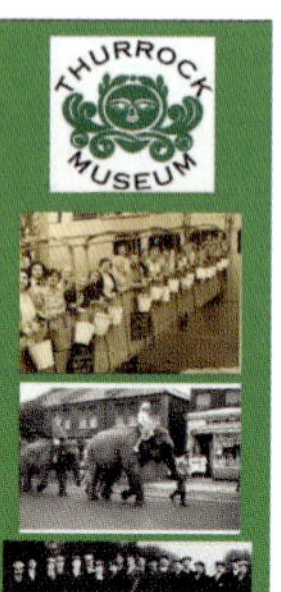

Fenland District Council

**Wisbech Tourist Information Centre**

2-3 Bridge Street,
Wisbech,
Cambridgehsire
PE13 1EW

Tel: 01945 583263

email: tourism@fenland.gov.uk
website: www.fenland.gov.uk

**Strawberry Wheelchair Accessible**
**VEHICLE HIRE LTD**

**Email info@strawberryvehiclehire**
**Tel /Fax: 0121 353 0660**

**Welcome to The Broads**

Go to our website and look under the Visiting section for easy access info.

**www.broads-authority.gov.uk**

## Rufford Abbey Country Park

- Historic parkland & abbey ruins
- Restaurant & cafe
- Contemporary sculpture & craft exhibitions
- Children's Garden

Open daily (except Xmas Day).
Free admission. Car parking £3.

**Tel: 01623 821338**
www.nottinghamshire.gov.uk/ruffordcp
Free loan of wheelchairs and mobility scooters.

**Nottinghamshire County Council**

With 45 shops and an indoor market we're the most convenient place to shop in Sutton-in-Ashfield.

Open Mon-Sat 8am-6pm, Sun 10am-4pm.
Tel: 01623 443368

**idlewells**
Shopping Centre

Explore.....Newark & Sherwood

**Outdoor activity centres, Country Parks, Museums, Historic Buildings, Craft Centres, Ancient Forests, Cafes/Restaurants, Cycles Hire, Market Towns, Garden Centres.....**

**And so much more.....**

Email: tourism@nsdc.info
Website: www.visitnewarkandsherwood.co.uk

Awaiting Rating

**Bircham, Norfolk**

Ranging from two to five bedroom units Norfolk Disabled Friendly Cottages caters for the disabled person their carers and families.

**All can be seen on our website at:-**

**www.norfolkdisabled-friendly cottages.co.uk**

**For further information please contact us by:**

**Email: bennion@paston.co.uk**

**Telephone: 01485 578354**

Awaiting Rating

## Need some ideas?

Big city buzz or peaceful panoramas? Take a fresh look at England and you may be surprised at what's right on your doorstep. Explore the diversity online at **visitbritain.com**

# South East England

Berkshire, Buckinghamshire, East Sussex, Hampshire, Isle of Wight, Kent, Oxfordshire, Surrey, West Sussex

Clockwise: Leeds Castle, Kent; RHS Garden Wisley, Surrey; Oxford

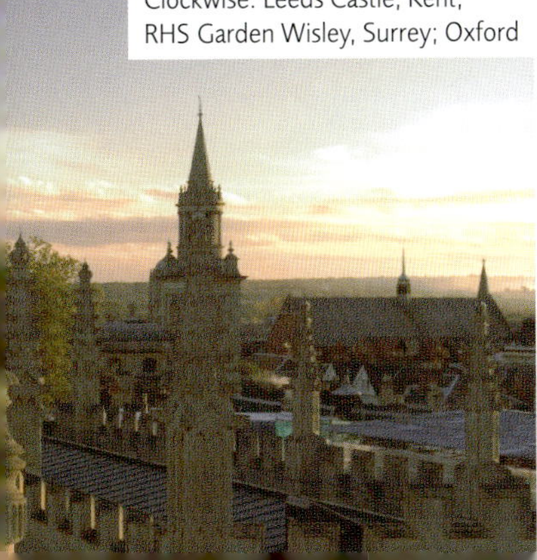

# Great days out

**The South East is your quintessential slice of England. Stroll around an English country garden, explore castles and sites on the frontline of history, experience colourful festivals and savour English wine. From 400 miles of glorious coastline to the dreaming spires of Oxford, there's so much to discover.**

## Making history

Explore a region that has witnessed some of the most momentous events of British history, from the Battle of Hastings in 1066 to the air raids of the Second World War. At **Battle Abbey**, stand on the exact spot where tradition says King Harold fell and take the interactive audio tour of the battlefield. Discover the world-famous **HMS Victory** at **Portsmouth Historic Dockyard**, where you can also go into battle with the Royal Marines at Action Stations, an interactive showcase of the modern navy. Then unlock a life of privilege at the South East's many awe-inspiring castles. **Windsor**, **Hever**, **Bodiam**, **Scotney** and **Arundel**, to name but five. Visit too the historic cities of **Oxford**, **Canterbury** and **Chichester** to admire elegant cathedrals and hear the gentle sound of evensong. Survey 'the finest view in England', according to Winston Churchill's mother, at stunning **Blenheim Palace** in Oxfordshire.

Marwell Zoological Park, Hampshire

## Full-on fun

Is the Queen at home? Peer into the windows of Buckingham Palace at **Legoland**, Windsor, or prepare for a wet and wild voyage on the Vikings' River Splash ride! Meet colourful characters at the imaginative new **Dickens World**, Chatham Maritime, themed around the life, books and times of the popular author. **Marwell Zoological Park**, Hampshire, is home to over 200 species of animals and offers facilities like shopmobility scooters for hire, manual wheelchairs and easy wheelchair accessibility across the site. You can also get nose to nose with a multitude of furry and feathered friends at **Drusillas Park**, Alfriston, where children can learn as they have fun with fascinating hands-on activities.

Left to right: Hever Castle, Kent; Royal Pavilion, Brighton, East Sussex

**did you know...** there's 80 million years of geological history along the White Cliffs of Dover?

## Shore pleasures

Leave the hurly-burly behind and head to the lovely **beaches** of the south coast. **Eastbourne**, **Bournemouth**, **Brighton** and **Margate** were all popular playgrounds for the Victorians – Queen Victoria would frequently stay at her Isle of Wight home, **Osborne House**. (Incidentally, in modern times Brighton has been one of the first cities in the UK to undergo a full city centre 'Destination Disability Audit'.) Save your small change for the slot machines on the **pier** where it's yummy hot doughnuts or fish and chips all round. If you prefer something more peaceful, you'll still find many gems on this stretch of coastline. Wander the sand dunes at **West Wittering**, just down the Sussex coast from **Bognor Regis**, or watch the zigzagging kite-surfers at **Pevensey Bay**. Try your hand at an unrivalled number of watersports, including sailing on the Solent at the Calshot Activities Centre.

New Forest ponies

## At one with nature

It's not for nothing that Kent is called the **Garden of England**. Sample the beauty of iconic places such as **Sissinghurst Castle Garden** near Cranbrook, the loving creation of Vita Sackville-West and her husband Sir Harold Nicolson. Garden 'compartments' here lead you through a magical series of colour schemes and moods. **Emmetts Garden**, also in Kent, is a charming Victorian affair bursting with year-round interest, from bluebell woods to summer roses and autumn leaves. Or head into West Sussex to **Wakehurst Place**, which displays plants from across the world and aims to house seeds from 10% of the world's flora by 2009 to save species from extinction in the wild. You can have a global experience at **Paradise Park** in East Sussex, too, touring Caribbean, desert, Italian and Oriental gardens to name a few – you might spot dinosaurs as well. Play hide and seek in and out of the paths and bridleways of the **New Forest**, now a National Park, and watch out for wild ponies as they contentedly graze. Follow the ancient tracks of the **South**

**why not...** visit the world's oldest and largest occupied castle – Windsor Castle?

Clockwise: Canterbury Cathedral, Kent; Cowes, Isle of Wight; Denbies Wine Estate, Surrey

**Downs Way** or the **Ridgeway** that eventually meets the **Thames Path**. Then relax and watch the river flow by.

## Never a dull moment

Catch the buzz of a **festival or event**, whatever the time of year. From rock 'n' pop to hops, from rowing to sailing, from Dickens to dancing round a maypole – the rich tapestry of life. The **Brighton Festival** comes to the hip seaside town every May and is a true celebration of the arts. If you're looking for the epitome of elegance, dress up for **Glyndebourne's season of opera**, and maybe take along a picnic too. Or see the streets of **Broadstairs** thronged with jolly folk in Victorian costumes during the **Dickens Festival** – the town was the author's favourite seaside resort. There's rock, pop and hip hop mixed with a liberal dose of mud at August's **Reading Festival**. And don't forget **Henley Royal Regatta**, another chance to pull on your best togs while rowers show off their sporting prowess. Then watch the internationally famous sailing event that is **Cowes Week** and breathe in some of that bracing sea air.

Above: Windsor Castle, Berkshire.
Below: The Roald Dahl Museum and Story Centre, Buckinghamshire

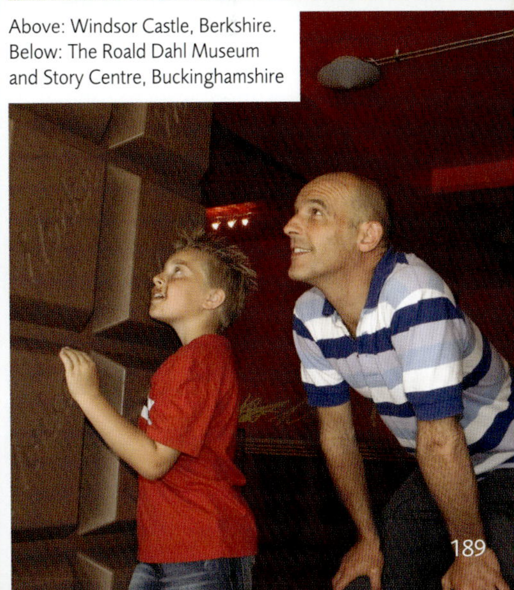

# South East England
## The warmest of welcomes

**Whatever type of accommodation you are looking for, you will find a welcome for all.**

From guest accommodation such as The Nurse's Cottage in the New Forest, or hotels and self catering cottages to Caravan Club sites such as Burford Caravan site or the YHA at Arundel, there is plenty of choice. Historic properties, gardens, family attractions and entire towns and cities are going the extra mile to ensure facilities are available whatever your needs. Investment is increasing in special facilities, adaptations and internal and external building work to improve accessibility across the South East.

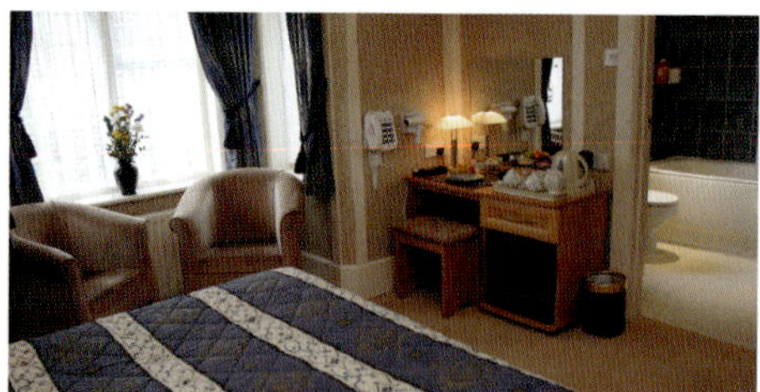

**Main:** Windsor, Berkshire
**Above:** The Nurse's Cottage, Hampshire

Just a few highlights are featured here that have already carried out that investment, but for more details on destinations, attractions and accommodation in South East England go to our website **visitsoutheastengland.com**.

Many historic properties and sites across the region have been modernised to offer excellent accessibility for all visitors including Waddesdon Manor in Buckinghamshire, Oxfordshire's Blenheim Palace and the Abbey and Battlefied at Hastings, Sussex. In 2006 Pallant House Gallery re-opened to the public following a £8.6million building and refurbishment project. This Grade I Listed Queen Anne townhouse now has a contemporary extension housing one of the best 20th century British art collections in the world and a courtyard garden. As a result of their work the Gallery has received the 'Adapt Award' for Excellence in Access and the 'Go Easy, Best Design' for Accessibility Award. They have developed picture descriptions for visually impaired people.

Outdoor attractions such as Marwell Zoo in Hampshire are also adapting their offer. The Hawk Conservancy Trust in Andover has areas reserved for wheelchairs at all its flying arenas and bird hides and special touching sessions, and the use of recorded bird calls can be provided for visually impaired people. Picnic and play areas have been adapted for wheelchair users to enjoy the areas with their family and friends.

For something completely different visit Dickens World at Chatham Maritime in Kent, Denbies Wine Estate in Surrey or Paradise Park in East Sussex.

Windsor recently followed Brighton's lead in undergoing a full city centre 'Destination Access Audit' – one of the spin-offs from this will be to benefit from the 2012 Paralympics and the welcome it offers to visitors at Dorney Lakes, the Rowing venue for the Olympics. Legoland Windsor's award winning facilities allow guests with disabilities and special needs the best possible enjoyment and accessibility. Buckinghamshire is also committed to providing an accessible welcome for all visitors, being the home of Stoke Mandeville which hosted the first Paralympics in 1948.

www.visitsoutheastengland.com

**Find out more:**
visitsoutheastengland.com
visitbrighton.com
visitwindsor.gov.uk
visitbuckinghamshire.org
dickensworld.co.uk
marwell.org.uk
blenheimpalace.com
waddesdon.org.uk
discoverhastings.co.uk
denbiesvineyard.co.uk
paradisepark.co.uk
hawk-conservancy.org
pallant.org.uk
caravanclub.co.uk
nursescottage.co.uk
yha.org.uk

**Below:** Waddesdon Manor, Buckinghamshire

# Useful regional contacts

**Tourism South East**
**t** (023) 8062 5400
**w** visitsoutheastengland.com

## Publications

### A Town Centre Shopping Guide For People With Disabilities

A Maidstone Borough Council publication available to download from digitalmaidstone.co.uk.

### Access Guide

A guide to Tunbridge Wells for people with disabilities. Available to download from tunbridgewells.gov.uk or call (01892) 526121 for alternative formats.

### Accessible Portsmouth – Guide For Visitors With Disabilities

Available to download from visitportsmouth.co.uk. For alternative formats, call (023) 9283 4109 or email tourism@portsmouthcc.gov.uk.

### Accessible Worthing

Information on accessibility in Worthing is available Tourist Information Centre. Call (01903) 239999 or visit visitworthing.co.uk.

### Places In And Around Eastbourne

Available from Eastbourne Tourist Information Centre. Call 0871 663 0031 or for textphone users (01323) 415111.

### Walks For All In Kent And Medway

A Kent County Council series of leaflets available to download from kent.gov.uk/explorekent.

Left to right: Broadstairs, Kent; Portsmouth Historic Dockyard, Hampshire; Sheffield Park, East Sussex

# Tourist Information Centres

When you arrive at your destination, visit an Official Partner Tourist Information Centre for quality assured help with accommodation and information about local attractions and events, or email your request before you go. To search for attractions and Tourist Information Centres on the move just text INFO to 62233, and a web link will be sent to your mobile phone. To find a Tourist Information Centre by region visit enjoyEngland.com/find-tic.

| | | | |
|---|---|---|---|
| **Bicester** | Unit 86a, Bicester Village | (01869) 369055 | bicester.vc@cherwell-dc.gov.uk |
| **Brighton** | Pavilion Buildings | 0906 711 2255** | brighton-tourism@brighton-hove.gov.uk |
| **Canterbury** | 12/13 Sun Street | (01227) 378100 | canterburyinformation@canterbury.gov.uk |
| **Chichester** | 29a South Street | (01243) 775888 | chitic@chichester.gov.uk |
| **Cowes** | 9 The Arcade | (01983) 813818 | info@islandbreaks.co.uk |
| **Dover** | The Old Town Gaol | (01304) 205108 | tic@doveruk.com |
| **Hastings** | Queens Square | (01424) 781111 | hic@hastings.gov.uk |
| **Newport** | High Street | (01983) 813818 | info@islandbreaks.co.uk |
| **Oxford** | 15/16 Broad Street | (01865) 726871 | tic@oxford.gov.uk |
| **Portsmouth** | Clarence Esplanade | (023) 9282 6722 | vis@portsmouthcc.gov.uk |
| **Portsmouth** | The Hard | (023) 9282 6722 | vis@portsmouthcc.gov.uk |
| **Rochester** | 95 High Street | (01634) 843666 | visitor.centre@medway.gov.uk |
| **Royal Tunbridge Wells** | The Pantiles | (01892) 515675 | touristinformationcentre @tunbridgewells.gov.uk |
| **Ryde** | 81-83 Union Street | (01983) 813818 | info@islandbreaks.co.uk |
| **Sandown** | 8 High Street | (01983) 813818 | info@islandbreaks.co.uk |
| **Shanklin** | 67 High Street | (01983) 813818 | info@islandbreaks.co.uk |
| **Southampton** | 9 Civic Centre Road | (023) 8083 3333 | tourist.information@southampton.gov.uk |
| **Winchester** | High Street | (01962 840500 | tourism@winchester.gov.uk |
| **Windsor** | Royal Windsor Central Station | (01753) 743900 | windsor.tic@rbwm.gov.uk |
| **Yarmouth** | The Quay | (01983) 813818 | info@islandbreaks.co.uk |

**calls to this number are charged at premium rate

where to stay in

# South East England

The following establishments participate in VisitBritain's Enjoy England quality assessment scheme and hold a National Accessible Scheme rating. YHA youth hostels in England and Wales are listed in a separate section, see page 40.

Place names in the blue bands with a map reference are shown on the maps at the front of this guide.

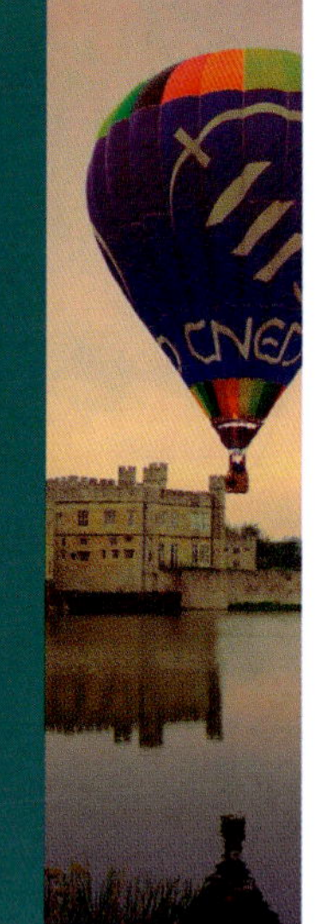

## Accommodation symbols

Symbols give useful information about services and facilities. You can find a key to these symbols on page 8.

**ABINGDON,** Oxfordshire — **GUEST ACCOMMODATION**

**Abbey Guest House** 136 Oxford Road, Abingdon OX14 2AG
**t** (01235) 537020
**e** info@abbeyguest.com
**w** abbeyguest.com

**BATTLE,** East Sussex Map ref 3B4 — **CAMPING, CARAVAN & HOLIDAY PARK**

(150)
£12.20–£25.10
(150)
£12.20–£25.10
150 touring pitches

## Normanhurst Court Caravan Club Site

Stevens Crouch, Battle TN33 9LR **t** (01424) 773808
**e** enquiries@caravanclub.co.uk **w** caravanclub.co.uk

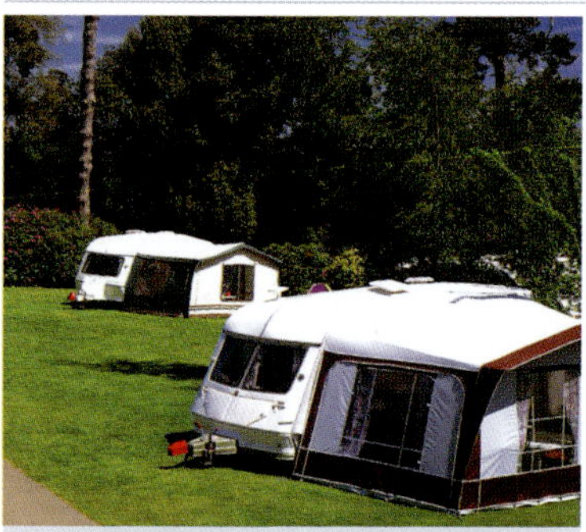

A gracious site in a former garden with magnificent specimen trees. There is a choice between pitches in open areas or in small groups surrounded with shrubs – the rhododendrons are a riot of colour in the spring. The site is located close to the 1066 Trail which will appeal to walkers, nature lovers and families.

**open** March 2009 to November 2009

*From Battle, turn left onto A271. Site is 3 miles on left.*

General

Leisure

Payment Credit/debit cards, cash, cheques

*Midweek discount; pitch fees reduced by 50% for stays on Mon, Tue, Wed or Thu outside peak season.*

**BIDDENDEN,** Kent Map ref 3B4 — **GUEST ACCOMMODATION**

GUEST ACCOMMODATION

B&B per room per night
**s £45.00–£55.00**
**d £55.00–£70.00**
Evening meal per person
**£18.50**

## Heron Cottage

Biddenden, Ashford TN27 8HH **t** (01580) 291358 **w** heroncottage.info

Peacefully set in five acres amidst unspoilt countryside, between Biddenden and Sissinghurst Castle. Ideal for visiting historical properties and gardens in Kent and Sussex.

**open** March to November
**bedrooms** 3 double, 2 twin, 2 family
**bathrooms** 6 en suite

Rooms
General
Payment Cash, cheques

**BOGNOR REGIS,** West Sussex Map ref 2C3 — **CAMPING, CARAVAN & HOLIDAY PARK**

TOURING & CAMPING PARK

(94) £12.20–£25.10
(94) £12.20–£25.10
94 touring pitches

## Rowan Park Caravan Club Site

Rowan Way, Bognor Regis PO22 9RP **t** (01243) 828515
**e** enquiries@caravanclub.co.uk **w** caravanclub.co.uk

General
Leisure
Payment Credit/debit cards, cash, cheques

*Midweek discount; pitch fees reduced by 50% for stays on Mon, Tue, Wed or Thu during saver and low seasons.*

This site is conveniently situated alongside the A29 and about two miles from the beach and is most attractive with its screen of trees in a park-like setting. The town of Bognor Regis is a traditional seaside resort with a shingle and sand beach and entertainments.

**open** April to November

*From roundabout on A29, 1 mile north of Bognor, turn left into Rowan Way, site 100yds on right, opposite Halfords superstore.*

**BOGNOR REGIS,** West Sussex

*See also entry on p202*

**BORTHWOOD,** Isle of Wight — **SELF CATERING**

★★★

SELF CATERING

**Borthwood Cottages contact** Mrs Anne Finch, Borthwood Cottages, Sandlin, Borthwood, Sandown PO36 0HH **t** (01983) 403967
**e** mail@netguides.co.uk **w** borthwoodcottages.co.uk

**BRACKLESHAM BAY,** West Sussex

*See entry on p202*

## BRACKNELL, Berkshire — HOTEL

**Coppid Beech Hotel** John Nike Way, Bracknell RG12 8TF
**t** (01344) 303333
**e** reservations@coppidbeech.com
**w** coppidbeech.com

## BRIGHTON & HOVE, East Sussex — CAMPING, CARAVAN & HOLIDAY PARK

TOURING & CAMPING PARK

**Sheepcote Valley Caravan Club Site** East Brighton Park, Brighton BN2 5TS
**t** (01273) 626546
**w** caravanclub.co.uk

## BURFORD, Oxfordshire Map ref 2B1 — CAMPING, CARAVAN & HOLIDAY PARK

★★★★★

TOURING PARK

(119) £14.00–£26.90
(119) £14.00–£26.90
119 touring pitches

# Burford Caravan Club Site

Bradwell Grove, Burford OX18 4JJ **t** (01993) 823080
**w** caravanclub.co.uk

General

Leisure

Payment Credit/debit cards, cash, cheques

*Midweek discount; pitch fees reducted by 50% for says on Mon, Tue, Wed or Thu night outside peak and value season.*

An attractive and spacious site – you can't miss it as it is located opposite the Cotswold Wildlife Park, a popular family attraction in the area. With rhinos, zebras and leopards, children love it and the brass rubbing centre, beautiful gardens and narrow gauge railway make this a good value and special day out.

**open** July to November

*From roundabout at A40/A361 junction in Burford, take A361 signposted Lechlade. Site on right after 2.5 miles. Site signposted from roundabout.*

## CHALE, Isle of Wight — SELF CATERING

★★★★

SELF CATERING

**Atherfield Green Farm Holiday Cottages contact** Mr & Mrs Alistair Jupe, Atherfield Green Farm Holiday Cottages, The Laurels, High Street, Newchurch PO36 0NN **t** (01983) 867613
**e** alistair.jupe@btinternet.com **w** btinternet.com/~alistair.jupe

## CHICHESTER, West Sussex — HOTEL

**Chichester Park Hotel** Madgwick Lane, Westhampnett, Chichester PO19 7QL
**t** (01243) 786351
**e** info@chichesterparkhotel.com **w** chichesterparkhotel.com

## CHICHESTER, West Sussex — SELF CATERING

★★★★ SELF CATERING

**Cornerstones contact** Viv & Roland Higgins, Greenacre, Goodwood Gardens, Chichester PO20 1SP **t** (01243) 839096
**e** v.r.higgins@dsl.pipex.com **w** cornercottages.com

## CHICHESTER, West Sussex

*See also entries on p202*

## DORKING, Surrey — SELF CATERING

★★★★ SELF CATERING

**Bulmer Farm contact** Mr & Mrs Graham & Sue Walker, Bulmer Farm, Holmbury St Mary, Dorking RH5 6LG **t** (01306) 731871
**e** enquiries@bulmerfarm.co.uk **w** bulmerfarm.co.uk

## EAST DEAN, East Sussex — SELF CATERING

★★★★ SELF CATERING

**Beachy Head Holiday Cottages contact** Jan Smith, Beachy Head Holiday Cottages, Upper Street, East Dean, Eastbourne BN20 0BS **t** (01323) 423878
**e** jan@beachyhead.org.uk **w** beachyhead.org.uk

## EASTBOURNE, East Sussex — HOTEL

★★★ HOTEL SILVER AWARD

**Hydro Hotel** Mount Road, Eastbourne BN20 7HZ
**t** (01323) 720643
**e** sales@hydrohotel.com
**w** hydrohotel.com

## EDENBRIDGE, Kent — SELF CATERING

★★★★ SELF CATERING

**Hay Barn & Straw Barn contact** Mr J Piers Quirk,
**t** (01892) 870701
**e** info@watstockbarns.co.uk **w** watstockbarns.co.uk

## FARNHAM, Surrey Map ref 2C2 — SELF CATERING

SELF CATERING

Units **1**
Sleeps **1–2**
Low season per wk
**£220.00**
High season per wk
**£265.00**

### High Wray, Farnham

**contact** Mrs Alexine G N Crawford, High Wray, 73 Lodge Hill Road, Lower Bourne, Farnham GU10 3RB **t** (01252) 715589
**e** alexine@highwray73.co.uk **w** highwray73.co.uk

Roomy and level ground-floor apartment specifically designed for wheelchair users. Wheel-in shower, parking close by. Sunny patio by large accessible garden. Wireless broadband available.

**open** All year
**nearest shop** 0.5 miles
**nearest pub** 0.5 miles

General

Unit

Payment Cash, cheques

## FELPHAM, West Sussex

*See entry on p203*

## FOLKESTONE, Kent — GUEST ACCOMMODATION

★★★★ GUEST ACCOMMODATION

**Garden Lodge** 324 Canterbury Road, Densole, Folkestone CT18 7BB
**t** (01303) 893147
**e** stay@garden-lodge.com **w** garden-lodge.com

## FOLKESTONE, Kent — CAMPING, CARAVAN & HOLIDAY PARK

★★★★★
TOURING & CAMPING PARK

**Black Horse Farm Caravan Club Site** 385 Canterbury Road, Densole, Folkestone CT18 7BG
**t** (01303) 892665
**w** caravanclub.co.uk

## HIGH HALDEN, Kent — SELF CATERING

★★★★
SELF CATERING

**The Granary and The Stables contact** Mrs Serena Maundrell, Vintage Years Company Ltd, Hales Place, High Halden, Ashford TN26 3JQ
**t** (01233) 850871 & 07715 488804
**e** serena@vintage-years.co.uk **w** vintage-years.co.uk

## HILL BROW, West Sussex — GUEST ACCOMMODATION

★★★★
INN
SILVER AWARD

**The Jolly Drover** London Road, Hill Brow, Liss GU33 7QL
**t** (01730) 893137
**e** thejollydrover@googlemail.com

## LECKHAMPSTEAD, Buckinghamshire — GUEST ACCOMMODATION

★★★★
FARMHOUSE

**Weatherhead Farm** Leckhampstead, Buckingham MK18 5NP
**t** (01280) 860502
**e** weatherheadfarm@aol.com

## LEWES, East Sussex Map ref 2D3 — SELF CATERING

★★★★
SELF CATERING

Units **2**
Sleeps **1–10**
Low season per wk
**£405.00–£490.00**
High season per wk
**£485.00–£655.00**

### Heath Farm, Plumpton Green, Lewes

**contact** Mrs Marilyn Hanbury, Heath Farm, South Road, Plumpton Green, Lewes BN8 4EA **t** (01273) 890712
**e** hanbury@heath-farm.com **w** heath-farm.com

General
Unit
Payment Cash, cheques

Former milking parlour and stables converted into luxury cottages on working family farm. Beautifully and comfortably furnished to highest standard. Level-entry showers. Wonderful countryside, easy access to Brighton, Gatwick, London, National Trust gardens and historic towns and villages. An ideal holiday base.

**open** All Year
**nearest shop** 1 mile
**nearest pub** < 0.5 miles

*Directions given at time of booking.*

## NEWCHURCH, Isle of Wight — CAMPING, CARAVAN & HOLIDAY PARK

★★★★★
TOURING & CAMPING PARK

**Southland Camping Park** Winford Road, Sandown PO36 0LZ
**t** (01983) 865385
**e** info@southland.co.uk
**w** southland.co.uk

## NORTON, Isle of Wight Map ref 2C3 — SELF CATERING

★★★★
SELF CATERING

Units **2**
Sleeps **2–4**

Low season per wk
**£175.00–£350.00**
High season per wk
**£350.00–£1,020.00**

### The Savoy, Norton

**contact** Mr Steve Deacon, The Savoy, Halletts Shute, Norton PO41 0RJ **t** (01983) 760355
**e** info@savoyholidays.co.uk **w** savoyholidays.com

General
Leisure
Unit
Payment Credit/debit cards, cash, cheques

Two quality, accessible, ground-floor cottages comprising two double bedrooms with twin beds in each, low level kitchen units, shower room with seat, hand rails, alarm and nearby parking spaces. Resort facilities include shop, spa, creche, laundry and swimming pool with hoist; all of which are wheelchair-friendly.

**open** All year
**nearest shop** < 0.5 miles
**nearest pub** 1 mile

*Just under 1 miles from the nearest ferry terminal at Yarmouth and close to beaches, The Needles and miles of unspoilt countryside.*

## PULBOROUGH, West Sussex — GUEST ACCOMMODATION

★★★★
INN

**The Labouring Man** Old London Road, Pulborough RH20 1LF
**t** (01798) 872215
**e** philip.beckett@btconnect.com **w** thelabouringman.co.uk

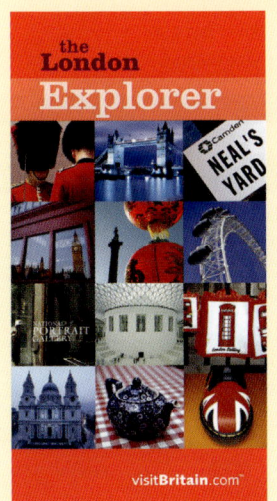



At-a-glance symbols are explained on page 8. 

**REDHILL,** Surrey Map ref 2D2 — **CAMPING, CARAVAN & HOLIDAY PARK**

★★★★
TOURING & CAMPING PARK

(150)
£12.20–£25.10
(150)
£12.20–£25.10
150 touring pitches

## Alderstead Heath Caravan Club Site

Dean Lane, Redhill RH1 3AH **t** (01737) 644629
**w** caravanclub.co.uk

General

Leisure

Payment Credit/debit cards, cash, cheques

*Midweek discount; pitch fees reduced by 50% for stays on Mon, Tue, Wed or Thu outside peak season.*

A quiet, level site, though the site drops away into rolling wooded countryside. Alderstead Heath is an ideal holiday in a picturesque setting. The Pilgrim's Way provides varied walking options. Its proximity to London makes this an obvious and delightful base to explore the capital (35 mins from Redhill).

**open** All year

*M25 jct 8, A217 towards Reigate, fork left after 300yds towards Merstham. 2.5 miles, left at T-junction onto A23. 0.5 miles turn right into Shepherds Hill (B2031). 1 mile, left into Dean Lane.*

**ROYAL TUNBRIDGE WELLS,** Kent — **HOTEL**

★★★★
HOTEL
SILVER AWARD

**The Brew House Hotel** 1 Warwick Park, Royal Tunbridge Wells TN2 5TA
**t** (01892) 520587
**e** frontoffice@brewhousehotel.com
**w** brewhousehotel.com

**SANDWICH,** Kent — **SELF CATERING**

★★★★
SELF CATERING

**Updown Park Farm contact** Mrs J R Mongomery, Updown Park Farm, Little Brooksend Farm, Birchington CT7 0JW **t** (01843) 841656
**e** info@montgomery-cottages.co.uk **w** montgomery-cottages.co.uk

**SELSEY,** West Sussex

*See entry on p203*

**SHANKLIN,** Isle of Wight Map ref 2C3 — **SELF CATERING**

★★★★
SELF CATERING

Units **1**
Sleeps **5**
Low season per wk
**£275.00–£375.00**
High season per wk
**£450.00–£695.00**

## Laramie, Shanklin

**contact** Mrs Sally Ranson, Laramie, Howard Road, Shanklin PO37 6HD
**t** (01983) 862905 **e** sally.ranson@tiscali.co.uk **w** laramieholidayhome.co.uk

Spacious bungalow minutes from tarmacked cliff path. Large, fitted, well-equppied kitchen/diner. Sunny lounge with patio doors. Two large bedrooms with double beds and one with additional single bed.

**nearest shop** < 0.5 miles
**nearest pub** 1 mile

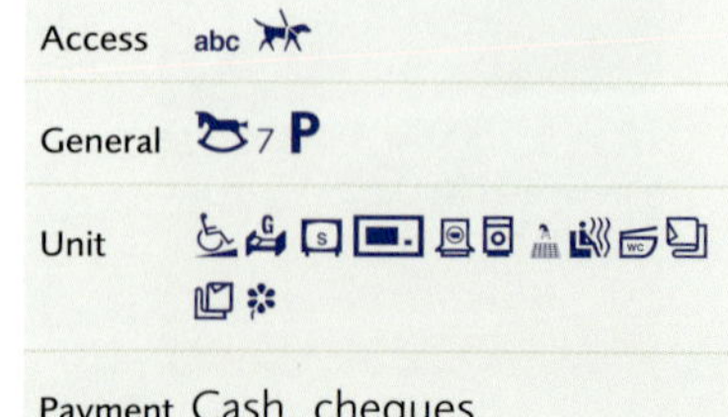

Access abc

General 7 P

Unit

Payment Cash, cheques

## SHANKLIN, Isle of Wight — SELF CATERING

★★★★
SELF CATERING

**Sunny Bay Apartments** **contact** Mrs Julia Nash, Sunny Bay Apartments, Alexandra Road, Shanklin PO37 6AF **t** (01983) 866379
**e** info@sunnybayapartments.com **w** sunnybayapartments.com

## SWAY, Hampshire — GUEST ACCOMMODATION

★★★★
GUEST ACCOMMODATION
SILVER AWARD

**The Nurse's Cottage** Station Road, Sway, Lymington SO41 6BA
**t** (01590) 683402

## TENTERDEN, Kent — HOTEL

★★★
HOTEL
SILVER AWARD

**Little Silver Country Hotel** Ashford Road, Tenterden TN30 6SP
**t** (01233) 850321
**e** enquiries@little-silver.co.uk
**w** little-silver.co.uk

## TONBRIDGE, Kent — SELF CATERING

★★★★★
SELF CATERING

**Goldhill Mill Cottages**
**t** (01732) 851626
**e** vernon.cole@virgin.net **w** goldhillmillcottages.com

## WINCHESTER, Hampshire — CAMPING, CARAVAN & HOLIDAY PARK

★★★
TOURING & CAMPING PARK

**Morn Hill Caravan Club Site** Morn Hill, Winchester SO21 2PH
**t** (01962) 869877
**w** caravanclub.co.uk

## WITNEY, Oxfordshire — GUEST ACCOMMODATION

★★★
FARMHOUSE

**Springhill Farm Bed & Breakfast** Cogges, Witney OX29 6UL
**t** (01993) 704919
**e** jan@strainge.fsnet.co.uk

## WITNEY, Oxfordshire Map ref 2C1 — SELF CATERING

★★★★
SELF CATERING

Units **1**
Sleeps **4**
Low season per wk
**£260.00–£330.00**
High season per wk
**£430.00–£450.00**

### Swallows Nest, Witney

**contact** Mrs Jan Strainge, Swallows Nest, Cogges, Witney OX29 6UL
**t** (01993) 704919 **e** jan@strainge.fsnet.co.uk

Cosy country barn conversion close to Witney, Oxford, Blenheim and nearby Cotswolds. Level access throughout including en suite showers. One zip/link double, one twin (low allergy). Shower chairs etc available.

**open** All year
**nearest shop** 1 mile
**nearest pub** 1 mile

General
Unit
Payment Cash, cheques, euros

## WORTHING, West Sussex — CAMPING, CARAVAN & HOLIDAY PARK

★★★★
TOURING PARK

**Northbrook Farm Caravan Club Site** Titnore Way, Worthing BN13 3RT
**t** (01903) 502962
**e** enquiries@caravanclub.co.uk **w** caravanclub.co.uk

At-a-glance symbols are explained on page 8.

# National Accessible Scheme ratings only

The following establishments hold a National Accessible Scheme rating as shown in their entry, but do not participate in a quality assessment scheme. However, to participate in the National Accessible Scheme accommodation must meet a minimum level of quality.

**BOGNOR REGIS,** West Sussex Map ref 2C3 **SELF CATERING**

Units **1**
Sleeps **2–8**
Low season per wk
Min £280.00
High season per wk
Max £520.00

**Awaiting NAS rating**

## Farrell House

**contact** Gail Lewis, Livability, PO Box 36, Cowbridge CF71 7GB
**t** 08456 584478 **e** selfcatering@livability.org.uk or glewis@livability.org.uk
**w** livabilityholidays.org.uk

Chalet bungalow, adapted and equipped for disabled people, sleeping up to eight. Ground-floor lounge, kitchen, bathroom, twin and single bedrooms and bathroom upstairs. Electric ceiling hoist, profiling bed and shower-chair. Ramp to garden.
**open** All year
**nearest shop** 1 mile
**nearest pub** 1 mile

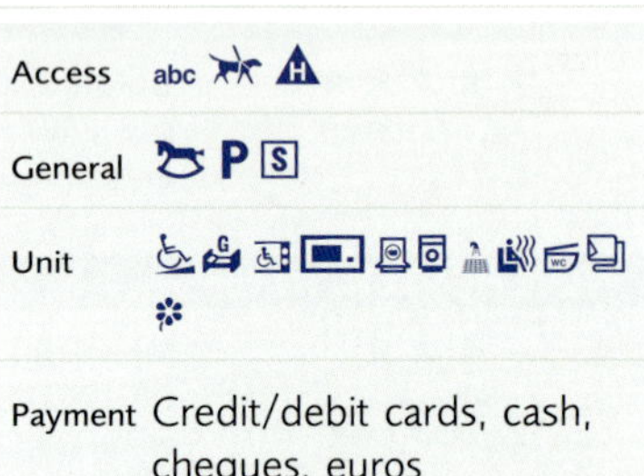


Payment Credit/debit cards, cash, cheques, euros

**BRACKLESHAM BAY,** West Sussex Map ref 2C3 **SELF CATERING**

Units **1**
Sleeps **2–6**
Low season per wk
Min £330.00
High season per wk
Max £540.00

**Awaiting NAS rating**

## Tamarisk, Bracklesham Bay

**contact** Gail Lewis, Livability, PO Box 36, Cowbridge CF71 7GB
**t** 08456 584478 **e** selfcatering@livability.org.uk or glewis@livability.org.uk
**w** livabilityholidays.org.uk

Bungalow near beach, adapted and equipped for disabled people. Three bedrooms, lounge/dining room, kitchen, roll-in and second shower rooms. Mobile and electric ceiling hoists, profiling bed and other equipment available.
**open** All year
**nearest shop** 1 mile
**nearest pub** 1 mile

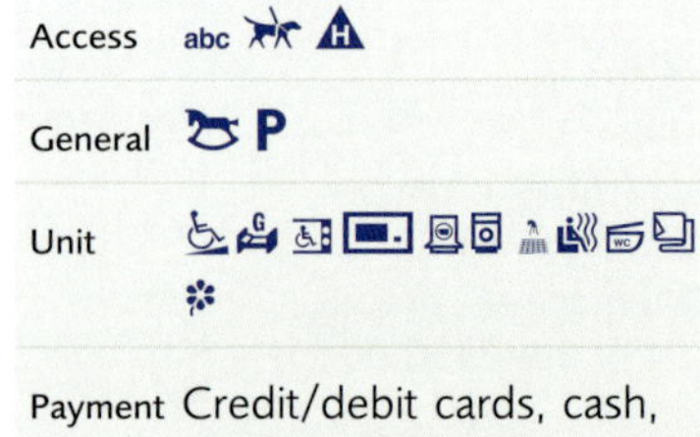


Payment Credit/debit cards, cash, cheques, euros

**CHICHESTER,** West Sussex **SELF CATERING**

**Compton Farm – The Barn contact** Mr & Mrs Robin & Melanie Bray, Compton Farm - The Barn, Church Lane, Compton, Chichester PO18 9HB
**t** (02392) 631022
**e** robinbray2@btopenworld.com **w** bookcottages.com

**CHICHESTER,** West Sussex **SELF CATERING**

**Compton Farm – The Bull Pen contact** Mr & Mrs Robin & Melanie Bray, Compton Farm - The Bull Pen, Church Lane, Compton, Chichester PO18 9HB
**t** (02392) 631022
**e** robinbray2@btopenworld.com **w** bookcottages.com

**FELPHAM,** West Sussex Map ref 2C3 **SELF CATERING**

Units **1**
Sleeps **2–9**
Low season per wk
Min £300.00
High season per wk
Max £495.00

Awaiting NAS rating

## Beach Lodge, Felpham

**contact** Gail Lewis, Livability, PO Box 36, Cowbridge CF71 7GB
**t** 08456 584478 **e** selfcatering@livability.org.uk or glewis@livability.org.uk
**w** livabilityholidays.org.uk

Detached house facing the sea, east of Bognor. Adapted for wheelchair users with a lift and roll-in shower. Sleeps up to nine people. Electric and mobile hoists available.

**open** All year
**nearest shop** 1 mile
**nearest pub** 1 mile

Access abc
General P
Unit

Payment Credit/debit cards, cash, cheques, euros

**SELSEY,** West Sussex Map ref 2C3 **SELF CATERING**

Units **1**
Sleeps **2–6**
Low season per wk
Min £280.00
High season per wk
Max £520.00

Awaiting NAS rating

## Seagulls

**contact** Gail Lewis, Livability, PO Box 36, Cowbridge CF71 7GB
**t** 08456 584478 **e** selfcatering@livability.org.uk or glewis@livability.org.uk
**w** livabilityholidays.org.uk

Bungalow, facing the sea at Selsey Bill, designed and equipped for disabled people. Lounge, kitchen and three bedrooms. Electric ceiling hoist, roll-in shower, shower-chair and profiling bed available. Ramp to beach.

**open** All year
**nearest shop** 2 miles
**nearest pub** 2 miles

Access abc
General P
Unit

Payment Credit/debit cards, cash, cheques, euros

## Key to symbols

Symbols at the end of each entry help you pick out the services and facilities which are most important for your stay. A key to the symbols can be found on page 8.

from ANTS to WHITE RHINOS and BATS to BIG CATS in 160 acres of Landscaped Parkland
• ADVENTURE PLAYGROUND
• CHILDRENS FARMYARD
• CAFETERIA • PICNIC AREAS
• NARROW GAUGE RAILWAY (RUNS FROM APR-OCT)
BURFORD • OXON • OX18 4JW
(MID-WAY BETWEEN OXFORD & CHELTENHAM)
COTSWOLD Wildlife Park and Gardens
INFORMATION HOTLINE: 01993 823006
OPEN DAILY FROM 10AM
www.cotswoldwildlifepark.co.uk

Mid Hants Railway
WATERCRESS LINE
More than just a Train Ride!
Open weekends Jan to end Oct
PLUS Bank Holidays and
Tues - Thurs from May to Sept.
Every day in August
Easy access for Wheelchair
passengers at Alresford station,
ramps available to board the trains.
Groups of 15+ must be pre-booked
Find us via A31 Winchester to
Alton Road in Hampshire.
Tel: 01962 733810
www.watercressline.co.uk

CANTERBURY
SIMPLY INSPIRATIONAL
www.canterbury.co.uk

ROYAL
Windsor
With 1000 years of history,
there's so much to pack in
SAVILL GARDEN
BOAT TRIPS
WINDSOR CASTLE
THEATRE ROYAL
Ascot
royal windsor
ETON COLLEGE
City Sightseeing
LEGOLAND WINDSOR
Royal Windsor
Call for a free brochure +44 (0)1753 743900
or visit www.windsor.gov.uk

Royal Horticultural Society
RHS
Garden
Wisley
A fabulous garden
for a fabulous day out
Something to see all
year round
Spring bulbs, summer
borders, autumnal leaves
and winter shapes
• Shop
• Plant Centre
• Cafés
• Restaurant
• Coffee Shop
Open all year and
accessible to all
On the A3 in Surrey north of
Guildford near J10 of the M25
Registered Charity No. 222879
RHS Garden Wisley, Woking, Surrey, GU23 6QB
Tel: 0845 260 9000 www.rhs.org.uk

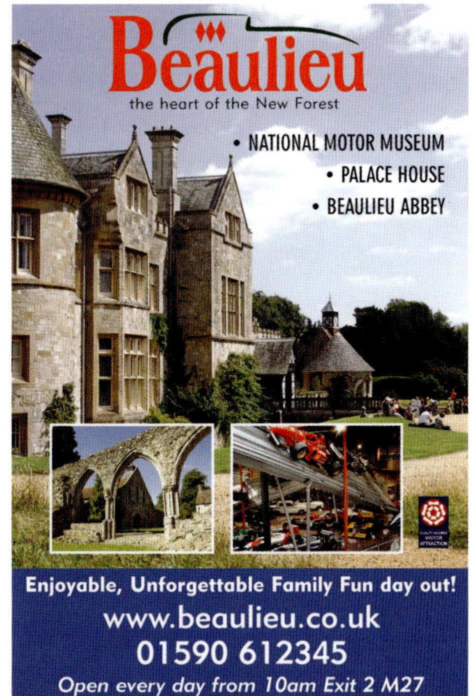
Beaulieu
the heart of the New Forest
• NATIONAL MOTOR MUSEUM
• PALACE HOUSE
• BEAULIEU ABBEY
Enjoyable, Unforgettable Family Fun day out!
www.beaulieu.co.uk
01590 612345
Open every day from 10am Exit 2 M27

CANTERBURY
SIMPLY INSPIRATIONAL
www.canterbury.co.uk

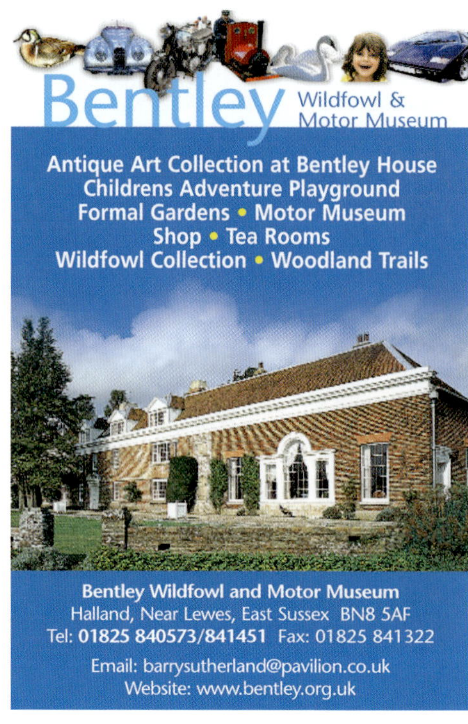
Bentley Wildfowl & Motor Museum
Antique Art Collection at Bentley House
Childrens Adventure Playground
Formal Gardens • Motor Museum
Shop • Tea Rooms
Wildfowl Collection • Woodland Trails
Bentley Wildfowl and Motor Museum
Halland, Near Lewes, East Sussex BN8 5AF
Tel: 01825 840573/841451 Fax: 01825 841322
Email: barrysutherland@pavilion.co.uk
Website: www.bentley.org.uk

Sussex Past Museums
Michelham Priory Explore beautiful gardens, visit the working watermill, Elizabethan great barn and the restored Tudor country house. Wheelchairs/electric buggies on site.
Fishbourne Roman Palace Discover in situ impressive early Roman mosaic floors and reconstructed garden. Tour the Collections Discovery Centre. Wheelchairs and hearing loop.
Café and convenient parking at both venues.
Marlipins Museum Fully accessible museum displaying maritime and local history.
Tour, concession and group rates available. See www.sussexpast.co.uk for details.
Michelham Priory, Upper Dicker, Hailsham, East Sussex BN27 3QS Tel: 01323 844224
Fishbourne Roman Palace, Salthill Rd, Fishbourne, Chichester, W Sussex PO19 3QR Tel: 01243 785859
Marlipins Museum, 36 High Street, Shoreham-by-Sea West Sussex BN43 5DA
Tel:01273 462994/01323 441279
Fishbourne Roman Palace won the Open Your Doors certificate recognising their excellent service to blind and partially sighted people in January 2007.
Guide Dogs
SUSSEX PAST

Katalan Travels Ltd
01494 580816
Holiday Services for People with Disabilities
Summer & Winter Holidays
*Supported Holidays
*Tailor made Holidays
*Equipment Hire in Resort
Helping you find the holiday
You deserve
www.katalantravels.com
katalan.travels@ntlworld.com

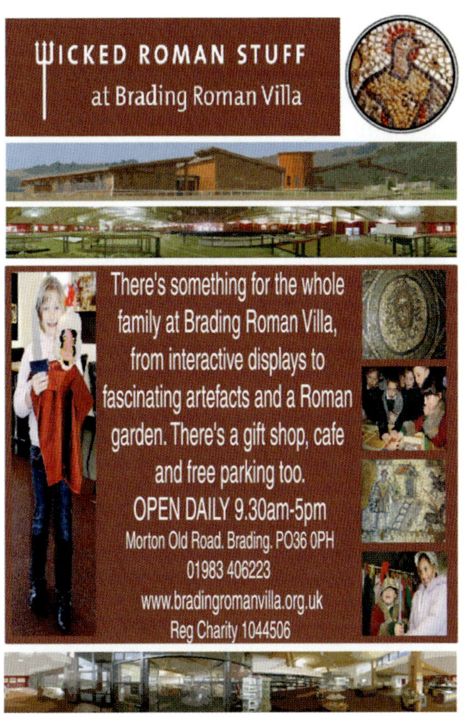

*Accessible Vehicles on Self-drive Hire*

- Medium and large minibuses, all lift equipped
- Hand controlled cars left or right-hand, also left foot throttle
- Delivery/collection service—short or long term hire
- Private hire service (driver included)

**www.wheelchairtravel.co.uk**
**Guildford, Surrey**
**Telephone: 01483 233 640**
**Fax:01483 234 845**

Horsham Shopmobility provides a selection of manual and powered wheelchairs along with motorised scooters to anyone , young or old, who has problems walking around Horsham Town Centre, giving them greater independence and access to the shopping areas and leisure facilities.
Horsham Shopmobility is situated in Level 2 of the Swan Walk Car Park in the area behind Marks & Spencer and is signposted both outside and inside the car park.
The opening hours are: 10.00am to 4.00pm Monday - Friday; 9.00am to 4.30pm Saturday (except Bank Holidays)

**Contact:01403 249015**

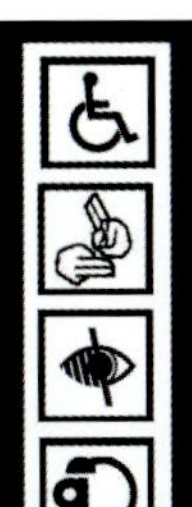

The Nuffield
southampton

Award-Winning Productions
Workshops | Sunday Night Specials
Poetry Evenings | Community Theatre
Community Theatre | Alternative
Theatre | Visiting Companies | Studio
Bar & Restaurant and so much more...

023 8067 1771 ww.nuffieldtheatre.co.uk

Call 01344 354400 for more information

**The Romney, Hythe & Dymchurch Railway**

- Level or Ramped Access
- Stairlift to museum
- Wheelchair Accessible Carriages.

To help us make your day out enjoyable and stress free, A phone call to our main station before your visit would be useful if you require the use of our accessible carriages.

Full Details for Disabled Visitors Please Contact:
RHDR, New Romney. Kent TN28 8PL
Tel: 01797 362353

**GUILDFORD CATHEDRAL**

In a peaceful rural setting with spacious parking.

Come and visit our lovely Cathedral, also our Restaurant, Gift Shop and Book Shop.

Guildford Cathedral
Stag Hill, Guildford
GU2 7UP
Tel: 01483 547860
Fax: 01483 303350

www.guildford-cathedral.org

Explore more than 1000 years of history in England's longest medieval cathedral.

Relax in the award-winning café and shop.

Open: 0830-1730 daily
*(Evensong at 1730 Mon-Sat, 1530 Sun)*

Admission: £5 Adults
£4 Concessions
Under 16s with family, free

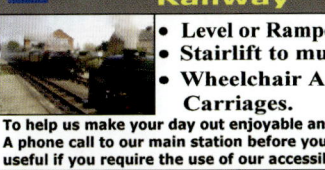

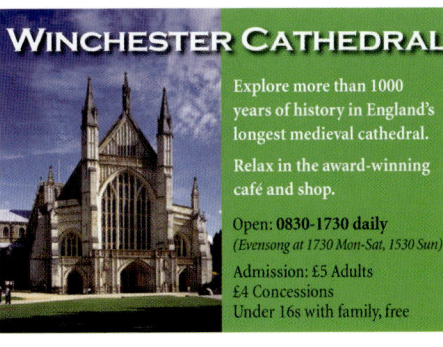

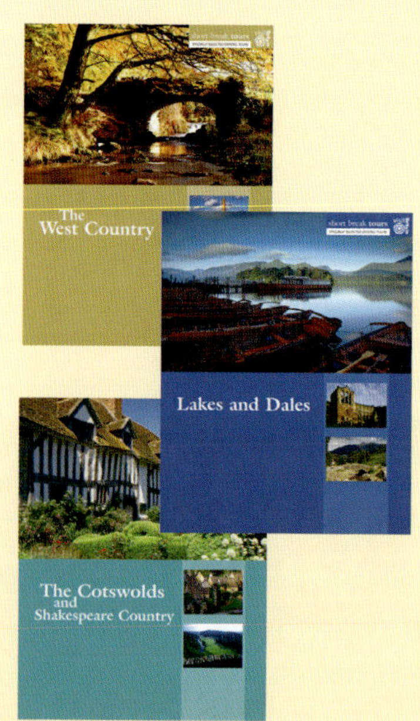

# Touring made easy

- Individual route maps
- Places of interest on route
- Gazetteer of key visitor sites and attractions
- Ideas for walks, pony trekking, boat trips and steam train rides

Make the best of your shortbreak with ready-made driving tours from VisitBritain. These attractive touring guides illustrate two to four-day circular routes with over 200 places to discover, including picturesque villages, heritage sites and cities, attractions and local beauty spots, historic houses and gardens.

Available in good bookshops and online at visitbritaindirect.com for just £6.99 each.

# London

Clockwise: Buckingham Palace; Shakespeare's Globe; Tower Bridge

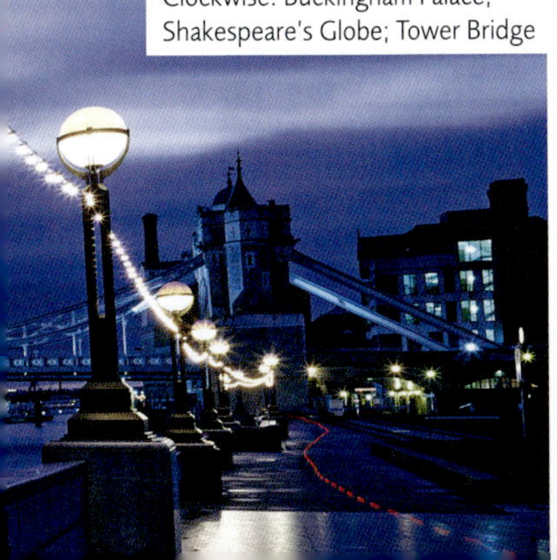

# Great days out

Enjoy a capital experience you'll never forget. From world-class museums, galleries and theatres to absolutely fabulous shopping and global dining. Getting around is easy, putting everything on your doorstep: royal palaces and gardens, ancient heritage and top sporting events.

## See the sights

View London's sights from the air, river and land – it's an exciting introduction to centuries of breathtaking city heritage. All **public buses** and **Docklands Light Railway** trains plus many tours are accessible to wheelchair users. Begin with a ride on the world's largest observation wheel, the **London Eye**, rising slowly into the sky to gaze on 55 famous landmarks across the city.

The British Museum

Then take a **cruise on the Thames**: departure points include the London Eye pier for a trip with commentary from the **Houses of Parliament** to the **Tower of London** and back. Join **Original London Sightseeing Tours** open-top buses for an entertaining guide through the city past and present (a third of vehicles are wheelchair accessible). And a personalised **London Taxi Tour** in an iconic black cab is truly memorable!

## Be a culture vulture

London is a true culture capital with some 70 large museums and over 30 major art galleries – a good number offer enhanced access facilities. Discover the works of man from prehistoric to modern times at the enthralling **British Museum**, where step-free access, sound guides and sign language interpreted talks make visiting a pleasure. Head for **Tate Britain** and browse over 500 years of British art, then compare **Tate Modern's** diverse modern and contemporary international art. Touch tours, audio guides, BSL interpreted events all feature at both galleries. And how about the **Natural**

**why not...** climb the Monument (311 steps) in the City for superb views?

Left to right: South Bank; London Eye

**did you know...** dozens of museums and galleries are free to visit, including Tate Britain?

**History Museum** with its hundreds of interactive exhibits, the **Science Museum** featuring superb science, technology and medicine collections, and an adventure through Britain's seafaring history at the **National Maritime Museum**?

## Retail heaven

Time now to check out London's legendary shopping scene and famous stores. Visit one of the largest toyshops in the world, **Hamley's** on Regent Street is a magical wonderland spread over seven floors, reached by lift or escalator. Along Oxford Street, sort out the latest sounds at **HMV** and **Zavvi** (both step-free access throughout) then update your wardrobe and lots more at **House of Fraser**, **John Lewis** and trendy **Top Shop**. After a book? **Foyles** on Charing Cross Road has been supplying them for over 100 years. **Fortnum & Mason** is a must for its celebrated fine food (step-free access via Piccadilly entrance) and you could spend hours roaming **Harrods** in Knightsbridge. Refuel at eateries with global appeal: **Wagamama** (Japanese), **Giraffe** (modern European and international) and **Nando's** (Portuguese) are among restaurants with accessible locations across London. Or relax with a picnic in one of the city's lovely green **parks**.

Tea at Harrods

## Show time

Drama, comedy, music – London's world-class theatres raise a curtain on them all. Be entranced by a magnificent performance at the **Royal Opera House**, Covent Garden, where surtitles, wheelchair spaces and guide dog sitting (among other services) make everyone welcome. The **Society of London Theatre** provides information on access and assisted performances in theatres throughout the capital (theatre-access.co.uk). Do catch the Bard at **Shakespeare's Globe**, Bankside, for an authentic experience of Tudor theatre. Or if you prefer rib-ticklers, join the comedy club circuit – **Jongleurs Comedy Club**, Bow Wharfe, and **The Comedy Store**, St James, will have you laughing all the way home.

**why not...** explore Regent's Canal from Little Venice to the Docklands?

## Attractions A to Z

From **London Aquarium** to **London Zoo**, there's something different to do every day. Once you've watched over 350 species of fascinating fish and over 12,000 amazing animals, soak up 500 years of history at majestic **Hampton Court Palace** (facilities include signed and captioned video presentations). Go green-fingered at the **Royal Botanic Gardens**, **Kew**, where you can tour via the Kew Explorer Bus (wheelchairs and electric mobility scooters also bookable in advance) and discover over 30,000 types of plants from around the world. Then raise a cheer at some top **sporting venues** – from **Lord's Cricket Ground** to **Wembley Stadium** and **Wimbledon** (all with facilities for wheelchair users and hearing and visually impaired spectators). Maybe round off with a wine tour at **Vinopolis** to learn about wine cultures around the globe and taste a few delicious samples.

Left to right: Covent Garden; Hampton Court Palace

# London 2012 – be there!

The countdown to the **London Paralympic Games 2012** is well and truly underway! From 29 August to 9 September 2012, 4,200 paralympians will compete in 20 sports across 21 venues – look out for tickets, on sale from 2011. Paralympics GB has already been talent scouting for more athletes with potential to add to its team and hopes are high.

The Paralympic Games are 'coming home': UK links date back to the Games' origins in Stoke Mandeville in 1948. Since then, the country has blazed a trail. What can you look forward to in London? Inspiring new venues are taking shape, to combine with established top locations. See track and road paralympic cycling in the slick **Olympic Park Velodrome** and **Regent's Park**, with 27 gold medals up for grabs. Discover Boccia, a skilful ball game that's unique to the Paralympics – watch it at **ExCeL**. British wheelchair tennis players are among the best in the world, while the atmosphere in the state-of-the-art new **Olympic Stadium** will be electric as athletes pit speed, strength, power and stamina for 160 golds.

**Come and share the experience of a lifetime.**

Above: Chinese New Year
Below: Kew Gardens

# Useful regional contacts

**Visit London**
**t** 0870 156 6366
**w** visitlondon.com

## Information

### Artsline
**t** (020) 7388 2227
**e** admin@artsline.org.uk
**w** artsline.org.uk
A resource for finding accessible attractions in London.

### City of London Access Group
Access Office, City of London,
PO Box 270, Guildhall,
London EC2P 2EJ
**t** (020) 7332 1995
**t** (020) 7332 3929 (textphone)
**e** access@cityoflondon.gov.uk
**w** cityoflondon.gov.uk/access
Information on access to buildings and special parking bays in the 'square mile' of the city. A booklet containing information on accessible toilets, dropped kerbs and transport is available for download.

### Congestion charge
**t** 0845 900 1234
**t** (020) 7649 9123 (textphone)
**w** cclondon.com
Blue badge holders are entitled to 100% discount for an initial registration of £10 – worthwhile if you pay more than two weekday visits to London in a year. Call for a registration pack.

### DisabledGo
**w** disabledgo.info
An online service with detailed information on access to premises and attractions in London, including Croydon, Lewisham, Richmond, Tower Hamlets and Wandsworth.

### London Eye
**t** 0870 500 0600
**t** 0870 990 8885 (disabled booking line)
**w** ba-londoneye.com
Operates a fast track policy for visitors with disabilities and older people, and can take up to eight wheelchairs per revolution, with a maximum of two in a capsule.

### Society of London Theatre
**t** (020) 7557 6751
**e** access@solttma.co.uk
**w** officiallondontheatre.co.uk/access
Runs Access London Theatre Guide, published three times a year, aiming to increase audiences with sensory impairments, as well as families and 16-25 year olds. There is a free brochure of audio-described, captioned and sign language performances.

### Taxis
**t** 07957 696673
**w** londonblackcabs.co.uk
London Black Cabs have space for a passenger in a manual wheelchair, and carry a ramp.

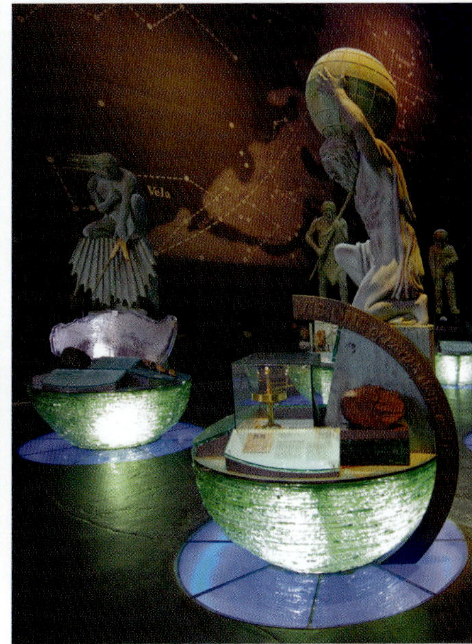


Clockwise: Hyde Park; Natural History Museum; Chelsea Flower Show

**Transport for London**
**t** (020) 7222 1234
**t** (020) 7918 3015 (textphone)
**w** tfl.gov.uk
Responsible for London's public transport. Search for accessible routes on tfl.gov.uk/journeyplanner. See also their shared information on directenquiries.com.

## Tourist Information Centres

| | | | |
|---|---|---|---|
| **Britain & London Visitor Centre** | 1 Regent Street | 0870 156636 | blvcenquiries@visitlondon.com |
| **Croydon** | Katharine Street | (020) 8253 1009 | tic@croydon.gov.uk |
| **Greenwich** | 2 Cutty Sark Gardens | 0870 608 2000 | tic@greenwich.gov.uk |
| **Lewisham** | 199-201 Lewisham High Street | (020) 8297 8317 | tic@lewisham.gov.uk |
| **Swanley** | London Road | (01322) 614660 | touristinfo@swanley.org.uk |

where to stay in

# London

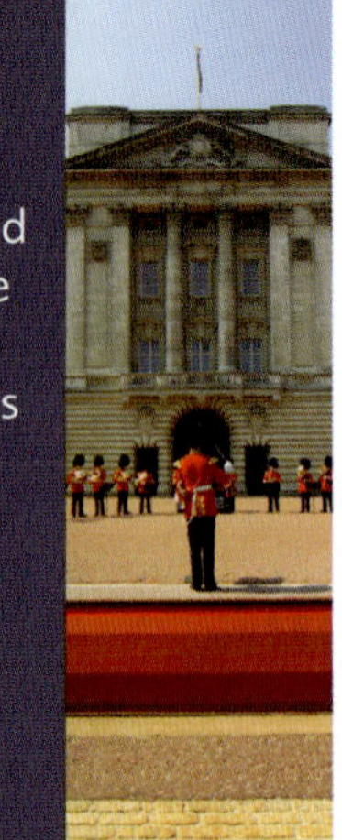

The following establishments participate in a quality assessment scheme and either hold a National Accessible Scheme rating, or have bedrooms suitable for wheelchair users and have been audited on behalf of the London Development Agency by Direct Enquiries (see page 10). YHA youth hostels in England and Wales are listed in a separate section, see page 40.

For maps of inner and outer London, see the front of this guide.

### Accommodation symbols

Symbols give useful information about services and facilities. You can find a key to these symbols on page 8.

## INNER LONDON

### LONDON E1 — HOTEL

BUDGET HOTEL

**Express by Holiday Inn Limehouse** 469-475 The Highway, Limehouse, London E1W 3HN **t** (020) 77913850
**e** jcniclas@exhi-limehouse.co.uk **w** hiexpress.com/limehouse

### LONDON E1 — HOTEL

Rating Applied For

**Ibis London City** 5 Commercial St, Whitechapel, London E1 6BF
**t** (020) 7422 8400
**w** ibishotel.com

### LONDON E1 — HOTEL

BUDGET HOTEL

**Travelodge London Liverpool Street** 1 Harrow Place, London E1 7DB
**t** 0870 191 1689
**w** travelodge.co.uk

### LONDON E4 — HOTEL

BUDGET HOTEL

**Express by Holiday Inn Chingford** 5 Walthamstow Avenue, Chingford, London E4 8ST **t** 0870 444 2789
**e** dgmchingford@expressholidayinn.co.uk **w** ichotelsgroup.com

### LONDON E14 — HOTEL

★★★★ QUALITY-ASSESSED HOTEL

**Hilton London Canary Wharf** South Quay, Marsh Wall, London E14 9SH
**t** (020) 3002 2300
**e** reservations.canarywharf@hilton.com **w** hilton.co.uk/canarywharf

### LONDON E14 — HOTEL

★★★★ HOTEL SILVER AWARD

**Radisson Edwardian New Providence Wharf** 5 Fairmont Avenue, London E14 9PQ
**t** (020) 7987 2050
**e** resnpw@radisson.com

### LONDON E14 — HOTEL

BUDGET HOTEL

**Travelodge London Docklands** Coriander Avenue, East India Dock Road, Docklands, London E14 2AA **t** 0870 191 1691
**w** travelodge.co.uk

## LONDON E15 — HOTEL

BUDGET HOTEL

**Express By Holiday Inn London Stratford** 196 High Street, Stratford, London E15 2NE **t** 0870 240 5708
**w** ichotelsgroup.com

## LONDON E15 — HOTEL

BUDGET HOTEL

**Ibis London Stratford** 1a Romford Road, Stratford, London E15 4JL
**t** (020) 8535 3700
**e** h3099@accor.com **w** ibishotel.com

## LONDON E16 — HOTEL

★★★★
HOTEL

B&B per room per night
**s £99.00–£250.00**
**d £99.00–£250.00**
HB per person per night
**£129.00–£280.00**

# Crowne Plaza London – Docklands

Royal Victoria Dock, Western Gateway, London E16 1AL
**t** 0870 990 9692
**e** sales@crowneplazadocklands.co.uk **w** crowneplazadocklands.co.uk

Access

Rooms

General

Leisure

Payment Credit/debit cards, cash

*The Docklands Bar & Grill is our newly opened, brasserie-style, destination restaurant & bar within the hotel.*

A contemporary, deluxe hotel next to the ExCel exhibition centre and close to London City Airport, the $0_2$ and Canary Wharf. We boast 210 comfortable bedrooms, 11 of which are accessible. Furthermore, we boast the newly opened Docklands Bar & Grill and the Quad Heath & Fitness Club with swimming pool.

**open** All year
**bedrooms** 107 double, 76 twin, 12 family, 15 suites
**bathrooms** All en suite

*By car: from the M25, via the M11 or A13. By public transport: we are adjacent to Royal Victoria Station (fully accessible) on the Docklands Light Railway.*

## LONDON E16 — HOTEL

BUDGET HOTEL

**Express by Holiday Inn London Royal Docks** 1 Silvertown Way, Silvertown, London E16 1EA **t** (020) 7540 4040
**e** info@exhi-royaldocks.co.uk **w** sixcontinentshotels.com

## LONDON E16 — HOTEL

BUDGET HOTEL

**Ibis London ExCel** 9 Western Gateway, Royal Victoria Dock, London E16 1AB
**t** (020) 7055 2300
**e** H3655@accor-hotels.com **w** ibishotel.com

At-a-glance symbols are explained on page 8.

**LONDON E16** **HOTEL**

BUDGET HOTEL

**Premier Travel Inn – London Docklands** Royal Victoria Dock, London E16 1SL
**t** 0870 238 3322
**w** premierinn.com

**LONDON E16** **HOTEL**

BUDGET HOTEL

**Travelodge London City Airport** Hartman Road, Silvertown, London E16 2BZ
**t** 0870 085 0950
**w** travelodge.co.uk

**LONDON EC1** **HOTEL**

BUDGET HOTEL

**Express by Holiday Inn London City** 275 Old Street, London EC1V 9LN
**t** (020) 7300 4300
**e** reservationsfc@holidayinnlondon.com **w** sixcontinentshotels.com

**LONDON EC1** **HOTEL**

BUDGET HOTEL

**Travelodge London City Road** 1-23 City Road, London EC1Y 1AE **t** 0871 984 6333
**w** travelodge.co.uk

**LONDON EC4** **HOTEL**

★★★★ HOTEL

**Crowne Plaza City** 19 New Bridge Street, London EC4V 6DB **t** 0870 400 9190
**w** ichotelsgroup.com

**LONDON N1** **HOTEL**

QUALITY-ASSESSED HOTEL

**Hilton London Islington** 53 Upper Street, Islington, London N1 0UY
**t** (020) 7354 7700
**e** reservations.islington@hilton.com **w** hilton.co.uk/islington

**LONDON N1** **HOTEL**

★★★ HOTEL

**Jurys Inn Islington** 60 Pentonville Road, London N1 9LA **t** (020) 7282 5500
**w** jurysinns.com

**LONDON NW1** **HOTEL**

★★★★ HOTEL

**Holiday Inn Camden Lock** 28 Jamestown Road, Camden Town, London NW1 7BY
**t** (020) 7485 4343
**e** info@holidayinncamden.co.uk **w** holidayinncamden.co.uk

**LONDON NW1** **HOTEL**

★★★★ HOTEL

**Novotel London Euston** 100 -110 Euston Road, Euston, London NW1 2AJ
**t** (020) 7666 9000
**e** H5309@accor-hotels.com **w** novotel.com

**LONDON NW2** **HOTEL**

★★★★ HOTEL

**Crown Moran** 142-152 Cricklewood Broadway, Cricklewood, London NW2 3ED
**t** (020) 8452 4175
**e** crownres@morangroup.ie **w** crownmoranhotel.co.uk

**LONDON NW2** **HOTEL**

★★★ HOTEL

**Holiday Inn Brent Cross** Tilling Road, Brent Cross, London NW2 1LP
**t** 0870 400 9112
**e** yvonne.charles2@ichotelsgroup.com **w** london-brentcross.holiday-inn.com

**LONDON NW3** **HOTEL**

BUDGET HOTEL

**Premier Travel Inn – London Hampstead** 215 Haverstock Hill, Hampstead, London NW3 4RB **t** 0870 850 6328
**w** premierinn.com

**LONDON NW7** — HOTEL

BUDGET HOTEL

**Days Hotel London North** Welcome Break Services, Mill Hill, Nr Wembley, London NW7 3HU **t** (020) 8906 7000
**w** daysinn.com

**LONDON SE1** — HOTEL

BUDGET HOTEL

**Days Hotel Waterloo** 54 Kennington Rd, Waterloo, London SE1 7BJ
**t** (020) 7922 1331
**e** waterloo@khl.uk.com **w** daysinn.com

**LONDON SE1** — HOTEL

BUDGET HOTEL

**Express by Holiday Inn Southwark** 103 Southwark St, London SE1 0JQ
**t** (020) 7401 2525
**w** hiexpress.com/lon-southwark

**LONDON SE1** — HOTEL

★★★★ HOTEL

**London Bridge Hotel** 8-18 London Bridge Street, London Bridge, London SE1 9SG
**t** (020) 7855 2200
**e** sales@london-bridge-hotel.co.uk **w** londonbridgehotel.com

**LONDON SE1** — HOTEL

★★★★ HOTEL

**Mercure London City Bankside Hotel** 77 Southwark Street, Southwark, London SE1 0JA **t** (020) 7902 0800
**e** H2814@accor-hotels.com **w** mercure.com

**LONDON SE1** — HOTEL

★★★★ HOTEL

**Novotel London City South** 53-61 Southwark Bridge Road, Southwark, London SE1 9HH **t** (020) 7089 0400
**e** H3269@accor-hotels.com **w** novotel.com

**LONDON SE1** — HOTEL

★★★ HOTEL

**Novotel London Waterloo** 113 Lambeth Road, Waterloo, London SE1 7LS
**t** (020) 7793 1010
**e** H1785@accor-hotels.com **w** novotel.com

**LONDON SE1** — HOTEL

BUDGET HOTEL

**Premier Travel Inn – London County Hall** Belvedere Road, London, London SE1 7PB **t** 0870 238 3300
**w** premierinn.com

**LONDON SE1** — HOTEL

BUDGET HOTEL

**Premier Travel Inn – London Southwark** Anchor, 34 Park Street, London SE1 9EF
**t** 0870 990 6402
**w** premierinn.com

## Accessibility accommodation in London

Establishments in London are assessed by Direct Enquiries which rates properties against a wide range of accessible categories. For more information go to directenquiries.com.

**LONDON SE2** — **CAMPING, CARAVAN & HOLIDAY PARK**

★★★★★
TOURING & CAMPING PARK

(202) £14.90–£28.90
(202) £14.90–£28.90
202 touring pitches

# Abbey Wood Caravan Club Site

Federation Road, Abbey Wood, London SE2 0LS **t** (020) 8311 7708
**w** caravanclub.co.uk

General

Leisure

Payment Credit/debit cards, cash, cheques

*Midweek discount; pitch fees reduced by 50% for stays on Mon, Tue, Wed or Thu night outside peak season.*

It feels positively rural when you reach this verdant, gently sloping, secure site with its mature-tree screening and spacious grounds. Good railway connections (35 mins) into central London's attractions are within walking distance of the site. As an alternative to the busy city centre, nearby Greenwich offers its own blend of fascinating attractions.

**open** All year

*On M2 turn off at A221. Then turn right into McLeod Road, right into Knee Hill and the site is the 2nd turning on the right.*

**LONDON SE3** — **HOTEL**

★★★
HOTEL

**Clarendon Hotel** 8-16 Montpelier Row, Blackheath, London SE3 0RW
**t** (020) 8318 4321
**e** relax@clarendonhotel.com **w** clarendonhotel.com

**LONDON SE19** — **CAMPING, CARAVAN & HOLIDAY PARK**

★★★★★
TOURING & CAMPING PARK

**Crystal Palace Caravan Club Site** Crystal Palace Parade, London SE19 1UF
**t** (020) 8778 7155
**w** caravanclub.co.uk

**LONDON SW1** — **HOTEL**

**City Inn Westminster** 30 John Islip Street, Belgravia, London SW1P 4DD
**t** (020) 7630 1000
**e** westminster.res@cityinn.com **w** cityinn.com/london

**LONDON SW1** — **HOTEL**

★★★★
HOTEL

**Crowne Plaza London St James** 45-51 Buckingham Gate, St James, London SW1E 6AF **t** (020) 7834 6655
**e** sales@cplonsj.co.uk **w** london.crowneplaza.com

**LONDON SW1** — **HOTEL**

BUDGET HOTEL

**Express by Holiday Inn Victoria** 106-110 Belgrave Road, Victoria, London SW1V 2BJ **t** (020) 7630 8888
**e** info@hiexpressvictoria.co.uk **w** sixcontinentshotels.com

## LONDON SW1 — HOTEL

★★★★ HOTEL

**Park Plaza Victoria** 239 Vauxhall Bridge Road, Victoria, London SW1V 1EQ
**t** (020) 7769 9999
**e** info@victoriaparkplaze.com **w** victoriaparkplaza.com

## LONDON SW6 — HOTEL

BUDGET HOTEL

**Ibis London Earl's Court** 47 Lillie Road, West Brompton, London SW6 1UD
**t** (020) 7610 0880
**e** h5623-re@accor-hotels.com **w** ibishotels.com

## LONDON SW6 — HOTEL

★★★★ HOTEL

**Millennium & Copthorne Hotels at Chelsea Football Club** Stamford Bridge, Fulham Road, London SW6 1HS **t** 0870 300 1212
**e** reservations.chelsea@mill-cop.com **w** millenniumhotels.com

## LONDON SW6 — HOTEL

**Premier Travel Inn – London Putney Bridge** 3 Putney Bridge Approach, London, London SW6 3JD **t** 0870 238 3302
**w** premierinn.com

## LONDON SW7 — HOTEL

★★★★

B&B per room per night
**d £99.00–£250.00**

# Holiday Inn London – Kensington Forum

97 Cromwell Road, London SW7 4DN
**t** 0870 400 9100 & 0870 40 50 60
**w** holidayinn.com

The Holiday Inn London Kensingon Forum offers 906 modern bedrooms with a choice of suites, executive rooms and accessible rooms. All rooms equipped with high-speed internet, AC, pay TV and complimentary tea- and coffee-making facilities.

**open** All year
**bedrooms** 638 double, 264 twin, 4 suites
**bathrooms** All en suite

Access abc

Rooms

General

Leisure

Payment Credit/debit cards, cash, cheques

## LONDON SW7 — HOSTEL

★★★★ HOSTEL

**Meininger City Hostel & Hotel London** 65-67 Queen's Gate, London SW7 5JS
**t** (020) 3051 8173
**e** welcome@meininger-hostels.com **w** meininger-hostels.com

At-a-glance symbols are explained on page 8.

## LONDON SW8 — HOTEL

★★★★ HOTEL

**Comfort Inn Vauxhall** 87 Lambeth Road, Vauxhall, London SW8 1RN
**t** (020) 7735 9494
**e** stay@comfortinnvx.co.uk **w** comfortinnvx.co.uk

## LONDON SW11 — HOTEL

BUDGET HOTEL

**Travelodge London Battersea** Southampton House, 192-206 York Road, London SW11 3SA **t** 0870 191 1688
**w** travelodge.co.uk

## LONDON SW18 — HOTEL

BUDGET HOTEL

**Express by Holiday Inn Wandsworth** Smuggler's Way, Battersea, London SW18 1EG **t** 0870 720 1298
**e** wandsworth@oriel-leisure.co.uk **w** sixcontinentshotel.com

## LONDON SW19 — HOTEL

BUDGET HOTEL

**Express by Holiday Inn Wimbledon South** 200 High Street, South Wimbledon, London SW19 2BH **t** (020) 8545 7300
**e** info@exhiwimbledon.co.uk **w** exhiwimbledon.co.uk

## LONDON SW19 — HOTEL

BUDGET HOTEL

**Premier Travel Inn – London Wimbledon South** 27 Chapter Way, London SW19 2RF **t** 0870 990 6342
**w** premierinn.com

## LONDON W1 — HOTEL

★★★★★ HOTEL

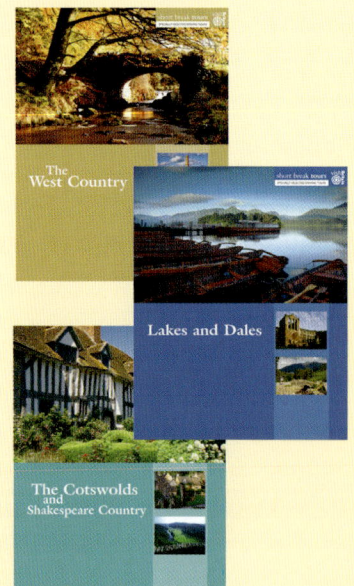

**Brown's Hotel** Albemarle Street, Mayfair, London W1S 4BP **t** (020) 7493 6020
**e** sales.browns@roccofortecollection.com **w** roccofortecollection.com

**LONDON W1** **HOTEL**

★★★★ HOTEL

B&B per room per night
**s £150.00–£320.00**
**d £150.00–£320.00**
HB per person per night
**£170.00–£340.00**

## Holiday Inn London – Regent's Park

Carburton Street, London W1W 5EE **t** 0870 400 9111
**e** reservations-londonregentspark@ihg.com
**w** holidayinn.co.uk/regentspark

Access

Rooms

General

Payment Credit/debit cards, cash, cheques

*Hotel includes 6 fully accessible bedrooms. Hearing loops and blue badge parking available.*

Fully accessible, modern hotel in London's West End with outstanding meeting facilities and transport links. Many local attractions including: Madame Tussaud's, London Zoo, Oxford Street, Regent's Park and Theatre District, all within easy reach. Restaurant, bar and car park on site. Fully licensed.

**open** All year
**bedrooms** 216 double, 111 twin, 5 single
**bathrooms** All en suite

*Great Portland Street underground station 100m (Circle, Metropolitan and Hammersmith & City lines). Warren Street 400m (Northern and Victoria Lines). Regent's Park 500m (Bakerloo line).*

**LONDON W1** **HOTEL**

★★★★ HOTEL

**Holiday Inn London Mayfair** 3 Berkeley Street, Oxford Street, London W1J 8NE
**t** (020) 7493 8282
**w** ichotelsgroup.com

**LONDON W1** **HOTEL**

★★★★★ HOTEL

**The InterContinental Hotel** 1 Hamilton Place, Park Lane, London W1J 7QY
**t** (020) 7409 3131
**e** london@interconti.com **w** intercontinental.com

**LONDON W1** **HOTEL**

★★★★ HOTEL

**Thistle Marble Arch** Bryanston Street, Marble Arch, London W1H 7EH
**t** 0871 376 9027
**e** MarbleArch@Thistle.co.uk **w** thistle.com/hotels/marble-arch

**LONDON W2** **HOTEL**

QUALITY-ASSESSED HOTEL

**Hilton London Metropole** 225 Edgware Road, Church Street, London W2 1JU
**t** (020) 7402 4141
**e** cbs.londonmet@hilton.com **w** hilton.co.uk/londonmet

**LONDON W2** **HOTEL**

★★★★ HOTEL

**Ramada Hyde Park** 150 Bayswater Road, Bayswater, London W2 4RT
**t** (020) 7229 1212
**e** jihydepark@jarvis.co.uk **w** jarvis.co.uk

At-a-glance symbols are explained on page 8. 

**LONDON W6** HOTEL

BUDGET HOTEL

**Express by Holiday Inn Hammersmith** 124 King Street, Hammersmith, London W6 0QU **t** (020) 8746 5100
**e** gsm.hammersmith@expressholidayinn.co.uk

**LONDON W6** HOTEL

★★★★ HOTEL

**Novotel London West** Hammersmith International Centre, 1 Shortlands, London W6 8DR **t** (020) 8741 1555 & (020) 8237 7474
**e** H0737@accor.com **w** novotellondonwest.co.uk

**LONDON W6** HOTEL

BUDGET HOTEL

**Premier Travel Inn – London Hammersmith** 255 King Street, Hammersmith, London W6 9LU **t** 0870 850 6310
**w** premierinn.com

**LONDON W8** HOTEL

★★★★ HOTEL

B&B per room per night
**d Max £225.00**

## Copthorne Tara Hotel

Scarsdale Place, Kensington, London W8 5SR **t** (020) 7937 7211
**e** reservations.tara@milleniumhotels.co.uk **w** milleniumhotels.co.uk/tara

The Copthorne Tara Hotel is ideally located in a corner of Kensington and is proud to be one of the UK's award-winning hotels for providing high specification, specially adapted bedrooms and facilities.

**open** All year
**bedrooms** 427 double, 378 twin, 3 family, 7 suites
**bathrooms** All en suite

Access
Rooms
General
Payment Credit/debit cards, cash, cheques

**LONDON W14** HOTEL

BUDGET HOTEL

**Express by Holiday Inn Earls Court** North End Road, West Kensington, London W14 9NS **t** (020) 7384 5151
**e** info@exhiearlscourt.co.uk **w** hiexpress.com/lonearlscourt

**LONDON WC1** HOTEL

★★★★ HOTEL

**Holiday Inn King's Cross** 1 King's Cross Road, King's Cross, London WC1X 9HX
**t** (020) 7833 3900
**e** reservations@holidayinnlondon.com **w** ichotelsgroup.com

## It's all quality-assessed accommodation

Our commitment to quality involves wide-ranging accommodation assessment. Ratings and awards were correct at the time of going to press but may change following a new assessment. Please check at time of booking.

**LONDON WC1** **HOTEL**

★★★★
HOTEL

B&B per room per night
**s £150.00–£320.00**
**d £150.00–£320.00**
HB per person per night
**£170.00–£340.00**

## Holiday Inn London – Bloomsbury

Coram Street, London WC1N 1HT **t** 0870 400 9222
**e** reservations-bloomsbury@ihg.com **w** holidayinn.co.uk/bloomsbury

Access

Rooms

General

Payment Credit/debit cards, cash, cheques

*Hotel includes 8 fully accessible bedrooms. Hearing loops, braille menus and blue badge parking all available.*

Fully accessible, modern hotel in Central London with outstanding meeting facilities and transport links. Many local attractions including: British Museum, Brunswick Shopping Centre, Covent Garden and Theatre District, all within easy reach. Restaurant, lounge bar, Irish pub and car park on site. Fully Licensed. Winner of M&IT 'Best Disabled Facilities' Award 2007.

**open** All year
**bedrooms** 218 double, 70 twin, 21 family, 2 suites
**bathrooms** All en suite

*Russell Square underground station 100m (Piccadilly line). Euston 600m (Northern and Victoria lines). King's Cross/ St Pancras International 1km.*

**LONDON WC1** **HOTEL**

BUDGET HOTEL

**Premier Travel Inn – London Euston** 1 Dukes Road, Euston, London WC1H 9PJ
**t** 0870 238 3301
**w** premierinn.com

**LONDON WC1** **HOTEL**

BUDGET HOTEL

**Travelodge London Kings Cross** Gray's Inn Road, Kings Cross, London WC1X 8BH
**t** 0870 191 1757
**w** travelodge.co.uk

**LONDON WC2** **HOTEL**

BUDGET HOTEL

**Travelodge London Covent Garden** 10 Drury Lane, Covent Garden, London WC2B 5RE
**t** (020) 7208 9988

**LONDON WC2** **HOTEL**

QUALITY-ASSESSED HOTEL

**The Waldorf Hilton** Aldwych, Aldwych, London WC2B 4DD
**t** 0870 400 8484
**e** enquiry.waldorflondon@hilton.com **w** hilton.co.uk/waldorf

At-a-glance symbols are explained on page 8.

## OUTER LONDON

### BARKING — HOTEL

**Etap East Barking** Highbridge Road, Barking, London IG11 7BA
**t** (020) 8507 8500
**w** etaphotel.com

### BARKING — HOTEL

BUDGET HOTEL

**Premier Travel Inn – Barking** Highbridge Road, Barking, London IG11 7BA
**t** 0870 990 6318
**w** premierinn.com

### BEXLEY — HOTEL

★★★ HOTEL

**Holiday Inn Bexley** Black Prince Interchange, London DA5 1ND **t** 0870 400 9006
**e** bexley@ichotelsgroup.com **w** holiday-inn.co.uk

### BRENTFORD — HOTEL

★★★★ HOTEL

**Holiday Inn London Brentford Lock** High Street, Brentford, London TW8 8JZ
**t** (020) 8232 2000
**e** info@holidayinnbrentford.com **w** holidayinnbrentford.co.uk

### BRENTFORD — HOTEL

BUDGET HOTEL

**Premier Travel Inn – London Kew** 52 High Street, Brentford, London TW8 0BB
**t** 0870 990 6304
**w** premierinn.com

### CHESSINGTON — HOTEL

★★★★ HOTEL

**Holiday Inn London Chessington** Leatherhead Road, London KT9 2NE
**t** 0870 890 0567
**w** holidayinnchessington.co.uk

### CHESSINGTON — HOTEL

BUDGET HOTEL

**Premier Travel Inn – Chessington** Leatherhead Road, Chessington, London KT9 2NE **t** 0870 197 7057
**w** premierinn.com

### CROYDON — HOTEL

★★★ HOTEL

**Jurys Inn Croydon** 26 Wellesley Road, London CR0 9XY **t** (020) 8448 6000
**e** jurysinncroydon@jurysdoyle.com **w** jurysdoyle.com

### CROYDON — HOTEL

BUDGET HOTEL

**Premier Travel Inn – Croydon South** 104 Coombe Road, Croydon, London CR0 5RB **t** 0870 197 7069
**w** premierinn.com

### CROYDON — HOTEL

BUDGET HOTEL

**Premier Travel Inn – Croydon West** The Colonnades Leisure Park, 619 Purley Way, London CR0 4RQ **t** (020) 8633 9300
**w** premierinn.com

## Key to symbols

Symbols at the end of each entry help you pick out the services and facilities which are most important for your stay. A key to the symbols can be found on page 8.

## EDGWARE — HOTEL

BUDGET HOTEL

**Premier Travel Inn – London Edgware** 435 Burnt Oak Broadway, Edgware HA8 5AQ **t** 0870 990 6522
**w** premierinn.com

## ENFIELD — HOTEL

BUDGET HOTEL

**Premier Travel Inn – Enfield** Innova Park, Corner of Solar Way, London EN3 7XY
**t** 0870 238 3306
**w** premierinn.com

## FELTHAM — HOTEL

BUDGET HOTEL

**Travelodge Feltham** High Street, Feltham, London TW13 4EX
**t** 0870 191 1819
**w** travelodge.co.uk

## GREENFORD — HOTEL

BUDGET HOTEL

**Premier Travel Inn – London Greenford** Western Avenue, Greenford, London UB6 8TE **t** (020) 8998 8820
**w** premierinn.com

## HAYES — HOTEL

Rating Applied For

**Holiday Inn London Heathrow Ariel** 118 Bath Road, Hayes, London UB3 5AJ
**t** 0870 400 9040
**w** holiday-inn.com

## HAYES — HOTEL

BUDGET HOTEL

**Ibis London Heathrow Airport** 112-114 Bath Road, Hayes, London UB3 5AL
**t** (020) 8759 4888
**e** h0794@accor-hotels.com **w** ibishotel.com

## HAYES — HOTEL

BUDGET HOTEL

**Premier Travel Inn – Hayes Heathrow** 362 Uxbridge Road, Hayes, London UB4 0HF **t** 0870 197 7132
**w** premierinn.com

## HAYES — HOTEL

BUDGET HOTEL

**Premier Travel Inn – Heathrow (M4)** Shepiston Lane, Heathrow, Hayes UB3 1RW
**t** 0870 990 6612
**w** premierinn.com

## HAYES — HOTEL

★★★★ HOTEL SILVER AWARD

**Radisson Edwardian Heathrow Hotel** 140 Bath Rd, Hayes, London UB3 5AW
**t** 0800 374411
**e** resreh@radisson.com **w** radissonedwardian.com/heathrow

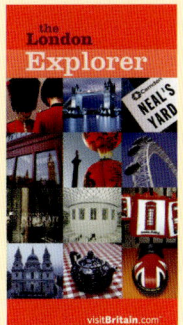



At-a-glance symbols are explained on page 8.

**HEATHROW** **HOTEL**

★★★★ HOTEL

B&B per room per night
**s £93.00–£476.00**
**d £105.00–£476.00**
HB per person per night
**£58.00–£253.00**

## Crowne Plaza London Heathrow

Stockley Road, West Drayton UB7 9NA **t** 0870 400 9140
**e** lonha.reservations@ihg.com **w** crowneplaza.co.uk

Crowne Plaza London Heathrow: close to motorway links, Heathrow Airport and Stockley Park. An ideal base from which to explore central London, Windsor, Wembley and Twickenham.

**open** All year
**bedrooms** 201 double, 259 twin, 3 suites
**bathrooms** All en suite

Access abc
Rooms
General
Leisure
Payment Credit/debit cards, cash, cheques, euros

**HEATHROW** **HOTEL**

QUALITY-ASSESSED HOTEL

**Hilton London Heathrow Airport** Terminal Four, Heathrow, London TW6 3AF
**t** (020) 8759 7755
**e** reservations.heathrow@Hilton.com **w** hilton.co.uk/heathrow

**HEATHROW** **HOTEL**

★★★★ HOTEL

**Holiday Inn London Heathrow** Bath Road, Corner of Sipson Way, West Drayton, London UB7 0DP **t** (020) 899 00000
**e** rm-heathrowm4@ichotelsgroup.com **w** holiday-inn.com

**HEATHROW** **HOTEL**

★★★ HOTEL

**Holiday Inn London Heathrow M4 (Jct 4)** Sipson Road, West Drayton, London UB7 0JU **t** 0870 400 8595
**w** ichotelsgroup.com

**HEATHROW** **HOTEL**

★★★ HOTEL

**Novotel London Heathrow** Cherry Lane, West Drayton, London UB7 9HB
**t** (01895) 431431
**e** H1551@accor.com **w** novotel.com

**ILFORD** **HOTEL**

BUDGET HOTEL

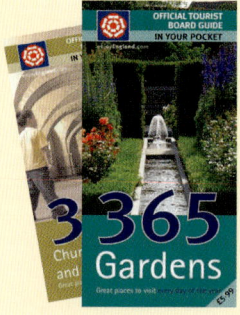

**Travelodge London Ilford** Clements Road, Ilford, London IG1 1BA
**t** 0870 191 1693
**w** travelodge.co.uk

## MORDEN — HOTEL

BUDGET HOTEL

**Travelodge London Wimbledon (Morden)** Epsom Road, Morden, London SM4 5PH **t** 0870 191 1695
**w** travelodge.co.uk

## ROMFORD — HOTEL

BUDGET HOTEL

**Premier Travel Inn – Romford Central** Mercury Gardens, Romford, London RM1 3EN **t** 0870 197 7220
**w** premierinn.com

## ROMFORD — HOTEL

BUDGET HOTEL

**Premier Travel Inn – Romford West** Whalebone Lane North, Chadwell Heath, Romford RM6 6QU **t** 0870 990 6450
**w** premierinn.com

## ROMFORD — HOTEL

BUDGET HOTEL

**Travelodge Romford Central Hotel** Market Link, Romford, London RM1 1XJ
**t** 0870 191 1756
**w** travelodge.co.uk

## SURBITON — HOTEL

BUDGET HOTEL

**Travelodge Chessington Tolworth** Tolworth Tower, Ewell Road, Surbiton KT6 7EL
**t** 0870 085 0950
**w** travelodge.co.uk

## SUTTON — HOTEL

★★★
HOTEL

**Holiday Inn London Sutton** Gibson Road, London SM1 2RF **t** 0870 400 9113
**w** ichotelsgroup.com

## TWICKENHAM — HOTEL

BUDGET HOTEL

**Premier Travel Inn – Twickenham** Chertsey Road, Whitton, London TW2 6LS
**t** 0870 990 6416
**w** premierinn.com

## WEMBLEY — HOTEL

BUDGET HOTEL

**Premier Travel Inn – London Wembley** 151 Wembley Park Drive, Wembley, London HA9 8HQ **t** 0870 990 6484
**w** premierinn.com

## WENNINGTON — HOTEL

BUDGET HOTEL

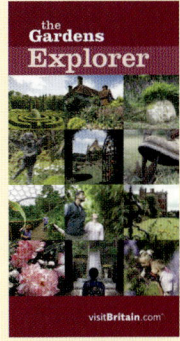

**Premier Travel Inn – Rainham** New Road, Wennington, London RM13 9ED
**t** 0870 197 7217
**w** premierinn.com

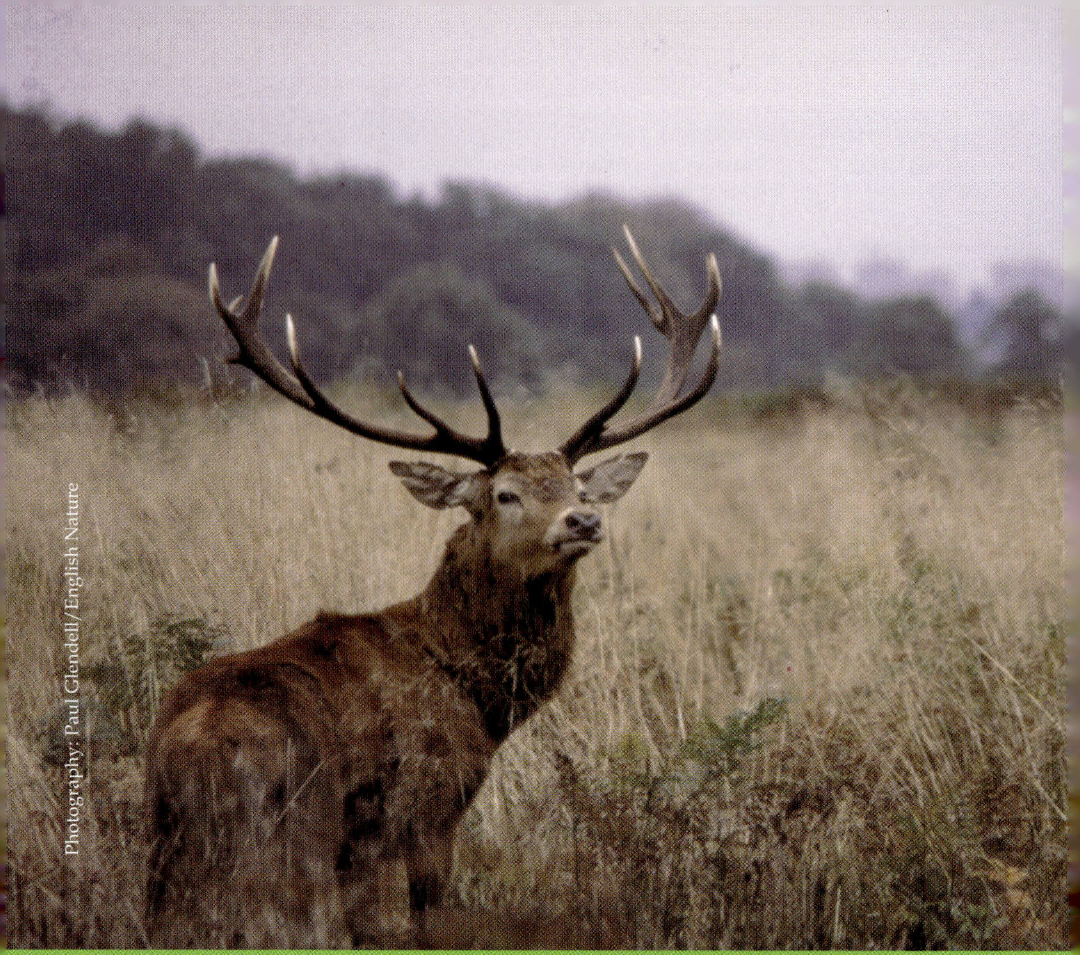
Photography: Paul Glendell/English Nature

# Get the most from your Tube

London Underground produce a range of guides and maps to help you plan your journey around London.

**Tube Access Guide**
A Tube map to help you plan journeys avoiding stairs and escalators.

**Large print Tube maps (in colour or black and white)**
Large scale Tube maps for those with impaired vision. Braille and audio Tube maps are also available.

**Getting around London - Your guide to accessibility**
An accessibility guide covering all modes of transport in London. Also available in audio and large print formats.

For copies call 020 7222 1234. To plan your journey visit tfl.gov.uk/journeyplanner or for detailed accessibility information at Tube stations visit directenquiries.com

**MAYOR OF LONDON**

**Transport for London**

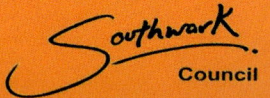

The Houses of Parliament
Summer Opening 2009
August - September
Booking line now open
Please call 0870 906 3773
for further information
Groups call 020 7014 8444
Coaches call 020 7014 8440

National Portrait Gallery
'There shall be but one mistress here and no master'
Ascribed to Elizabeth I
in response to the Earl of Leicester
www.npg.org.uk
Open daily 10.00 – 18.00
Thursdays and Fridays until 21.00
St Martin's Place, London
Leicester Square
History Art Biography Fame
Discover them for Free
Queen Elizabeth I (detail) by an unknown artist, c.1600
© National Portrait Gallery, London

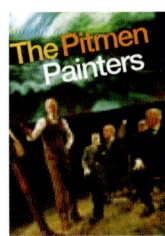

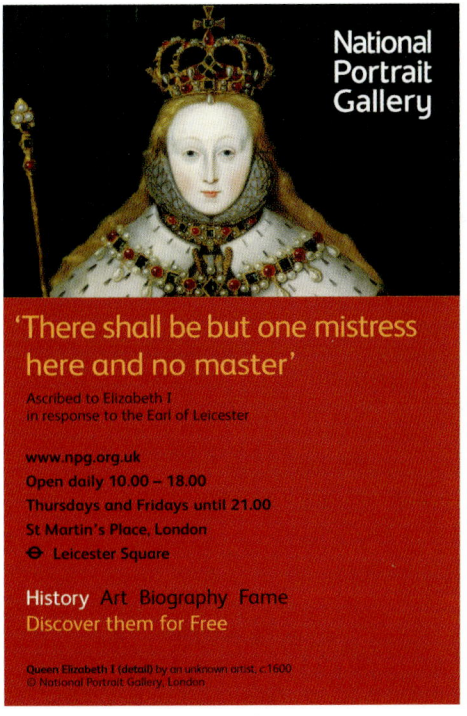

# Visit Greenwich

## – where time begins.

Maritime Greenwich World Heritage Site is a great place to take a break with many attractions nearby, including Firepower, the Royal Artillery Museum; Eltham Palace and The $O_2$ entertainment venue.

For information on attractions, events, tickets, transport and accommodation contact:
Greenwich Tourist Information Centre
46 Greenwich Church Street
London SE10 9BL
Tel: 0870 608 2000
Email: tic@greenwich.gov.uk
Web: www.greenwich.gov.uk/tourism
www.greenwichwhs.org.uk

**Our Mobility Section manages or is involved in several schemes to help elderly people and people with disabilities with mobility problems.**

**The various schemes help people who are living in the community stay independent by providing travel opportunities that may not otherwise be available to them.**

## Contact

**Mobility Services**
**90 Stour Road**
**Dagenham**
**RM10 7JD**
**www.barking-dagenham.gov.uk**

**Walk through time**

Discover 400 years of chairs, stairs, plates, grates, tables, fables, walls, stalls, jugs, rugs, flooring, storing, candles, handles, knives, lives, books, nooks, lights, sights, doors and more in the English home.

GEFFRYE MUSEUM
400 Years of English Domestic Interiors

136 Kingsland Road, London E2 8EA Telephone 020 7739 9893
ADMISSION FREE Open Tue-Sat 10-5, Sun / Bank Hols 12-5
*Tube:* Liverpool Street / Old Street. *Bus:* 149, 242, 243, 67
www.geffrye-museum.org.uk

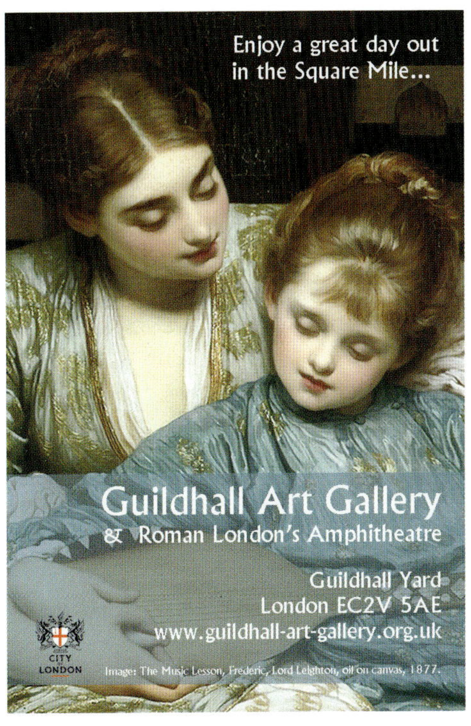
Enjoy a great day out
in the Square Mile...
Guildhall Art Gallery
& Roman London's Amphitheatre
Guildhall Yard
London EC2V 5AE
www.guildhall-art-gallery.org.uk
CITY
LONDON
Image: The Music Lesson, Frederic, Lord Leighton, oil on canvas, 1877.

HORNIMANMUSEUM

INTRODUCING
ADAPTEDCAR HIRE
Car hire for disabled drivers and passengers
Broad range of cars and adaptations
Cars with push pull hand controls
Wheelchair Accessible Vehicles (WAV)
Cars with flip down left foot accelerators
Automatic vehicles
Online and telephone booking
Door-to-door delivery and collection service
Insurance included
Reasonable rates
Unlimited mileage
Brand new vehicles
Adapted Car Hire provides a broad range of specially adapted vehicles to cater for the needs of disabled drivers and passengers.
Vehicles can be hired on a daily, weekly and monthly basis and we provide a door-to-door delivery and collection service.
We run a variety of rental schemes tailored to the needs of the individual customer, as well as regular promotional and special offers.
All vehicles supplied and adapted by Motability accredited suppliers.
Please visit our website www.adaptedcarhire.co.uk, email us at info@adaptedcarhire.co.uk or call us on 0845 68 62 007 for further information.
www.adaptedcarhire.co.uk

Tel: 020 7713 0836
LONDON CANAL MUSEUM
LONDON CANAL MUSEUM
www.canalmuseum.org.uk
A charming waterside museum near King's Cross station - and fully accessible!
Canals, the Victorian ice trade, and more. New Wharf Road N1 9RT
Open Tuesday-Sunday & BH Mons

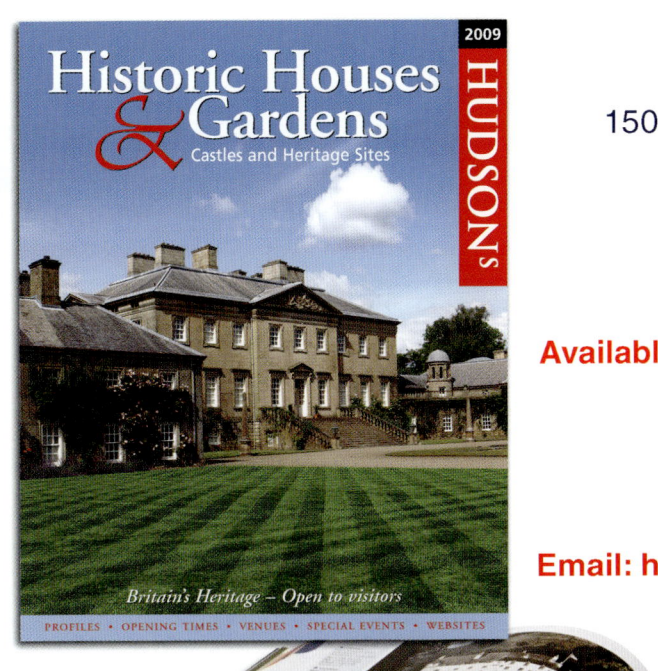

# South West England

Bristol, Cornwall, Devon, Dorset, Gloucestershire, Isles of Scilly, Somerset, Wiltshire

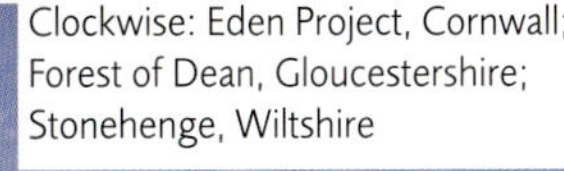

Clockwise: Eden Project, Cornwall; Forest of Dean, Gloucestershire; Stonehenge, Wiltshire

# Great days out

Indulge your love of cream teas and clotted cream fudge. Explore the South West Coast Path, Exmoor, Dartmoor and honey-coloured Cotswold villages. Wonder at the mysteries of Avebury and Stonehenge and stunning gardens across the region. There's so much to experience in South West England.

## Secret gardens

The South West boasts three of the most extraordinary gardens in Britain. Its balmy, subtropical climate is perfect for more exotic flora. Start with the remarkable **Eden Project**, near St Austell, home to thousands of plants. Wander around the enormous biomes, where nature and technology meet, or set the children off on one of the fun, interactive trails. Delight in the **Lost Gardens of Heligan** at Pentewan – an 80-acre garden neglected for more than 70 years until 1991 – or take a helicopter ride to Tresco, one of the Scilly Isles, to see more unexpected exotic plants at the **Abbey Gardens**. For more inspiration, follow the **Forest of Dean Sculpture Trail** where you can discover thought-provoking works of art nestling between the trees. Or stroll around **Westonbirt**: **The National Arboretum** in Gloucestershire and allow the colours to mesmerise you whatever the season.

## Feeling free

Find your bearings along sections of the **South West Coast Path** which stretches for 630 miles from Minehead to Poole, with dramatic views of the coastline along the way. A selection of short walks are suitable for people with limited mobility, wheelchairs or motor scooters (southwestcoastpath.com). Catch a glimpse of wild red deer or grazing ponies in the stunning **Exmoor National Park** and gaze at reflections in beautiful lake-like reservoirs on heather-clad **Dartmoor**.

Torquay, Devon

After all that fresh air, indulge in the South West's delicious specialities. A Cornish pasty tastes especially good washed down with a pint of sweet cider. Or take afternoon tea with mouthwatering scones straight from the oven, topped with indulgent clotted cream!

Left to right: Exmoor, Somerset; Westonbirt: The National Arboretum, Gloucestershire

**did you know...** there are over 240 resident and migrating bird species on Exmoor?

## Down by the sea

How's this for the perfect antidote to modern life? The South West has more Blue Flag beaches than anywhere else in England. The region's sandy bays and sheltered coves are perfect for building sandcastles and enjoying secluded picnics. If you are seeking adventure, the hip centres of **Newquay**, **Bude**, **Croyde** and **Woolacombe** are great places for watersports. Discover Devon's English Riviera – the bustling seaside towns of **Torquay**, **Paignton** and **Brixham** – and get acquainted with coastal creatures from penguins to puffins at **Living Coasts** in Torquay. Away from the beach, charming fishing villages, such as **Clovelly**, **Port Isaac** and **Beer**, are the perfect setting for a relaxing lunch.

Looking for something different? Take a fossil hammer for an ammonite hunt on the **Jurassic Coast**, a World Heritage Site, where you can see 185 million years of earth history along 95 miles of spectacular coastline.

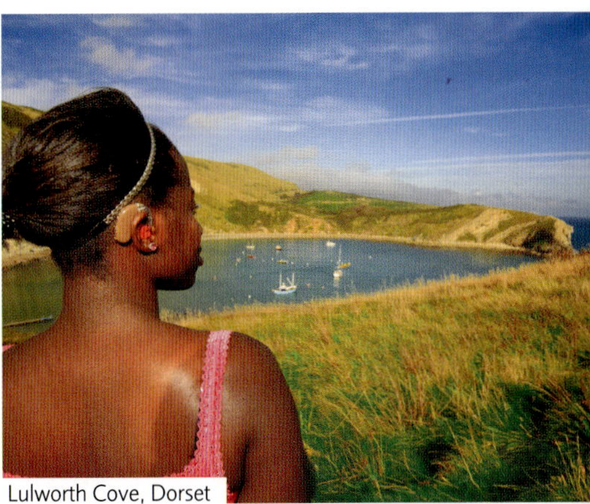

Lulworth Cove, Dorset

## Out and about

If you're looking for a great day out, try these for starters! Uncover the history of the railway at Swindon's interactive attraction **Steam – Museum of the Great Western Railway** and meet colourful butterflies, snakes and exotic insects at **Studley Grange**.

See how many animals the kids can spot at **Longleat's** famous Safari Park and enjoy a close encounter with friendly mute swans and their fluffy cygnets at **Abbotsbury Swannery**. Relive the seafaring history of the South West at the **National Maritime Museum Cornwall** in Falmouth, or catch a performance at the stunning cliffside setting of the **Minack Theatre** at Porthcurno. Ponder the mysteries of the ancient stone circles of **Stonehenge** and **Avebury** or try to spot Gwyn ap Nudd, King of the Fairies, at **Glastonbury Tor** (not wheelchair accessible). Take a tour around the honey-coloured limestone villages of the **Cotswolds**, exploring the beautiful towns of **Cheltenham** and **Cirencester**, and the lovely villages of **Bourton-on-the-Water** and **Castle Combe** on the way. Saddle up on Exmoor, Dartmoor or **Bodmin** (disabled riding is available), or soar skywards in a hot-air balloon (not suitable for wheelchair users).

**why not...** look for the Fossil Forest revealed at low tide near Little Bindon, Dorset?

Clockwise: Salisbury Cathedral, Wiltshire; Castle Combe, Wiltshire; Abbotsbury Swannery, Dorset

## City splendours

The buzzing cities of **Bristol** and **Bath** are filled with attractions. Revel in the Georgian beauty of Bath; tour round the best-preserved Roman religious spa from the ancient world, lying under the watchful gaze of **Bath Abbey**; or sink into the natural thermal waters of the newly opened **Thermae Bath Spa**. Sample Bristol's infectious vitality and head for the rejuvenated harbour front to discover vibrant bars and restaurants. Take an interactive adventure of a lifetime at magical **At-Bristol** – a unique destination bringing science, nature and art to life. Check out the feat of engineering that is the **Clifton Suspension Bridge**, the brainchild of Isambard Kingdom Brunel, and then continue your journey with a trip to some of the West's other great cathedral cities. Discover **Exeter**, **Wells** and **Gloucester** and marvel at **Salisbury Cathedral** with the tallest spire in Britain.

Above: ss Great Britain, Bristol
Below: Thermae Bath Spa, Bath

# Useful regional contacts

### South West Tourism
**t** 0870 442 0880
**w** visitsouthwest.co.uk

## Publications

### Access Salisbury
Available free from Salisbury Tourist Information Centre and Salisbury Shopmobility.
Call (01722) 328068.

### Easy Going Dartmoor and Access Guide to Dartmoor Towns and Villages
Available from the Dartmoor National Park Authority. Call (01822) 890414 or visit dartmoor-npa.gov.uk.

### The English Riviera: Access for All
An information leaflet on Torbay, Paignton and Brixham. Available from Tourist Information Centres and the English Riviera Tourist Board on (01803) 211211.

### South Somerset: A Guide for People with Disabilities
Available from South Somerset District Council. Call (01935) 845946 or visit visitsouthsomerset.com.

### West Dorset for Visitors with Additional Needs
Available from West Dorset District Council Tourist Information Centres. Email tourism@westdorset-dc.gov.uk.

## Information

### Accessible South West
**w** accessiblesouthwest.co.uk
A directory designed to assist visitors with disabilities travelling to the South West of England find suitable places to stay and visit.

### Forest of Dean Tourist Information
**w** visitforestofdean.co.uk
Has information for visitors with disabilities.

### South West Coastal Path
**w** southwestcoastpath.com
A national trail website with details of walks for everyone. Includes pictures so that you can assess whether a walk is right for you.

### Visit Kennet
**w** visitkennet.co.uk
Includes an online guide to assist and enable disabled visitors to enjoy Kennet and its attractions.

### Visit Somerset
**w** visitsomerset.co.uk
Contains information for disabled people, including where to find accessible toilets and accommodation.

# Tourist Information Centres

Official Partner Tourist Information Centres offer quality assured help with accommodation and information about local attractions and events. To search for attractions and Tourist Information Centres on the move just text INFO to 62233, and a web link will be sent to your mobile phone. To find a Tourist Information Centre by region visit enjoyEngland.com/find-tic.

| | | | |
|---|---|---|---|
| **Avebury** | Green Street | (01672) 539425 | all.tic's@kennet.gov.uk |
| **Bath** | Abbey Church Yard | 0906 711 2000** | tourism@bathtourism.co.uk |
| **Bodmin** | Mount Folly Square | (01208) 76616 | bodmintic@visit.org.uk |
| **Bourton-on-the-Water** | Victoria Street | (01451) 820211 | bourtonvic@btconnect.com |
| **Bridport** | 47 South Street | (01308) 424901 | bridport.tic@westdorset-dc.gov.uk |
| **Bristol** | Harbourside | 0906 711 2191** | ticharbourside@destinationbristol.co.uk |
| **Brixham** | The Quay | (01803) 211 211 | holiday@torbay.gov.uk |
| **Bude** | The Crescent | (01288) 354240 | budetic@visitbude.info |
| **Burnham-on-Sea** | South Esplanade | (01278) 787852 | burnham.tic@sedgemoor.gov.uk |
| **Camelford*** | The Clease | (01840) 212954 | manager@camelfordtic.eclipse.co.uk |
| **Cartgate** | A303/A3088 Cartgate Picnic Site | (01935) 829333 | cartgate.tic@southsomerset.gov.uk |
| **Cheddar** | The Gorge | (01934) 744071 | cheddar.tic@sedgemoor.gov.uk |
| **Chippenham** | Market Place | (01249) 665970 | tourism@chippenham.gov.uk |
| **Chipping Campden** | High Street | (01386) 841206 | information@visitchippingcampden.com |
| **Christchurch** | 49 High Street | (01202) 471780 | enquiries@christchurchtourism.info |
| **Cirencester** | Market Place | (01285) 654180 | cirencestervic@cotswold.gov.uk |
| **Coleford** | High Street | (01594) 812388 | tourism@fdean.gov.uk |
| **Corsham** | 31 High Street | (01249) 714660 | enquiries@corshamheritage.org.uk |
| **Devizes** | Market Place | (01380) 729408 | all.tic's@kennet.gov.uk |
| **Dorchester** | 11 Antelope Walk | (01305) 267992 | dorchester.tic@westdorset-dc.gov.uk |
| **Falmouth** | Prince of Wales Pier | (01326) 312300 | info@falmouthtic.co.uk |
| **Frome** | Justice Lane | (01373) 467271 | frome.tic@ukonline.co.uk |
| **Glastonbury** | 9 High Street | (01458) 832954 | glastonbury.tic@ukonline.co.uk |
| **Gloucester** | 28 Southgate Street | (01452) 396572 | tourism@gloucester.gov.uk |
| **Looe*** | Fore Street | (01503) 262072 | looetic@btconnect.com |
| **Lyme Regis** | Church Street | (01297) 442138 | lymeregis.tic@westdorset-dc.gov.uk |
| **Malmesbury** | Market Lane | (01666) 823748 | malmesburyip@northwilts.gov.uk |
| **Moreton-in-Marsh** | High Street | (01608) 650881 | moreton@cotswold.gov.uk |
| **Padstow** | North Quay | (01841) 533449 | padstowtic@btconnect.com |
| **Paignton** | The Esplanade | (01803) 211 211 | holiday@torbay.gov.uk |
| **Penzance** | Station Road | (01736) 362207 | pztic@penwith.gov.uk |

| | | | |
|---|---|---|---|
| **Plymouth Mayflower** | 3-5 The Barbican | (01752) 306330 | barbicantic@plymouth.gov.uk |
| **St Ives** | The Guildhall | (01736) 796297 | ivtic@penwith.gov.uk |
| **Salisbury** | Fish Row | (01722) 334956 | visitorinfo@salisbury.gov.uk |
| **Shelton Mallet** | 70 High Street | (01749) 345258 | sheptonmallet.tic@ukonline.co.uk |
| **Sherborne** | 3 Tilton Court, Digby Road | (01935) 815341 | sherborne.tic@westdorset-dc.gov.uk |
| **Somerset** | Sedgemoor Services | (01934) 750833 | somersetvisitorcentre@somerset.gov.uk |
| **Stow-on-the-Wold** | The Square | (01451) 831082 | stowvic@cotswold.gov.uk |
| **Street** | Farm Road | (01458) 447384 | street.tic@ukonline.co.uk |
| **Stroud** | George Street | (01453) 760960 | tic@stroud.gov.uk |
| **Swanage** | Shore Road | (01929) 422885 | mail@swanage.gov.uk |
| **Swindon** | 37 Regent Street | (01793) 530328 | infocentre@swindon.gov.uk |
| **Taunton** | Paul Street | (01823) 336344 | tauntontic@tauntondeane.gov.uk |
| **Tewkesbury** | 100 Church Street | (01684) 855043 | tewkesburytic@tewkesburybc.gov.uk |
| **Torquay** | Vaughan Parade | (01803) 211 211 | holiday@torbay.gov.uk |
| **Truro** | Boscawen Street | (01872) 274555 | tic@truro.gov.uk |
| **Wadebridge** | Eddystone Road | 0870 1223337 | wadebridgetic@btconnect.com |
| **Wareham** | South Street | (01929) 552740 | tic@purbeck-dc.gov.uk |
| **Warminster** | off Station Rd | (01985) 218548 | visitwarminster@btconnect.com |
| **Wells** | Market Place | (01749) 672552 | touristinfo@wells.gov.uk |
| **Weston-super-Mare** | Beach Lawns | (01934) 888800 | westontouristinfo@n-somerset.gov.uk |
| **Weymouth** | The Esplanade | (01305) 785747 | tic@weymouth.gov.uk |
| **Winchcombe** | High Street | (01242) 602925 | winchcombetic@tewkesbury.gov.uk |
| **Yeovil** | Hendford | (01935) 845946/7 | yeoviltic@southsomerset.gov.uk |

*seasonal opening

**calls to this number are charged at premium rate

Left to right: The Bishop's Palace & Gardens, Somerset; Minack Theatre, Cornwall

where to stay in

# South West England

The following establishments participate in VisitBritain's Enjoy England quality assessment scheme and hold a National Accessible Scheme rating. YHA youth hostels in England and Wales are listed in a separate section, see page 40.

Place names in the blue bands with a map reference are shown on the maps at the front of this guide.

## Accommodation symbols

Symbols give useful information about services and facilities. You can find a key to these symbols on page 8.

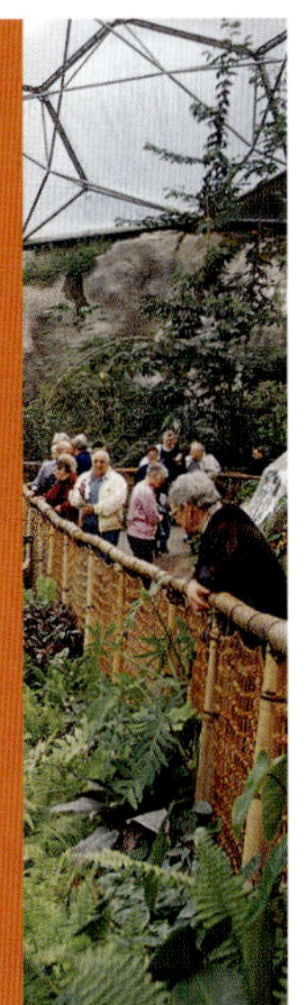

### ABBOTSBURY, Dorset — SELF CATERING

★★★★ SELF CATERING

**Gorwell Farm Cottages** **contact** Mrs Mary Pengelly, Gorwell Farm Cottages, Gorwell, Abbotsbury, Weymouth DT3 4JX **t** (01305) 871401
**e** mary@gorwellfarm.co.uk **w** gorwellfarm.co.uk

### ALBASTON, Cornwall — SELF CATERING

★★★★ SELF CATERING

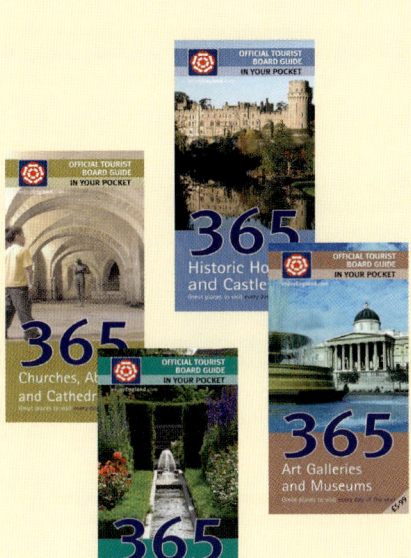

**Todsworthy Farm Holidays** **contact** Mr Pellow, Todsworthy Farm Holidays, Albaston, Gunnislake PL18 9AW
**t** (01822) 834744
**w** todsworthyfarmholidays.co.uk

## ALTON PANCRAS, Dorset Map ref 2B3 — SELF CATERING

★★★★–★★★★★
SELF CATERING

Units **4**
Sleeps **4–10**
Low season per wk
£335.00–£560.00
High season per wk
£655.00–£1,195.00

### Bookham Court, Dorchester

**contact** Mr & Mrs Andrew Foot, Whiteways, Bookham, Alton Pancras, Dorchester DT2 7RP **t** (01300) 345511
**e** andy.foot1@btinternet.com **w** bookhamcourt.co.uk

Access

General

Unit

Payment Cash, cheques

*Ground-floor bedrooms and games room. View amazing wildlife from your cottage or from our hide.*

Bookham Court lies in an Area of Outstanding Natural Beauty, on the edge of the South Wessex Downs. These handsomely converted cottages sleep 4-10 and are equipped to a high standard. Great Coombe and Crowthorne have wooden floors and ground-floor twin bedrooms with flush-to-floor shower rooms (M2).

**open** All Year
**nearest shop** 1 mile
**nearest pub** 1 mile

*Bookham Court is signposted off the B3143, between Alton Pancras and Buckland Newton, 9 miles north of Dorchester.*

## ALVERTON, Cornwall — HOSTEL

★★
HOSTEL

**Penzance Youth Hostel** Castle Horneck, Alverton, Penzance TR18 4LP
**t** (01736) 362666
**e** penzance@yha.co.uk

## ASHBURTON, Devon — SELF CATERING

★★★★
SELF CATERING

**Wren & Robin Cottages contact** Mrs Margaret Phipps, Wren & Robin Cottages, New Cott Farm, Poundsgate, Ashburton TQ13 7PD **t** (01364) 631421
**e** enquiries@newcott-farm.co.uk **w** newcott-farm.co.uk

## ASHWATER, Devon — SELF CATERING

★★★★–★★★★★
SELF CATERING

**Blagdon Farm Country Holidays contact** Mr & Mrs Clark, Blagdon Farm Country Holidays, Ashwater, Beaworthy EX21 5DF **t** (01409) 211509
**e** info@blagdon-farm.co.uk **w** blagdon-farm.co.uk

## AWRE, Gloucestershire — SELF CATERING

★★★★
SELF CATERING

**The Priory Cottages contact** Ian Cowan, The Priory Cottages, Awre, Newham GL14 1EQ
**t** 07919 407128
**e** rigc@onetel.com

**BARNSTAPLE,** Devon — **SELF CATERING**

SELF CATERING

**Country Ways contact** Mrs Kate Price, Country Ways, Little Knowle Farm, High Bickington, Umberleigh EX37 9BJ **t** (01769) 560503
**e** kate@country-ways.net **w** country-ways.net

**BATH,** Somerset Map ref 2B2 — **GUEST ACCOMMODATION**

GUEST ACCOMMODATION

B&B per room per night
**s £71.00–£81.00**
**d £99.00–£150.00**
Evening meal per person
**£8.50–£16.50**

## The Carfax

13-15 Great Pulteney Street, Bath BA2 4BS **t** (01225) 462089
**e** reservations@carfaxhotel.co.uk **w** carfaxhotel.co.uk

A trio of Georgian townhouses in the centre of Bath. Lifts to all floors, private car park and garages, wheelchair access to public rooms and affordable prices.

**open** All year
**bedrooms** 13 double, 7 twin, 6 single, 4 family, 1 suite
**bathrooms** All en suite

*From M4 jct 18, A4 to London Road. At city traffic lights over Cleveland Bridge, sharp right at Holburne Museum.*

Access abc

Rooms

General

Payment Credit/debit cards, cash, cheques

**BATH,** Somerset — **SELF CATERING**

★★★★

SELF CATERING

**Church Farm Country Cottages contact** Mrs Trish Bowles, Church Farm, Winsley, Bradford-on-Avon BA15 2JH **t** (01225) 722246
**e** stay@churchfarmcottages.com **w** churchfarmcottages.com

**BATH,** Somerset — **SELF CATERING**

SELF CATERING

**Greyfield Farm Cottages contact** Mrs June Merry, Greyfield Farm Cottages, Greyfield Road, High Littleton, Bristol BS39 6YQ **t** (01761) 471132
**e** june@greyfieldfarm.com **w** greyfieldfarm.com

**BEAMINSTER,** Dorset — **SELF CATERING**

★★★★

SELF CATERING

**Lewesdon Farm Holidays contact** Mr & Mrs Michael & Linda Smith, Lewesdon Farm Holidays, Lewesdon Farm, Stoke Abbott, Beaminster DT8 3JZ
**t** (01308) 868270
**e** lewesdonfarmholiday@tinyonline.co.uk **w** lewesdonfarmholidays.co.uk

## Has every property been assessed?

All accommodation in this guide has been rated for quality, or is awaiting assessment, by a professional national tourist board assessor.

## BEAMINSTER, Dorset Map ref 2A3 — SELF CATERING

SELF CATERING

Units **1**
Sleeps **2–3**
Low season per wk
Min £200.00
High season per wk
Max £400.00

### Stable Cottage, Beaminster

**contact** Mrs Diana Clarke, Stable Cottage, Meerhay Manor, Beaminster DT8 3SB **t** (01308) 862305 **e** meerhay@aol.com **w** meerhay.co.uk

Ground-floor conversion of old barn in grounds of old manor. Wheelchair accessible. Idyllic setting in 40 acres of farmland. Plantsman's garden, tennis court, stabling. Seven miles coast.

**open** All year
**nearest shop** 1 mile
**nearest pub** 1 mile

General
Leisure
Unit
Payment Cash, cheques

## BEESON, Devon — SELF CATERING

★★★★
SELF CATERING

**Beeson Farm Holiday Cottages contact** Mr & Mrs Robin & Veronica Cross, Beeson Farm Holiday Cottages, Beeson Farm, Beeson, Kingsbridge TQ7 2HW
**t** (01548) 581270
**e** info@beesonhols.co.uk **w** beesonhols.co.uk

## BEETHAM, Somerset — CAMPING, CARAVAN & HOLIDAY PARK

★★★★
TOURING PARK

**Five Acres Caravan Club Site** Giants Grave Road, Chard TA20 3QA
**t** (01460) 234519
**e** enquiries@caravanclub.co.uk **w** caravanclub.co.uk

## BIDEFORD, Devon — SELF CATERING

★★★★
SELF CATERING

**West Hele contact** Mrs Lorna Hicks, West Hele, Buckland Brewer, Bideford EX39 5LZ **t** (01237) 451044
**e** lorna.hicks@virgin.net **w** westhele.co.uk

## BLANDFORD FORUM, Dorset — SELF CATERING

★★★★★
SELF CATERING

**Houghton Lodge contact** Mrs Clarice Fiander-Norman, Houghton Lodge, Winterborne Houghton, Blandford Forum DT11 0PE **t** (01258) 882170
**e** enquiries@houghtonlodge.com **w** houghtonlodge.com

## BODMIN, Cornwall — HOTEL

★★★
HOTEL

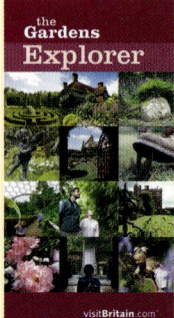

**Lanhydrock Hotel and Golf Club** Lostwithiel Road, Bodmin PL30 5AQ
**t** (01208) 262570
**e** info@lanhydrockhotel.com **w** lanhydrockhotel.com

## BOSCASTLE, Cornwall Map ref 1B2 — GUEST ACCOMMODATION

GUEST ACCOMMODATION

B&B per room per night
**s £40.00–£50.00**
**d £56.00–£60.00**

### The Old Coach House

Tintagel Road, Boscastle PL35 0AS **t** (01840) 250398
**e** jackiefarm@btinternet.com **w** old-coach.co.uk

Stay in our beautifully situated 300-year-old coach house. Breakfast served in large conservatory overlooking gardens, patio area and coastline. Tastefully furnished en suite rooms available on ground floor.

**open** All year except Christmas
**bedrooms** 4 double, 2 twin, 2 family
**bathrooms** All en suite

Access
Rooms
General
Payment Credit/debit cards, cash, cheques

## BOSCASTLE, Cornwall — GUEST ACCOMMODATION

★★★★★
GUEST ACCOMMODATION
SILVER AWARD

**Reddivallen Farm** Trevalga, Boscastle PL35 0EE
**t** (01840) 250854
**e** liz@redboscastle.com
**w** redboscastle.com

## BRATTON, Somerset Map ref 1D1 — SELF CATERING

★★★★
SELF CATERING

Units **8**
Sleeps **2–11**
Low season per wk
**Min £170.00**
High season per wk
**Max £1,250.00**

### Woodcombe Lodges, Minehead

**contact** Mrs Nicola Hanson, Woodcombe Lodges, Bratton Lane, Minehead TA24 8SQ **t** (01643) 702789 & 07860 667325
**e** nicola@woodcombelodge.co.uk **w** woodcombelodge.co.uk

Cherry Lodge and Holly Lodge are both wheelchair accessible, with Cherry Lodge being M1 and Holly Lodge M2. Holly Lodge has the additional benefit of a wheel-in shower with seat. Both lodges are very comfortable with wonderful views.

**open** All year
**nearest shop** 1 mile
**nearest pub** 1 mile

General
Unit

Payment Credit/debit cards, cash, cheques

## BRIDGWATER, Somerset — GUEST ACCOMMODATION

★★★★
FARMHOUSE
SILVER AWARD

**Apple View** Temple Farm, Chedzoy TA7 8QR
**t** (01278) 423201
**e** temple_farm@hotmail.com
**w** apple-view.co.uk

## BRIDGWATER, Somerset — SELF CATERING

★★★★
SELF CATERING

**Ash-Wembdon Farm Cottages** **contact** Mr Clarence Rowe, Ash-Wembdon Farm Cottages, Ash-Wembdon Farm, Hollow Lane, Bridgwater TA5 2BD
**t** (01278) 453097
**e** c.a.rowe@btinternet.com **w** ukcottageholiday.com

At-a-glance symbols are explained on page 8. 

**BRISTOL,** City of Bristol — **CAMPING, CARAVAN & HOLIDAY PARK**

★★★★
TOURING PARK

**Baltic Wharf Caravan Club Site** Cumberland Road, Southville BS1 6XG
**t** (0117) 926 8030
**e** enquiries@caravanclub.co.uk **w** caravanclub.co.uk

**BRIXHAM,** Devon Map ref 1D2 — **CAMPING, CARAVAN & HOLIDAY PARK**

★★★★★
TOURING & CAMPING PARK

(239) £14.90–£35.00
(239) £14.90–£35.00
239 touring pitches

# Hillhead Caravan Club Site

Hillhead, Brixham TQ5 0HH **t** (01803) 853204
**w** caravanclub.co.uk

Set in 22 acres of Devon countryside this site offers some of the finest facilities on the network. In a great location with many pitches affording stunning views of the sea. There's plenty of entertainment, including an outdoor heated swimming pool, games room, play area, bar and restaurant.

**open** March 2009 to January 2010

*Right off A380 (Newton Abbot). Three miles onto ring road (Brixham). Seven miles turn right, A3022. In 0.75 miles, right onto A379. Two miles keep left onto B3025. Site entrance on left.*

General

Leisure

Payment Credit/debit cards, cash, cheques

**BROADCLYST,** Devon — **SELF CATERING**

★★★★
SELF CATERING

**Hue's Piece contact** Mrs Anna Hamlyn, Hue's Piece, Paynes Farm, Broadclyst, Exeter EX5 3BJ
**t** (01392) 466720
**e** annahamlyn@paynes-farm.co.uk **w** paynes-farm.co.uk

**BUDE,** Cornwall — **SELF CATERING**

★★★★–★★★★★
SELF CATERING

**Forda Lodges & Cottages contact** Mr & Mrs Jim & Gillian Chibbett, Forda Lodges & Cottages, Kilkhampton, Bude EX23 9RZ
**t** (01288) 321413
**e** info@forda.co.uk **w** forda.co.uk

## CALLINGTON, Cornwall Map ref 1C2

SELF CATERING

★★★★
SELF CATERING

Units 2
Sleeps 2–4
Low season per wk
£240.00–£320.00
High season per wk
£330.00–£660.00

### Berrio Mill Farm Holiday Cottages, Callington

**contact** Ivan & Carolyn Callanan, Berrio Mill Farm Holiday Cottages, Golberdon, Callington PL17 7NL **t** (01579) 363252
**e** enquiries@berriomill.co.uk **w** berriomill.co.uk

These cottages are a conversion of an old stone-built shippen in the grounds of Berrio Mill, which nestles in the peace and tranquillity of the undiscovered Lynher Valley. Approached via a quiet country lane, these cottages have been created for those who really want to escape from it all.

**open** All year
**nearest shop** 2 miles
**nearest pub** 3 miles

*A30 to Launceston, then A388 towards Callington. After 8 miles turn right towards Golberdon. Drive through Golberdon, at bottom of hill turn right to Berrio Mill.*

General P

Unit

Payment Credit/debit cards, cash, cheques

*Trout and salmon fishing available in season. Guests must provide their own fishing tackle and permits.*

## CANNINGTON, Somerset

GUEST ACCOMMODATION

★★★★
FARMHOUSE

**Blackmore Farm** Blackmore Lane, Bridgwater TA5 2NE
**t** (01278) 653442
**e** dyerfarm@aol.com **w** dyerfarm.co.uk

## CASTLE CARY, Somerset

SELF CATERING

★★★★
SELF CATERING

**Clanville Manor Tallet and Lone Oak Cottage contact** Mrs Snook, Clanville Manor Tallet and Lone Oak Cottage, Clanville Manor, Clanville BA7 7PJ
**t** (01963) 350124
**e** info@clanvillemanor.co.uk **w** clanvillemanor.co.uk

## CHAPEL AMBLE, Cornwall

SELF CATERING

★★★–★★★★
SELF CATERING

**The Olde House contact** Mr A Hawkey, The Olde House,Chapel Amble, The Olde House, Chapel Amble, Wadebridge PL27 6EN **t** (01208) 813219
**e** info@theoldehouse.co.uk **w** theoldehouse.co.uk

## CHARMOUTH, Dorset

SELF CATERING

★★★
SELF CATERING

**The Poplars contact** Mrs Jane Bremner, Wood Farm Caravan Park, Axminster Road, Bridport DT6 6BT **t** (01297) 560697
**e** holiday@woodfarm.co.uk **w** woodfarm.co.uk

## CHELTENHAM, Gloucestershire

GUEST ACCOMMODATION

★★★★
GUEST ACCOMMODATION

**Prestbury House** The Burgage, Prestbury, Cheltenham GL52 3DN
**t** (01242) 529533
**e** enquiries@prestburyhouse.co.uk **w** prestburyhouse.co.uk

At-a-glance symbols are explained on page 8.

**COLYTON,** Devon — GUEST ACCOMMODATION

**Smallicombe Farm** Northleigh, Colyton EX24 6BU
**t** (01404) 831310
**e** maggie_todd@yahoo.com
**w** smallicombe.com

**COLYTON,** Devon — SELF CATERING

**Smallicombe Farm contact** Mrs Maggie Todd, Smallicombe Farm, Northleigh, Colyton EX24 6BU **t** (01404) 831310
**e** maggie_todd@yahoo.com **w** smallicombe.com

**CORFE CASTLE,** Dorset Map ref 2B3 — HOTEL

B&B per room per night
**s £75.00–£140.00**
**d £149.00–£169.00**
HB per person per night
**£88.00–£112.00**

## Mortons House Hotel

East Street, Corfe Castle, Wareham BH20 5EE **t** (01929) 480988
**e** stay@mortonshouse.co.uk **w** mortonshouse.co.uk

Access

Rooms

General

Payment Credit/debit cards, cash, cheques

*Four specially adapted rooms. 25% discount during January and February (Sun-Thu), excludes school holidays.*

16thC Elizabethan manor in the beautiful Purbeck village of Corfe Castle. Two AA Rosettes for Fine Dining. The 'Dacombe' rooms are set in secluded gardens and equipped with high quality walk-in showers, and adjustable washbasins. The hotel was awarded 'Small Hotel of the Year 2005' and 'Silver Award for Accessible Accommodation 2007' by South West Tourism.

**open** All year
**bedrooms** 13 double, 5 twin, 1 family, 2 suites
**bathrooms** All en suite

*On the A351 between Wareham and Swanage.*

**CREDITON,** Devon — SELF CATERING

★★★★ SELF CATERING

**Creedy Manor contact** Mrs Sandra Turner, Creedy Manor, Long Barn Farm, Crediton EX17 4AB **t** (01363) 772684
**e** sandra@creedymanor.com **w** creedymanor.com

**DEERHURST,** Gloucestershire — SELF CATERING

**Deerhurst Cottages contact** Mrs Nicole Samuel, Deerhurst Cottages, Abbots Court Farm, Deerhurst, Tewkesbury GL19 4BX **t** (01684) 275845
**e** enquiries@deerhurstcottages.co.uk **w** deerhurstcottages.co.uk

**DULVERTON,** Somerset — **CAMPING, CARAVAN & HOLIDAY PARK**

★★★★
TOURING PARK

**Exmoor House Caravan Club Site** Dulverton TA22 9HL
**t** (01398) 323268
**w** caravanclub.co.uk

**EXFORD,** Somerset — **SELF CATERING**

★★★
SELF CATERING

**Westermill Farm contact** Mr Oliver Edwards, Westermill Farm, Porlock Road, Exford TA24 7NJ
**t** (01643) 831238
**e** swt@westermill.com **w** westermill.com

**FIFEHEAD MAGDALEN,** Dorset — **SELF CATERING**

★★★
SELF CATERING

**Top Stall contact** Mrs Kathleen Jeanes, Top Stall, Factory Farm, Fifehead Magdalen, Gillingham SP8 5RS **t** (01258) 820022
**e** kath@topstallcottage.co.uk **w** topstallcottage.co.uk

**GOLANT,** Cornwall — **SELF CATERING**

★★★★–★★★★★
SELF CATERING

**Penquite Farm Holidays contact** Mrs Ruth Varco, Penquite Farm Holidays, Penquite Farm, Golant, Fowey PL23 1LB **t** (01726) 833319
**e** ruth@penquitefarm.co.uk **w** penquitefarm.co.uk

**GOLANT,** Cornwall — **SELF CATERING**

★★★★
SELF CATERING

**South Torfrey Farm contact** Mr & Mrs Andrews, South Torfrey Farm, Golant, Fowey PL23 1LA **t** (01726) 833126
**e** debbie.andrews@southtorfreyfarm.com **w** southtorfreyfarm.com

**HAMWORTHY,** Dorset

*See entry on p281*

**HELSTON,** Cornwall — **SELF CATERING**

★★★★
SELF CATERING

**Tregoose Farmhouse contact** Mrs Hazel Bergin, Tregoose Farmhouse, Southern Cross, Boundervean Lane, Camborne TR14 0QB **t** (01209) 714314
**e** hazel.bergin@dsl.pipex.com **w** tregooselet.co.uk

**HORSINGTON,** Somerset — **GUEST ACCOMMODATION**

★★★
INN

**Half Moon Inn** Off Higher Road, Templecombe BA8 0EF
**t** (01963) 370140
**e** halfmoon@horsington.co.uk **w** horsington.co.uk

**ISLES OF SCILLY** — **GUEST ACCOMMODATION**

★★★
GUEST HOUSE

**Isles of Scilly Country Guest House** Sage House, High Lanes TR21 0NW
**t** (01720) 422440
**e** scillyguesthouse@hotmail.co.uk **w** scillyguesthouse.co.uk

## Using map references

The map references refer to the colour maps at the front of this guide. The first figure is the map number, the letter and figure that follow indicate the grid reference on the map.

**LANGTON HERRING,** Dorset Map ref 2A3 **SELF CATERING**

★★★★
SELF CATERING

Units **7**
Sleeps **2–9**
Low season per wk
£225.00–£550.00
High season per wk
£380.00–£1,000.00

## Character Farm Cottages, Weymouth

**contact** Mrs Ann Mayo, Character Farm Cottages, Higher Farm, Rodden DT3 4JE **t** (01305) 871347 **e** jane@characterfarmcottages.co.uk
**w** characterfarmcottages.co.uk

Nestling on the World Heritage Jurassic Coast between picturesque Abbotsbury and Weymouth, our personally-run, quality character cottages are suitable for the less mobile. 'Chestnuts' is suitable for wheelchair access, and three cottages have ground-floor bedrooms and showers/bathrooms.

**open** All year
**nearest shop** 2 miles
**nearest pub** 1 mile

Access
General P
Leisure
Unit
Payment Cash, cheques

**LONG BREDY,** Dorset **SELF CATERING**

★★★★
SELF CATERING

**Whatcombe Stables contact** Ms Margarette Stuart-Brown, Whatcombe Stables, Long Bredy, Dorchester DT2 9HN
**t** (01305) 789000

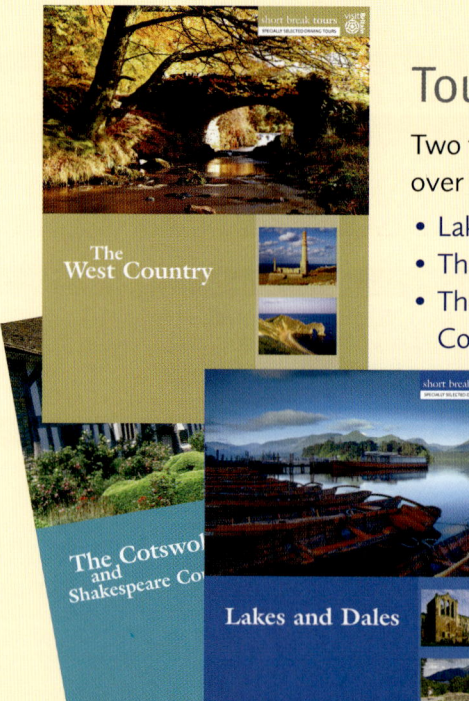

**LOOE,** Cornwall Map ref 1C2 — SELF CATERING

SELF CATERING

Units **3**
Sleeps **4–5**

Low season per wk
£200.00–£400.00
High season per wk
£400.00–£680.00

## Bocaddon Holiday Cottages, Looe

**contact** Mrs Alison Maiklem, Bocaddon Holiday Cottages, Bocaddon Farm, Lanreath PL13 2PG **t** (01503) 220192
**e** holidays@bocaddon.com **w** bocaddon.com

General

Leisure

Unit

Payment Credit/debit cards, cash, cheques

*All cottages have close parking, level entry, wide doors. Bathrooms have level-entry showers with hoist available over bath and shower.*

Unwind, relax and enjoy our tastefully converted barns, nestling peacefully in beautiful countryside. Bocaddon is a 350-acre working farm close to clean beaches, fishing harbours and smugglers' coves! Also close to fabulous gardens and historic houses. All cottages are very wheelchair friendly.

**open** All Year
**nearest shop** 2 miles
**nearest pub** 2 miles

*From A38, take A390 (East Taphouse). Left onto B3359. After 4 miles, right (Shillamill Lakes). We are 0.25 miles on left-hand side.*

**LOOE,** Cornwall — SELF CATERING

SELF CATERING

**Bucklawren Farm contact** Jean Henly, Bucklawren Farm, St Martin, Looe PL13 1NZ
**t** (01503) 240738
**e** bucklawren@btopenworld.com **w** bucklawren.com

**LOOE,** Cornwall — SELF CATERING

★★★★

SELF CATERING

**Tudor Lodges contact** Mr & Mrs Tudor, Tudor Lodges, Northwood, St Neot PL14 6QN **t** (01579) 320344
**e** mollytudor@aol.com **w** tudorlodges.co.uk

## What do the star ratings mean?

For a detailed explanation of the quality and facilities represented by the stars, please refer to the information pages at the back of this guide.

**LOSTWITHIEL,** Cornwall Map ref 1B2 **SELF CATERING**

★★★★★
SELF CATERING

Units 1
Sleeps 8
Low season per wk
Min £850.00
High season per wk
Max £2,195.00

## Brean Park, Lostwithiel

**contact** Mrs Janet Hoskin, Brean Park, Brean Park Farm, Lostwithiel PL22 0LP **t** (01208) 872184
**e** breanpark@btconnect.com **w** breanpark.co.uk

General

Unit

Payment Cash, cheques

*Single-storey property, two en suite wetrooms.*

The perfect choice for those seeking quality and luxury in a rural idyll. Our luxurious mobility-assisted property is situated in a picturesque valley with breathtaking views of the Lanhydrock estate and parkland within easy reach of Eden. Spaciously accommodates eight plus cot. Four en suite bedrooms.

**open** All year

*From A30 Bodmin exit, 3rd left, T-junction turn left, roundabout 1st exit, next roundabout 3rd exit towards Lostwithiel, 1st left towards Respryn. After bridge 0.75 miles on left.*

**LOSTWITHIEL,** Cornwall **SELF CATERING**

★★★★
SELF CATERING

**Chark Country Holidays contact** Mrs Jenny Littleton, Chark Country Holidays, Redmoor, Bodmin PL30 5AR **t** (01208) 871118
**e** charkholidays@tiscali.co.uk **w** charkcountryholidays.co.uk

**LOSTWITHIEL,** Cornwall **SELF CATERING**

★★★★
SELF CATERING

**Hartswheal Barn**
**t** (01208) 873419
**w** connexions.co.uk/hartswheal/index.htm

**LYDNEY,** Gloucestershire Map ref 2B1 **SELF CATERING**

★★★
SELF CATERING

Units 1
Sleeps 6
Low season per wk
£400.00–£500.00
High season per wk
£500.00–£595.00

## 2 Danby Cottages, Lydney

**contact** Gareth Lawes, c/o 23 Cotham Road South, Bristol BS6 5TZ
**t** (0117) 942 2301 **e** glawes@tiscali.co.uk

Upstairs there are two double bedrooms and bathroom. Downstairs there is a double bedroom with wetroom, kitchen and large living/dining room with folding glass doors opening onto decking and garden.

**open** All Year
**nearest shop** 0.5 miles
**nearest pub** 0.5 miles

General

Unit

Payment Cash, cheques

## MARAZION, Cornwall — SELF CATERING

★★★★ SELF CATERING

**Ocean Studios contact** Mrs Heather Wenn, Ocean Studios, Mounts Bay House, Turnpike Hill, Marazion TR17 0AY **t** (01736) 711040
**e** enquiries@mountsbayhouse.co.uk **w** mountsbayhouse.co.uk

## MINEHEAD, Somerset

*See entry on p282*

## MODBURY, Devon Map ref 1C3 — CAMPING, CARAVAN & HOLIDAY PARK

★★★★ TOURING PARK

(112)
£12.20–£25.30
(112)
£12.20–£25.30
112 touring pitches

THE CARAVAN CLUB

# Broad Park Caravan Club Site

Higher East Leigh, Modbury, Ivybridge PL21 0SH **t** (01548) 830714
**w** caravanclub.co.uk

General

Leisure

Payment Credit/debit cards, cash, cheques

Situated between moor and sea, not far from the ancient village of Modbury – a splendid base from which to explore South Devon. Make for Dartmoor and the silence and solitude, the tumbling streams and the long views, or go south and seek out the small villages of the South Hams.

**open** March to November

*From B3027 (signposted Modbury), site on left after 1 mile.*

## MORETON-IN-MARSH, Gloucestershire Map ref 2B1 — CAMPING, CARAVAN & HOLIDAY PARK

★★★★★ TOURING PARK

(182)
£14.90–£28.30
(182)
£14.90–£28.30
182 touring pitches

THE CARAVAN CLUB

# Moreton-in-Marsh Caravan Club Site

Bourton Road, Moreton-in-Marsh GL56 0BT **t** (01608) 650519
**w** caravanclub.co.uk

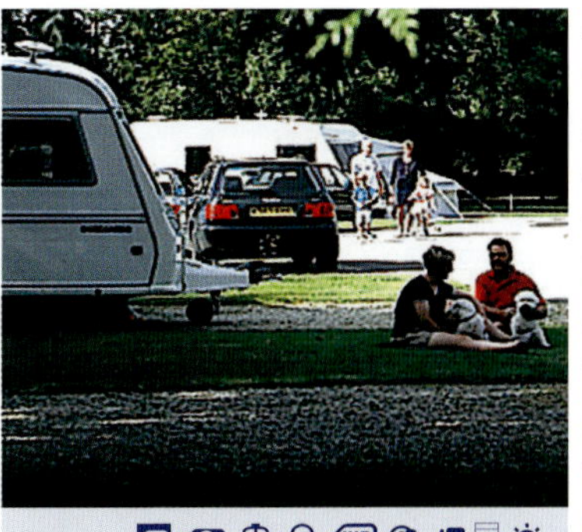

General

Leisure

Payment Credit/debit cards, cash, cheques

A well-wooded site with a pleasant openness nonetheless, and within easy walking distance of an interesting, lively market town. Moreton-in-Marsh nestles in the heart of beautiful Cotswold countryside. This attractive town with many interesting shops, is perhaps today most famous for the Tuesday street market.

**open** All year

*From Moreton-in-Marsh on A44 the site entrance is on the right 250yds past the end of the speed limit sign.*

## MORETONHAMPSTEAD, Devon — SELF CATERING

★★★ SELF CATERING

**Budleigh Farm contact** Mr Arthur Harvey, Budleigh Farm, Moretonhampstead, Newton Abbott TQ13 8SB **t** (01647) 440835
**e** harvey@budleighfarm.co.uk **w** budleighfarm.co.uk

## MOUNT HAWKE, Cornwall — SELF CATERING

★★★★ SELF CATERING

**Ropers Walk Barns contact** Mrs Elizabeth Pollard, Ropers Walk Barns, Rope Walk, Mount Hawke, Truro TR4 8DW **t** (01209) 891632
**e** peterandliz@roperswalkbarns.co.uk **w** roperswalkbarns.co.uk

## OKEHAMPTON, Devon — SELF CATERING

★★★★ SELF CATERING

**Beer Farm contact** Bob & Sue Annear, Beer Farm, Okehampton EX20 1SG
**t** (01837) 840265
**e** info@beerfarm.co.uk **w** beerfarm.co.uk

## PADSTOW, Cornwall — GUEST ACCOMMODATION

★★★★★ GUEST ACCOMMODATION GOLD AWARD

**Woodlands Country House** Treator, Padstow PL28 8RU
**t** (01841) 532426
**e** enquiries@woodlands-padstow.co.uk **w** woodlands-padstow.co.uk

## PADSTOW, Cornwall Map ref 1B2 — SELF CATERING

★★★–★★★★★ SELF CATERING

Units **6**
Sleeps **1–6**
Low season per wk
**£285.00–£465.00**
High season per wk
**£525.00–£700.00**

### Yellow Sands Cottages, Padstow

**contact** Mrs Sharon Keast, Yellow Sands Cottages, Harlyn Bay, Padstow PL28 8SE **t** (01637) 881548 **e** yellowsands@btinternet.com
**w** yellowsands.co.uk

Lerryn Cottage, Harlyn Bay has one double or twin room. Spacious bath/wet room and central heating. Very comfortable for couple or young family. Level access throughout. Local proprietors. Idyllic, quiet location.

**open** All Year
**nearest shop** 1 mile
**nearest pub** 0.5 miles

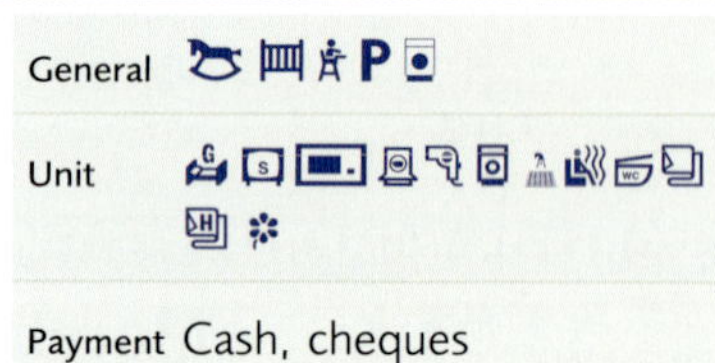

General
Unit

Payment Cash, cheques

## PARKEND, Gloucestershire — GUEST ACCOMMODATION

★★★ INN

**The Fountain Inn** Parkend, Lydney GL15 4JD
**t** (01594) 562189
**e** thefountaininn@aol.com

## PENZANCE, Cornwall — HOTEL

★★★ HOTEL SILVER AWARD

**Hotel Penzance** Britons Hill, Penzance TR18 3AE
**t** (01736) 363117
**e** enquiries@hotelpenzance.com
**w** hotelpenzance.com

## PLYMOUTH, Devon — HOTEL

★★★ HOTEL

**Kitley House Hotel and Restaurant** Kitley Estate, Yealmpton, Plymouth PL8 2NW
**t** (01752) 881555
**e** sales@kitleyhousehotel.com **w** kitleyhousehotel.com

## PLYMOUTH, Devon — SELF CATERING

★★★ SELF CATERING

**Haddington House Apartments contact** Mr Fairfax Luxmoore, 42 Haddington Road, Stoke, Plymouth PL2 1RR **t** 07966 256984
**e** luxmoorf@hotmail.com **w** abudd.co.uk

## PLYMOUTH, Devon — CAMPING, CARAVAN & HOLIDAY PARK

★★★★★ TOURING PARK

**Plymouth Sound Caravan Club Site** Bovisand Lane, Down Thomas, Plymouth PL9 0AE **t** (01752) 862325
**w** caravanclub.co.uk

## POLZEATH, Cornwall — SELF CATERING

★★★★ SELF CATERING

**Manna Place contact** Mrs Ann Jones, Manna Place, 14 Trenant Close, Polzeath, Wadebridge PL27 6SW **t** (01208) 863258
**e** anniepolzeath@hotmail.com **w** mannaplace.co.uk

## POOLE, Somerset — CAMPING, CARAVAN & HOLIDAY PARK

★★★★ TOURING PARK

**Cadeside Caravan Club Site** Nynehead Road, Wellington TA21 9HN
**t** (01823) 663103
**e** enquiries@caravanclub.co.uk **w** caravanclub.co.uk

## PORTHTOWAN, Cornwall — SELF CATERING

★★★★★ SELF CATERING

**Rosehill Lodges contact** Mr John Barrow, Rosehill Lodges, Porthtowan TR4 8AR
**t** (01209) 891920
**e** reception@rosehilllodges.com **w** rosehilllodges.com

## PORTREATH, Cornwall Map ref 1B3 — SELF CATERING

★★★★★ SELF CATERING

Units **3**
Sleeps **1–5**
Low season per wk
£220.00–£300.00
High season per wk
£300.00–£750.00

### Higher Laity Farm, Redruth

**contact** Mrs Lynne Drew, Higher Laity Farm, Portreath Road, Redruth TR16 4HY **t** (01209) 842317
**e** info@higherlaityfarm.co.uk **w** higherlaityfarm.co.uk

Tastefully converted luxury barns set amidst the Cornish countryside. One cottage, offering master bedroom with en suite and second twin-bedded room, has a fully adapted accessible bathroom with level-access shower. The exceptional accommodation and its proximity to the A30 makes this an ideal base from which to explore. Service dogs welcome.

**open** All Year
**nearest shop** 1 mile
**nearest pub** 0.5 miles

*From M5 take A30 to Redruth/Porthtowan slip road towards Redruth. For full travel directions please contact us directly.*

General P

Unit

Payment Credit/debit cards, cash, cheques

*Special weekend and mid-week breaks available.*

## PORTREATH, Cornwall — SELF CATERING

★★★–★★★★★ SELF CATERING

**Trengove Farm Cottages contact** Mrs Lindsey Richards, Trengove Farm, Cot Road, Illogan, Redruth TR16 4PU **t** (01209) 843008 **e** richards@farming.co.uk **w** trengovefarm.co.uk

## PORTSCATHO, Cornwall — SELF CATERING

★★★★–★★★★★ SELF CATERING

**Pollaughan Farm contact** Mrs Valerie Penny, Pollaughan Farm, Portscatho, St Mawes TR2 5EH **t** (01872) 580150 **e** pollaughan@yahoo.co.uk **w** pollaughan.co.uk

## RUAN HIGH LANES, Cornwall Map ref 1B3 — SELF CATERING

★★★★ SELF CATERING

Units **1**
Sleeps **1–5**
Low season per wk **£250.00–£400.00**
High season per wk **£350.00–£750.00**

### Trelagossick Farm – Barnowl Cottage, Truro

**contact** Mrs Rachel Carbis, Trelagossick Farm - Barnowl Cottage, Trelagossick Farm, Truro TR2 5JU **t** (01872) 501338 **e** enquiries@trelagossickfarm.co.uk **w** trelagossickfarm.co.uk

Detached barn conversion on traditional farm. All rooms on ground floor. Level-access shower/wc. Cosy all year with underfloor heating. Level, secluded garden/patio. Adjacent parking. Service dogs welcome.

**open** All Year
**nearest shop** 1 mile
**nearest pub** 3 miles

## ST AUSTELL, Cornwall Map ref 1B3 — SELF CATERING

★★★★ SELF CATERING

Units **1**
Sleeps **2–5**
Low season per wk **£300.00–£450.00**
High season per wk **£650.00–£800.00**

### Owls Reach, Roche, St Austell

**contact** Diana Pride, Owls Reach, Colbiggan Farm, Roche PL26 8LJ **t** (01208) 831597 **e** info@owlsreach.co.uk **w** owlsreach.co.uk

Spacious, detached, luxury cottage, designed for accessibility needs on single level. Three bedrooms, wheel-in shower room and second bathroom. Parking very close to doors. Peaceful country location.

**open** All year
**nearest shop** 2 miles
**nearest pub** 2 miles

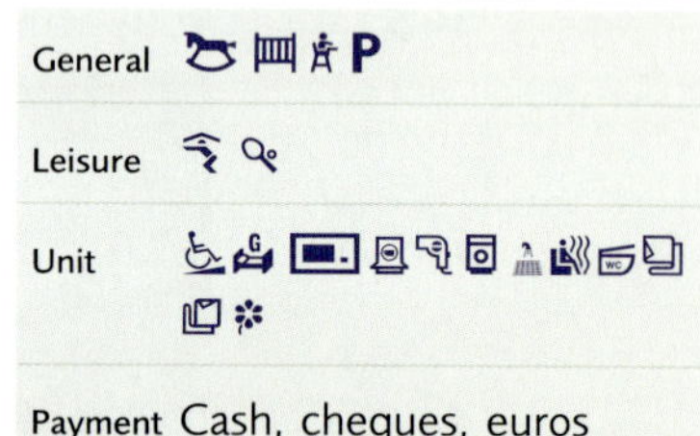


## ST ENDELLION, Cornwall — SELF CATERING

★★★★ SELF CATERING

**Tolraggott Farm Cottages contact** Mrs Harris, Tolraggott Farm Cottages, Tolraggott Farm, St Endellion, Port Isaac PL29 3TP **t** (01208) 880927

## Don't forget www.

Web addresses throughout this guide are shown without the prefix www. Please include www. in the address line of your browser. If a web address does not follow this style it is shown in full.

## ST JUST-IN-PENWITH, Cornwall Map ref 1A3

SELF CATERING

★★★★
SELF CATERING

Units 1
Sleeps 2–4

Low season per wk
£200.00–£350.00
High season per wk
£450.00–£595.00

### Swallow's End, Bosworlas

**contact** Mr David Beer, Swallow's End, Kelynack Moor Farmhouse, Bosworlas TR19 7RQ **t** (01736) 787011
**e** enquiries@westcornwalllets.co.uk **w** westcornwalllets.co.uk

Access abc

General

Unit

Payment Credit/debit cards, cash, cheques

*Special reductions for short breaks for 2 people out of season. Special Christmas-break offers.*

Modern annexe to traditional farmhouse in peaceful valley with lovely countryside views. Close to Sennen and Land's End. Lovely garden with private patio and barbecue. One double room and one twin room. All one level. Specialist equipment available. Low-level kitchen.

**open** All Year
**nearest shop** 1 mile
**nearest pub** 1 mile

*Turn off the A30 Land's End road onto the A3071 towards St Just, then B3306 towards Sennen. Turn left before Kelynack village. Third house on the right.*

## ST VEEP, Cornwall

SELF CATERING

★★★
SELF CATERING

**A Little Bit of Heaven Manelly Fleming contact** Mrs Daphne Rolling, Manelly Fleming Farm, St Veep, Lostwithiel PL22 0NS **t** (01208) 872564
**e** daphne@alittlebitofheaven.co.uk **w** alittlebitofheaven.co.uk

## SALISBURY, Wiltshire

SELF CATERING

★★★★
SELF CATERING

**The Old Stables contact** Mr Giles Gould, The Old Stables, Bridge Farm, Lower Road, Britford, Salisbury SP5 4DY **t** (01722) 349002
**e** mail@old-stables.co.uk **w** old-stables.co.uk

## SANDFORD, Devon

GUEST ACCOMMODATION

★★★★
BED & BREAKFAST

**Ashridge Farm** Sandford EX17 4EN
**t** (01363) 774292
**e** info@ashdridgefarm.co.uk **w** ashridgefarm.co.uk

## SHAFTESBURY, Dorset

SELF CATERING

★★★–★★★★★
SELF CATERING

**Hartgrove Farm contact** Mrs Susan Smart, Hartgrove Farm, Hartgrove, Shaftesbury SP7 0JY **t** (01747) 811830
**e** smart@hartgrovefarm.co.uk **w** hartgrovefarm.co.uk

At-a-glance symbols are explained on page 8.

**SIDBURY,** Devon Map ref 1D2 — **CAMPING, CARAVAN & HOLIDAY PARK**

TOURING PARK

(117)
£12.20–£25.30
(117)
£12.20–£25.30
117 touring pitches

## Putts Corner Caravan Club Site

Sidbury, Sidmouth EX10 0QQ **t** (01404) 42875
**w** caravanclub.co.uk

General

Leisure

Payment Credit/debit cards, cash, cheques

A quiet site in pretty surroundings high up but sheltered from the wind. Spring brings a fantastic display of bluebells followed by foxgloves, and you'll see a wide variety of birds and even the occasional deer. There is a choice of walks from the site and Sidmouth is a restful resort with a long pebble beach.

**open** March to November

*From M5 jct 25, A375 signposted Sidmouth. Turn right at Hare and Hounds onto B3174. In about 0.25 miles turn right into site entrance.*

**SOUTH MOLTON,** Devon — **SELF CATERING**

★★★★★
SELF CATERING

**Stable Cottage** **contact** Mrs Victoria Huxtable, Stable Cottage, Stable Cottages, Stitchpool Farm, South Molton EX36 3EZ
**t** (01598) 740130

**STATHE,** Somerset — **SELF CATERING**

★★★★
SELF CATERING

**Walkers Farm Cottages** **contact** Mrs Dianne Tilley, Walkers Farm Cottages, Walkers Farm, Stathe, Bridgwater TA7 0JL **t** (01823) 698229
**e** info@walkersfarmcottages.co.uk **w** walkersfarmcottages.co.uk

**STOKE ST GREGORY,** Somerset — **SELF CATERING**

★★★★
SELF CATERING

**Holly Farm Cottages** **contact** Mr & Mrs Robert & Liz Hembrow, Holly Farm Cottages, Meare Green, Stoke St Gregory, Taunton TA3 6HS
**t** (01823) 490828
**e** robhembrow@btinternet.com **w** holly-farm.com

**SWANAGE,** Dorset — **SELF CATERING**

★★★
SELF CATERING

**9 Quayside Court** **contact** Mr Graham Hogg, 9 Quayside Court, Lilliput Avenue, Chipping Sodbury BS37 6HX **t** (01454) 311178
**e** graham.hogg@blueyonder.co.uk **w** bythequayholidays.co.uk

**SWANAGE,** Dorset — **CAMPING, CARAVAN & HOLIDAY PARK**

TOURING PARK

**Haycraft Caravan Club Site** Haycrafts Lane, Swanage BH19 3EB
**t** (01929) 480572
**e** enquiries@caravanclub.co.uk **w** caravanclub.co.uk

## TAUNTON, Somerset — SELF CATERING

★★★★ SELF CATERING

**Linnets contact** Mrs Patricia Grabham, Linnets, Church Road, Wivliscombe TA4 3JX
**t** (01823) 400658
**e** patricia.grabham@onetel.net **w** linnetsfitzhead.co.uk

## TAUNTON, Somerset

*See also entry on p282*

## TEWKESBURY, Gloucestershire — CAMPING, CARAVAN & HOLIDAY PARK

★★★★ TOURING & CAMPING PARK

**Tewkesbury Abbey Caravan Club Site** Gander Lane, Tewkesbury GL20 5PG
**t** (01684) 294035
**w** caravanclub.co.uk

## TINCLETON, Dorset — SELF CATERING

★★★★★ SELF CATERING

**Tincleton Lodge and Clyffe Dairy Cottage contact** Mrs Jane Coleman, Tincleton Lodge and Clyffe Dairy Cottage, Eweleaze Farm, Tincleton, Dorchester DT2 8QR **t** (01305) 848391
**e** enquiries@dorsetholidaycottages.net **w** dorsetholidaycottages.net

## TINTAGEL, Cornwall — CAMPING, CARAVAN & HOLIDAY PARK

★★★★★ TOURING & CAMPING PARK

**Trewethett Farm Caravan Club Site** Trethevy, Tintagel PL34 0BQ
**t** (01840) 770222
**w** caravanclub.co.uk

## TORQUAY, Devon Map ref 1D2 — GUEST ACCOMMODATION

★★★★ GUEST ACCOMMODATION

B&B per room per night
**s £50.00–£70.00**
**d £59.00–£79.00**
Evening meal per person
**£14.95**

# Crown Lodge

83 Avenue Road, Torquay TQ2 5LH **t** (01803) 298772
**e** stay@crownlodgehotel.co.uk **w** crownlodgehotel.co.uk

Rooms

General 9

Payment Credit/debit cards, cash

*Includes two disabled-friendly rooms, a double with wheelchair-accessible en suite and a twin suitable for ambulant disabled.*

Charming guest accommodation less than one mile from the very centre of Torquay and a level walk to the seafront. We guarantee a quality service. Ample on-site parking is available for guests' use.

**open** All year
**bedrooms** 4 double, 1 twin, 1 family
**bathrooms** All en suite

*A380 onto A3022. After approx 1.5 miles fork right at lights by Torre Station into Avenue Road. Crown Lodge is 220yds on left.*

**TORQUAY,** Devon Map ref 1D2 **SELF CATERING**

★★★–★★★★★
SELF CATERING

Units **6**
Sleeps **2–5**
Low season per wk
£200.00–£290.00
High season per wk
£310.00–£650.00

## Atlantis Holiday Apartments, Torquay

**contact** Mrs Pauline Roberts, Atlantis Holiday Apartments, Solsbro Road, Chelston, Torquay TQ2 6PF **t** (01803) 607929
**e** enquiry@atlantistorquay.co.uk **w** atlantistorquay.co.uk

Near seafront. Wheelchair access. Car park. Double, twin and family apartments. Full central heating, no meters. Wi-Fi. Apartments have dishwasher and washing machine. Heated pool with 'Multidome' all-weather cover.

**open** All year
**nearest shop** < 0.5 miles
**nearest pub** < 0.5 miles

Access abc
General
Leisure
Unit
Payment Credit/debit cards, cash, cheques

**TORQUAY,** Devon **SELF CATERING**

★★★
SELF CATERING

**South Sands Apartments contact** Mr & Mrs Paul & Deborah Moorhouse, South Sands Apartments, Torbay Road, Livermead, Torquay TQ2 6RG
**t** (01803) 293521
**e** info@southsands.co.uk **w** southsands.co.uk

**TORQUAY,** Devon

*See also entry on p282*

**TRURO,** Cornwall **GUEST ACCOMMODATION**

★★★★
GUEST ACCOMMODATION

**Tregoninny Farm** Tresillian, Truro TR2 4AR
**t** (01872) 520529
**e** tregoninny.farm@btopenworld.com **w** tregoninny.com

**UGBOROUGH,** Devon **SELF CATERING**

★★★★
SELF CATERING

**Venn Farm contact** Mrs Stephens, Venn Farm, The Farmhouse, Venn Farm, Ugborough, Ivybridge PL21 0PE
**t** (01364) 73240

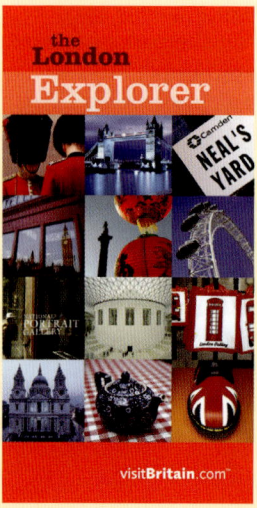

**VERYAN,** Cornwall Map ref 1B3 **SELF CATERING**

★★★★
SELF CATERING

Units **1**
Sleeps **6**

Low season per wk
**£275.00–£360.00**
High season per wk
**£360.00–£790.00**

## Trenona Farm Holidays, Veryan

**contact** Mrs Pamela Carbis, Trenona Farm, Ruan High Lanes, Truro TR2 5JS **t** (01872) 501339
**e** pam@trenonafarmholidays.co.uk **w** trenonafarmholidays.co.uk

General

Unit

Payment Credit/debit cards, cash, cheques

*Short breaks Oct-Mar. 2 bedrooms accessible for wheelchair users.*

Chy Whel is a single-storey cottage with three en suite bedrooms (a double and two twin-bedded rooms). The open-plan lounge/kitchen/diner has all modern comforts and conveniences. The property also has a private garden with patio and lawn area.

**open** All Year
**nearest shop** 1 mile
**nearest pub** 2 miles

*A30 past Bodmin, A391 to St Austell, A390 towards Truro. Just beyond Probus take A3078 to St Mawes. After 8 miles pass Jet garage, Trenona Farm 2nd on left.*

**WARMINSTER,** Wiltshire Map ref 2B2 **CAMPING, CARAVAN & HOLIDAY PARK**

★★★★★
TOURING PARK

(165)
**£14.90–£28.90**
(165)
**£14.90–£28.90**
165 touring pitches

## Longleat Caravan Club Site

Longleat, Warminster BA12 7NL **t** (01985) 844663
**w** caravanclub.co.uk

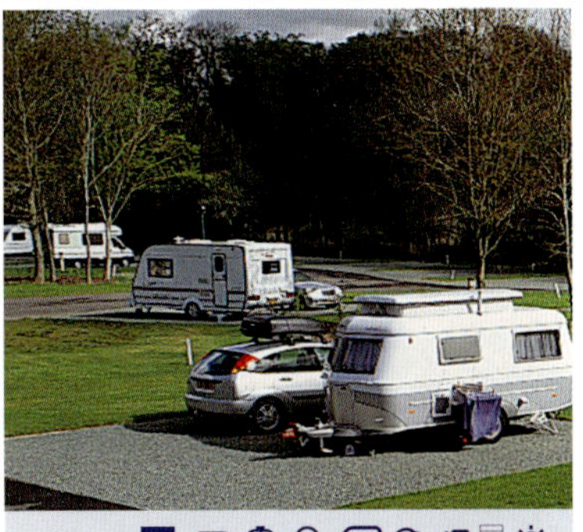

General

Leisure

Payment Credit/debit cards, cash, cheques

The only Club site where you can hear lions roar at night. Longleat is one of the Club's most beautiful parkland sites, in the middle of the lovely Longleat estate, with miles of paths to walk amid the pleasures of woodland, bluebell, azalea and rhododendron.

**open** March to November

*Take A362, signed for Frome, 0.5 miles at roundabout turn left (1st exit) onto Longleat Estate. Through toll booths, follow caravan and camping pennant signs for 1 mile.*

At-a-glance symbols are explained on page 8.

**WELLINGTON,** Somerset **SELF CATERING**

**Old Lime Kiln Cottages contact** Mrs Sue Gallagher, Old Lime Kiln Cottages, Holcombe Rogus, Wellington TA21 0NA **t** (01823) 672339
**e** bookings@oldlimekiln.freeserve.co.uk **w** oldlimekilncottages.co.uk

**WELLS,** Somerset Map ref 2A2 **GUEST ACCOMMODATION**

B&B per room per night
**s £60.00–£65.00**
**d £70.00–£80.00**
Evening meal per person
**£15.00**

## Double-Gate Farm

Godney, Nr Wells BA5 1RX **t** (01458) 832217
**e** doublegatefarm@aol.com **w** doublegatefarm.com

Access abc

Rooms

General

Payment Credit/debit cards, cash, cheques

Well known for providing accessible accommodation. AA Accessible Hotel runner-up 2001. Play table-tennis or snooker in the games room, or watch your own DVDs in well-equipped, en suite bedrooms. Free internet access. Delicious breakfasts, home-grown and local produce. Evening meals at selected times. New for summer 2009: four ground-floor triple, en suite bedrooms plus a lovely garden dining room.

**open** All year except Christmas and New Year
**bedrooms** 1 double, 1 twin, 1 family, 4 triple
**bathrooms** All en suite

*From Wells take A39 south. At Polsham turn right, signed Godney/Polsham. Continue 3 miles. Farmhouse on left after the Sheppey Inn.*

**WELLS,** Somerset **SELF CATERING**

**St Marys Lodge contact** Mrs Jane Hughes, St Marys Lodge, Long Street, Croscombe, Wells BA5 3QL **t** (01749) 342157
**e** janehughes@trtopbox.net **w** st-marys-lodge.co.uk

## Key to symbols

Symbols at the end of each entry help you pick out the services and facilities which are most important for your stay. A key to the symbols can be found on page 8.

**WELLS,** Somerset Map ref 2A2 — **SELF CATERING**

★★★★
SELF CATERING

Units **1**
Sleeps **6**

Low season per wk
£350.00–£500.00
High season per wk
£600.00–£750.00

## Swallow Barn, Godney, Wells

**contact** Mrs Hilary Millard, Swallow Barn, Double Gate Farm, Godney, Nr Wells BA5 1RX **t** (01458) 832217
**e** doublegatefarm@aol.com **w** doublegatefarm.com

Access abc

General P

Unit

Payment Credit/debit cards, cash, cheques

Lovely barn conversion designed for full accessibility. Ground-floor en suite bedroom with roll-in shower. Two en suite bedrooms upstairs. All with Freeview/DVD TVs. Inglenook sitting room. Fully accessible, dual height, fitted kitchen. Very pretty, shared flower garden. Own patio. Breakfast and evening meals available at selected times. Service dogs welcome.

**open** All year
**nearest shop** 3 miles
**nearest pub** < 0.5 miles

*From Wells take A39 south. At Polsham turn right, signed Godney/Polsham. Continue 3 miles. Farmhouse on left after The Sheppey Inn.*

**WEST BEXINGTON,** Dorset Map ref 2A3 — **SELF CATERING**

★★★–★★★★★
SELF CATERING

Units **5**
Sleeps **4–7**

Low season per wk
Min £375.00
High season per wk
Max £980.00

## Tamarisk Farm Cottages, Dorchester

**contact** Mrs Josephine Pearse, Tamarisk Farm Cottages, Beach Road, West Bexington, Dorchester DT2 9DF **t** (01308) 897784
**e** holidays@tamariskfarm.com **w** tamariskfarm.com

Beautiful views of Lyme Bay – Portland to Start Point, Devon. Quiet, extensive patios. Roll-in showers, low-level stove and sink. Extra aids available. Two bungalows suitable for disabled guests; three bungalows, each with three steps outside.

**open** All year
**nearest shop** 3 miles
**nearest pub** < 0.5 miles

Access

General P S

Leisure

Unit

Payment Credit/debit cards, cash, cheques, euros

**WEST DOWN,** Devon — **CAMPING, CARAVAN & HOLIDAY PARK**

★★★★
TOURING PARK

**Brook Lea** Brooklea Caravan Club Site, Woolacombe EX34 8NE
**t** (01271) 862848
**e** enquiries@caravanclub.co.uk **w** caravanclub.co.uk

At-a-glance symbols are explained on page 8.

## WEST QUANTOXHEAD, Somerset — GUEST ACCOMMODATION

**Stilegate Bed and Breakfast** Staple Close, Williton TA4 4DN
**t** (01984) 639119
**e** stilegate@aol.com
**w** stilegate.co.uk

## WESTON-SUPER-MARE, Somerset Map ref 1D1 — HOTEL

B&B per room per night
**s Min £69.00**
**d £89.00–£140.00**

# Royal Hotel

South Parade, Weston-super-Mare BS23 1JP **t** (01934) 423100
**e** reservations@royalhotelweston.com **w** royalhotelweston.com

Access 

Rooms 

General 

Payment Credit/debit cards, cash, cheques

*Special seasonal offers and packages now available. Please contact our reservations team for more details.*

Situated in the heart of Weston, the Royal Hotel is set in its own extensive lawns which extend to the promenade, offering views across the bay.

**open** All year
**bedrooms** 19 double, 3 twin, 6 single, 7 family, 4 suites
**bathrooms** All en suite

*M5 jct 21 follow signs to seafront, past the pier next door to Winter Gardens Pavilion.*

## WESTON-SUPER-MARE, Somerset — GUEST ACCOMMODATION

**Milton Lodge Guest House** 15 Milton Road, Weston-super-Mare BS23 2SH
**t** (01934) 623161
**e** info@milton-lodge.co.uk **w** milton-lodge.co.uk

## WESTON-SUPER-MARE, Somerset — GUEST ACCOMMODATION

**Spreyton Guest House** 72 Locking Road, Weston-super-Mare BS23 3EN
**t** (01934) 416887
**e** info@spreytonguesthouse.com **w** spreytonguesthouse.com

## WESTON-SUPER-MARE, Somerset

*See also entries on p282*

**WEYMOUTH,** Dorset Map ref 2B3 **CAMPING, CARAVAN & HOLIDAY PARK**

TOURING PARK

(120)
**£11.40–£23.60**
(120)
**£11.40–£23.60**
120 touring pitches

## Crossways Caravan Club Site

Crossways, Dorchester DT2 8BE **t** (01305) 852032
**w** caravanclub.co.uk

General

Leisure

Payment Credit/debit cards, cash, cheques

*Midweek discount; pitch fees reduced by 50% for stays on Mon, Tue, Wed or Thu night outside peak and value season.*

A most imaginatively landscaped site in 35 acres of woodland, with pitching in open groves linked by a snaking road which leads you round the site from Iron Horse Meadows to Poacher's Paradise. If you want to leave the car behind for the day, the railway station is just 5 minutes' walk from the site.

**open** April to October

*North from A35 or south from A352, join B3390. Site on right within 1 mile. Entrance to site by forecourt of filling station.*

**WEYMOUTH,** Dorset

*See also entry on p283*

**WOOLLAND,** Dorset **SELF CATERING**

★★★★
SELF CATERING

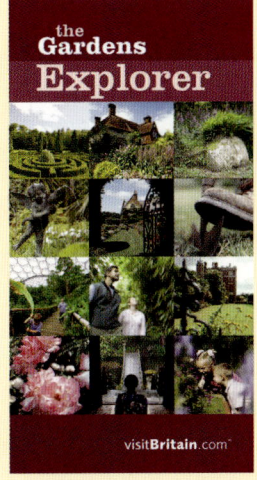

**Ellwood Cottages contact** Mr & Mrs John & Ann Heath, Ellwood Cottages, Woolland, Blandford Forum DT11 0ES **t** (01258) 818196
**e** admin@ellwoodcottages.co.uk **w** ellwoodcottages.co.uk

**YELLVERTON,** Devon Map ref 1C2 **GUEST ACCOMMODATION**

★★★★
**GUEST ACCOMMODATION**

B&B per room per night
**s £37.50–£45.00**
**d £70.00–£80.00**

## Overcombe House

Old Station Road, Yelverton PL20 7RA **t** (01822) 853501
**e** enquiries@overcombehotel.co.uk **w** overcombehotel.co.uk

Access abc

Rooms

General 5

Payment Credit/debit cards, cash

*Access to property by ramp. 2 ground-floor bedrooms, double with standard en suite, twin with totally flat-floored facilities.*

Offering a warm, friendly welcome in relaxed comfortable surroundings with a substantial breakfast using local and home-made produce. Situated between Tavistock and Plymouth with beautiful views over the village and Dartmoor. Conveniently located for exploring both Devon and Cornwall, in particular Dartmoor National Park and the adjacent Tamar Valley.

**open** All year except Christmas
**bedrooms** 4 double, 3 twin, 1 single
**bathrooms** All en suite

*Situated between Plymouth and Tavistock. Located on the edge of the village of Horrabridge and just over a mile north-west of Yelverton heading towards Tavistock.*

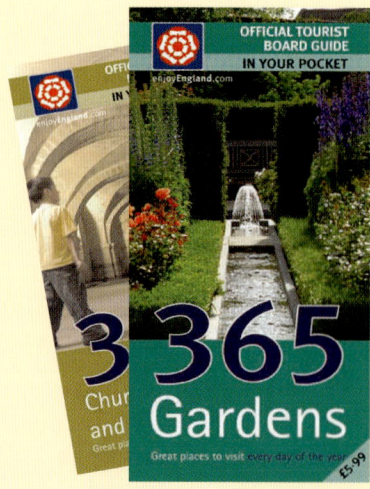

# National Accessible Scheme ratings only

The following establishments hold a National Accessible Scheme rating as shown in their entry, but do not participate in a quality assessment scheme. However, to participate in the National Accessible Scheme accommodation must meet a minimum level of quality.

**HAMWORTHY,** Dorset Map ref 2B3 **SELF CATERING**

Units **1**
Sleeps **2–6**
Low season per wk
Min £405.00
High season per wk
Max £520.00

Awaiting NAS rating

## Grooms Chalet Rockley Park

**contact** Gail Lewis, Livability, PO Box 36, Cowbridge CF71 7GB
**t** 08456 584478 **e** selfcatering@livability.org.uk or glewis@livability.org.uk
**w** livabilityholidays.org.uk

Chalet adapted for disabled holidaymakers. Sleeps up to six in two bedrooms, plus sofa bed in lounge. Roll-in shower and shower-chair, and mobile hoist.
**open** April to October
**nearest shop** 1 mile
**nearest pub** 1 mile

Access
General
Leisure
Unit

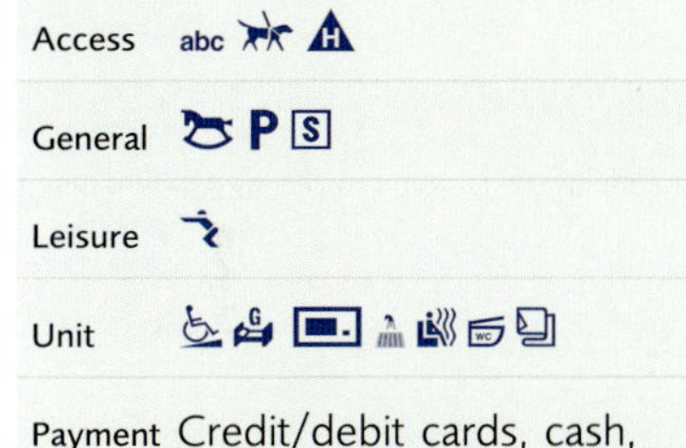


Payment Credit/debit cards, cash, cheques, euros

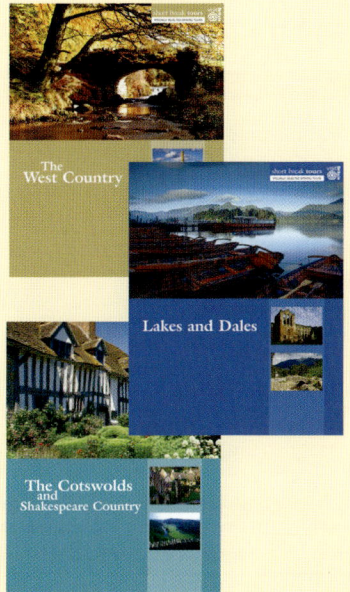



At-a-glance symbols are explained on page 8. 

**MINEHEAD,** Somerset Map ref 1D1 — **GUEST ACCOMMODATION**

## The Promenade

HB per person per night
**£36.61–£62.90**

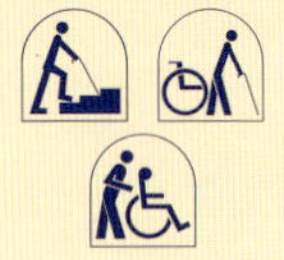

The Esplanade, Minehead TA24 5QS **t** (01643) 702572
**e** promenade@livability.org.uk or SAtkins@livability.org.uk
**w** livabilityholidays.org.uk

Access abc

Rooms

General

Payment Credit/debit cards, cash, cheques, euros

*Turkey and Tinsel breaks (Nov). Spring Harvest breaks (Feb, Mar).*

Property owned by Grooms Holidays specially adapted for disabled guests. Eleven bedrooms with eight fully accessible. Some equipment available, including fixed and manual hoists. Guests needing personal help should be accompanied or make arrangements through local agency.

**open** All year
**bedrooms** 9 twin, 1 single, 1 family
**bathrooms** All en suite

*A358 from Taunton. Collections from Taunton railway station can be arranged.*

**TAUNTON,** Somerset — **GUEST ACCOMMODATION**

**Redlands** Trebles Holford, Combe Florey, Taunton TA4 3HA
**t** (01823) 433159
**e** redlandshouse@hotmail.com **w** escapetothecountry.co.uk

**TORQUAY,** Devon Map ref 1D2 — **SELF CATERING**

## Park House, St Mary Church, Babbacombe

Units **1**
Sleeps **2–6**
Low season per wk
**Min £180.00**
High season per wk
**Max £445.00**

Awaiting NAS rating

**contact** Gail Lewis, Livability, PO Box 36, Cowbridge CF71 7GB
**t** 08456 584478 **e** selfcatering@livability.org.uk or glewis@livability.org.uk
**w** livabilityholidays.org.uk

Ground-floor flat. Double bedroom and two sofa beds in lounge. Fully adapted for wheelchair users. Roll-in shower. Mobile hoist and shower-chair available.

**open** All year
**nearest shop** 1 mile
**nearest pub** 1 mile

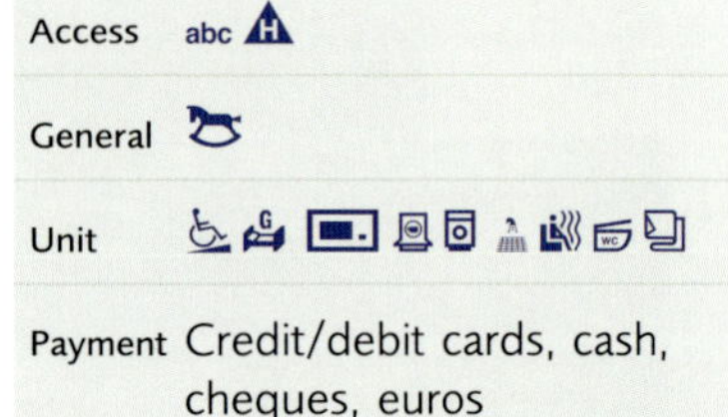

Access abc

General

Unit

Payment Credit/debit cards, cash, cheques, euros

**WESTON-SUPER-MARE,** Somerset — **GUEST ACCOMMODATION**

**Beverley Guest House** 11 Whitecross Road, Weston-super-Mare BS23 1EP
**t** (01934) 622956
**e** beverley11@hushmail.com **w** beverleyguesthouse.co.uk

**WESTON-SUPER-MARE,** Somerset Map ref 1D1 **SELF CATERING**

Units **1**
Sleeps **1–8**
Low season per wk
Min £235.00
High season per wk
Max £480.00

Awaiting NAS rating

## Villa Ryall, Worle

**contact** Gail Lewis, Livability, PO Box 36, Cowbridge CF71 7GB
**t** 08456 584478 **e** selfcatering@livability.org.uk or glewis@livability.org.uk
**w** livabilityholidays.org.uk

Newly-adapted property, with four bedrooms, large lounge, dining area and decked area. Fully fitted kitchen. Electric mobile hoist, shower-chair and profiling bed. Three miles from Weston-super-Mare seafront.

**open** All year
**nearest shop** 1 mile
**nearest pub** 1 mile

Access abc
General P S
Unit
Payment Credit/debit cards, cash, cheques, euros

**WEYMOUTH,** Dorset Map ref 2B3 **SELF CATERING**

Units **1**
Sleeps **2–10**
Low season per wk
Min £395.00
High season per wk
Max £595.00

Awaiting NAS rating

## Anchor House

**contact** Gail Lewis, Livability, PO Box 36, Cowbridge CF71 7GB
**t** 08456 584478 **e** selfcatering@livability.org.uk or glewis@livability.org.uk
**w** livabilityholidays.org.uk

Victorian house owned by Grooms Holidays, adapted for wheelchair users. Ramp to entrance. Lift to first floor. Accommodation for up to ten people in six bedrooms of which three are accessible. Roll-in shower, shower-chair, profiling bed and mobile hoist available.

**open** All year
**nearest shop** 1 mile
**nearest pub** 1 mile

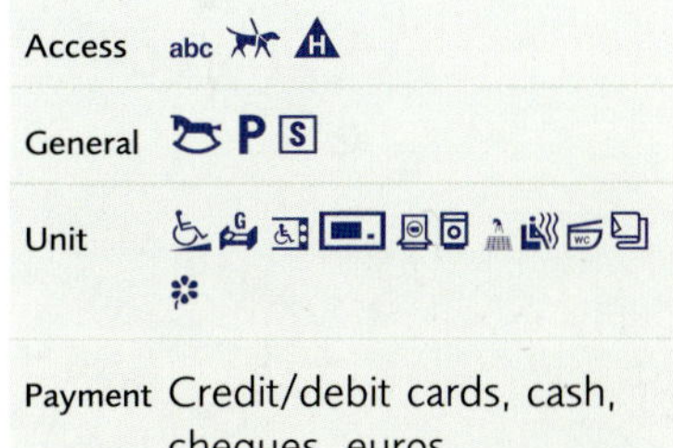

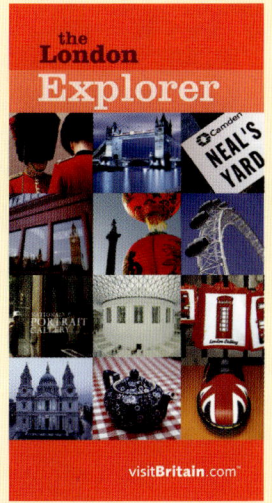

The ultimate designer day out
With designer and high street brands reduced by up to 50% at all seven centres throughout th
UK, McArthurGlen Designer Outlets are sure to be a hit with your passengers anytime
of the year. And with free 10% discount cards, free meal vouchers for drivers,
and dedicated parking, they're sure to be a winner with you too.
For more information on the ultimate designer day out,
email tourism@mcarthurglen.com
**Ashford** M20 Junction 9 or 10
**Bridgend** M4 Junction 36
**Cheshire Oaks** M53 Junction 10
**East Midlands** M1 Junction 28
**Livingston** M8 Junction 3
**Swindon** M4 Junction 16 or M5 Junction 11a
**York** A19/A64 interchange, south of York
Livingston
York
East Midlands
Cheshire Oaks
Swindon
Bridgend
Ashford
ARMANI COLLECTIONS
GAP OUTLET
KAREN MILLEN
NIKE FACTORY STORE
MARKS & SPENCER OUTLET
TED BAKER
loveoutletshopping.com
McArthur Glen
Designer Outlet

# Discover Falmouth

**Falmouth Tourist Information Centre** offers an accommodation booking service and has a comprehensive list of accessible accommodation in Falmouth and the surrounding area. The centre stocks a good range of maps and guides and can provide detailed information for visitors with specific needs on what to do, where to go and how to get around the area.

**ACCESSIBILITY** information is available from Falmouth Tourist Information Centre **info@falmouthtic.co.uk** tel 01326 312300
11 Market Strand, Prince of Wales Pier, Falmouth TR11 3DF

For information on arts and museums and historic buildings in Falmouth visit **www.falmouthtowncouncil.co.uk**

**SHOPMOBILITY SCOOTERS** are available 10am - 2pm Mon to Fri. Book through Specsavers 24hrs in advance tel 01326 212733

**ALL-TERRAIN WHEELCHAIR** for easy access onto Gyllyngvase beach and into the sea available through Gylly Beach Café
tel 01326 312884 or email **cafe@gyllybeach.com**

**FOR WHERE TO STAY** what to do and how to get around visit **www.acornishriver.co.uk**. Details can also be found on Falmouth and District Hotels Association website **www.visitfalmouth.com**

The Lost Gardens of
# HELIGAN

**Open Daily 10am**
**www.heligan.com**

**Victorian Productive Gardens, Pleasure Grounds, Sub-tropical Jungle, Ancient Woodland, a pioneering Wildlife Project and beyond...**

The Lost Gardens of Heligan, seat of the Tremayne family for over 400 years, is one of the most mysterious estates in England. At the end of the nineteenth century its thousand acres were at their zenith, but only a few years after the Great War of 1914 bramble and ivy were already drawing a green veil over this 'Sleeping Beauty'. Today "the nation's favourite garden" offers over 200 acres for exploration, from Victorian Productive Gardens and the surrounding Pleasure Grounds to a sub-tropical Jungle valley brimming with exotic foliage; sustainably managed woodland and farm walks through beautiful Cornish countryside, and a pioneering Wildlife Project.Visitors who are less able would be advised to focus their visit on the Northern Gardens, incorporating plantings from around the world throughout the Pleasure Grounds and boasting over 200 varieties of fruit and vegetables grown in the Productive Gardens. The Wildlife Project situated at the heart of the Lost Gardens is also accessible to all offering visitors an intimate view of native wildlife abundant throughout the Heligan estate. Areas of the Outer Estate and gardens, which are less accessible, can be experienced visually via the armchair tour situated close to the Heligan Shop, Plant Sales and Tearoom. Manual wheelchairs are available from the Visitor Reception on a first-come first-served basis and the Heligan Access Guide may be downloaded from the Heligan website (www.heligan.com) or obtained from the Heligan Visitor Reception.

**Pentewan, St Austell, Cornwall PL26 6EN Tel: 01726 845100 Email: info@heligan.com**

WWT Wildfowl & Wetlands Trust
Tourism for all across the UK
For information on WWT wetland visitor centres, events and highlights, visit us at
www.wwt.org.uk
WWT Slimbridge,
T 01453 891900
Caerlaverock
Washington
Castle Espie
Martin Mere
Welney
Llanelli
Slimbridge
London
Arundel
Registered charity number 1030884
Celebrating 60 years of conservation 1946 – 2006

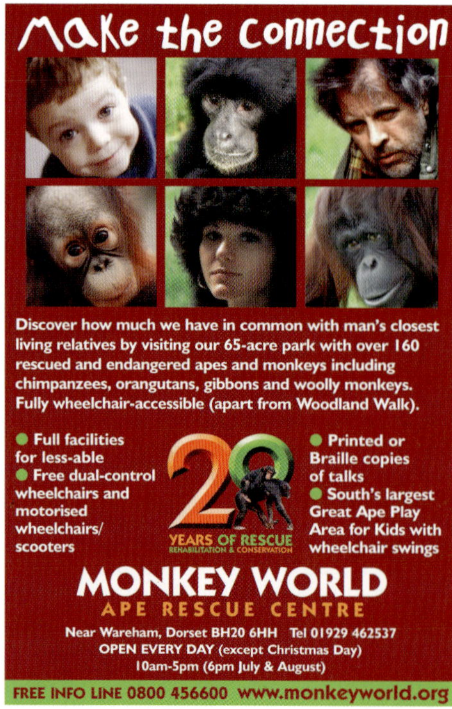
Make the connection
Discover how much we have in common with man's closest living relatives by visiting our 65-acre park with over 160 rescued and endangered apes and monkeys including chimpanzees, orangutans, gibbons and woolly monkeys. Fully wheelchair-accessible (apart from Woodland Walk).
Full facilities for less-able
Free dual-control wheelchairs and motorised wheelchairs/ scooters
20 YEARS OF RESCUE
REHABILITATION & CONSERVATION
Printed or Braille copies of talks
South's largest Great Ape Play Area for Kids with wheelchair swings
MONKEY WORLD
APE RESCUE CENTRE
Near Wareham, Dorset BH20 6HH Tel 01929 462537
OPEN EVERY DAY (except Christmas Day)
10am-5pm (6pm July & August)
FREE INFO LINE 0800 456600 www.monkeyworld.org

Every day's a fun day!
50p off
per person
up to 4 max
Rescue, Rehabilitation
& Re-homing
Whitchurch, Bristol
Just off A37 Tel 01275 540173
HorseWorld
THE FRIENDS OF BRISTOL HORSES SOCIETY
Registered Charity no.1121920
www.horseworld.org.uk

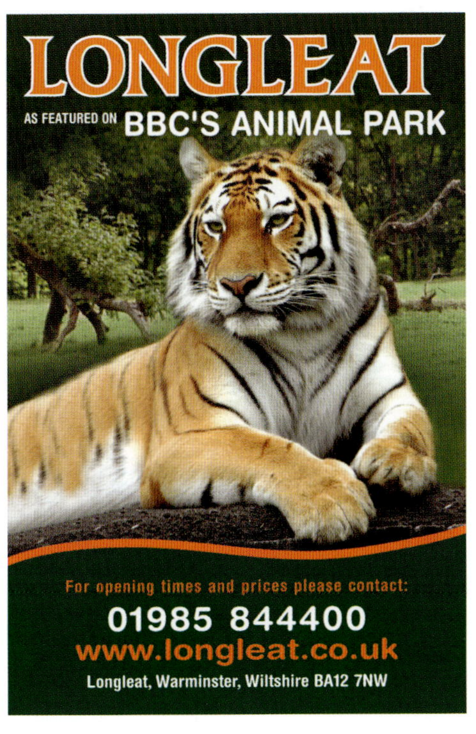
LONGLEAT
AS FEATURED ON BBC'S ANIMAL PARK
For opening times and prices please contact:
01985 844400
www.longleat.co.uk
Longleat, Warminster, Wiltshire BA12 7NW

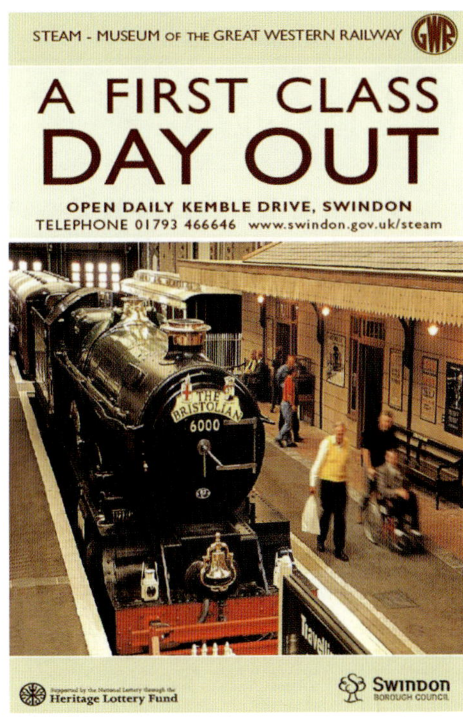
STEAM - MUSEUM OF THE GREAT WESTERN RAILWAY
GWR
A FIRST CLASS
DAY OUT
OPEN DAILY KEMBLE DRIVE, SWINDON
TELEPHONE 01793 466646 www.swindon.gov.uk/steam
THE BRISTOLIAN
6000
Heritage Lottery Fund
Swindon
Borough Council

Devon
County Council

TOWER PARK
LET YOURSELF GO...
TOWER PARK
part of
X-LEISURE
www.x-leisure.co.uk
EAT
FITNESS
CINEMA
AMUSEMENTS
BINGO
WATERPARK
DRINK
BOWL
01202 723671
WWW.TOWERPARKCENTRE.CO.UK
TOWER PARK YARROW ROAD
POOLE BH12 4NY
EXCHANGE
EMPIRE
REEL•TIME
TOWER PARK

SO MUCH TO ENJOY AT
CHEW
VALLEY LAKE
For a relaxing day out Chew Valley Lake has such a lot to enjoy. Situated in an area of outstanding natural beauty, the lake is a haven for wildlife and a delight for visitors.
Two lakeside nature trails meander through meadows & reedbeds, one suitable for buggies & wheelchairs • Viewing points & bird hide • Many species of wildfowl • Landscaped picnic sites overlooking the lake • Watch the sailing and fishing • Tea shop for snacks, hot lunches & ice creams • Gift shop & visitor centre • Woodford Lodge licensed restaurant for breakfast, lunch & dinners (01275 331365 for bookings).
Bristol Water
Leisure
Chew Valley Lake is 5 miles south of Bristol off the A368. More information on 01275 333345 or www.bristolwater.co.uk

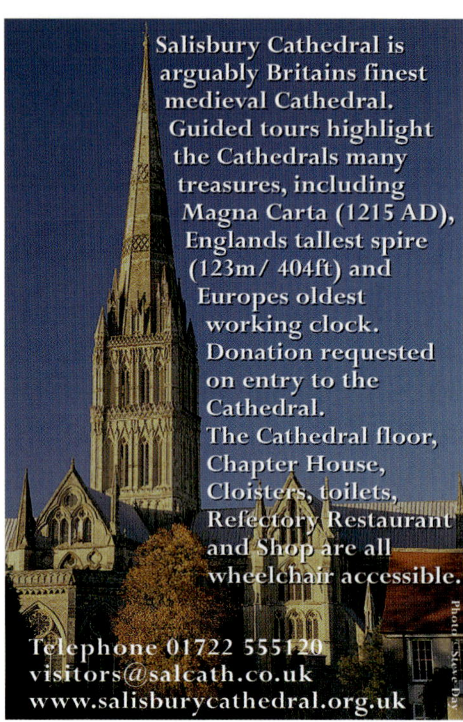
Salisbury Cathedral is arguably Britains finest medieval Cathedral. Guided tours highlight the Cathedrals many treasures, including Magna Carta (1215 AD), Englands tallest spire (123m/ 404ft) and Europes oldest working clock. Donation requested on entry to the Cathedral.
The Cathedral floor, Chapter House, Cloisters, toilets, Refectory Restaurant and Shop are all wheelchair accessible.
Telephone 01722 555120
visitors@salcath.co.uk
www.salisburycathedral.org.uk

SEE
SOMETHING AMAZING,
DISCOVER SOMETHING NEW
Torquay Museum
Agatha Christie
Kents Cavern Collection
Devon Farmhouse

Heritage
LOTTERY FUNDED

SOUTH SOMERSET DISTRICT COUNCIL

Beacon Authority

THERMAE
BATH SPA
hot baths, cool views
In the heart of Bath, Thermae Bath Spa is Britain's original and only natural thermal Spa
Telephone: 0844 888 0844 www.thermaebathspa.com

(01297) 560697
www.woodfarm.co.uk
THE POPLARS
WOOD FARM CARAVAN PARK
CHARMOUTH • DORSET DT6 6BT
• Two bedroom self catering flat
• We aim to offer every possible comfort
• Spacious Kitchen and Dining Area
• Bath and separate wheel-in shower area
• Comfortable lounge
• Breathtaking Views and Spectacular Heritage Coast
★★★
SELF CATERING

THE BRISTOL
HIPPODROME
MUSICALS • BALLET • OPERA • FAMILY • COMEDY • CONCERTS
Welcoming all visitors with Access requirements
Telephone: 0117 302 3222 • Mon - Fri 10am-6pm • Voice or minicom
email: trish.hodson@livenation.co.uk
www.bristolhippodrome.org.uk for show and venue info

ROYAL SIGNALS MUSEUM

Cotswold Charm

Scope Inclusion Team
"Scope's inclusion team offers much-needed support to help disabled people achieve inclusion in the wider community."
therapy
nursing
care
education support
For more information please contact Scope's inclusion team on:
01752 840059, by fax on: 01752 846162
or email: andrew.mullen@scope.org.uk
scope
Time to get equal

www.cornwall.gov.uk
CORNWALL
COUNTY COUNCIL
CORNWALL
Celebrating Diversity

BROADWINDSOR
CRAFT AND DESIGN CENTRE
Shopping for all the family ~ the main shop & individual craft studios are the ideal place to shop or browse.
Meals and refreshments are served in the relaxed atmosphere of the restaurant and conservatory. For lunch, homemade soups, hot dishes and salads are created daily using local produce. Fine coffee, teas, homemade cakes and Dorset cream teas are served throughout the day.
The attractive setting is well complemented by the warm and friendly serves.
The main shop, restaurant and conservatory are now fully air-conditioned.
Open daily all year 10am – 5pm
Large free car park
Coaches welcome
Broadwindsor DT8 3PX
Tel; 01308 868362
www.broadwindsorcrafts.co.uk

ROYAL AIR FORCE museum COSFORD
FREE fun 4 all!
Just 3 minutes drive from Jnct 3 on the M54
FREE ADMISSION
Cosford, Shifnal, Shropshire, TF11 8UP
Tel: 01902 376 200
www.rafmuseum.org/fun4all
www.nationalcoldwarexhibition.org.uk

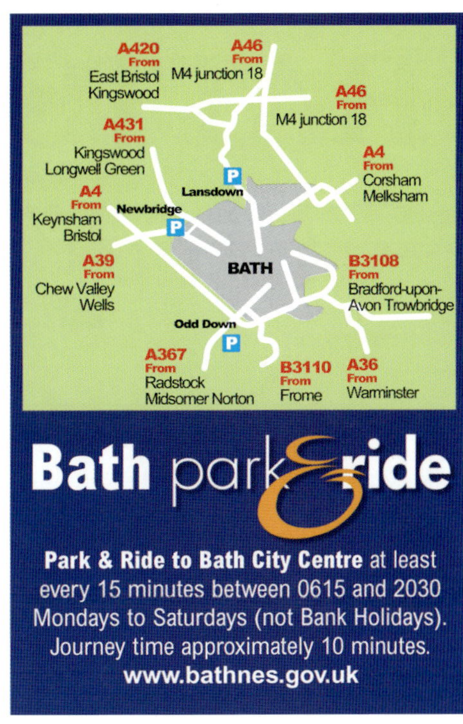
A420 From East Bristol Kingswood
A46 From M4 junction 18
A46 From M4 junction 18
A431 From Kingswood Longwell Green
A4 From Corsham Melksham
A4 From Keynsham Bristol
Lansdown
Newbridge
BATH
A39 From Chew Valley Wells
B3108 From Bradford-upon-Avon Trowbridge
Odd Down
A367 From Radstock Midsomer Norton
B3110 From Frome
A36 From Warminster
Bath park&ride
Park & Ride to Bath City Centre at least every 15 minutes between 0615 and 2030 Mondays to Saturdays (not Bank Holidays).
Journey time approximately 10 minutes.
www.bathnes.gov.uk

1793
PLYMOUTH
The Smooth ENGLISH GIN
DISTILLERY & TOUR · BRASSERIE COCKTAIL LOUNGE · SHOP
Discover gin's colourful history and over 200 years of distilling at Black Friars Distillery - the working home of Plymouth Gin since 1793.
Take a guided tour and learn about the art of making the world famous Plymouth Gin and discover more secrets behind the taste of this unique and original gin.
Plymouth Gin Black Friars Distillery
60 Southside Street,
Plymouth, PL1 2LQ
T: 01752 665292
E: rose@plymouthgin.com
W: www.plymouthgin.com
The distillery is open from 10 am - 5.30pm Monday to Saturday and 11am - 5.00pm Sunday, except for Christmas.
PLYMOUTH
DRINKAWARE.CO.UK

Discover East Devon's glorious Axe Valley - from the top of a heritage tram
Enclosed saloons operate during bad weather
Journey from Seaton, gateway town to the World Heritage Jurassic Coast through two nature reserves alongside the Axe estuary to historic Colyton, Devon's most rebellious town.
SEATON TRAMWAY
It's electric
2008 OPENING TIMES
OPEN DAILY 9th - 24th February, 15th March - 2nd November,
OPEN WEEKENDS
1st - 9th March &
8th November - 13th December
Halloween Tram of Terror: 31st October
Bird Watching Trips February - May & September - December
Children's Birthday Parties and Tram Driving Lessons available all year round
Santa Specials 14th, 21st, 23rd & 24th December
HARBOUR ROAD, SEATON, DEVON EX12 2NQ
T: 01297 20375
E: info@tram.co.uk www.tram.co.uk

An award winning day out
DairyLand FARM WORLD
incorporating The Bull Pen
Seven Days for the Price of One!
Unlimited Weekly Entry
(Valid on full paying admission tickets only)
Open Daily
10am - 5pm
28 Mar-28 Oct
Pony & Hayrides • Bottle Feeding • Pat-a-pet • Pet Parade
Astra Slides • Drop Slides • Ball Pool & so much more...
INFOLINE 01872 510349
On the A3058 4 miles from Newquay

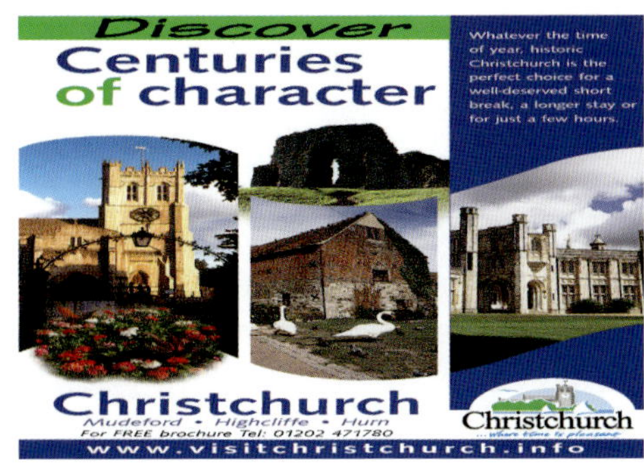
Discover
Centuries of character
Whatever the time of year, historic Christchurch is the perfect choice for a well-deserved short break, a longer stay or for just a few hours.
Christchurch
Mudeford • Highcliffe • Hurn
For FREE brochure Tel: 01202 471780
Christchurch
www.visitchristchurch.info

THE ROSES
TEWKESBURY
The best in live entertainment & film throughout the year, at Gloucestershire's friendliest theatre
Brum
Sun Street, Tewkesbury, Gloucestershire GL20 5NX
01684 295074 www.rosestheatre.org

Registered Charity no. 262158
BRUNEL'S
ss GREAT BRITAIN™
enjoyEngland
Awards for Excellence 2007
GOLD WINNER
0117 926 0680
ssgreatbritain.org

Bath CitySightseeing
If you're local or visiting the area, you'll be amazed what you learn on our two Bath CitySightseeing tours
01225 330444

Gloucester Cathedral
The Cathedral Church of St. Peter and the Holy and Invisible Trinity
Gloucester Cathedral welcomes disabled visitors
• There is a "touch and hear" centre for visually impaired visitors. We provide audio guides, large print and Braille guides and a leaflet to help visitors with disabilities
• Wheelchair lifts & a toilet for disabled visitors
• A loop system operates during services.
Open every day 07.30-18.00
Please check website for Services
+44 (0)1452 528095 www.gloucestercathedral.org.uk

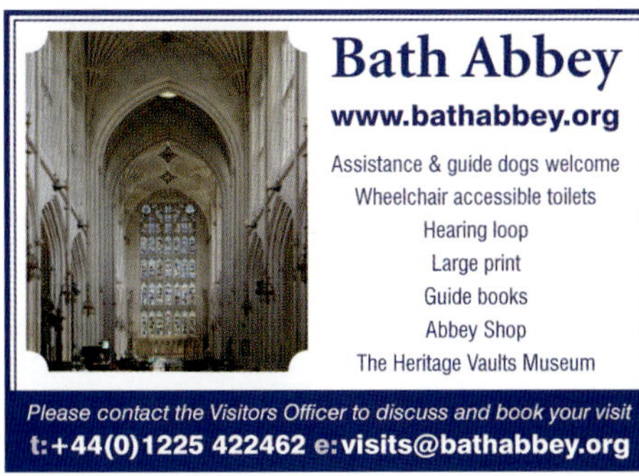
Bath Abbey
www.bathabbey.org
Assistance & guide dogs welcome
Wheelchair accessible toilets
Hearing loop
Large print
Guide books
Abbey Shop
The Heritage Vaults Museum
Please contact the Visitors Officer to discuss and book your visit
t:+44(0)1225 422462 e:visits@bathabbey.org

RHS GARDEN
Rosemoor
Royal Horticultural Society
Reg. Charity no. 222879/SC038262
www.rhs.org.uk/rosemoor
01805 624067

DZP
Dartmoor Zoological Park
Where the wild things are...
Largest collection of big cats in the south west as well as otters, bears, wolves, snakes, owls, flamingos, parrots, tigers, lynx, and more...
OPEN DAILY - ALL YEAR
Summer opening hours
10am - 6pm from 31st March 2008
Winter opening hours
10am - 4pm from 1st November 2008
Adults - £8.95
Concessions - £7.95
Child (4-16) - £6.95
Children under 4 Free
Weekly & Annual passes also available. See the website or call us direct for further information and special events.
Dartmoor Zoological Park
Sparkwell, Plymouth
Devon, PL7 5DG
01752 837645
www.dartmoorzoo.co.uk
The Book "We Bought a Zoo" by Benjamin Mee
AVAILABLE NOW
Ben's Zoo - As seen on BBC2

St Michaels WITHOUT
Welcome to St. Michael's Without
Come and visit us in our beautiful church. All are welcome; find a peaceful spot away from the bustle of the city, enjoy our café, explore our building or find out about forthcoming concerts and events.
St. Michael's Without, Broad Street, Bath, BA1 5LJ (Next to the main post office and Podium shopping centre)
Open 10.00am – 4.00pm Monday to Saturday, Sunday services at 9.00am and 10.30am
www.stmichaelsbath.org.uk
tel:01225 447103

The Devon Guild of Craftsmen
Jubilee Gallery, The Terrace café and large Craft Shop
Riverside Mill, Bovey Tracey, Devon
Free Admission
01626 832223
www.crafts.org.uk
EXCELLENT ACCESS FOR ALL
THE DEVON GUILD OF CRAFTSMEN

Access All Areas
See the world's best collection of tanks in a new, world class home.
To find out more, click; www.tankmuseum.org
MLA
MUSEUMS LIBRARIES ARCHIVES
THE TANK MUSEUM
An indepdendent Museum and registered charity no: 1102661

YATE SHOPPING CENTRE
OVER 100 SHOPS
1400 FREE PARKING SPACES
OPEN 7 DAYS A WEEK
EVENTS THROUGHOUT THE YEAR
Visit www.yateshoppingcentre.co.uk for store opening times.

EXETER

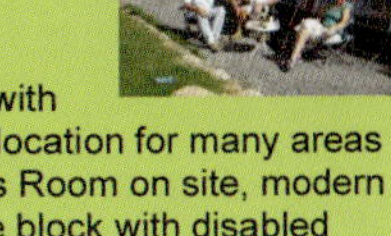

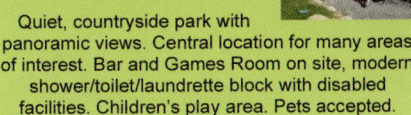

## Where can I get help and advice?

Tourist Information Centres offer friendly help with accommodation and holiday ideas as well as suggestions of places to visit and things to do. You'll find contact details at the beginning of each regional section.

# Scotland

Clockwise: Edinburgh Military Tattoo; St Andrews, Fife; Castle Stalker, Argyll and Bute

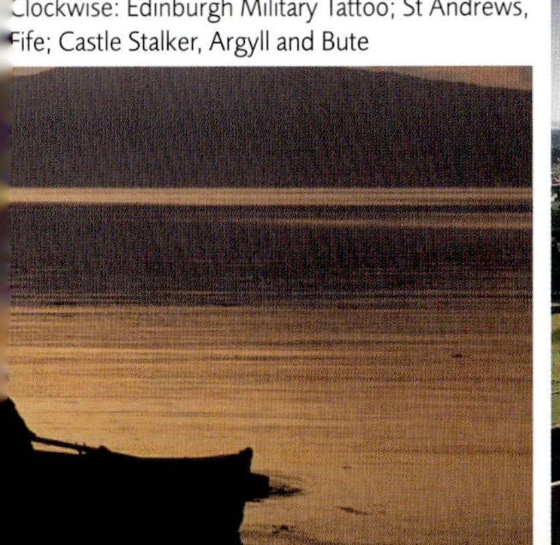

# Scotland
## For the holiday of a lifetime

### Scotland is a destination which draws people from many countries.

The breath-taking scenery, fascinating castles, historic houses, beautiful gardens, traditional culture, great places to stay, good food from natural produce (and whisky!), and friendly people are all part of the magical mix which is Scotland. Wherever you go, there are memories waiting to be captured – the glimpse of a castle on the hillside, a stunning garden in June, a Scottish ceilidh in full swing, or a pipe band at one of the Highland games.

**Main:** Loch Garry, Highlands
**Above:** Culzean Castle, Ayrshire

Scotland may be a small country but within a day's travel you can pass through fertile farmlands, wooded glens, seaside villages, market towns and rugged mountains. A good network of roads makes it easy to get around, so you can choose to have one or two central bases and explore from there each day.

When you plan your holiday, remember that, while Edinburgh and Glasgow have museums, art galleries and entertainment in abundance, many of the smaller towns and the villages have fine museums and interesting visitor attractions which highlight the local heritage.

Scotland has festivals of all kinds – as well as the famous Edinburgh International Festival, there are film festivals, folk music and rock music festivals, science festivals, walking festivals, story-telling festivals and, of course, the Highland Games! These take place throughout the summer months. 2009 is the Year of the Homecoming, when there will be special events for Scots and for visitors from all over the world. As well as some major events, there will be smaller happenings from Burns' Night (25 January) to St. Andrew's Night (30 November). For the latest information check homecomingscotland2009.com.

Scotland prides itself on its food, with the emphasis on fresh produce, locally sourced. The beef, lamb, and sea-food are among the best in the world and part of our traditional fare; restaurants and pubs often concentrate on these when they put together their menus. But the cosmopolitan mix of Scotland's people provides a range of restaurants, from Italian to Chinese, from Indian to American, so you can dine out in a different country every night!

The accommodation includes hotels, guest houses, bed and breakfasts, self-catering cottages, hostels, apartments and caravan holiday homes. Look out for the VisitScotland star grading logo, which means that the accommodation is part of the VisitScotland grading scheme; it will be visited once a year, so you can be sure that the high standards are maintained.

Spend a week in Scotland and you'll gather memories for a lifetime!

**VisitScotland, the national tourist board, has published a guide which lists over 1,000 places to stay and to visit, all of them accessible to visitors with mobility impairments.** For information and a free copy of "Accessible Scotland", call VisitScotland.com on + 44 1506 832 121 (from outside the UK) or 1800 22 55 121 (from the Republic of Ireland) or 0845 22 55 121 (from within the UK); or e.mail on info@visitscotland.com or check the website visitscotland.com/accommodation/accessiblescotland where you can search by town and by category of accessibility.

Business Tourism: If you are considering Scotland for a meeting or a conference, then our city conference centres are wheelchair accessible, with top-class hotels nearby. Check out www.conventionscotland.com or e.mail: businesstourism@visitscotland.com or call + 44 (0) 131 472 2355.

Live it. Visit Scotland.
visitscotland.com 0845 22 55 121
The No.1 booking and information service for Scotland.


**Left:** Edinburgh Castle

# Great days out

## Base yourself in a vibrant city, explore romantic castles and gardens, learn the secrets of whisky making, or admire the dramatic scenery of the Highlands and the Cairngorms. Scotland is bursting with memorable experiences and 2009, the Year of the Homecoming and Robert Burns' 250th anniversary, is more eventful than ever.

### Historic Edinburgh

Visit Scotland's capital, **Edinburgh**, and enjoy a tale of two cities: the wonderful blend of the medieval Old Town and the New Town built at the end of the 18th century and full of elegant streets and crescents. Getting around is easy because so many must-sees are within a few minutes of the main thoroughfare, Princes Street, including **Edinburgh Castle**, the **National Museum of Scotland**, the **Palace of Holyroodhouse** and the **Scotch Whisky Experience**. Discover other highlights like the **Royal Botanic Garden** and **Royal Yacht Britannia** just a short trip away by bus or taxi.

Kelvingrove Art Gallery and Museum, Glasgow

**Regular buses** with on-board guide and informative commentary tour the city's main attractions – hop off and back on again as often as you like during the day. Some buses are wheelchair accessible; simply ask the Tourist Information Centre to check for you.

### Lively Glasgow

Switch scenes to **Glasgow**, only an hour away from Edinburgh on Scotland's west coast. It's a much bigger city, with a well-justified reputation for **fantastic shops**, **buzzing nightlife** and captivating places to visit. Browse in **Kelvingrove Museum and Art Gallery**, a treasure trove of art collections and eclectic natural history displays. Put on your wish list, too, the **Gallery of Modern Art**, the **St Mungo Museum of Religious Life and Art** plus **Pollok House** and its surrounding park. And don't miss the **Museum of Transport**, a fascinating collection of cars and trams, bicycles, fire engines and ship models from the past. **Hop-on, hop-off buses** with guide and commentary offer a stress-free way to explore, exactly as in Edinburgh.

Left to right: Royal Botanic Garden, Edinburgh; Urquhart Castle, Loch Ness

**why not...** cruise the Caledonian Canal and lochs linking Scotland's east and west coasts?

## Castle adventures

There are so many thrilling castles and historic houses in Scotland that you will want to come back again and again. **Historic Scotland** alone cares for more than 70 properties, including grand old **Stirling Castle**, and **Urquhart Castle** on the shores of Loch Ness – an ideal spot to look for the legendary **Loch Ness Monster**! Check out **The National Trust for Scotland's** 'Access Guide for Visitors with Disabilities' for detailed information about historic houses, castles and gardens in its care. Then add to your holiday itinerary: **Newhailes** on the outskirts of Edinburgh and romantic **Culzean Castle and Country Park** near Ayr on the west coast. There is also the evocative **Culloden Battlefield**, where a new visitor centre brings vividly to life the story of the battle in 1746 when Bonnie Prince Charlie and his army were defeated by the forces of the British Government.

Glencoe, Highlands

## Glorious gardens and scenery

Come any time from June to October to admire gardens at their best. Among the most colourful are **Crathes Castle Gardens** on Royal Deeside – look out for its world-renowned June border. At **Castle Kennedy Gardens** near Stranraer you can explore a rich history of horticultural development that continues to this day. Meanwhile **Kailzie Gardens** in the Borders boast both wild and walled gardens, alive with spring bluebells and daffodils, as well as beautiful summer roses. Savour more memorable moments amid the country's breathtaking scenery, especially the mountains and glens of the **Highlands**, where rugged, heather-clad slopes are home to red deer. Travel to the Highlands and the **Cairngorm National Park** – the UK's largest – for the most spectacular landscapes.

## Take a wee dram

Whisky distilleries are a must-do for an authentic flavour of Scotland, although their layout can make accessibility for less mobile visitors difficult. However, at **Dewar's World of Whisky** near Aberfeldy, wheelchair users can see most of the distillery, as they can at **Auchentoshan Distillery** on the

**why not...** enjoy Sir Walter Scott's favourite spot, Scott's View on to the Eildon Hills?

Clockwise: Crathes Castle Gardens, Royal Deeside; The Falkirk Wheel; Auchentoshan Distillery, Glasgow

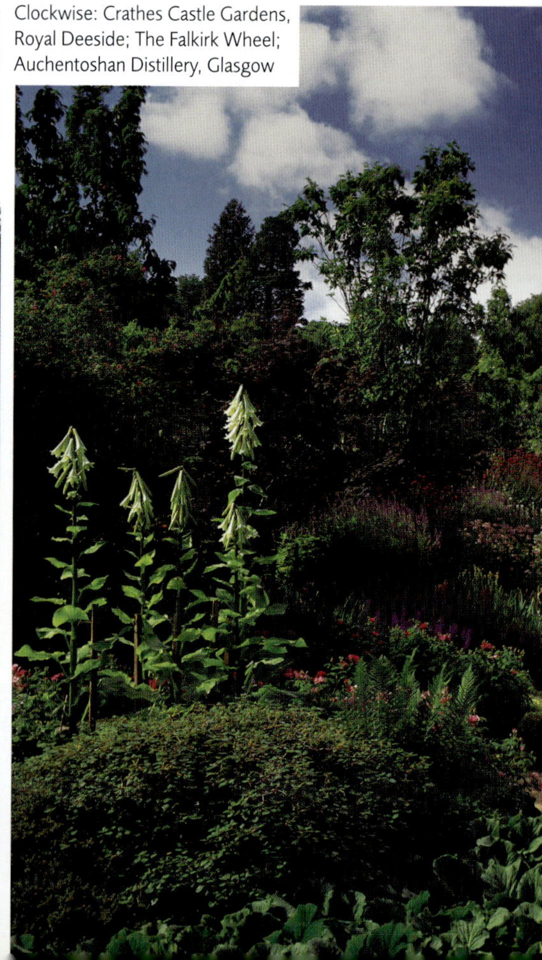

outskirts of Glasgow, and at **Dallas Dhu** on Speyside. Once you've learnt some of the secrets behind uisge-beatha, the 'water of life', treat yourself to a wee dram.

## Scotland for all seasons

When is the best time for a trip? **Attractions** in main towns and cities are open all year and in rural areas usually from Easter until the end of October. Weather can be changeable – from day to day and hour to hour – but in the summer you can enjoy long evenings when the sun doesn't set until after ten o'clock. And do make a date to visit in 2009, the **Year of the Homecoming** and the 250th anniversary of the birth of Scotland's national poet **Robert Burns**. Special events are being staged all over Scotland, to welcome home Scots, people of Scottish ancestry – and everyone else! Check what's happening at homecomingscotland2009.com and make a date to celebrate everything the country is famous for: from whisky and golf to great minds, innovations and music. Also, pick up VisitScotland's **Accessible Scotland** guide for information and details of facilities at all the places mentioned here: see overleaf to get your free copy.

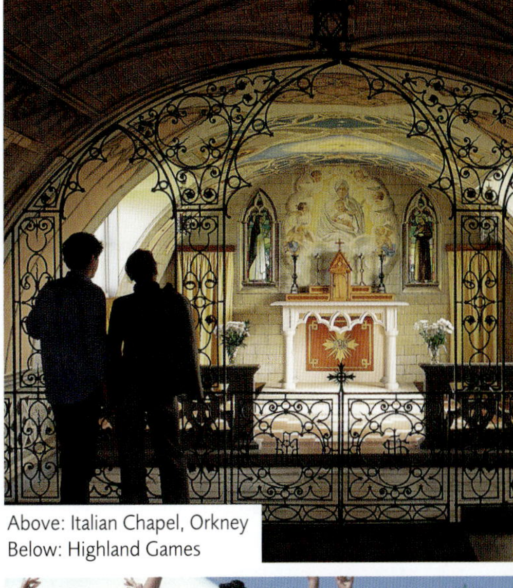

Above: Italian Chapel, Orkney
Below: Highland Games

# Useful national contacts

## VisitScotland
**t** 0845 22 55 121
**t** 1800 22 55 121 (if calling from the Republic of Ireland)
**t** +44 1506 832 121 (from outside the UK)
**e** info@visitscotland.com
**w** visitscotland.com
To browse or book accessible accommodation online go to visitscotland.com/accommodation /accessiblescotland.

## Publications

### Accessible Scotland

VisitScotland's guide to accessible accommodation and visitor attractions for people with physical disabilities. To order a copy call 0845 22 55 121 or email info@visitscotland.com.

## Information

### British Airports Authority Scotland
Operates three airports in Scotland:

Aberdeen Airport
**t** 0870 040 0006
**w** aberdeenairport.com

Edinburgh Airport
**t** 0870 040 0007
**w** edinburghairport.com

Glasgow Airport
**t** 0870 040 0008
**w** glasgowairport.com

The textphone for all three airports is (0141) 585 6161.

There are also airports in Shetland, Orkney, Wick, Prestwick, Inverness, Dundee and the Outer Hebrides.

### Caledonian MacBrayne
**t** (01475) 650100
CalMac operates ferries to the islands off the west coast of Scotland. For information on accessibility, visit calmac.co.uk/customers-requiring-assistance.html and calmac.co.uk/facilities-lounges-disability-amenities-pet-areas-.htm.

### First ScotRail
**t** 0800 912 2901
**w** firstgroup.com/scotrail/specialneeds/index.html
Operates trains throughout Scotland and has a dedicated department to help travellers with mobility impairment. It is recommended that, when possible, arrangements are made in advance to ensure that First ScotRail is able to meet your needs.

## Historic Scotland

Longmore House, Salisbury Place, Edinburgh EH9 1SH
**t** (0131) 668 8600
**e** hs.explorer@Scotland.gsi.gov.uk
**w** historic-scotland.gov.uk
Historic Scotland has more than 70 castles, abbeys and historic monuments in its care, including Edinburgh, Stirling and Urquhart Castles. Accessibility details are on the website under the entry for each property.

## National Trust for Scotland

Wemyss House, 28 Charlotte Square, Edinburgh EH2 4ET
**t** (0131) 243 9300
**e** information@nts.org.uk
**w** nts.org.uk
The Trust looks after castles, historic houses, gardens and wilderness areas. They publish a free guide describing accessibility at each property and detailed information is on the website under the entry for each property.

## Scottish Borders Rangers Service

Harestanes Visitor Centre, Ancrum, Jedburgh, Roxburghshire TD8 6UQ
**t** 01835 830281
**w** scotborders.gov.uk
The Rangers Service helps people enjoy and understand the Borders countryside. It has been working with the Ability Centre, Galashiels to produce a list of places to visit with easy access. For more information visit bordersdisabilityforum.org.uk/news/rangers.

If you have any queries about the VisitScotland scheme or wish to give feedback on any of the accommodation listed in the Scotland section of this guide, call the Quality and Standards Department of VisitScotland on (01463) 244111, email qainfo@visitscotland.com or write to Quality and Standards Department, VisitScotland, Cowan House, Inverness Retail and Business Park, Inverness IV2 7GF.

Loch Lomond

# Tourist Information Centres

When you are in Scotland, the best source of information and advice are the tourist information centres. Many are wheelchair-accessible with help, but, as they are usually in the town centre, it may not be possible to park outside and it is recommended that you telephone in advance. You can book accommodation on visitscotland.com or call 0845 22 55 121 or email info@visitscotland.com.

| | | |
|---|---|---|
| **Aberdeen** | 23 Union Street | (01224) 252212 |
| **Aberfeldy** | The Square | (01887) 820276 |
| **Aberfoyle*** | Trossachs Discovery Centre, Main Street | (01877) 382352 |
| **Abington** | Junction 13, M74 Services | (01864) 502436 |
| **Alford*** | Old Station Yard, Main Street | (01975) 562052 |
| **Anstruther*** | Harbourhead | (01333) 311073 |
| **Arbroath** | Harbour Visitor Centre, Fishmarket Quay | (01241) 872609 |
| **Ardgarten*** | Glen Croe, By Arrochar | (01301) 702432 |
| **Aviemore** | 7 The Parade, Grampian Road | (01479) 810930 |
| **Ayr** | 22 Sandgate | (01292) 290300 |
| **Ballater** | Old Royal Station, Station Square | (01339) 755306 |
| **Balloch** | Old Station Building, Balloch Road | (01389) 753533 |
| **Banchory*** | Bridge Street | (01330) 822000 |
| **Banff*** | Collie Lodge, St Mary's Car Park, Low Street | (01261) 812419 |
| **Biggar*** | 155 High Street | (01899) 221066 |
| **Blairgowrie** | 26 Wellmeadow | (01250) 872960 |
| **Bo'ness*** | Bo'ness Station, Union Street | (01506) 826626 |
| **Bowmore** | The Square, Main Street | (01496) 810254 |
| **Braemar** | The Mews, Mar Road | (01339) 741600 |
| **Brechin*** | Pictavia Centre, Brechin Castle Centre | (01356) 623050 |
| **Brodick** | The Pier | (01770) 303774/776 |
| **Callander** | Ancaster Square | (01877) 330342 |
| **Campbeltown** | MacKinnon House, The Pier | (01586) 552056 |
| **Castle Douglas*** | Market Hill Car Park | (01556) 502611 |
| **Castlebay*** | Main Street | (01871) 810336 |
| **Craignure** | The Pierhead | (01680) 812377 |
| **Crail*** | Museum and Heritage Centre, 62-64 Marketgate | (01333) 450869 |
| **Crathie*** | The Car Park | (01339) 742414 |
| **Crieff** | High Street | (01764) 652578 |
| **Daviot Wood*** | The Picnic Area, A9 | (01463) 772971 |
| **Drumnadrochit** | The Car Park | (01456) 459086 |
| **Dufftown*** | The Clock Tower | (01340) 820501 |

| | | |
|---|---|---|
| **Dumbarton (Milton)*** | A82 Northbound | (01389) 742306 |
| **Dumfries** | 64 Whitesands | (01387) 253862 |
| **Dunbar*** | 143A High Street | (01368) 863353 |
| **Dundee** | Discovery Point, Discovery Quay | (01382) 527527 |
| **Dunfermline** | 1 High Street | (01383) 720999 |
| **Dunkeld** | The Cross | (01350) 727688 |
| **Dunoon** | 7 Alexandra Parade | (01369) 703785 |
| **Dunvegan** | 2 Lochside | (01470) 521878 |
| **Durness** | Sango | (01971) 511368 |
| **Edinburgh** | 3 Princes Street | (0131) 473 3846 |
| **Edinburgh Airport** | Edinburgh International Airport | (0131) 473 3231/3142 |
| **Elgin** | 17 High Street | (01343) 542666/543388 |
| **Eyemouth*** | Auld Kirk, Manse Road | (01890) 750678 |
| **Falkirk** | Falkirk Wheel, Lime Road, Tamfourhill | (01324) 620244 |
| **Fort William** | 15 High Street | (01397) 701801 |
| **Fraserburgh*** | 3 Saltoun Square | (01346) 518315 |
| **Glasgow** | 11 George Square | (0141) 204 4400 |
| **Glasgow Airport** | International Arrivals Hall | (0141) 848 4440 |
| **Grantown-on-Spey*** | 54 High Street | (01479) 872242 |
| **Gretna** | Unit 38, Gateway Outlet Village, Glasgow Road | (01461) 337834 |
| **Hawick** | Heart of Hawick, Tower Mill, Kirkstile | (01450) 373993 |
| **Helensburgh*** | Clock Tower, East Clyde Street | (01436) 672642 |
| **Huntly*** | 9A The Square | (01466) 792255 |
| **Inveraray** | Front Street | (01499) 302063 |
| **Inverness** | Castle Wynd | (01463) 252401 |
| **Inverurie*** | 18 High Street | (01467) 625800 |
| **Jedburgh** | Murrays Green | (01835) 863171/864099 |
| **Kelso** | Town House, The Square | (01573) 228055 |
| **Kinross*** | High Street | (01577) 863680 |
| **Kirkcaldy** | The Merchant's House, 339 High Street | (01592) 267775 |
| **Kirkcudbright*** | Harbour Square | (01557) 330494 |
| **Kirkwall** | The Travel Centre, West Castle Street | (01856) 872856 |
| **Lanark** | Horsemarket, Ladyacre Road | (01555) 661661 |
| **Largs*** | The Railway Station Booking Office | (01475) 689962 |
| **Lerwick** | Market Cross | (01595) 693434 |
| **Lochboisdale*** | The Pier Road | (01878) 700286 |
| **Lochgilphead*** | 29 Lochnell Street | (01546) 602344 |
| **Lochinver*** | Assynt Visitor Centre | (01571) 844373 |
| **Lochmaddy*** | The Pier Road | (01876) 500321 |
| **Melrose** | Abbey House, Abbey Street | (01896) 822283 |
| **Moffat*** | Churchgate | (01683) 220620 |

| | | |
|---|---|---|
| **Newton Stewart*** | Dashwood Square | (01671) 402431 |
| **Newtongrange*** | Scottish Mining Museum, Lady Victoria Gallery | (0131) 663 4262 |
| **North Berwick** | 1 Quality Street | (01620) 892197 |
| **North Kessock*** | Picnic Site | (01463) 731836 |
| **Oban** | Albany Street | (01631) 563122 |
| **Paisley** | 9A Gilmour Street | (0141) 889 0711 |
| **Peebles** | 23 High Street | (01721) 723159 |
| **Perth** | Lower City Mills, West Mill Street | (01736) 450600/636103 |
| **Pirnhall** | Junction 9 Service Area, M9/M80 | (01786) 814111 |
| **Pitlochry** | 22 Atholl Road | (01796) 472215 |
| **Portree** | Bayfield House, Bayfield Road | (01478) 614906 |
| **Rothesay** | Isle of Bute Discovery Centre, Victoria Street | (01700) 502151 |
| **St Andrews** | 70 Market Street | (01334) 472021/474609 |
| **Selkirk*** | Halliwells House | (01750) 20054 |
| **Southwaite** | M6 Service Area | (01697) 473445 |
| **Stirling** | 41 Dumbarton Road | (01786) 475019 |
| **Stonehaven*** | 66 Allardice Street | (01569) 762806 |
| **Stornoway** | 26 Cromwell Street | (01851) 703088 |
| **Stranraer** | 28 Harbour Street | (01776) 702595 |
| **Stromness*** | Ferry Terminal Building, Pier Head | (01856) 850716 |
| **Strontian*** | Strontian | (01967) 402382 |
| **Sumburgh** | Sumburgh Airport, Wilsness Terminal | (01595) 693434 |
| **Tarbert** | The Pier | (01859) 502001 |
| **Tarbert Loch Fyne*** | Harbour Street | (01880) 820429 |
| **Tarbet*** | Tarbet Loch Lomond, By Arrochar | (01301) 702260 |
| **Thurso*** | Riverside Road | (01847) 893155 |
| **Tillicoultry** | Unit 22, Sterling Mills Outlet Village | (01259) 769696 |
| **Tobermory*** | The Pier, Main Street | (01688) 302182/302610 |
| **Tyndrum** | 6 Main Street | (01838) 400324 |
| **Ullapool*** | Argyle Street | (01854) 612486 |

*seasonal opening

where to stay in

# Scotland

The following establishments participate in VisitScotland's quality assessment scheme and have been awarded one of three mobility categories. If you have a visual or hearing requirements, please contact the accommodation directly.

Place names in the blue bands with a map reference are shown on the maps at the front of this guide.

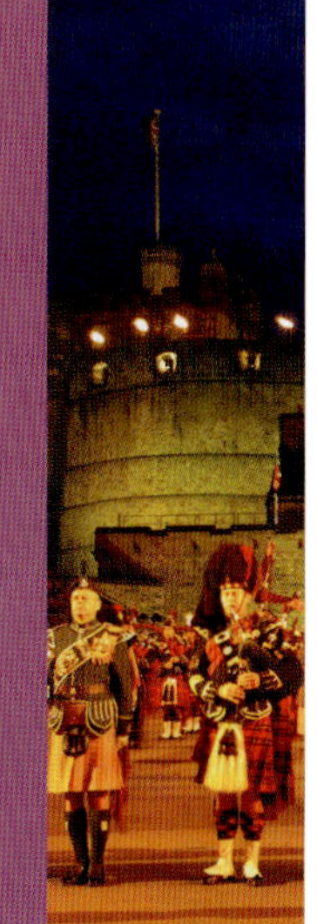

## Accommodation symbols

Symbols give useful information about services and facilities. You can find a key to these symbols on page 8.

**ABERDEEN,** Aberdeenshire **HOTEL**

★★★★ HOTEL

**Aberdeen Patio Hotel** Beach Boulevard, Aberdeen AB24 5EF
**t** (01224) 633339
**e** info@patiohotels.com **w** patiohotels.com

**ABERDEEN,** Aberdeenshire **HOTEL**

★★★★ HOTEL

**Ardoe House Hotel** South Deeside Road, Blairs, Aberdeen AB12 5YP
**t** (01224) 860600
**e** h6626@accor.com **w** mercure-uk.com

**ABERDEEN,** Aberdeenshire **HOTEL**

★★★★ HOTEL

**Copthorne Hotel** 122 Huntly Street, Aberdeen AB10 1SU
**t** (01224) 630404
**e** reservations.aberdeen@mill-cop.com **w** millenniumhotels.com

**ABERDEEN,** Aberdeenshire **HOTEL**

★★★ METRO HOTEL

**Express by Holiday Inn** Chapel Street, Aberdeen AB10 1SQ
**t** (01224) 623500
**e** info@hieaberdeen.co.uk **w** hieaberdeen.co.uk

**ABERDEEN,** Aberdeenshire **HOTEL**

★★★★ HOTEL

**Holiday Inn Aberdeen West** Westhill Drive, Westhill, Aberdeen AB32 6TT
**t** (01224) 270300
**e** reservations@hiaberdeenwest.co.uk **w** holiday-inn.com/aberdeenwest

**ABERDEEN,** Aberdeenshire **HOTEL**

★★★★★ HOTEL

**The Marcliffe Hotel and Spa** North Deeside Road, Pitfodels, Aberdeen AB15 9YA
**t** (01224) 861000
**e** stewart@marcliffe.com **w** marcliffe.com

**ABERDEEN,** Aberdeenshire **HOTEL**

★★★ HOTEL

**Speedbird Inn** Argyll Road, Dyce, Aberdeen AB21 0AF
**t** (01224) 772883
**e** reception@speedbirdinns.co.uk **w** speedbirdinns.co.uk

**ABERDEEN,** Aberdeenshire — **HOTEL**

★★★★ HOTEL

**Thistle Aberdeen Airport Hotel** Argyll Road, Aberdeen AB21 0AF
**t** (01224) 725252
**e** Aberdeen.Airport@Thistle.co.uk

**ABERDEEN,** Aberdeenshire — **HOTEL**

★★★ HOTEL

**Thistle Aberdeen Altens** Souterhead Road, Altens, Aberdeen AB12 3LF
**t** (01224) 877000

**ABERDEEN,** Aberdeenshire — **SELF CATERING**

★★ SELF CATERING

**Hillhead Halls contact** Stephanie Millar, Conference & Event Office, University of Aberdeen, Aberdeen AB24 3FX **t** (01224) 272660
**e** accommodation@abdn.ac.uk **w** abdn.ac.uk/summeraccommodation

**ABERDEEN,** Aberdeenshire — **SELF CATERING**

★★ SELF CATERING

**Woolmanhill Flats contact** The Robert Gordon University, Schoolhill, Aberdeen AB10 1FR **t** (01224) 262134
**e** accommodation@rgu.ac.uk **w** scotland2000.com/rgu

**ABERDEEN,** Aberdeenshire — **CAMPUS**

★★ CAMPUS

**Crombie House** University of Aberdeen, Aberdeen AB24 3TS
**t** (01224) 273444
**e** accommodation@abdn.ac.uk **w** abdn.ac.uk/summeraccommodation

**ABERDEEN,** Aberdeenshire — **CAMPUS**

★★ CAMPUS

**King's Hall** University of Aberdeen, Aberdeen AB24 3FX
**t** (01224) 273444
**e** j.tuckwell@abdn.ac.uk **w** abdn.ac.uk/kingshall

**ABERFELDY,** Perth and Kinross — **GUEST ACCOMMODATION**

★★★ FARMHOUSE

**Tomvale** Tom of Cluny, Aberfeldy PH15 2JT
**t** (01887) 820171
**e** tomvale@aol.com **w** tomvale.co.uk

**ABERFELDY,** Perth and Kinross — **SELF CATERING**

★★★★ SELF CATERING

**Drumcroy Lodges contact** Mrs Nicola McDiarmid, Mains of Murthly, Aberfeldy PH15 2EA **t** (01887) 820978
**e** info@highland-lodges.com **w** highland-lodges.com

**ABERFELDY,** Perth and Kinross — **SELF CATERING**

★★★ SELF CATERING

**Loch Tay Lodges contact** Mr & Mrs J Duncan Millar, Remony, Aberfeldy PH15 2HR **t** (01887) 830209
**e** remony@btinternet.com **w** lochtaylodges.co.uk

**ABERFELDY,** Perth and Kinross — **SELF CATERING**

★★★ SELF CATERING

**Tomvale contact** Mrs Hazel Kennedy, Tomvale, Tom of Cluny Farm, Aberfeldy PH15 2JT **t** (01887) 820171
**e** tomvale@aol.com **w** tomvale.co.uk

**ABERFOYLE,** Stirling — **HOTEL**

★★★★ HOTEL

**Forest Hills Hotel** Kinlochard, By Aberfoyle FK8 3TL
**t** (01877) 387277
**e** forest_hills@macdonald-hotels.co.uk **w** foresthills-hotel.com

## ABERFOYLE, Stirling — GUEST ACCOMMODATION

★★★ GUEST HOUSE

**Crannaig House** Trossachs Road, Aberfoyle FK8 3SR
**t** (01877) 382276
**e** crannaighouse@aol.com **w** crannaighouse.com

## ABOYNE, Aberdeenshire — SELF CATERING

★★–★★★★★ SELF CATERING

**Glen Tanar Estate contact** Mrs Fiona Martin, Glen Tanar Estate, Brooks House, Aboyne AB34 5EU **t** (013398) 86451
**e** info@glentanar.co.uk **w** glentanar.co.uk

## ACHNASHEEN, Highland — HOTEL

★★★★ COUNTRY HOUSE HOTEL

**The Torridon** Torridon, Achnasheen IV22 2EY
**t** (01445) 791242
**e** info@thetorridon.com **w** thetorridon.com

## ACHNASHEEN, Highland — SELF CATERING

★★★★ SELF CATERING

**31 Mellon Charles contact** Mr R MacKenzie, 8 Ormiscaig, Aultbea, Achnasheen IV22 2JJ
**t** (01445) 731382
**e** randcmackenzie@aol.com

## ALEXANDRIA, West Dunbartonshire — HOTEL

★★★★★ HOTEL

**De Vere Cameron House** Loch Lomond, Alexandria G83 8QZ
**t** (01389) 755565
**e** reservations@cameronhouse.co.uk **w** cameronhouse.co.uk

## ALEXANDRIA, West Dunbartonshire — SELF CATERING

★★★★ SELF CATERING

**Greystonelea Lodge contact** Mr Gerry Woods, Greystonelea, Gartocharn, Alexandria G83 8SD **t** (01389) 830419
**e** contact@greystonelealodge.com **w** greystonelealodge.com

## ALLOWAY, South Ayrshire — SELF CATERING

★★★ SELF CATERING

**South Lodge contact** Mr M Dunlop, Brigend House, Doonside Estate, Alloway KA7 4EB
**t** (01292) 441313

## ANSTRUTHER, Fife — SELF CATERING

★★★★ SELF CATERING

**Lobster Pot Cottage contact** Mrs Kim Kirkaldy, Inchardie Farmhouse, Kilconquhar KY9 1JU **t** (01333) 340640
**e** kirkaldy2004@hotmail.com **w** lobster-pot.co.uk

## APPIN, Argyll and Bute — SELF CATERING

★★★★ SELF CATERING

**Appin House Apartments**
**contact** Mrs D Mathieson, Appin House Apartments & Lodges, Appin House, Appin PA38 4BN **t** (01631) 730207
**e** denys@appinhouse.co.uk **w** appinhouse.co.uk

## ARDMADDY, Argyll and Bute — SELF CATERING

★★★★ SELF CATERING

**Ardmaddy Castle Holiday Cottages**
**contact** Mrs C H Struthers, Castle Holiday Cottages, Ardmaddy Castle, By Oban PA34 4QY **t** (01852) 300353
**e** ardmaddycastle@btopenworld.com **w** scottish-country-cottages.co.uk

At-a-glance symbols are explained on page 8.

## ASHKIRK, Scottish Borders — SELF CATERING

★★★ SELF CATERING

**Synton Mains Farm** **contact** Mrs W Davies, The Davies Partnership, Synton Mains Farm, Ashkirk TD7 4PA **t** (01750) 32388
**e** syntonmains@onetel.com **w** syntonmains-holidaycottages.co.uk

## AUCHTERARDER, Perth and Kinross — HOTEL

★★★★★ HOTEL

**The Gleneagles Hotel** Auchterarder PH3 1NF
**t** (01764) 662231
**e** resort.sales@gleneagles.com **w** gleneagles.com

## AUCHTERARDER, Perth and Kinross — SELF CATERING

★★★★★ SELF CATERING

**Duchally Country Estate** **contact** Mr Graeme MacDonald, Duchally Country Estate, By Gleneagles, Auchterarder PH3 1PN **t** (01764) 663071
**e** duchally@clublacosta.com **w** duchally.com

## AULDEARN, Highland — GUEST ACCOMMODATION

★★★ INN

**Covenanters' Inn** High Street, Auldearn IV12 5TG
**t** (01667) 452456
**e** covenanters@aol.com **w** covenanters-inn.co.uk

## AVIEMORE, Highland — GUEST ACCOMMODATION

★★★ LODGE

**Macdonald Academy** Aviemore Highland Resort, Aviemore PH22 1PF
**t** (01479) 810781
**w** aviemorehighlandresort.co.uk

## AVIEMORE, Highland — SELF CATERING

★★★ SELF CATERING

**Badaguish** **contact** Mrs Dylis Stretton, Badaguish, Cairngorm Outdoor Centre, Aviemore PH22 1QU **t** (01479) 861285
**e** dylis.s@badaguish.org **w** badaguish.org

## AVIEMORE, Highland — SELF CATERING

★★★–★★★★★ SELF CATERING

**High Range Self Catering Chalets** **contact** Mr F Vastano, High Range Holiday Lodges, Grampian Road, Aviemore PH22 1PT **t** (01479) 810636
**e** info@highrange.co.uk **w** highrange.co.uk

## AVIEMORE, Highland — SELF CATERING

★★★ SELF CATERING

**The Highland Council @ Badaguish** **contact** Mr Phil Swainson, The Highland Council at Badaguish, Sluggan, Aviemore PH22 1QU **t** (01479) 861734
**e** badaguish@highland.gov.uk

## AVIEMORE, Highland — SELF CATERING

★★★ SELF CATERING

**Silverglades Holiday Homes** **contact** Miss P MacKenzie, Silverglades Holiday Homes, Dalnabay, Aviemore PH22 1TD **t** (01479) 810165
**e** info@silverglades.co.uk **w** silverglades.co.uk

## AVIEMORE, Highland — HOSTEL

★★★★ HOSTEL

**Aviemore Bunkhouse** Dalfaber Road, Aviemore PH22 1PU
**t** (01479) 811181
**e** sales@aviemore-bunkhouse.com **w** aviemore-bunkhouse.com

## AVIEMORE, Highland — HOSTEL

★★★★ HOSTEL

**Aviemore SYHA** 25 Grampian Road, Aviemore PH22 1PR
**t** (01479) 810345
**e** reservations@syha.org.uk **w** syha.org.uk

**AYR,** South Ayrshire — HOTEL

★★★ HOTEL

**Horizon Hotel** Esplanade, Ayr KA7 1DT
t (01292) 264384
e reception@horizonhotel.com w horizonhotel.com

**AYR,** South Ayrshire — HOTEL

★★★ HOTEL

**Ramada Jarvis** Dalblair Road, Ayr KA7 1UG
t (01292) 269331
w jarvis.co.uk

**AYR,** South Ayrshire — HOTEL

★★★★ HOTEL

**Western House Hotel** 2 Whitletts Road, Ayr KA9 0JE
t 0870 850 5666
e sjardine@ayr-racecource.co.uk w ayr-racecource.co.uk

**BACK,** Western Isles — GUEST ACCOMMODATION

★★★★★ GUEST HOUSE

**Broad Bay House** Back HS2 0LQ
t (01851) 820990
e stay@broadbayhouse.co.uk w broadbayhouse.co.uk

**BALLACHULISH,** Argyll and Bute — HOTEL

★★★ HOTEL

**The Ballachulish Hotel** Ballachulish PH49 4JY
t (01855) 811606
w foliohotels.com/ballachulish

**BALLACHULISH,** Argyll and Bute — HOTEL

★★★ HOTEL

**Isles of Glencoe Hotel & Leisure Centre** Ballachulish PH49 4HL
t (01855) 811602
e gm.glencoe@foliohotels.com w foliohotels.com

**BALLANTRAE,** South Ayrshire — HOTEL

★★★★★ HOTEL

**Glenapp Castle** Ballantrae KA26 0NZ
t (01465) 831212
e info@glanappcastle.com w glenappcastle.com

**BALLATER,** Aberdeenshire — GUEST ACCOMMODATION

★★★ GUEST HOUSE

**Glenernan** 37 Braemar Road, Ballater AB35 5RQ
t (01339) 753111
e enquiries@gleneranguesthouse.com w glenernanguesthouse.com

**BALLATER,** Aberdeenshire — SELF CATERING

★★★★ SELF CATERING

**Bonn-na Coille contact** Mr & Mrs Hughes, Bonn-Na Coille, 8 Braemar Road, Ballater AB35 5RL
t (01339) 755414
e ballaterbnc@btinternet.com

## Accessibility accommodation in Scotland

Establishments in Scotland are awarded one or more of three mobility categories. If you have visual or hearing requirements, please contact the accommodation directly.

At-a-glance symbols are explained on page 8.

**BALLATER,** Aberdeenshire Map ref 7D3 — **SELF CATERING**

SELF CATERING

Units **4**
Sleeps **4–6**
Low season per wk
£305.00–£400.00
High season per wk
£405.00–£640.00

## Crathie Opportunity Holidays, Crathie, Royal Deeside

The Manse Courtyard, Crathie, Ballater AB35 5UL **t** (013397) 42100
**e** info@crathieholidays.org.uk **w** crathieholidays.org.uk

Access abc

General

Unit

Payment Credit/debit cards, cash, cheques

*Short breaks available from Nov-Mar from £70 per cottage per night (excl Christmas and New Year).*

Four lovely cottages designed and equipped to the highest standard of accessibility. Facilities include wheel-in shower, height-adjustable sink, Clos-o-Mat toilet and adjustable bed. We also have a range of other equipment available. In the heart of the Cairngorms National Park and within easy reach of the famous whisky and castle trails.

**open** All Year
**nearest shop** 1 mile
**nearest pub** 4 miles

*Crathie is in the heart of Royal Deeside situated halfway between Ballater and Braemar on the A93, approximately 50 miles west of Aberdeen.*

**BALNAIN,** Highland — **SELF CATERING**

SELF CATERING

**Lochletter Lodges contact** Miss M Brook, Lochletter Lodges, Balnain, Drumnadrochit IV63 6TJ **t** (01456) 476313
**e** info@lochletter.com **w** lochletter.com

**BALQUHIDDER,** Stirling — **SELF CATERING**

★★★★
SELF CATERING

**Lochside Cottages contact** Mrs Catriona Oldham, Muirlaggan, Balquhidder, Lochearnhead FK19 8PB **t** (01877) 384219
**e** info@lochsidecottages.co.uk **w** lochsidecottages.co.uk

**BANCHORY,** Aberdeenshire — **SELF CATERING**

★★★–★★★★★
SELF CATERING

**Woodend Chalet Holidays contact** Mrs Ursula George, Laigh Riggs, Kincardine Road, Torphins, Banchory AB31 4GH **t** (01339) 882562
**e** info@woodendchalets.co.uk **w** woodendchalets.co.uk

**BENDERLOCH,** Argyll and Bute — **HOTEL**

★★★★★
COUNTRY HOUSE HOTEL

**Isle of Eriska Hotel** Benderloch PA37 1SD
**t** (01631) 720371
**e** office@eriska-hotel.co.uk **w** eriska-hotel.co.uk

**BIGGAR,** South Lanarkshire — GUEST ACCOMMODATION

★★★ GUEST HOUSE

**The Glenholm Centre** Broughton, by Biggar ML12 6JF
**t** (01899) 830408
**e** info@glenholm.co.uk **w** glenholm.co.uk

**BIXTER,** Isle of Shetland — SELF CATERING

★★★ SELF CATERING

**Langbiggin contact** Mrs J P Adamson, Langbiggin, Bixter ZE2 9NA
**t** (01595) 810361

**BLAIRGOWRIE,** Perth and Kinross — SELF CATERING

★★★–★★★★ SELF CATERING

**Glenbeag Mountain Lodges contact** Mr D Stewart, Glenbeag Mountain Lodges, Spittal of Glenshee PH10 7QE **t** (01250) 885204
**e** glenbeag@aol.com **w** glenbeag.co.uk

**BONNYRIGG,** Midlothian — HOTEL

★★★ SMALL HOTEL

**The Retreat Castle** Cockpen Road, Bonnyrigg EH19 3HS
**t** (0131) 660 3200
**e** info@theretreatcastle.com **w** theretreatcastle.com

**BRECHIN,** Angus — HOTEL

★★★ SMALL HOTEL

**Northern Hotel** 2 Clerk Street, Brechin DD9 6AE
**t** (01356) 625400
**e** info@northern-hotel.co.uk **w** northern-hotel.co.uk

**BRESSAY,** Isle of Shetland — GUEST ACCOMMODATION

★★★★ GUEST HOUSE

**Northern Lights Holistic Spa** Sound View Uphouse, Bressay ZE2 9ES
**t** (01595) 820733
**e** northernlightsholisticspa@fsmail.net

**BRIDGE OF ALLAN,** Stirling — HOTEL

★★★★ SMALL HOTEL

**The Queen's Hotel** 24 Henderson Street, Bridge of Allan FK9 4HP
**t** (01786) 833268
**e** info@queenshotelscotland.com **w** queenshotelscotland.com

**BRODICK,** North Ayrshire — HOTEL

★★★★ HOTEL

**Auchrannie Country House Hotel** Brodick KA27 8BZ
**t** (01770) 302234
**e** hotel@auchrannie.co.uk **w** auchrannie.co.uk

**BRODICK,** North Ayrshire — HOTEL

★★★★ HOTEL

**Auchrannie Spa Resort** Brodick KA27 8BZ
**t** (01770) 302234
**e** resort@auchrannie.co.uk **w** auchrannie.co.uk

**BRORA,** Highland — GUEST ACCOMMODATION

★★★★ BED & BREAKFAST

**Glenaveron** Golf Road, Brora KW9 6QS
**t** (01408) 621601
**e** alistair@glenaveron.co.uk **w** glenaveron.co.uk

**BROUGHTY FERRY,** Dundee — HOTEL

★★ SMALL HOTEL

**The Fisherman's Tavern Hotel** 10-16 Fort Street, Broughty Ferry, Dundee DD5 2AD **t** (01382) 775941
**w** fishermanstavern.co.uk

At-a-glance symbols are explained on page 8.

## BROUGHTY FERRY, Dundee — SELF CATERING

★★★★ SELF CATERING

**Forbes of Kingennie** contact Mr M Forbes, Omachie Farm, Kingennie, By Dundee DD5 3RE t (01382) 350777
e info@forbesofkingennie.com w forbesofkingennie.com

## BURNTISLAND, Fife — HOTEL

★★★ SMALL HOTEL

**Kingswood Hotel** Kinghorn Road, Burntisland KY3 9LL
t (01592) 872329
e rankin@kingswoodhotel.co.uk w kingswoodhotel.co.uk

## CAMPBELTOWN, Argyll and Bute — SELF CATERING

★★★★ SELF CATERING

**The Dairy, Rhoin Farm** contact Mrs Catherine Ralston, Rhoin Holidays, Rhoin Farm, Campbeltown PA28 6NT t (01856) 820220
e info@rhoinholidays.co.uk w rhoinholidays.co.uk

## CARRADALE, Argyll and Bute — GUEST ACCOMMODATION

★★★★ RESTAURANT WITH ROOMS

**Dunvalanree** Portrigh Bay, Carradale PA28 6SE
t (01583) 431226
e stay@dunvalanree.com w dunvalanree.com

## CARRBRIDGE, Highland — HOSTEL

★★★★ HOSTEL

**Slochd Mhor Lodge** Slochd, Carrbridge PH23 3AY
t (01479) 841666
e slochd666@aol.com w slochd.co.uk

## CARRUTHERSTOWN, Dumfries & Galloway — HOTEL

★★★ HOTEL

**Hetland Hall Hotel** Carrutherstown DG1 4JX
t (01387) 840201
e info@hetlandhallhotel.co.uk w hetlandhallhotel.co.uk

## CASTLE DOUGLAS, Dumfries & Galloway — HOTEL

★★★ COUNTRY HOUSE HOTEL

**Balcary Bay Hotel** Auchencairn, Auchencairn, by Castle Douglas DG7 1QZ
t (01556) 640217
e reservations@balcary-bay-hotel.co.uk w balcary-bay-hotel.co.uk

## CASTLE DOUGLAS, Dumfries & Galloway — GUEST ACCOMMODATION

★★★★ BED & BREAKFAST

**Douglas House B&B** 63 Queen Street, Castle Douglas DG7 1HS
t (01556) 503262
e info@douglas-house.com w douglas-house.com

## CASTLE DOUGLAS, Dumfries & Galloway — SELF CATERING

★★–★★★ SELF CATERING

**Barncrosh Farm** contact Mr Mickey Ball, Barncrosh Leisure, Barncrosh Farm, Ringford, Castle Douglas DG7 1TX t (01556) 680216
e enq@barncrosh.co.uk w barncrosh.co.uk

## CASTLE DOUGLAS, Dumfries & Galloway — SELF CATERING

★★★★ SELF CATERING

**Chapelerne Farmhouse** contact Mr and Mrs Thomas Brown, Trowdale, Bridge of Urr, Castle Douglas DG7 3BY t (01556) 650270 & 07977 763780
e brown.trowdale@virgin.net w chapelerne.com

## CASTLE DOUGLAS, Dumfries & Galloway — SELF CATERING

★★★★ SELF CATERING

**Craigadam Lodge** contact Mrs C Pickup, Craigadam, Kirkpatrick Durham, Castle Douglas DG7 3HU t (01556) 650233
e inquiry@craigdam.com w craigadam.com

**CLYDEBANK,** West Dunbartonshire — **HOTEL**

★★★★ HOTEL

**The Beardmore Hotel & Conference Centre** Beardmore Street, Clydebank G81 4SA **t** (0141) 951 6000
**e** info@beardmore.scot.nhs.uk **w** thebeardmore.com

**COCKSBURNPATH,** Scottish Borders — **CAMPING, CARAVAN & HOLIDAY PARK**

★★★★★ HOLIDAY PARK

**Pease Bay Caravan Park** Cocksburnpath TD13 5YP
**t** (01368) 830206
**e** info@peasebay.co.uk **w** peasebay.co.uk

**COLDINGHAM,** Scottish Borders — **CAMPING, CARAVAN & HOLIDAY PARK**

★★★★★ HOLIDAY PARK

**Crosslaw Caravan Park** Coldingham TD14 5NS
**t** (01890) 771316
**w** crosslaw.co.uk

**COLDSTREAM,** Scottish Borders — **SELF CATERING**

★★★ SELF CATERING

**Little Swinton Cottages, Cotoneaster & Honeysuckle contact** Mrs S Brewis, Leet Villa, Leet Street, Coldstream TD12 4BJ **t** (01890) 882173
**e** suebrewis@tiscali.co.uk **w** littleswinton.co.uk

**COMRIE,** Perth and Kinross — **SELF CATERING**

★★★★ SELF CATERING

**Highland Heather Lodges contact** Mr John Davidson, Highland Heather Lodges, South Crieff Road, Comrie PH6 2JA **t** (01764) 670440
**e** enquiries@highlandheatherlodges.co.uk **w** highlandheatherlodges.co.uk

**CRIEFF,** Perth and Kinross — **HOTEL**

★★★ HOTEL

**Murraypark Hotel** Connaught Terrace, Crieff PH7 3DJ
**t** (01764) 658000
**e** enquiries@murraypark.com **w** murraypark.com

**CRIEFF,** Perth and Kinross — **GUEST ACCOMMODATION**

★★★ GUEST HOUSE

**Comely Bank Guest House** 32 Burrell Street, Crieff PH7 4DT
**t** (01764) 653409
**e** marion@comelybank.demon.co.uk

**CRIEFF,** Perth and Kinross — **SELF CATERING**

★★★–★★★★★ SELF CATERING

**Crieff Hydro Hotel Chalets contact** Mr C Dalton, Crieff Hydro Hotel, Crieff PH7 3LQ **t** (01764) 655555
**e** enquiries@crieffhydro.com **w** crieffhydro.com

**CULRAIN,** Highland — **HOSTEL**

★★★★ HOSTEL

**Carbisdale Castle Youth Hostel** Culrain IV24 3DP
**t** (01549) 921232
**e** reservations@syha.org.uk **w** syha.org.uk

**DAVIOT,** Highland — **GUEST ACCOMMODATION**

★★★★★ BED & BREAKFAST

**The Lodge at Daviot Mains** Daviot IV2 5ER
**t** (01463) 772215
**e** margaret.hutcheson@btopenworld.com **w** daviotlodge.co.uk

**DEERNESS,** Orkney Islands — **SELF CATERING**

★★★★ SELF CATERING

**Deersound Cottage contact** Mr G E Coates, Mossquoy, Deerness KW17 2QL
**t** (01856) 741331
**e** eric.coates@ukgateway.net **w** orkney.org/deersound

At-a-glance symbols are explained on page 8.

## DIRLETON, East Lothian — SELF CATERING

★★★★ SELF CATERING

**Denis Duncan House contact** Miriam Toosey, Eastgate House, Upper East Street, Sudbury CO10 1UB **t** (01787) 372343
**e** info@thelinberwicktrust.org.uk **w** thelinberwicktrust.org.uk

## DOLLAR, Clackmannanshire — SELF CATERING

★★★★ SELF CATERING

**Arndean Cottages contact** Mr Stewart, Arndean Cottages, Arndean, Dollar FK14 7NH **t** (01259) 743525
**e** johnny@farmltr.fsnet.co.uk **w** arndean.co.uk

## DRUMNADROCHIT, Highland — GUEST ACCOMMODATION

★★★★ GUEST HOUSE

**Woodlands** East Lewiston, Drumnadrochit IV63 6UJ
**t** (01456) 450356
**e** stay@woodlands-lochness.co.uk **w** woodlands-lochness.co.uk

## DRYMEN, Stirling — HOTEL

★★★ HOTEL

**Winnock Hotel** The Square, Drymen G63 0BL
**t** (01360) 660245
**e** info@winnockhotel.com **w** winnockhotel.com

## DRYMEN, Stirling — SELF CATERING

★★★★★ SELF CATERING

**Foxglove Cottages contact** Mr & Mrs J Bowman, Foxglove Cottages, Gartness Road, Drymen, Loch Lomond G63 0DW **t** (01360) 661128
**e** jean@foxglovecottages.co.uk **w** foxglovecottages.co.uk

## DRYMEN, Stirling — HOSTEL

★★★ HOSTEL

**Rowardennan Youth Hostel** Rowardennan, By Drymen G63 0AR
**t** 0870 004 1148
**e** reservations@syha.org.uk **w** syha.org.uk

## DUMFRIES, Dumfries & Galloway — HOTEL

★★★ HOTEL

**Aston Hotel** The Crichton, Bankend Road, Dumfries DG1 4ZZ
**t** 0845 634 0205
**e** enquiries@astonhotels.co.uk **w** astonhotels.co.uk

## DUMFRIES, Dumfries & Galloway — SELF CATERING

★★★★ SELF CATERING

**Alder and Acorn contact** Mr and Mrs Robert Broatch, The Cedars, Clarencefield, Dumfries DG1 4NF **t** (01387) 870608
**e** suebroatch@aol.com

## DUMFRIES, Dumfries & Galloway Map ref 6C3 — SELF CATERING

★★★★ SELF CATERING

Units **1**
Sleeps **8**
High season per wk
£250.00–£600.00

### The Byre, Dunscore

**contact** Mr Joe Kirk, The Byre, Auldgirth DG2 0SP **t** (01387) 820258
**e** lowkirkbridebyre@btinternet.com **w** lowkirkbridebyre.com

Warm, comfortable, new byre conversion. Spacious and modern yet full of character, set on an organic farm. Beautiful countryside, large garden with patio. Games room.

**open** All year
**nearest shop** 2.5 miles
**nearest pub** 3 miles

General P S
Unit
Payment Cash, cheques

**DUMFRIES,** Dumfries & Galloway — SELF CATERING

★★★–★★★★★ SELF CATERING

**Conheath Gatelodge** **contact** Mrs J D Murray, Conheath, Glencaple, Dumfries DG1 4UB **t** (01387) 770205
**e** conheath@btconnect.com

**DUMFRIES,** Dumfries & Galloway — SELF CATERING

★★–★★★ SELF CATERING

**Gubhill Farm** **contact** Mrs G Stewart, Gubhill Farm, Ae, Dumfries DG1 1RL
**t** (01387) 860648
**w** aefarmcottages.co.uk

**DUMFRIES,** Dumfries & Galloway — SELF CATERING

★★★–★★★★★ SELF CATERING

**Nunland Country Holidays** **contact** Mr & Mrs Chambers, Nunland Country Holidays, By Lochfoot, Dumfries DG2 8PZ **t** (01387) 730214
**e** mail@nunland.co.uk **w** nunland.co.uk

**DUNBAR,** East Lothian — CAMPING, CARAVAN & HOLIDAY PARK

★★★★ HOLIDAY PARK

**Belhaven Bay Caravan Park** Belhaven Bay, Dunbar EH42 1TU
**t** (01368) 865956
**e** belhaven@meadowhead.co.uk **w** meadowhead.co.uk

**DUNBAR,** East Lothian — CAMPING, CARAVAN & HOLIDAY PARK

★★★★★ HOLIDAY PARK

**Thurston Manor Holiday Home Park** Innerwick, Dunbar EH42 1SA
**t** (01368) 840643
**e** mail@thurstonmanor.co.uk **w** thurstonmanor.co.uk

**DUNDEE** — GUEST ACCOMMODATION

★★ LODGE

**Your Hotel** 296a Strathmore Avenue, Dundee DD3 6SP
**t** (01382) 826000
**e** dundeesales@revpar.co.uk

**DUNDEE** — CAMPUS

★★★ CAMPUS

**West Park Centre** 319 Perth Road, Dundee DD2 1NN
**t** (01382) 647177
**e** info@dundee.ac.uk **w** westparkcentre.com

**DUNFERMLINE,** Fife — HOTEL

★★★ COUNTRY HOUSE HOTEL

**Best Western Keavil House Hotel** Crossford, Dunfermline KY12 8QW
**t** (01383) 736258
**e** sales@keavilhouse.co.uk **w** keavilhouse.co.uk

**DUNFERMLINE,** Fife — HOTEL

★★★ METRO HOTEL

**Express By Holiday Inn Dunfermline** Halbeath, Dunfermline KY11 8DY
**t** (01383) 748220
**e** info@hiexpressdunfermline.co.uk **w** hiexpress.co.uk/dunfermline

**DUNFERMLINE,** Fife — HOTEL

★★★★ HOTEL

**Garvock House Hotel** St John's Drive, Transy, Dunfermline KY12 7TU
**t** (01383) 621067
**e** sales@garvock.co.uk **w** garvock.co.uk

**DUNNING,** Perth and Kinross — SELF CATERING

★★★★–★★★★★ SELF CATERING

**Duncrub Holidays Ltd** **contact** Mrs W Marshall, Duncrub Holidays Ltd, Dalreoch, Dunning PH2 0QJ **t** (01764) 684368
**e** reservations@duncrub-holidays.com **w** duncrub-holidays.com

At-a-glance symbols are explained on page 8.

**DUNOON,** Argyll and Bute — **HOSTEL**

★★–★★★★ GROUP ACCOMMODATION

**Bernice Farmhouse & Cottage** Bernice, By Dunoon PA23 8QX
**t** (01369) 706337
**e** benmorecentre@benmorecentre.co.uk **w** benmorecentre.co.uk

**DUNS,** Scottish Borders — **SELF CATERING**

★★★ SELF CATERING

**Green Hope contact** Mr & Mrs Landale, Green Hope, Ellemford, Duns TD11 3SG
**t** (01361) 890242

**EDINBURGH** — **HOTEL**

★★★★★ HOTEL

**Caledonian Hilton Hotel** Princes Street, Edinburgh EH1 2AB
**t** (0131) 222 8888
**e** ednchhirm@hilton.com **w** hilton.uk.com

**EDINBURGH** — **HOTEL**

BUDGET HOTEL

**Edinburgh City Centre (Morrison St) Premier Inn** 1 Morrison Link, Edinburgh EH3 8DN **t** 0870 238 3319
**e** edinburghccmorrisonstpti@whitbread.com **w** premiertravelinn.com

**EDINBURGH** — **HOTEL**

★★★★ HOTEL

**Edinburgh Marriott** 111 Glasgow Road, Edinburgh EH12 8NF
**t** 0870 400 7293
**e** reservations.edinburgh@marriotthotels.co.uk **w** marriott.co.uk/edib

**EDINBURGH** — **HOTEL**

★★★ METRO HOTEL

**Express By Holiday Inn** Britannia Way, Ocean Drive, Edinburgh EH6 6LA
**t** (0131) 555 4422
**e** andrew@hiex-edinburgh.com **w** hiex-edinburgh.com

**EDINBURGH** — **HOTEL**

★★★ METRO HOTEL

**Express By Holiday Inn** 16-22 Picardy Place, Edinburgh EH1 3JT
**t** (0131) 558 2300
**e** info@hieedinburgh.co.uk **w** hiexpress.co.uk

**EDINBURGH** — **HOTEL**

★★★ HOTEL

**Hilton Edinburgh Airport** Edinburgh International Airport, Edinburgh EH28 8LL
**t** (0131) 519 4400
**w** hilton.com

**EDINBURGH** — **HOTEL**

★★★ HOTEL

**Hilton Edinburgh Grosvenor** 7-21 Grosvenor Street, Edinburgh EH12 5EF
**t** (0131) 226 6001
**w** hilton.com

**EDINBURGH** — **HOTEL**

HOTEL

**Holiday Inn Edinburgh** Corstorphine Road, Edinburgh EH12 6UA
**t** 0870 400 9026
**e** edinburgh@ihg.com **w** edinburgh.holiday-inn.com

**EDINBURGH** — **HOTEL**

★★★ HOTEL

**Holiday Inn Edinburgh-North** 107 Queensferry Road, Edinburgh EH4 3HL
**t** 0870 400 9025
**e** reservations-edinburghnorth@ihg.com **w** edinburgh-north.holiday-inn.com

**EDINBURGH** HOTEL

★★★ HOTEL

**Jurys Inn Edinburgh** 43 Jeffrey Street, Edinburgh EH1 1DH
**t** (0131) 200 3300
**e** bookings@jurysdoyle.com **w** jurysdoyle.com

**EDINBURGH** HOTEL

★★★★ HOTEL

**Novotel Edinburgh Centre** 80 Lauriston Place, Edinburgh EH3 9DE
**t** (0131) 656 3500
**e** h3271@accor.com

**EDINBURGH** HOTEL

★★★ HOTEL

**Ramada Mount Royal Hotel** 53 Princes Street, Edinburgh EH2 2DG
**t** (0131) 225 7161

**EDINBURGH** HOTEL

★★★ METRO HOTEL

**Salisbury Green Hotel Conference Centre** University of Edinburgh, Pollock Halls, 18 Holyrood Park Road, Edinburgh EH16 5AY **t** (0131) 662 2000
**e** salisbury.green@ed.ac.uk **w** salisburygreen.com

**EDINBURGH** HOTEL

★★★ HOTEL

**Thistle Edinburgh** 107 Leith Street, Edinburgh EH1 3SW
**t** (0131) 556 0111
**w** thistlehotels.com/edinburgh

**EDINBURGH** GUEST ACCOMMODATION

★★★ GUEST HOUSE

**Ardgarth Guest House** 1 St Mary's Place, Portobello, Edinburgh EH15 2QF
**t** (0131) 669 3021
**e** stay@ardgarth.com **w** ardgarth.com

**EDINBURGH** GUEST ACCOMMODATION

★★★ GUEST HOUSE

**Gillis** 100 Strathearn Road, Edinburgh EH9 1BB
**t** (0131) 623 8933
**e** gilliscentre@staned.org.uk **w** gilliscentre.org.uk

**EDINBURGH** GUEST ACCOMMODATION

★★★ LODGE

**Toby Carvery & Innkeepers Lodge Edin/Wes** 114-116 St Johns Road, Edinburgh EH12 8AX **t** 0870 243 0500
**w** innkeeperslodge.com

**EDINBURGH** GUEST ACCOMMODATION

LODGE

**Travelodge Edinburgh Central** 33 St Mary Street, Edinburgh EH1 1TA
**t** 0871 984 6137

**EDINBURGH** SELF CATERING

★★★★ SELF CATERING

**Atholl Brae contact** Mr and Mrs Ernie Bentley, Atholl Brae, c/o 20 Bellfield Crescent, Eddleston, Peebles EH45 8RQ **t** 07732 730177
**e** stay@athollbrae.co.uk **w** athollbrae.co.uk

**EDINBURGH** SELF CATERING

★★ SELF CATERING

**Napier University contact** Mrs H Crocker, Napier University, Sighthill Campus, 9 Sighthill Court, Edinburgh EH11 4BN **t** (0131) 455 3738
**e** vacation.lets@napier.ac.uk **w** napier.ac.uk/cca

At-a-glance symbols are explained on page 8.

## EDINBURGH — CAMPING, CARAVAN & HOLIDAY PARK

★★★★ HOLIDAY PARK

**Mortonhall Caravan Park** 38 Mortonhall Gate, Frogston Road East, Edinburgh EH16 6TJ **t** (0131) 664 1533
**e** mortonhall@meadowhead.com **w** meadowhead.co.uk

## EDINBURGH — HOSTEL

★★★★ BACKPACKERS

**Budget Backpackers** 37-39 Cowgate, Edinburgh EH1 1JR
**t** (0131) 226 6351
**e** hi@budgetbackpackers.com **w** budgetbackpackers.com

## EDINBURGH — CAMPUS

★★★ CAMPUS

**Edinburgh First**
Chancellor Court, Pollock Halls,18 Holyrood Park Road, Edinburgh EH16 5AY
**t** (0131) 651 2007
**e** edinburgh.first@ed.ac.uk **w** edinburghfirst.com

## ELGIN, Moray — SELF CATERING

★★★–★★★★ SELF CATERING

**Carden Self-Catering contact** Mrs S Mackessack-Leitch, Carden Self-Catering, Old Steading, Carden, Alves, Elgin IV30 8UP **t** (01343) 850222
**e** stb@carden.co.uk **w** carden.co.uk

## FARR, Highland — SELF CATERING

★★★★ SELF CATERING

**Dalvourn Holidays contact** Mr F M Forbes, Inverarnie House, Inverarnie IV2 6XA
**t** (01808) 521467 & (01808) 521747
**e** info@dalvourn.com **w** dalvourn.com

## FINSTOWN, Orkney Islands — SELF CATERING

★★★★ SELF CATERING

**Auldkirk Apartments contact** Mr Robert Clouston, 5 Clumly Avenue, Kirkwall KW15 1YU **t** (01856) 575498
**e** bob@r-clouston.co.uk **w** auldkirk-apt.co.uk

## FORGANDENNY, Perth and Kinross — GUEST ACCOMMODATION

★★★★ BED & BREAKFAST

**Battledown Bed & Breakfast** Off Station Road, Forgandenny PH2 9EL
**t** (01738) 812471
**e** i.dunsire@btconnect.com **w** battledownbb.co.uk

## FORRES, Moray — SELF CATERING

★★★–★★★★ SELF CATERING

**Tulloch Lodges contact** Mrs Mary Stewart, Tulloch Lodges, Rafford, Forres IV36 2RU **t** (01309) 673311
**e** enquiries@tullochlodges.com **w** tullochlodges.com

## FORT WILLIAM, Highland — HOTEL

★★★ HOTEL

**Clan MacDuff Hotel** Achintore Road, Fort William PH33 6RW
**t** (01397) 702341
**e** reception@clanmacduff.co.uk **w** clanmacduff.co.uk

## FOULDEN, Scottish Borders — SELF CATERING

★★★★ SELF CATERING

**The Paddock contact** Mr and Mrs John Hutchinson, Foulden Hagg, Foulden TD15 1UH **t** (01289) 386339
**e** johnhutch29@hotmail.com

## FRASERBURGH, Aberdeenshire — GUEST ACCOMMODATION

★★★ RESTAURANT WITH ROOMS

**Findlays Hotel & Restaurant** Smiddyhill Road, Fraserburgh AB43 9WL
**t** (01346) 519547

## GAILES, North Ayrshire — HOTEL

★★★ HOTEL

**The Gailes Lodge** Marine Drive, Gailes KA11 5AE
**t** (01294) 204040

## GAIRLOCH, Highland — SELF CATERING

★★★ SELF CATERING

**Willow Croft contact** Mrs B Leslie, 40 Big Sand, Gairloch IV21 2DD
**t** (01445) 712448
**e** bigsand@waitrose.com **w** sites.ecosse.net/iml/

## GATEHOUSE OF FLEET, Dumfries & Galloway Map ref 6B3 — SELF CATERING

SELF CATERING

Units **2**
Sleeps **1–6**
Low season per wk
£309.00–£399.00
High season per wk
£507.00–£645.00

### Rusko Holidays, Gatehouse of Fleet

Rusko Holidays, Gatehouse of Fleet, Castle Douglas DG7 2BS
**t** (01557) 814215
**e** info@ruskoholidays.co.uk **w** ruskoholidays.co.uk

Access abc

General

Leisure

Unit

Payment Credit/debit cards, cash, cheques

*Grade 1 cottage has wet-floor bathroom with bath and shower; and a second shower room for carers etc.*

Lovely, accessible and luxurious 'haven in the hills' (sleeps four-six) and charming Victorian cottage (sleeps four); with ambulant disabled facilities. Near historic towns, forests and the coast. Situated amid magnificent scenery and ideal for exploring this beautiful and unspoilt area of southern Scotland – without too long a journey. Wonderful accessible walking, bird watching, beaches and good restaurants.

**open** All year
**nearest shop** 4 miles
**nearest pub** 4 miles

*From the M74 just north of Carlisle, turn left onto A75 and then turn off at Gatehouse of Fleet. The cottages are just a few miles up the road, through the National Scenic Area – about 1.5 hours from Carlisle.*

## GLASGOW — HOTEL

★★★ HOTEL

**Campanile Glasgow** Tunnel Street, Glasgow G3 8HL
**t** (0141) 287 7700
**e** glasgow@campanile.com **w** campanile.com

## GLASGOW — HOTEL

★★★★ HOTEL

**Carlton George Hotel** 44 West George Street, Glasgow G2 1DH
**t** (0141) 353 6373
**e** george@carltonhotels.co.uk **w** carltonhotels.co.uk

At-a-glance symbols are explained on page 8.

## GLASGOW — HOTEL

★★★★ HOTEL

**Crowne Plaza Hotel** Congress Road, Glasgow G3 8QT
**t** 0870 443 4691
**e** cpglasgow@qmh-hotels.com **w** crowneplaza.co.uk

## GLASGOW — HOTEL

★★★★★ HOTEL

**Glasgow Hilton** 1 William Street, Glasgow G3 8HT
**t** (0141) 204 5555
**w** hilton.co.uk/glasgow

## GLASGOW — HOTEL

★★★★ HOTEL

**Glasgow Marriott** 500 Argyle Street, Glasgow G3 8RR
**t** (0141) 226 5577
**e** london.regional.reservations@marriott.com **w** glasgowmarriott.co.uk

## GLASGOW — HOTEL

★★★★ HOTEL

**Holiday Inn** 161 West Nile Street, Glasgow G1 2RL
**t** (0141) 352 8300
**e** reservations@higlasgow.com **w** higlasgow.com

## GLASGOW — HOTEL

★★ HOTEL

**Ibis Hotel Glasgow** 220 West Regent Street, Glasgow G2 4DQ
**t** (0141) 225 6000
**e** h3139@accor-hotels.com **w** ibishotel.com

## GLASGOW — HOTEL

★★★ HOTEL

**Jurys Inn Glasgow** Jamaica Street, Glasgow G1 4QE
**t** (0141) 314 4800
**w** jurysinn.com

## GLASGOW — HOTEL

★★★ HOTEL

**Novotel Glasgow Centre** 181 Pitt Street, Glasgow G2 4DT
**t** (0141) 222 2775
**e** h3136@accor-hotels.com **w** novotel.com

## GLASGOW — HOTEL

★★★ HOTEL

**Premier Inn Glasgow City Centre South** 80 Ballater Street, Glasgow G5 0TW
**t** 0870 423 6452
**e** glasgowccsouth.pi@premierinn.com **w** premierinn.com

## GLASGOW — SELF CATERING

★★★★ SERVICED APARTMENTS

**Fraser Suites Glasgow contact** Ms Heather Gilchrist, Fraser Suites Glasgow, 1-19 Albion Street, Glasgow G1 1NY **t** (0141) 553 4288
**e** sales.glasgow@fraserhospitality.com **w** frasershospitality.com

## GLASGOW — HOSTEL

★★★ HOSTEL

**Cairncross House** 20 Kelvinhaugh Place, Glasgow G3 8NH
**t** (0141) 330 5385
**e** enquiries@cvso.co.uk **w** cvso.co.uk

## GLASGOW — CAMPUS

★★ CAMPUS

**Queen Margaret Hall** 55 Bellshaugh Road, Glasgow G12 0SQ
**t** (0141) 334 2192
**e** enquiries@cvso.co.uk **w** cvso.co.uk

## GLASGOW — CAMPUS

★ CAMPUS

**Wolfson Hall** Kelvin Campus, West Scotland Science Park, Maryhill Road, Glasgow G20 0TH
**t** (0141) 330 3773
**w** cvso.co.uk

## GLENROTHES, Fife — HOTEL

★★★★ HOTEL

**Balbirnie House Hotel** Balbirnie Park, Markinch, by Glenrothes KY7 6NE
**t** (01592) 610066
**e** info@balbirnie.co.uk **w** balbirnie.co.uk

## GOREBRIDGE, Midlothian — GUEST ACCOMMODATION

★★★★ GUEST HOUSE

**Ivory House** 14 Vogrie Road, Gorebridge EH23 4HH
**t** (01875) 820755
**e** barbara@ivory-house.co.uk **w** ivory-house.co.uk

## GRANGEMOUTH, Stirling — HOTEL

★★★ HOTEL

**Leapark Hotel** 130 Bo'ness Road, Grangemouth FK3 9BX
**t** (01324) 486733

## GRANTOWN-ON-SPEY, Highland — HOTEL

★★★ COUNTRY HOUSE HOTEL

**Muckrach Lodge Hotel** Dulnain Bridge, Grantown-on-Spey PH26 3LY
**t** (01479) 851257
**e** info@muckrach.co.uk **w** muckrach.co.uk

## GREENOCK, Inverclyde — HOTEL

★★★ METRO HOTEL

**Express by Holiday Inn** Cartsburn, Greenock PA15 4RT
**t** (01475) 786666
**e** greenock@expressbyholidayinn.net

## GREENOCK, Renfrewshire — CAMPUS

★★ CAMPUS

**James Watt College** Waterfront Campus, Customhouse Way, Greenock PA15 1EN
**t** (01475) 731360

## GRETNA, Dumfries & Galloway — HOTEL

★★★ HOTEL

**The Garden House Hotel** Sarkfoot Road, Gretna DG16 5EP
**t** (01461) 337621
**w** gardenhouse.co.uk

## GRETNA, Dumfries & Galloway — HOTEL

★★★ SMALL HOTEL

**Hunters Lodge Hotel** Annan Road, Gretna DG16 5DL
**t** (01461) 338214
**e** reception@hunterslodgehotel.co.uk **w** hunterslodgehotel.co.uk

## GRETNA, Dumfries & Galloway — GUEST ACCOMMODATION

★★★ BED & BREAKFAST

**The Willows** Loanwath Road, Gretna DG16 5ES
**t** (01461) 337996
**e** gary@lynwilliams.freeserve.co.uk

## GRETNA GREEN, Dumfries & Galloway — HOTEL

★★★★ HOTEL

**Smiths @ Gretna Green** Gretna Green DG16 5EA
**t** 0845 3676768
**e** info@smithsgretnagreen.com **w** smithsgretnagreen.com

At-a-glance symbols are explained on page 8.

## GRETNA GREEN, Dumfries & Galloway — GUEST ACCOMMODATION

LODGE

**Days Inn** Welcome Break Service Area, M74, Gretna Green DG16 5HQ
**t** (01461) 337566

## HADDINGTON, East Lothian — HOTEL

★★★★ HOTEL

**Maitlandfield House Hotel** 24 Sidegate, Haddington EH41 4BZ
**t** (01620) 826513
**e** info@maitlandfieldhouse.co.uk **w** maitlandfieldhouse.co.uk

## HAWICK, Scottish Borders — HOTEL

★★★ SMALL HOTEL

**Elm House Hotel** 17 North Bridge Street, Hawick TD9 9BD
**t** (01450) 372866
**e** julie@elmhouse-hawick.fsnet.co.uk **w** elmhouse-hawick.fsnet.co.uk

## HAWICK, Scottish Borders — GUEST ACCOMMODATION

★★★ RESTAURANT WITH ROOMS

**Mosspaul** Teviothead, Hawick, Newburgh TD9 0LP
**t** (01450) 850245
**e** mosspaulinn@aol.com **w** mosspaulinn.com

## HAWICK, Scottish Borders — GUEST ACCOMMODATION

★★★ GUEST HOUSE

**Whitchester Guest House** Hawick TD9 7LN
**t** (01450) 377477
**e** enquiries@whitchester.org.uk **w** whitchester.org.uk

## HOY, Orkney Islands — HOTEL

★★★ SMALL HOTEL

**Stromabank** Hoy KW16 3PA
**t** (01856) 701494
**e** stromabankhotel@btconnect.com **w** stromabank.co.uk

## HUNTLY, Aberdeenshire — SELF CATERING

★★ SELF CATERING

**Drumdelgie house contact** Mrs Kate Martin, Drumdelgie House, Cairnie, Huntly AB54 4TH **t** (01466) 760346
**e** info@drumdelgiecottages.co.uk **w** drumdelgiecottages.co.uk

## INVERARAY, Argyll and Bute — HOTEL

★★★ HOTEL

**Loch Fyne Hotel** Newtown, Inveraray PA32 8XT
**t** (01499) 302148
**e** lochfyne@crerarhotels.com **w** crerarhotels.com

## INVERMORISTON, Highland — SELF CATERING

★★★–★★★★ SELF CATERING

**Invermoriston Holiday Chalets contact** Mr K E A Levings, Invermoriston Holiday Chalets, Invermoriston IV63 7YF **t** (01320) 351254
**e** erollevings@btconnect.com **w** invermoriston-holidays.co.uk

## INVERNESS, Highland — HOTEL

★★★★ HOTEL

**Kingsmills Hotel Inverness Ltd** Culcabock Road, Inverness IV2 3LP
**t** (01463) 237166
**e** info@kingsmillshotel.com **w** Kingsmillshotel.com

## INVERNESS, Highland — HOTEL

★★★★ HOTEL

**New Drumossie Hotel** Perth Road, Inverness IV1 2BE
**t** (01463) 236451
**e** stay@drumossiehotel.co.uk **w** drumossiehotel.co.uk

**INVERNESS,** Highland — HOTEL

★★★ HOTEL

**Ramada Jarvis Inverness** Church Street, Inverness IV1 1DX
**t** (01463) 235181
**e** gm.inverness@ramadajarvis.co.uk **w** ramadajarvis.co.uk/inverness

**INVERNESS,** Highland — GUEST ACCOMMODATION

★★★ GUEST HOUSE

**Glencairn and Ardross House** 18-19 Ardross Street, Inverness IV3 5NS
**t** (01463) 232965

**INVERNESS,** Highland — SELF CATERING

★★★★ SELF CATERING

**Firthview House, Links View & The Gatehouse contact** Mrs June Alexander, Blackpark Farm, Westhill, Inverness IV2 5BP **t** (01463) 790620
**e** i.alexander@blackpark.co.uk **w** blackpark.co.uk

**INVERNESS,** Highland — SELF CATERING

★★★ SELF CATERING

**Rookery Nook contact** Ms A Cole-Hamilton, 54 Culcabock Avenue, Inverness IV2 3RQ **t** (01463) 237085
**e** rook@cole-hamilton.co.uk **w** rookerynookinverness.co.uk

**INVERNESS,** Highland — HOSTEL

★★★★ HOSTEL

**Inverness Millburn Youth Hostel** Victoria Drive, Inverness IV2 3QB
**t** (01463) 231771
**e** inverness@syha.org.uk **w** syha.org.uk

**INVERURIE,** Aberdeenshire — GUEST ACCOMMODATION

★★★ INN

**Grant Arms Hotel** Monymusk, Inverurie AB51 7HJ
**t** (01467) 651226
**e** grantarmshotel@btconnect.com **w** monymusk.com

**ISLE OF HARRIS,** Western Isles — SELF CATERING

★★★★★ SELF CATERING

**Croft Cottage contact** Mrs Alice Read, 3 Diracleit, Isle of Harris HS3 3DP
**t** (01859) 502338
**e** alice.read1@btopenworld.com **w** croftcottageharris.co.uk

**ISLE OF ISLAY,** Argyll and Bute — SELF CATERING

★★★ SELF CATERING

**Glen-na-airidh & Blackpark Croft contact** Mr MacLugash, Blackpark, Bridgend PA44 7PL
**t** (01496) 810376

**ISLE OF LEWIS,** Western Isles — GUEST ACCOMMODATION

★★★ INN

**The Cross Inn** Cross Ness HS2 0SN
**t** (01851) 810152
**e** info@tcrossinn.com **w** crossinn.com

**ISLE OF MULL,** Argyll and Bute — GUEST ACCOMMODATION

★★★ GUEST HOUSE

**Ard Mhor House** Pier Road, Salen PA72 6JL
**t** (01680) 300255
**e** davidclowes@ardmhorhouse.fsnet.co.uk **w** ardmhorguesthouse.co.uk

**ISLE OF MULL,** Argyll and Bute — SELF CATERING

★★★–★★★★ SELF CATERING

**Treshnish & Haunn Cottages contact** Mrs C M Charrington, House of Treshnish, Treshnish Point, By Calgary, Isle of Mull PA75 6QX **t** (01688) 400249
**e** enquiries@treshnish.co.uk **w** treshnish.co.uk

At-a-glance symbols are explained on page 8.

## ISLE OF NORTH UIST, Western Isles — HOTEL

★★★★ SMALL HOTEL

**Tigh Dearg Hotel** Lochmaddy, Isle of North Uist HS6 5AE
**t** (01876) 500700
**e** tighdearghotel@aol.com **w** tighdearghotel.co.uk

## KEITH, Moray — SELF CATERING

★★★–★★★★★ SELF CATERING

**Parkmore Farm Holiday Cottages contact** Mr E A and Mrs H M Andrews, Parkmore Farm, Dufftown, Keith AB55 4DN **t** (01340) 820072
**e** enquiries@parkmorecottages.com **w** parkmorecottages.com

## KELSO, Scottish Borders — GUEST ACCOMMODATION

★★★ GUEST HOUSE

**Inglestone House** Abbey Row, Kelso TD5 7HQ
**t** (01573) 225800
**w** inglestonehouse.co.uk

## KILDONAN, North Ayrshire — HOTEL

★★★ SMALL HOTEL

**Kildonan Hotel** Kildonan KA27 8SE
**t** (01770) 820207
**e** info@kildonanhotel.com **w** kildonanhotel.com

## KILDONAN, North Ayrshire — SELF CATERING

★★★★ SELF CATERING

**The Beach House contact** Mr and Mrs Ian McMurdo, 33 Hoyle Crescent, Cumnock KA18 1RX **t** (01290) 421412 & 07793 495170
**e** ian@iqualconsultancy.co.uk

## KILDONAN, North Ayrshire — SELF CATERING

★★★★ SELF CATERING

**Island Properties contact** Mrs Denise Mann, Miodar Mor House, Shore Road, Kildonan KA27 8SE **t** (01770) 820624
**e** rmmann@fsmail.net **w** islandproperty.co.uk

## KILDONAN, North Ayrshire — SELF CATERING

★★★ SELF CATERING

**Kildonan School & Schoolhouse contact** Mr R M Wilson, Egmond Estates, Egmond, Torwoodhill Road, Rhu, Helensburgh G84 8LE **t** (01436) 820956
**e** egmond@btinternet.com **w** egmond-estates.co.uk

## KILKENZIE, Argyll and Bute — GUEST ACCOMMODATION

★★★★★ GUEST HOUSE

**Dalnaspidal Guest House** Tangy, Kilkenzie PA28 6QD
**t** (01586) 820466
**e** dalnaspidal@btconnect.com **w** dalnaspidal-guesthouse.com

## KILMARNOCK, East Ayrshire — HOTEL

★★★★ HOTEL

**Park Hotel** Rugby Park, Kilmarnock KA1 1UR
**t** (01563) 545999
**e** enquiries@theparkhotel.uk.com **w** theparkhotel.uk.com

## KILWINNING, North Ayrshire — SELF CATERING

★★★★ SELF CATERING

**Ailsa Craig View contact** Anne Adrain, High Smithstone Farm B&B, High Smithstone, Kilwinning KA13 6PG **t** (01294) 552361
**e** anne@bedandbreakfastayrshire.com **w** selfcateringayrshire.com

## KINCRAIG, Highland — SELF CATERING

★★–★★★ SELF CATERING

**Loch Insh Chalets contact** Mr C Freshwater, Insh Hall Lodge, Kincraig PH21 1NU
**t** (01540) 651272
**e** office@lochinsh.com **w** lochinsh.com

## KINGHORN, Fife — HOTEL

★★★ HOTEL

**Bay Hotel** Burntisland Road, Kinghorn KY3 9YE
**t** (01592) 892222
**e** info@pettycur.co.uk

## KINGUSSIE, Highland — HOTEL

★★★ SMALL HOTEL

**Columba House Hotel & Garden Restaurant** Manse Road, Kingussie PH21 1JF
**t** (01540) 661402
**e** relax@columbahousehotel.com **w** columbahousehotel.co.uk

## KINLOCH RANNOCH, Perth and Kinross — HOTEL

★★★ HOTEL

**Dunalastair Hotel** The Square, Kinloch Rannoch PH16 5PW
**t** (01882) 632323
**e** reservations@dunalastair.co.uk **w** dunalastair.co.uk

## KINLOCHLEVEN, Argyll and Bute — GUEST ACCOMMODATION

★★★★ GUEST HOUSE

**Tigh-Na-Cheo** Garbien Road, Kinlochleven PH50 4SE
**t** (01855) 831434
**e** reception@tigh-na-cheo.co.uk **w** tigh-na-cheo.co.uk

## KINLOCHLEVEN, Highland — HOSTEL

★★★★ HOSTEL

**Blackwater Hostel** Lab Road, Kinlochleven PH50 4SG
**t** (01855) 831253
**e** black.water@virgin.net **w** blackwaterhostel.co.uk

## KINROSS, Perth and Kinross — GUEST ACCOMMODATION

LODGE

**Travelodge Kinross M90** Turfhills Tourist Centre, Kinross KY13 7NQ
**t** 08719 846151

## KIRKCUDBRIGHT, Dumfries & Galloway — GUEST ACCOMMODATION

★★★★★ GUEST HOUSE

**Fludha Guest House** Tongland Road, Kirkcudbright DG6 4UU
**t** (01557) 331443
**e** info@fludha.com **w** fludha.com

## KIRKWALL, Orkney Islands — GUEST ACCOMMODATION

★★★★ GUEST HOUSE

**Lav'rockha Guest House** Inganess Road, Kirkwall KW15 1SP
**t** (01856) 876103
**e** lavrockha@orkney.com **w** lavrockha.co.uk

## KIRKWALL, Orkney Islands — SELF CATERING

★★★★ SELF CATERING

**Laingbrae Cottage** **contact** Mr and Mrs Graeme Wright, Laingbrae Cottage, 6 Bignold Park Road, Kirkwall KW15 1PT **t** (01856) 877573
**e** laingbraecottage@aol.com **w** laingbraecottage.co.uk

## KIRRIEMUIR, Angus — GUEST ACCOMMODATION

★★★★ RESTAURANT WITH ROOMS

**Lochside Lodge & Roundhouse Restaurant** Bridgend of Lintrathen, Kirriemuir DD8 5JJ **t** (01575) 560340
**e** enquiries@lochsidelodge.com **w** lochsidelodge.com

## KIRRIEMUIR, Angus — SELF CATERING

★–★★★ SELF CATERING

**Glenprosen Cottages** **contact** Mr Hector MacLean, Glenprosen Cottages, Balnaboth, Glenprosen DD8 4SA **t** (01575) 540302
**e** mail@glenprosen.co.uk **w** glenprosen.co.uk

At-a-glance symbols are explained on page 8.

**KIRRIEMUIR,** Angus — SELF CATERING

★★★★ SELF CATERING

**Pearsie Lodge contact** Mr Norman F Ogg, Pearsie Estate Co Ltd, West Kinwhirrie, Kirriemuir DD8 4QA **t** (01575) 540234
**e** norman.ogg@btclick.com

**KIRRIEMUIR,** Angus — HOSTEL

★★★ HOSTEL

**The Steading Bunkhouse** Glen Clova Hotel, Glen Clova, by Kirriemuir DD8 4QS
**t** (01575) 550 350
**e** hotel@clova.com **w** clova.com

**LAIDE,** Highland — SELF CATERING

★★★★ SELF CATERING

**Rocklea, Little Gruinard contact** Mr & Mrs A Gilchrist, Grassvalley Cottage, 12 Woodhall Road, Edinburgh EH13 0DX **t** (0131) 441 6053
**e** aandagilchrist@blueyonder.co.uk **w** heimdall-scot.co.uk/laide

**LAUDER,** Scottish Borders — SELF CATERING

★★★★–★★★★★ SELF CATERING

**Airhouses contact** Mrs Carol Houghton, Airhouses, Oxton, Lauder TD2 6PX
**t** (01578) 750642
**e** carol@airhousestudios.co.uk **w** airhouses.com

**LERWICK,** Isle of Shetland — HOTEL

★★★ HOTEL

**Shetland Hotel** Holmsgarth Road, Lerwick ZE1 0PW
**t** (01595) 695515
**e** reception@shetlandhotel.co.uk **w** shetlandhotels.com

**LERWICK,** Isle of Shetland — SELF CATERING

★★★ SELF CATERING

**63 Burgh Road & Decca contact** Mrs G Henry, Inches, Bells Road, Lerwick ZE1 0QB **t** (01595) 695354 & 07768 654 459
**e** gillian.scs@tiscali.co.uk **w** selfcateringshetland.com

**LEVERBURGH,** Western Isles — HOSTEL

★★★★★ HOSTEL

**Am Bothan Leverburgh Bunkhouse** Am Bothan, Leverburgh HS5 3UA
**t** (01859) 520251
**e** ruari@ambothan.com **w** ambothan.com

**LOCHCARNAN,** Western Isles — HOTEL

★★★ SMALL HOTEL

**Orasay Inn** Lochcarnan HS8 5PD
**t** (01870) 610298

**LOCHGILPHEAD,** Argyll and Bute — GUEST ACCOMMODATION

★★★ LODGE

**Empire Travel Lodge** Union Street, Lochgilphead PA31 8JS
**t** (01546) 602381
**e** enquiries@empirelodge.co.uk **w** empirelodge.co.uk

**LOCHINVER,** Highland — SELF CATERING

★★★★ SELF CATERING

**Mountview Self-Catering contact** Mrs S MacLeod, 70 Mountview, Baddidarroch, Lochinver IV27 4LP **t** (01571) 844648
**e** stay@mountview-lochinver.co.uk **w** mountview-lochinver.co.uk

**LOCHMABEN,** Dumfries & Galloway — GUEST ACCOMMODATION

★★ INN

**The Crown Hotel** 8 Bruce Street, Lochmaben DG11 1PD
**t** (01387) 811750

## LOCHWINNOCH, Renfrewshire — SELF CATERING

★★★★
SELF CATERING

**East Lochhead Cottages** **contact** Mrs V J Anderson, East Lochhead, Largs Road, Lochwinnoch PA12 4DX **t** (01505) 842610
**e** admin@eastlochhead.co.uk **w** eastlochhead.co.uk

## LOCKERBIE, Dumfries & Galloway — HOTEL

★★★★
HOTEL

**Dryfesdale Country House Hotel** Dryfebridge, Lockerbie DG11 2SF
**t** (01576) 202427
**e** reception@dryfesdalehotel.co.uk **w** dryfesdalehotel.co.uk

## LOSSIEMOUTH, Moray — GUEST ACCOMMODATION

★★★
BED & BREAKFAST

**Ceilidh B&B** 34 Clifton Road, Lossiemouth IV31 6DP **t** (01343) 815848
**e** ceilidh.b-b@whsmithnet.co.uk
**w** scottish-info.com/scotland/ceilidh.htm

## LUSS, Argyll and Bute Map ref 6B2 — SELF CATERING

★★★★–★★★★★
SELF CATERING

Units **7**
Sleeps **2–6**
High season per wk
£355.00–£925.00

### Loch Lomond Hideaways

Loch Lomond Hideaways **t** (01436) 860267
**w** lochlomondhideaways.co.uk

General

Unit

Payment Credit/debit cards, cash, cheques

Relax in beautiful surroundings on the edge of Luss village. Superbly appointed, luxury cottages available for short or long breaks. Ideally located for Loch Lomond and exploring the Highlands. Keepers Cottage features ramp access and level entry shower.

**open** All year
**nearest shop** 0.5 miles
**nearest pub** < 0.5 miles

## MADDISTON, Falkirk — SELF CATERING

★★★
SELF CATERING

**Avon Glen Lodges** **contact** Mrs D Seaton, Avon Glen Lodges, Melons Place, Maddiston FK2 0BT
**t** (01324) 861166

## MAYBOLE, South Ayrshire — SELF CATERING

★
SELF CATERING

**Royal Artillery Cottage** **contact** Ms Anne Campbell, National Trust for Scotland, 28 Charlotte Square, Edinburgh EH2 4ET **t** (0131) 243 9331
**e** holidays@nts.org.uk **w** ntsholidays.com

## MELROSE, Scottish Borders — SELF CATERING

★★★–★★★★★
SELF CATERING

**Dimpleknowe Mill & Cottage** **contact** Mrs A M J Cameron, Dimpleknowe, Lilliesleaf, Melrose TD6 9JU **t** (01835) 870333
**w** dimpleknowe.co.uk

At-a-glance symbols are explained on page 8.

**MELROSE,** Scottish Borders — **SELF CATERING**

★★★–★★★★★
SELF CATERING

**Eildon Holiday Cottages contact** Mrs Jill Hart, Eildon Holiday Cottages, Dingleton Mains, Melrose TD6 9HS **t** (01896) 823258
**e** info@eildon.co.uk **w** eildon.co.uk

**MILLPORT,** North Ayrshire — **GUEST ACCOMMODATION**

★★★
GUEST HOUSE

**The Cathedral of the Isles** The College, Millport KA28 0HE
**t** (01475) 530353
**e** tccumbrae@argyll.anglican.org **w** island-retreats.org

**MINARD,** Argyll and Bute — **GUEST ACCOMMODATION**

★★★★
BED & BREAKFAST

**Minard Castle** Minard PA32 8YB
**t** (01546) 886272
**e** info@minardcastle.com **w** minardcastle.com

**MOFFAT,** Dumfries & Galloway — **GUEST ACCOMMODATION**

★★★
BED & BREAKFAST

**Lochhouse Farm Retreat Centre** Beattock, Moffat DG10 9SG
**t** (01683) 300451
**w** lochhousefarm.com

**MOFFAT,** Dumfries & Galloway — **SELF CATERING**

★★★
SELF CATERING

**Lochhouse Farm Retreat Centre contact** Mrs Brown, Lochhouse Farm Retreat Centre, Beattock, Moffat DG10 9SG **t** (01683) 300451
**e** cottages@lochhousefarm.com **w** lochhousefarm.com

**MOTHERWELL,** North Lanarkshire — **HOTEL**

★★★★
HOTEL

**The Alona Hotel** Strathclyde Country Park, Motherwell ML1 3RT
**t** 0870 112 3888
**e** info@alonahotel.co.uk **w** alonahotel.co.uk

**MOTHERWELL,** North Lanarkshire — **HOTEL**

★★★
METRO HOTEL

**Express By Holiday Inn** Strathclyde Park M74 Jct 5, Motherwell ML1 3RB
**t** (01698) 852375
**e** isabella.little@ihg.com **w** hiexpress.com/strathclyde

**MOTHERWELL,** North Lanarkshire — **HOTEL**

★★★
HOTEL

**Moorings Hotel** 114 Hamilton Road, Motherwell ML1 3DG
**t** (01698) 258131
**e** enquiries@morringsmotherwell.co.uk **w** mooringsmotherwell.co.uk

**MOTHERWELL,** North Lanarkshire — **CAMPUS**

★
CAMPUS

**Motherwell College Stewart Hall** Dalzell Drive, Motherwell ML1 2DD
**t** (01698) 261890
**e** mcol@motherwell.co.uk **w** motherwell.ac.uk

**NAIRN,** Highland — **HOTEL**

Rating Applied For
HOTEL

**Windsor Hotel** 16 Albert Street, Nairn IV12 4HP
**t** (01667) 453108
**e** windsorres@btconnect.com **w** windsor-hotel.co.uk

**NAIRN,** Highland — **SELF CATERING**

★★–★★★★★
SELF CATERING

**Hidden Glen Holidays contact** Mrs Muskus, Laikenbuie Holidays, Grantown Road, Nairn IV12 5QN **t** (01667) 454630
**e** muskus@bigfoot.com **w** hiddenglen.co.uk

**NAIRN,** Highland — **SELF CATERING**

★★★★ SELF CATERING

**Mill Lodge & Burnside Lodge contact** Mr D M Buchanan, Raitloan, Geddes, Nairn IV12 5SA **t** (01667) 454635
**e** bookings@geddesmill.co.uk **w** geddesmill.co.uk

**NETHY BRIDGE,** Highland — **HOTEL**

★★★ HOTEL

**Nethybridge Hotel** Nethybridge PH25 3DP
**t** (01479) 821203
**e** salesnethybridge@strathmorehotels.com **w** strathmorehotels.com

**NETHY BRIDGE,** Highland — **SELF CATERING**

★★★★ SELF CATERING

**Cluny-Mhore contact** Mr Hamish Jack, Rhuarden, Seafield Avenue, Grantown-on-Spey PH26 3JF
**t** (01479) 872675

**NETHY BRIDGE,** Highland — **SELF CATERING**

★★★★ SELF CATERING

**Fhuarain Forest Cottages contact** Mrs V Dean, Badanfhuarain, Nethybridge PH25 3ED **t** (01479) 821642
**e** visits@forestcottages.com **w** forestcottages.com

**NETHY BRIDGE,** Highland — **HOSTEL**

★★★★ HOSTEL

**Lazy Duck Hostel** Nethybridge PH25 3ED
**t** (01479) 821642
**e** lazyduckhostel@googlemail.com **w** lazyduck.co.uk

**NEW LANARK,** South Lanarkshire — **HOTEL**

★★★ HOTEL

**New Lanark Mill Hotel** New Lanark ML11 9DB
**t** (01555) 667200
**e** hotel@newlanark.org **w** newlanark.org

**NEWTONMORE,** Highland — **GUEST ACCOMMODATION**

★★★★ GUEST HOUSE

**Crubenbeg House** Falls of Truim PH20 1BE
**t** (01540) 673300
**e** enquiries@crubenbeghouse.com **w** crubenbeghouse.com

**NEWTONMORE,** Highland — **HOSTEL**

★★★ ACTIVITY ACCOMMODATION

**Craigower Lodge** Golf Course Road, Newtonmore PH20 1AT
**t** 08450 505052
**e** info@activeoutdoorpursuits.com **w** activeoutdoorpursuits.com

**NEWTONMORE,** Highland — **HOSTEL**

★★★ HOSTEL

**Strathspey Mountain Hostel** Main Street, Newtonmore PH20 1DR
**t** (01540) 673694
**e** strathspey@newtonmore.com **w** newtonmore.com/strathspey

**NORTH BERWICK,** East Lothian — **CAMPING, CARAVAN & HOLIDAY PARK**

★★★★ HOLIDAY PARK

**Tantallon Caravan Park** Dunbar Road, North Berwick EH39 5NJ
**t** (01620) 893348
**e** tantallon@meadowhead.co.uk **w** meadowhead.co.uk

**NORTH RONALDSAY,** Orkney Islands — **GUEST ACCOMMODATION**

★★★ GUEST HOUSE

**Observatory Guest House** North Ronaldsay KW17 2BE
**t** (01857) 633200
**e** bookings@nrbo.prestel.co.uk **w** nrbo.f2s.com

At-a-glance symbols are explained on page 8.

**OBAN,** Argyll and Bute — GUEST ACCOMMODATION

★★★
RESTAURANT WITH ROOMS

**Wide Mouthed Frog** Dunstaffnage Marina, Connel, by Oban PA37 1PX
**t** (01631) 567005
**e** frogenqs@aol.com **w** widemouthedfrog.com

**OBAN,** Argyll and Bute — SELF CATERING

★★★–★★★★★
SELF CATERING

**Cologin Country Chalets contact** Mr & Mrs LJ Battison, Cologin Farmhouse, Lerags Glen, By Oban PA34 4SE **t** (01631) 564501
**e** info@cologin.co.uk **w** cologin.co.uk

**OBAN,** Argyll and Bute — HOSTEL

★★★★
HOSTEL

**Oban Youth Hostel** Esplanade, Oban PA34 5AF
**t** 0870 004 1144
**e** reservations@syha.org.uk **w** syha.org.uk

**ONICH,** Highland — HOSTEL

★★★★
HOSTEL

**Corran Bunkhouse** Corran, Onich PH33 6SE
**t** (01855) 821000
**e** info@corranbunkhouse.co.uk **w** corranbunkhouse.co.uk

**ORKNEY,** Orkney Islands — SELF CATERING

★★★
SELF CATERING

**14 Buttquoy Park contact** Mr R Peace, New Voy, Toab, Orkney KW17 2QG
**t** (01856) 861267
**e** raymondpeace@btinternet.com

**ORMSARY,** Argyll and Bute Map ref 6A2 — SELF CATERING

★★★
SELF CATERING

Units **1**
Sleeps **11**
Low season per wk
**£710.00–£865.00**
High season per wk
**£1,100.00–£1,350.00**

## Barnlongart, Lochgilphead

Ormsary Estate Holidays **t** (01880) 770222 **e** enquiries@ormsary.co.uk
**w** ormsary.com

Single-storey, spacious, well-equipped lodge, delightful views, own woodland setting, close to sandy beach. Six bedrooms, six bathrooms (four en suite), full disabled shower room with facilities for wheelchair use.

**open** All year
**nearest shop** 12 miles
**nearest pub** 6 miles

General
Unit
Payment Credit/debit cards, cash, cheques

**ORPHIR,** Orkney Islands — SELF CATERING

★★★★
SELF CATERING

**Owlswood Lodge contact** Mrs Carol Mainland, South Greenigoe, Orphir KW17 2RA
**t** (01856) 873596

**PAISLEY,** Renfrewshire — HOTEL

★★★
METRO HOTEL

**Express by Holiday Inn Glasgow Airport** St Andrews Drive, Paisley PA3 2TJ
**t** (0141) 842 1100
**e** info@hiex-glasgow.com

**PAISLEY,** Renfrewshire — HOTEL

★★★ HOTEL

**Ramada Glasgow Airport** Marchburn Drive, Abbotsinch, Paisley PA3 2SJ
**t** (0141) 840 2200
**w** ramadaglasgowairport.com

**PAISLEY,** Renfrewshire — GUEST ACCOMMODATION

★★★ LODGE

**Travelodge Glasgow Airport** Marchburn Drive,
Paisley PA3 2SJ
**t** 08719 846335

**PAPA WESTRAY,** Orkney Islands — SELF CATERING

★★★★ SELF CATERING

**Holm View contact** Mr T P Hughes, Bayview, Papa Westray KW17 2BU
**t** (01857) 644211
**e** tomhughes@scotnet.co.uk

**PEEBLES,** Scottish Borders — HOTEL

★★★★ HOTEL

**Cardrona Hotel Golf & Country Club** Cardrona, Near Peebles EH45 6LZ
**t** (01896) 831144
**e** general.cardrona@macdonald-hotels.co.uk **w** cardrona-hotel.co.uk

**PEEBLES,** Scottish Borders — HOTEL

★★★★ COUNTRY HOUSE HOTEL

**Cringletie House Hotel** Edinburgh Road, Peebles EH45 8PL
**t** (01721) 725750
**e** enquiries@cringletie.com **w** cringletie.com

**PERTH,** Perth and Kinross — HOTEL

★★★ HOTEL

**Huntingtower Hotel** Crieff Road, Perth PH1 3JT
**t** (01738) 583771
**e** reservations@huntingtowerhotel.co.uk **w** huntingtowerhotel.co.uk

**PERTH,** Perth and Kinross — GUEST ACCOMMODATION

Rating Applied For
INN

**Glencarse Hotel** Glencarse, By Perth PH2 7LX
**t** (01738) 860206
**e** alistair.robb@btconnect.com

**PETERHEAD,** Aberdeenshire — GUEST ACCOMMODATION

★★★ GUEST HOUSE

**Invernettie Guest House** South Road, Burnhaven,
Peterhead AB42 0YX
**t** (01779) 473530

**PIRNHALL,** Stirling — GUEST ACCOMMODATION

LODGE

**Travelodge Stirling** Service Area, Pirnhall FK7 8EU
**t** 08719 846178

**PITLOCHRY,** Perth and Kinross — GUEST ACCOMMODATION

★★★ GUEST HOUSE

**Cuil -an- Daraich Guest House** 2 Cuil -An- Daraich, Logierait, Pitlochry PH9 0LH
**t** (01796) 482750
**e** nimarachel@aol.com **w** scottishguesthouse.com

**PITLOCHRY,** Perth and Kinross — SELF CATERING

★★★★ SELF CATERING

**Dalshian Chalets contact** Mr & Mrs David Bartholomew, Dalshian Chalets,
Old Perth Road, Pitlochry PH16 5TD **t** (01796) 473080
**e** info@dalshian-chalets.co.uk **w** dalshian-chalets.co.uk

At-a-glance symbols are explained on page 8.

**PITLOCHRY,** Perth and Kinross — **SELF CATERING**

★★★-★★★★★ SELF CATERING

**Dunalastair Holiday Houses** **contact** Mrs Rose La Terriere, Lochgarry House, Kinloch Rannoch PH16 5PD **t** (01882) 632314
**e** dunalastair@sol.co.uk **w** dunalastair.com

**POLMONT,** Stirling — **HOTEL**

★★★★ HOTEL

**Inchyra Grange Hotel** Grange Road, Polmont FK2 0YB
**t** (01324) 711911
**e** inchyra@macdonald-hotels.co.uk **w** macdonald-hotels.co.uk

**PORTREE,** Highland — **HOTEL**

★★★★ COUNTRY HOUSE HOTEL

**Cuillin Hills Hotel** Portree IV51 9QU
**t** (01478) 612003
**e** info@cuillin-hotel-skye.co.uk **w** cuillinhills-hotel-skye.co.uk

**PORTREE,** Highland — **GUEST ACCOMMODATION**

★★★ GUEST HOUSE

**Auchendinny** Treaslane, Portree IV51 9NX
**t** (01470) 532470
**e** auchendinnygh@aol.com **w** auchendinny.co.uk

**PORTREE,** Highland — **SELF CATERING**

★★★ SELF CATERING

**Brescalan Cottage** **contact** Mr Alastair Nicolson, 3 Borve, Portree IV51 9PE
**t** (01470) 532425
**e** info@brescalan.co.uk **w** brescalan.co.uk

**PORTREE,** Highland — **SELF CATERING**

★★★ SELF CATERING

**Number 6** **contact** Mrs Margaret MacDonald, Maligan, Achachork, Portree IV51 9HT **t** (01478) 613167
**e** no6chalet@aol.com **w** no6achachork.co.uk

**POTTERTON,** Aberdeenshire — **SELF CATERING**

★★★ SELF CATERING

**The Byre** **contact** Mrs A Shipton, Butterywells, Potterton, Aberdeen AB23 8UY
**t** (01358) 742673

**PRESTWICK,** South Ayrshire — **HOTEL**

★★★ HOTEL

**Parkstone Hotel** Esplanade, Prestwick KA9 1QN
**t** (01292) 477286

**RENDALL,** Orkney Islands — **SELF CATERING**

★★★★ SELF CATERING

**Widefirth Cottages** **contact** Mr Greig Sinclair, The Riff Cottage, Rendall, Orkney KW17 2PB **t** (01856) 761028
**e** greig31@btinternet.com **w** orkney-selfcatering.com

**RHU,** Argyll and Bute — **HOTEL**

★★★ HOTEL

**Rosslea Hall Hotel** Ferry Road, Rhu G84 8NF
**t** (01436) 439955
**e** reception@rossleahall.co.uk **w** rossleshall.co.uk

**ROSEWELL,** Midlothian — **SELF CATERING**

★★★ SELF CATERING

**Hunter Holiday Cottages** **contact** Mr D J Hunter, Thornton Farm, Rosewell EH24 9EF **t** (0131) 448 0888
**e** info@edinburghcottages.com **w** edinburghcottages.com

**ROY BRIDGE,** Highland — **HOTEL**

★★★ SMALL HOTEL

**The Stronlossit Inn** Roy Bridge PH31 4AG
**t** (01397) 712253
**e** stay@stronlossit.co.uk **w** stronlossit.co.uk

**ST ANDREWS,** Fife — **HOTEL**

★★★★ COUNTRY HOUSE HOTEL

**Rufflets Country House Hotel** Strathkinness Low Road, St Andrews KY16 9TX
**t** (01334) 472594
**e** reservations@rufflets.co.uk **w** rufflets.co.uk

**ST ANDREWS,** Fife — **GUEST ACCOMMODATION**

★★★★ GUEST HOUSE

**The Old Station, Country Guest House** Stratvithie Bridge, St Andrews KY16 8LR
**t** (01334) 880505
**e** info@theoldstation.co.uk **w** theoldstation.co.uk

**ST ANDREWS,** Fife — **SELF CATERING**

★★★★ SELF CATERING

**Balmashie Holiday Cottages contact** Mr Andrew Pirie,
Balmashie Holiday Cottages, By St Andrews KY16 8PN **t** (01334) 880666
**e** andrew@balmashie.co.uk **w** balmashie.co.uk

**SANQUHAR,** Dumfries & Galloway — **GUEST ACCOMMODATION**

★★★ FARMHOUSE

**Newark** Sanquhar DG4 6HN
**t** (01659) 50263
**e** info@newarkfarm.com **w** newarkfarm.com

**SANQUHAR,** Dumfries & Galloway — **SELF CATERING**

★★★ SELF CATERING

**Nith Riverside Lodges contact** Mr and Mrs Ian McAndrew,
Blackaddie House Hotel, Blackaddie Road, Sanquhar DG4 6JJ **t** (01659) 50270
**e** enquiries@blackaddiehotel.co.uk **w** blackaddiehotel.co.uk

**SELKIRK,** Scottish Borders — **SELF CATERING**

★★★★ SELF CATERING

**Crook Cottage and Elspinhope contact** Mrs Daphne Jackson,
Ettrick Holidays, Cossarshill Farm, Ettrick Valley, Selkirk TD7 5JB **t** (01750) 62259
**e** ettrickholidays@btinternet.com **w** ettrick-holidays.co.uk

**SOUTH UIST,** Western Isles — **GUEST ACCOMMODATION**

★★★ BED & BREAKFAST

**Crossroads** Stoneybridge,
South Uist HS8 5SD
**t** (01870) 620321

**SOUTHERNESS,** Dumfries & Galloway — **CAMPING, CARAVAN & HOLIDAY PARK**

★★★★ HOLIDAY PARK

**Southerness Holiday Village** Southerness DG2 8AZ
**t** (01387) 880256
**e** enquiries@parkdeanholidays.co.uk **w** parkdeanholidays.co.uk

**SPEAN BRIDGE,** Highland — **HOTEL**

★★★ SMALL HOTEL

**Old Pines Hotel and Restaurant** Gairlochy Road, Spean Bridge PH34 4EG
**t** (01397) 712324
**e** enquiries@oldpines.co.uk **w** oldpines.co.uk

**STIRLING** — **HOTEL**

★★★ METRO HOTEL

**Express by Holiday Inn – Stirling** Springkerse Business Park, Stirling FK7 7XH
**t** (01786) 449922
**e** info@hiex-stirling.com **w** hiex-stirling.com

At-a-glance symbols are explained on page 8.

## STIRLING — HOTEL

★★★ HOTEL

**Stirling Management Centre** University of Stirling, Stirling FK9 4LA
**t** (01786) 451666
**e** smc.sales@stir.ac.uk **w** smc.stir.ac.uk

## STIRLING — SELF CATERING

★★★★ SELF CATERING

**Hawthorn Cottage contact** Mrs Graham, West Drip Farm, Stirling FK9 4UJ
**t** (01786) 472523
**e** enquiries@westdripfarm.com **w** westdripfarm.com

## STIRLING — HOSTEL

★★★★ HOSTEL

**Stirling Youth Hostel** St John Street, Stirling FK8 1EA
**t** 0870 004 1149
**e** reservations@syha.org.uk **w** syha.org.uk

## STORNOWAY, Western Isles — SELF CATERING

★★★★–★★★★★ SELF CATERING

**Herbridean Self Catering contact** Mr G A McLennan, Hebrides Self Catering, 29 Kenneth Street, Stornoway HS1 2DR **t** (01851) 700100
**e** info@hebrides-selfcatering.co.uk **w** hebrides-selfcatering.co.uk

## STRAITON, Midlothian — SELF CATERING

★★★–★★★★★ SELF CATERING

**Balbeg House contact** Mrs Lynne E Sinclair, Balbeg House, Balbeg, Straiton KA19 7NN **t** (01655) 770665
**e** enquiries@balbeg.co.uk **w** balbeg.co.uk

## STRANRAER, Dumfries & Galloway — SELF CATERING

★★★★ SELF CATERING

**Culmore Bridge contact** Mrs Marilyn Sime, West Cottage, Culgroat, Stoneykirk, Stranraer DG9 9DZ **t** (01776) 830539
**w** culmorebridge.co.uk

## STROMNESS, Orkney Islands — SELF CATERING

★★★ SELF CATERING

**Old Hall Cottage contact** Mrs L Hardcastle, Old Hall Cottage, Longhope, Stromness KW16 3PQ **t** (01856) 701213
**e** oldhall@freeuk.com **w** oldhallcottage.co.uk

## STRONTIAN, Highland — SELF CATERING

★★★★★ SELF CATERING

**Bluebell Croft contact** Susanna Barber, Bluebell Croft, 15 Anaheilt, Strontian PH36 4JA **t** (01967) 402226
**w** bluebellcroft.co.uk

## STRONTIAN, Highland — HOSTEL

★★★★ HOSTEL

**Ariundle Bunkhouse** Ariundle, Strontian PH36 4JA
**t** (01967) 402279
**e** info@ariundle.co.uk **w** ariundle.co.uk

## SWINTON, Scottish Borders — GUEST ACCOMMODATION

★★★★ RESTAURANT WITH ROOMS

**The Wheatsheaf at Swinton** Main Street, Swinton TD11 3JJ
**t** (01890) 860257
**e** reception@wheatsheaf-swinton.co.uk **w** wheatsheaf-swinton.co.uk

## TAIN, Highland — GUEST ACCOMMODATION

★★★ INN

**Edderton Inn** Station Road, Edderton, Edderton, Tain IV19 1LB
**t** (01862) 821588
**e** enquiries@eddertoninn.co.uk **w** eddertoninn.co.uk

**TALMINE,** Highland — **GUEST ACCOMMODATION**

★★★★
BED & BREAKFAST

**Cloisters** Church Holme, Talmine IV27 4YP
**t** (01847) 601286
**e** reception@cloistertal.demon.co.uk **w** cloistertal.demon.co.uk

**TAYNUILT,** Argyll and Bute — **GUEST ACCOMMODATION**

★★★★
BED & BREAKFAST

**Roineabhal Country House** Kilchrenan, By Taynuilt PA35 1HD
**t** (01866) 833207
**e** maria@roineabhal.com **w** roineabhal.com

**TAYNUILT,** Argyll and Bute — **SELF CATERING**

★★★–★★★★
SELF CATERING

**Airdeny Chalets contact** Mrs Jenifer Moffat, Airdeny Chalets, Glen Lonan, Taynuilt PA35 1HY **t** (01866) 822648
**e** jenifer.moffat@airdenychalets.co.uk **w** airdenychalets.co.uk

**TAYNUILT,** Argyll and Bute — **SELF CATERING**

★★★★
SELF CATERING

**Sithean contact** Mrs Leonie Charlton, Bunanta, Barguillean, Taynuilt PA35 1HY
**t** (01866) 822110
**e** leoniecharlton@talktalk.net **w** sitheanselfcatering.co.uk

**TAYNUILT,** Argyll and Bute — **SELF CATERING**

★★★★–★★★★★
SELF CATERING

**Tigh an Daraich contact** Mr J Holden, Tigh an Daraich, Bridge of Awe, Taynuilt PA35 1HR **t** (01866) 822693
**e** info@tighandaraich.co.uk **w** tighandaraich.co.uk

**THORNHILL,** Dumfries & Galloway — **SELF CATERING**

★★★
SELF CATERING

**Templand Cottages contact** Mr and Mrs Lenny Chambers, Templand Cottages, Templand Mains, Thornhill DG3 5AB **t** (01848) 330775
**e** andrew@templandcottages.co.uk **w** templandcottages.co.uk

**THURSO,** Highland — **HOTEL**

★★★
SMALL HOTEL

**Park Hotel** Oldfield, Thurso KW14 8RE
**t** (01847) 893251
**e** reception@parkhotelthurso.co.uk **w** parkhotelthurso.co.uk

**THURSO,** Highland — **HOTEL**

★★★
HOTEL

**Weigh Inn Hotel** Burnside, Thurso KW14 7UG
**t** (01847) 893722
**e** reception@weighinn.co.uk **w** weighinn.co.uk

**THURSO,** Highland — **GUEST ACCOMMODATION**

★★★★
GUEST HOUSE

**Pentland Lodge House** Granville Street, Thurso KW14 7JN
**t** (01847) 895103
**e** sandys@fwi.co.uk **w** pentlandlodgehouse.co.uk

**TOBERMORY,** Argyll and Bute — **SELF CATERING**

★★★
SELF CATERING

**Beech & Willow, Cill-Mhoire contact** Mr Andrew Stevens, Cill-Mhoire, Dervaig, Tobermory PA75 6QN **t** (01688) 400445
**e** info@isle-mull-self-catering.co.uk **w** isle-mull-self-catering.co.uk

**TROON,** South Ayrshire — **HOTEL**

★★★★
HOTEL

**Barcelo Troon Marine Hotel** Crosbie Road, Troon KA10 6HE
**t** (01292) 314444
**e** marine@barcelo-hotels.co.uk **w** barcelo-hotels.co.uk

At-a-glance symbols are explained on page 8.

**TROON,** South Ayrshire — HOTEL

★★★ HOTEL

**South Beach Hotel** South Beach, Troon KA10 6EG
**t** (01292) 312033
**e** info@southbeach.co.uk **w** southbeach.co.uk

**TUMMEL BRIDGE,** Perth and Kinross — HOTEL

★★★ HOTEL

**Kynachan Loch Tummel Hotel** Tummel Bridge PH16 5SB
**t** (01796) 484848
**w** lochlandglens.com

**TURNBERRY,** South Ayrshire — HOTEL

★★★★★ HOTEL

**The Westin Turnberry Resort** Turnberry KA26 9LT
**t** (01655) 331000
**e** turnberry@westin.com **w** westin.com/turnberry

**TURRIFF,** Aberdeenshire — GUEST ACCOMMODATION

★★★★ GUEST HOUSE

**Deveron Lodge B&B Guesthouse** Bridgend Terrace, Turriff AB53 4ES
**t** (01888) 563613
**e** info@deveronlodge.com **w** deveronlodge.com

**TURRIFF,** Aberdeenshire — SELF CATERING

★★★ SELF CATERING

**Delgatie Castle contact** Mrs Johnston, Delgatie Castle, Turriff AB53 5TD
**t** (01888) 563479
**e** jjohnson@delgatie-castle.freeserve.co.uk **w** delgatiecastle.com

**TURRIFF,** Aberdeenshire — SELF CATERING

★★★★ SELF CATERING

**Garden Cottage contact** Mr Windsor, Byth House, New Byth AB53 5XN
**t** (01888) 544230
**e** a.windsor@farming.co.uk **w** gardencottagebyth.com

**UIG,** Western Isles — SELF CATERING

★★★★ SELF CATERING

**Riof Ocean Cottage contact** Mr Norman MacKay, Tigh a Mhuil, 7a Reef, Miavaig, Uig HS2 9HU **t** (01851) 672732 & (01851) 672354
**e** mackaynorry@aol.com **w** riofoceancottage.com

**UIG,** Western Isles — SELF CATERING

★★★–★★★★ SELF CATERING

**Tigh-a-Ghoba & Tigh-nan-Eilean contact** Mr Murdo MacLeod, 17 Uigen, Uig, Stornoway HS2 9HX **t** (01851) 672377 & 07785 524826
**e** murdomac@btinternet.com **w** holidays-scotland.co.uk/705.htm

**ULLAPOOL,** Highland — SELF CATERING

★★★★ SELF CATERING

**Rubha Mor Self Catering contact** Mr & Mrs Paul Copestake, Rubha Mor Self Catering, Peacock House, Garve Road, Ullapool IV26 2SX
**t** (01854) 612323
**e** kate.copestake@btinternet.com

## What if I need to cancel?

It is advisable to check the proprietor's cancellation policy in case you have to change your plans at a later date.

**UNST,** Isle of Shetland — **HOSTEL**

★★★ HOSTEL

**Gardiesfauld Youth Hostel** Uyeasound, Unst ZE2 9DW
**t** (01975) 755279
**e** anything@gardiesfauld.shetland.co.uk **w** gardiesfauld.shetland.co.uk

**WALLS,** Isle of Shetland — **GUEST ACCOMMODATION**

★★★★ GUEST HOUSE

**Burrastow House** Walls ZE2 9PD
**t** (01595) 809307
**e** burr.hs@zetnet.co.uk **w** users.zetnet.co.uk/burrastow-house

**WATERNISH,** Highland — **SELF CATERING**

★★★★ SELF CATERING

**Auld Orwell Cottage contact** Mrs L Hartwell, Auld Orwell Cottage, 17 Lochbay, Waternish IV55 8GD **t** (01470) 592363
**e** lydia@auld-orwell-skye.co.uk **w** auld-orwell-skye.co.uk

**WATERNISH,** Highland — **SELF CATERING**

★★★★ SELF CATERING

**La Bergerie contact** Mrs Chantal MacLeod, La Bergerie, 33 Lochbay, Waternish IV55 8GD **t** (01470) 592282
**e** chantalmac@lineone.net **w** la-bergerie-skye.co.uk

**WEST CALDER,** West Lothian — **SELF CATERING**

★★★–★★★★★ SELF CATERING

**Crosswoodhill Farm contact** Mrs G Hamilton, Crosswoodhill Farm, By West Calder EH55 8LP **t** (01501) 785205
**e** cottages@crosswoodhill.co.uk **w** fivestarholidaycottage.co.uk

**WEST FISHWICK,** Scottish Borders — **SELF CATERING**

★★★★★ SELF CATERING

**Bunnahabhain, Strathisla and Tomatin contact** Mr Pilling, Strathmore, West Fishwick, Berwick-upon-Tweed TD15 1XQ **t** (01289) 386279
**e** info@lazydaycottages.co.uk **w** lazydaycottages.co.uk

**WEST LINTON,** Scottish Borders — **GUEST ACCOMMODATION**

★★★★ BED & BREAKFAST

**Drochil Castle Farm** West Linton EH46 7DD
**t** (01721) 752249
**e** black.drochil@talk21.com **w** drochilcastle.co.uk

**WHITBURN,** West Lothian — **HOTEL**

★★★ HOTEL

**Best Western Hilcroft Hotel** East Main Street, Whitburn EH47 0JU
**t** (01501) 740818
**e** hilcroft@bestwestern.co.uk **w** hilcrofthotel.com

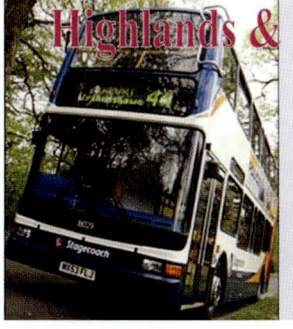



At-a-glance symbols are explained on page 8.

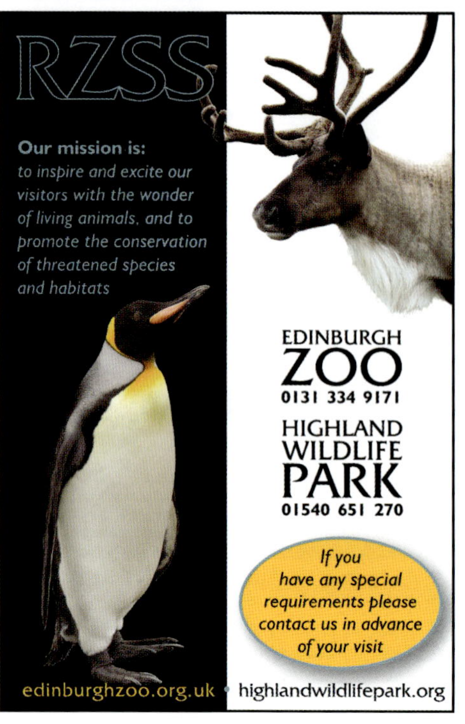
RZSS
Our mission is:
to inspire and excite our visitors with the wonder of living animals, and to promote the conservation of threatened species and habitats
EDINBURGH
ZOO
0131 334 9171
HIGHLAND
WILDLIFE
PARK
01540 651 270
If you have any special requirements please contact us in advance of your visit
edinburghzoo.org.uk • highlandwildlifepark.org

DEEP SEA WORLD
Scotland's Shark Capital
SCOTLANDS NATIONAL AQUARIUM
DEEP SEA WORLD
EVERYONE IS WELCOME
UNDER THE SEA
Fully Wheelchair Accessible
The UK's longest Underwater Safari home to 12ft Sharks
Cafe, gift shop
Carers go free*
*with ID
www.deepseaworld.com

Ionad Ealain
Arts Centre
an Lanntair
an Lanntair
Exhibitions
Live Events
Cinema & Shop
Workshops
Bar & Restaurant
Sràid Choinnich Kenneth Street,
Steòrnabhagh Stornoway,
Eilean Leòdhais Isle of Lewis,
Innse Gall Western Isles
01851 703307
www.lanntair.com
LOTTERY FUNDED
Scottish Arts Council
PÀIRT MAOINICHTE LEIS AN AONADH EORPACH
Eorpa agus Alba ag obair còmhla
HIE Innse Gall

KIRKCALDY INDOOR MARKET
Kircaldy Indoor Market
234-242 High Street Kdy,
01592 597051 Come along and enjoy a great day out at Fife's premier shopping experience with over 50 retail outlets under one roof.
Including 90 seater cafeteria
(Lite - Bite). Souvenirs
A complete A-Z, of merchandise
SCOTTISH SOUVENIRS FOR ALL
Fife's premier
shopping experience
Open 7 Days
Mon-Sat 09-30am -5-30pm
Sunday 11-00am - 4-00pm

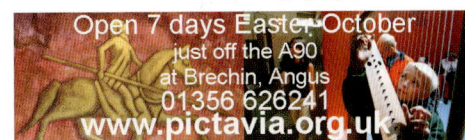

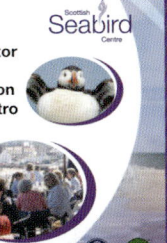

tigh an daraich
luxury lodges
Tigh an Daraich Luxury Lodges
Taynuilt,
PA35 1HR
Tel: 01866 822693
Fax: 01866 822339
info@tighandaraich.co.uk or sales@tighandaraich.co.uk
www.tighandaraich.co.uk

RSPB
Mersehead
Nature Reserve
lapwing
barnacle goose
Southwick,
Dumfries DG2 8AH
Tel: 01387 780579/01387 780298
www.rspb.org.uk/scotland
for birds for people for ever

The Scottish Parliament
Visit our
"Landmark for
21st Century
Democracy"
0131 348 5200
sp.bookings@scottish.parliament.uk
www.scottish.parliament.uk
The Scottish Parliament
Pàrlamaid na h-Alba

Shetland Islands Council – Ferry Services
Meet the Local Wildlife And See the Sights
With Shetland's Inter-Island Ferries,
95 Sailings Daily to
8 Islands
You'll have a whale of a time...
www.shetland.gov.uk/ferries

East Ayrshire
COUNCIL
Our public toilet facilities are at,
Burns Mall Kilmarnock and
Tanyard Cumnock
All facilities are at ground level with
no steps

at Strathclyde Country Park
enjoy:
• Woodland & Lochside trails.
• Roman Ruins
• Watersports to learn or for fun
• Mountain Bikes for hire
• Visitor Centre and Cafe
• Conditioning Gym
• Caravan & Campsite
• M&D's theme park - Scotland's first
• Hotel, restaurant & bar
366 Hamilton Road, Motherwell ML1 3ED
Tel: (01698) 402060
E.mail: strathclydepark@northlan.gov.uk

• Entry ticket valid all day
• Over 30 fascinating marine displays
• Feeding demonstrations throughout the day
• Restaurant
• Free Parking, Coaches Welcome
• Call 016321 720386 to ask about our special rates for groups and schools
Quote TFA Guide to get a 50% discount
Or go online to book tickets at
www.sealsanctuary.co.uk
The Scottish Sealife Sanctuary, Barcaldine,
Oban, Argyll PA37 1SE, Scotland
SCOTTISH
SEA LIFE
SANCTUARY

Atholl Centre
PITLOCHRY PERTHSHIRE
SCOTLAND
Holidays, Bed & Breakfast
Equipped for people with a disability
and their carers
Atholl Road, Pitlochry, PH16 5BX
Tel. 01796 473044
E/mail; admin@athollcentre.org.uk
Website; www.athollcentre.org.uk

Awaiting Rating

# Wales

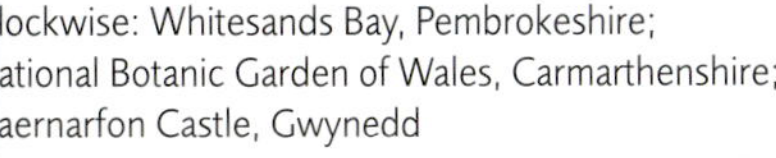

lockwise: Whitesands Bay, Pembrokeshire; ational Botanic Garden of Wales, Carmarthenshire; aernarfon Castle, Gwynedd

# Great days out

For a small country Wales is big on things to see and do. To start with it has three National Parks, each one featuring very different landscapes, and a turbulent history which comes alive in its many castles. Search out Wales' fascinating industrial heritage and discover its myths and legends.

## Nature at its best

In big, bold **Snowdonia National Park** ascend to the summit of **Mount Snowdon** on the little mountain railway for dazzling views across North Wales. In the south, travel in style on a vintage steam locomotive through beautiful **Brecon Beacons** – you can board the **Brecon Mountain Railway** near Merthyr Tydfil. Wales has 750 miles of coastline so it's not surprising that it offers a succession of award-winning beaches, bays, headlands and harbours. Let the sea air fill your lungs and the wildlife capture your attention in **Pembrokeshire** where you'll find Britain's only coastal-based **National Park**, or discover the hundreds of miles of seashore which have been declared Areas of Outstanding Natural Beauty and Heritage Coast. Take a boat from **New Quay** or **St Davids** to spot bottlenose dolphins along the coast of **Cardigan Bay**.

Cardiff Castle

## Cybermen and science

Europe's youngest capital and home of Dr Who, **Cardiff** is just a stone's throw from the Beacons' wide open spaces. It's cosmopolitan, lively and busy. Join in the cafe culture and don't miss the stunning new waterfront along **Cardiff Bay**. Make sure you visit the fabulous city-centre castle and the attractive glass-canopied Victorian and Edwardian shopping arcades.

Take a trip to **Swansea** for the largest indoor market in Wales, where you can sample and buy local delicacies such as cockles, laverbread and traditional welshcakes. Then set your course for the Maritime Quarter to visit Wales' newest museum, the **National Waterfront Museum**. Pushing the boundaries of technology in an interactive interpretation of Wales' industry and innovation, it showcases new technologies in science, manufacturing and medicine.

Left to right: Tenby, Pembrokeshire; St Davids Cathedral, Pembrokeshire

**why not...** enjoy some of Britain's best sunsets, at Whitesands Bay, Pembrokeshire?

## Great creations

Clough Williams-Ellis aimed to integrate man-made beauty with natural beauty. See the results for yourself at **Portmeirion Village and Gardens** where a romantic Italian-style village is set in sub-tropical woodlands. Pick up a piece of the attractive Portmeirion Pottery whilst you're there. Make a bee-line for one of the most fascinating gardens in the UK – **The National Botanic Garden of Wales** in Carmarthenshire where The Great Glasshouse protects and conserves some of the most endangered plants on the planet. Include on your must-see list **St Davids** where the magnificent cathedral and imposing ruins of its Bishop's Palace are accessible via ramps and lifts. Stroll the enchanting cloister, pool and walled gardens at **Aberglasney**, tucked away in the lovely Tywi Valley and an inspiration to poets since1477.

Want to entertain the kids? Set them on the Childen's Puzzle Trail at dramatic **Lake Vyrnwy**, west of **Welshpool**, where they can seek out beautifully crafted wooden animals hidden in the trees.

Portmeirion, Gwynedd

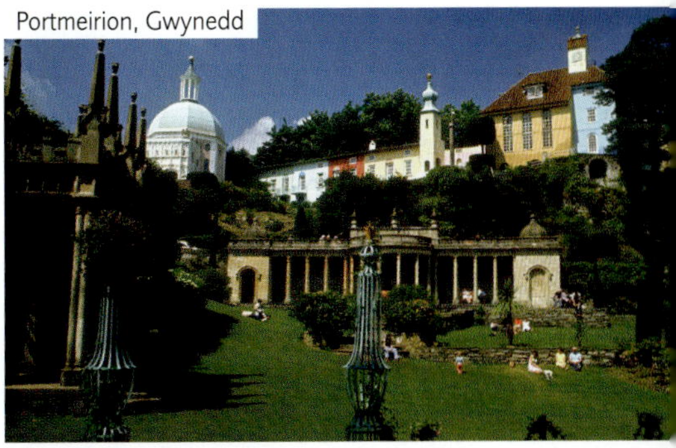

## Past and future

Wales can stake a strong claim to King Arthur. In the south, **Caerleon's** magnificent **Roman amphitheatre** is said to have served as Arthur's Round Table and the castle above **Llangollen** in the north is the reputed hiding place for the Holy Grail. Discover the legends for yourself. Castles, of course, are what Wales does very well, ranging from **Harlech**, **Beaumaris**, **Caernarfon** and **Conwy**, in the north, to romantic hilltop fortresses such as **Carreg Cennen** near **Llandeilo**. If you want to venture inside do check access before you go. Experience the country's fascinating industrial heritage first-hand in places like the **Llechwedd Slate Caverns** and the **Big Pit at Blaenavon** where you can go underground.

For all its history, Wales doesn't live in the past. It's an exciting, forward-looking country, full of discovery and adventure. At the **Centre for Alternative Technology** in mid Wales fill your head with ideas of how to conserve the earth's natural resources: wind, water and solar power, energy conservation, organic growing and more. Or test out the interactive, hands-on exhibits at **Techniquest**, a collection of four amazing science

**did you know...** the unique Snowdon Lily has survived on Mount Snowdon for 10,000 years?

Clockwise: Snowdonia; Wales Millennium Centre, Cardiff; Beaumaris Castle, Anglesey

centres across Wales; and see stars in the planetarium.

## It's all happening

There's plenty going on all over Wales. Begin by checking out sporting fixtures and concerts at **Cardiff's Millennium Stadium**. Take the tour to imagine being greeted by 74,500 people as you exit the tunnel or see how it feels to sit in the Queen's seat.

Give your taste buds a treat in September at the **Abergavenny Food Festival** or at **Caerphilly's Big Cheese** extravaganza in July. If words are your inspiration, celebrate great writing in every medium at the world-famous **Hay Festival** at the end of May.

As you would expect, there is music everywhere. Get with the beat at the renowned **Brecon International Festival of Jazz** or immerse yourself in all things Welsh at the **National Eisteddfod**, both in August. And in July, join the cosmopolitan gathering at **Llangollen International Musical Eisteddfod**. For ballet, opera, dance and musicals you can't do better than the **Wales Millennium Centre**.

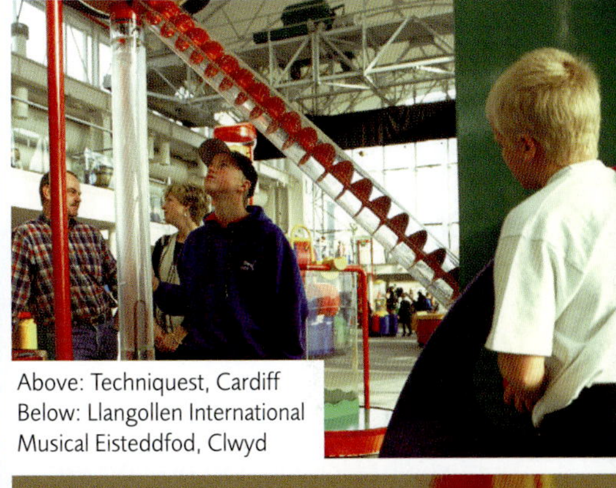

Above: Techniquest, Cardiff
Below: Llangollen International Musical Eisteddfod, Clwyd

# Useful national contacts

**Visit Wales**
**t** 0870 121 1251
**t** 0870 121 1255 (minicom)
**w** visitwales.com

## Information

### Brecon Beacons National Park Authority

Plas y Ffynnon, Cambrian Way, Brecon LD3 7DP
**t** (01874) 624437
**e** enquiries@breconbeacons.org
**w** breconbeacons.org
Produces Places to Visit With Easier Access, a guide to short walks and trails, and places of interest suitable for people with limited mobility.

### Red Cross North Wales

Red Cross House, North Wales Business Park, Abergele LL22 8LJ
**t** (01745) 828330
**e** northwales@redcross.org.uk
**w** redcross.org.uk
Provides wheelchairs and equipment on short-term loan across North Wales, and transport and escort services in North West Wales only.

### Cadw: Welsh Historic Monuments

Welsh Assembly Government, Plas Carew,Unit 5/7 Cefn Coed, Parc Nantgarw, Cardiff CF15 7QQ
**t** (01443) 336000
**e** Cadw@Wales.gsi.gov.uk
**w** cadw.wales.gov.uk
Responsible for protecting the built heritage of Wales, including over 130 historic sites. A guide to Cadw sites for disabled visitors is available to download from the website.

### Disability Wales (Head Office)

Bridge House, Caerphilly Business Park, Van Road, Caerphilly CF83 3GW
**t** (029) 2088 7325
**e** info@disabilitywales.org
**w** disabilitywales.org
A national association of disability groups in Wales.

### Pembrokeshire Coast National Park Authority

Llanion Park, Pembroke Dock SA72 6DY
**t** 0845 345 7245
**e** info@pembrokeshirecoast.org.uk
**w** pembrokeshirecoast.org.uk
Produces Easy Access Routes, a guide to 20 walks on the coast, along with other information about the area, views and beaches. Available by post by calling (01834) 845040.

### Snowdonia National Park Authority

Penrhyndeudraeth LL48 6LF
**t** (01766) 770274
**e** parc@snowdonia-npa.gov.uk
Produces Enjoying Eryri, a booklet, available in print or on CD, on the national park and attractions in Snowdonia.

# Tourist Information Centres

When you arrive at your destination, visit a Tourist Information Centre for help with accommodation and information about local attractions and events, or email your request before you go.

| | | | |
|---|---|---|---|
| **Aberaeron** | The Quay | (01545) 570602 | aberaerontic@ceredigion.gov.uk |
| **Aberdulais Falls** | The National Trust | (01639) 636674 | aberdulaistic@nationaltrust.org.uk |
| **Aberdyfi*** | The Wharf Gardens | (01654) 767321 | tic.aberdyfi@eryri-npa.gov.uk |
| **Abergavenny** | Monmouth Road | (01873) 853254 | abergavennyic@breconbeacons.org |
| **Aberystwyth** | Terrace Road | (01970) 612125 | aberystwythtic@ceredigion.gov.uk |
| **Bala*** | Pensarn Road | (01678) 521021 | bala.tic@gwynedd.gov.uk |
| **Bangor*** | Deiniol Road | (01248) 352786 | bangor.tic@gwynedd.gov.uk |
| **Barmouth** | Station Road | (01341) 280787 | barmouth.tic@gwynedd.gov.uk |
| **Barry Island*** | The Promenade | (01446) 747171 | barrytic@valeofglamorgan.gov.uk |
| **Beddgelert*** | Canolfan Hebog | (01766) 890615 | tic.beddgelert@eryri-npa.gov.uk |
| **Betws y Coed** | Royal Oak Stables | (01690) 710426 | tic.byc@eryri-npa.gov.uk |
| **Blaenau Ffestiniog*** | Unit 3, High Street | (01766) 830360 | tic.blaenau@eryri-npa.gov.uk |
| **Blaenavon*** | Church Road | (01495) 742333 | blaenavon.tic@torfaen.gov.uk |
| **Borth*** | Cambrian Terrace | (01970) 871174 | borthtic@ceredigion.gov.uk |
| **Brecon** | Cattle Market Car park | (01874) 622485 | brectic@powys.gov.uk |
| **Bridgend** | Bridgend Designer Outlet | (01656) 654906 | bridgendtic@bridgend.gov.uk |
| **Builth Wells** | The Groe Car Park | (01982) 553307 | builtic@powys.gov.uk |
| **Caerleon** | 5 High Street | (01633) 422656 | caerleon.tic@newport.gov.uk |
| **Caernarfon** | Castle Street | (01286) 672232 | caernarfon.tic@gwynedd.gov.uk |
| **Caerphilly** | The Twyn | (029) 2088 0011 | tourism@caerphilly.gov.uk |
| **Cardiff** | The Old Library | 0870 121 1258 | visitor@cardiff.gov.uk |
| **Cardigan** | Bath House Road | (01239) 613230 | cardigantic@ceredigion.gov.uk |
| **Carmarthen** | 113 Lammas Street | (01267) 231557 | carmarthentic@carmarthenshire.gov.uk |
| **Chepstow** | Bridge Street | (01291) 623772 | chepstow.tic@monmouthshire.gov.uk |
| **Conwy** | Castle Buildings | (01492) 592248 | conwytic@conwy.gov.uk |
| **Dolgellau** | Eldon Square | (01341) 422888 | tic.dolgellau@eryri-npa.gov.uk |
| **Fishguard Harbour** | The Parrog | (01348) 872037 | fishguardharbour.tic@pembrokeshire.gov.uk |
| **Fishguard Town** | Market Square | (01437) 776636 | fishguard.tic@pembrokeshire.gov.uk |
| **Harlech*** | High Street | (01766) 780658 | tic.harlech@eryri-npa.gov.uk |
| **Haverfordwest** | Old Bridge | (01437) 763110 | haverfordwest.tic@pembrokeshire.gov.uk |

| | | | |
|---|---|---|---|
| **Holyhead** | Stena Line, Terminal 1 | (01407) 762622 | holyhead@nwtic.com |
| **Knighton** | West Street | (01547) 528753 | oda@offasdyke.demon.co.uk |
| **Llanberis*** | 41b High Street | (01286) 870765 | llanberis.tic@gwynedd.gov.uk |
| **Llandovery** | Kings Road | (01550) 720693 | llandovery.ic@breconbeacons.org |
| **Llandudno** | Mostyn Street | (01492) 876413 | llandudnotic@conwy.gov.uk |
| **Llanelli** | North Dock | (01554) 777744 | DiscoveryCentre@ carmarthenshire.gov.uk |
| **Llanfairpwllgwyngyll** | Station Site | (01248) 713177 | llanfairpwll@nwtic.com |
| **Llangollen** | Castle Street | (01978) 860828 | llangollen@nwtic.com |
| **Machynlleth** | Penrallt Street | (01654) 702401 | mactic@powys.gov.uk |
| **Merthyr Tydfil** | 14a Glebeland Street | (01685) 379884 | tic@merthyr.gov.uk |
| **Milford Haven*** | 94 Charles Street | (01646) 690866 | milford.tic@pembrokeshire.gov.uk |
| **Mold** | Earl Road | (01352) 759331 | mold@nwtic.com |
| **Monmouth** | Agincourt Square | (01600) 713899 | monmouth.tic@monmouthshire.gov.uk |
| **Mumbles** | Mumbles Road | (01792) 361302 | info@mumblestic.co.uk |
| **New Quay*** | Church Street | (01545) 560865 | newquaytic@ceredigion.gov.uk |
| **Newport** | John Frost Square | (01633) 842962 | newport.tic@newport.gov.uk |
| **Newport (pembs)*** | Long Street | (01239) 820912 | newportTIC@pembrokeshirecoast.org.uk |
| **Oswestry Mile End** | Mile End Services | (01691) 662488 | tic@oswestry-bc.gov.uk |
| **Oswestry Town** | 2 Church Terrace | (01691) 662753 | ot@oswestry-welshborders.org.uk |
| **Pembroke*** | Commons Road | (01646) 622388 | pembroke.tic@pembrokeshire.gov.uk |
| **Penarth*** | Penarth Pier | (029) 2070 8849 | penarthtic@valeofglamorgan.gov.uk |
| **Porthcawl*** | John Street | (01656) 786639 | porthcawltic@bridgend.gov.uk |
| **Porthmadog** | High Street | (01766) 512981 | porthmadog.tic@gwynedd.gov.uk |
| **Presteigne*** | Broad Street | (01544) 260650 | presteignetic@powys.gov.uk |
| **Pwllheli** | Station Square | (01758) 613000 | pwllheli.tic@gwynedd.gov.uk |
| **Rhyl** | West Parade | (01745) 355068 | rhyl.tic@denbighshire.gov.uk |
| **St Davids** | 1 High Street | (01437) 720392 | enquiries@ stdavids.pembrokeshirecoast.org.uk |
| **Saundersfoot*** | Harbour Car Park | (01834) 813672 | saundersfoot.tic@pembrokeshire.gov.uk |
| **Swansea** | Plymouth Street | (01792) 468321 | tourism@swansea.gov.uk |
| **Tenby** | Unit 2, The Gateway Complex | (01834) 842402 | tenby.tic@pembrokeshire.gov.uk |
| **Tywyn*** | High Street | (01654) 710070 | tywyn.tic@gwynedd.gov.uk |
| **Welshpool** | Church Street | (01938) 552043 | weltic@powys.gov.uk |
| **Wrexham** | Lambpit Street | (01978) 292015 | tic@wrexham.gov.uk |

* seasonal opening

where to stay in

# Wales

The following establishments participate in the Visit Wales quality assessment scheme and are required to provide Access Statements describing their facilities. YHA youth hostels in England and Wales are listed in a separate section, see page 40.

Place names in the blue bands with a map reference are shown on the maps at the front of this guide.

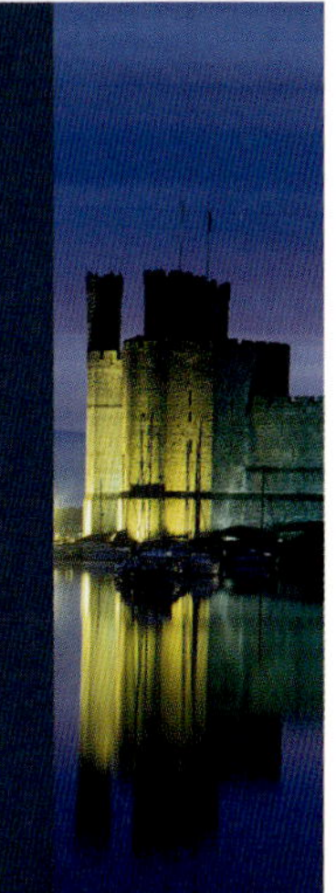

## Accommodation symbols

Symbols give useful information about services and facilities. You can find a key to these symbols on page 8.

**ABERAERON,** Ceredigion — **GUEST ACCOMMODATION**

★★★★★ INN

ACCESS STATEMENT

**Harbour Master Hotel** Pencei, Aberaeron SA46 0BA
**t** (01545) 570755
**e** menna@harbour-master.com **w** harbour-master.com

**ABERGAVENNY,** Monmouthshire — **SELF CATERING**

★★★ SELF CATERING

ACCESS STATEMENT

**Homefield contact** Mrs Hounsome,
**t** (01981) 240859
**e** ltm3castles@aol.com **w** homefield.me.uk

**AMROTH,** Pembrokeshire — **SELF CATERING**

★★★★ SELF CATERING

ACCESS STATEMENT

**Sunflower Cottage contact** Mr N Clark,
**t** (01834) 831259
**e** pendeiloholidays@aol.com **w** pendeilo.co.uk

## Where can I get help and advice?

Tourist Information Centres offer friendly help with accommodation and holiday ideas as well as suggestions of places to visit and things to do. You'll find contact details at the beginning of this section.

**BORTH,** Ceredigion Map ref 8A2 **SELF CATERING**

★★★–★★★★★
SELF CATERING

Units **5**
Sleeps **2–10**
Low season per wk
£189.00–£309.00
High season per wk
£369.00–£829.00

## Aberleri Seaside Cottages, Borth

Aberleri Farm Cottages, Maramba, Cliff Road, Borth SY24 5NN
**t** (01970) 871722
**e** info@aberlericottages.co.uk **w** aberlericottages.co.uk

General

Leisure

Unit

Payment Credit/debit cards, cash, cheques

*Wales Tourist Board-approved. Accessibility Statement on request.*

Peacefully situated adjoining nature reserve and golf course and a few minutes from sandy beaches. Farmhouse and four cottages, superbly appointed. Luxury bathrooms, three with jacuzzi. Sky Digital/Freeview LCD TVs, DVD, some bedrooms have TV. Broadband connection. Convenient for places of interest, restaurants, pubs and shopping. Owners' personal supervision.

**open** All year
**nearest shop** 1.5 miles
**nearest pub** 1.5 miles

*From A487 take B4350 to Borth. Shared entrance with Swn-y-Mor Holiday Park at northern end of village at Ynyslas. Adjoining golf course.*

**CAERNARFON,** Gwynedd **HOTEL**

★★★
HOTEL

ACCESS STATEMENT

**Celtic Royal Hotel** Bangor Street, Caernarfon LL55 1AY
**t** (01286) 674477
**w** celtic-royal.co.uk

**CAERNARFON,** Gwynedd Map ref 8A1 **HOTEL**

B&B per room per night
**s £75.00–£130.00**
**d £85.00–£180.00**
HB per person per night
**£72.50–£125.00**

ACCESS STATEMENT

## Seiont Manor

Llanrug, Caernarfon LL55 2AQ **t** 0845 072 7550
**e** seiontmanor@handpicked.co.uk **w** handpicked.co.uk/seiontmanor

Seiont Manor sits peacefully within the countryside of Snowdonia, some of the most stunning scenery in north Wales. Surrounded by 150 acres of mature farmland, Seiont offers a complete escape from the pressures of everyday life.

**open** All year
**bedrooms** 18 double, 1 twin, 2 family, 7 suites
**bathrooms** All en suite

Access abc

Rooms

General

Leisure

Payment Credit/debit cards, cash, cheques, euros

**CARDIFF** HOTEL

★★★★★
HOTEL

ACCESS STATEMENT

**Cardiff Hilton** Kingsway, Cardiff CF10 3HH
**t** (02920) 646300
**e** mark.walker@hilton.com **w** hilton.co.uk/cardiff

**CARDIFF** HOTEL

★★★★
HOTEL

ACCESS STATEMENT

**Copthorne Hotel Cardiff/Caerdydd** Copthorne Way, Culverhouse Cross, Cardiff CF5 6DH **t** (02920) 599100
**e** sales@mill-cop.com **w** millenniumhotels.co.uk

**CARDIGAN,** Ceredigion Map ref 8A2 SELF CATERING

SELF CATERING

Units **5**
Sleeps **4–9**
Low season per wk
**£250.00–£300.00**
High season per wk
**£540.00–£720.00**

## The Mews, Saddleback, Ladderloft, The Mansion & Granary, Boncath

**contact** Mr Jim Bowen, Clynfyw, Abercych, Boncath SA37 0HF
**t** (01239) 841236
**e** jim.clynfyw@virgin.net **w** clynfyw.co.uk

Access abc

General P S

Unit

Payment Cash, cheques, euros

We have provided award-winning accommodation on our family's organic farm here in Pembrokeshire for over 20 years. Some guests have revisited us almost every year since then. Set in converted Victorian farm buildings, the sensitively designed, all-access cottages provide a wonderfully peaceful base for a countryside holiday. Dogs welcome.

**open** All Year
**nearest shop** 2 miles
**nearest pub** 1 mile

*Clynfyw is on the B4332 between Boncath and Cenarth at the top of the hill above Abercych, North Pembrokeshire.*

## Accessibility accommodation in Wales

Establishments in Wales are not inspected under the National Accessible Scheme, however they are required to provide access statements describing their facilities.

## CONWY — HOTEL

★★★★
HOTEL

ACCESS STATEMENT

**The Quay Hotel** Deganwy Quay, Deganwy, Conwy LL31 9DJ
**t** (01492) 564100
**e** info@quayhotel.com **w** quayhotel.com

## CONWY, Conwy Map ref 8B1 — SELF CATERING

★★
SELF CATERING

Units **1**
Sleeps **6**
Low season per wk
**Min £325.00**
High season per wk
**Max £775.00**

ACCESS STATEMENT

### Y Beudy, Conwy

North Wales Holiday Cottages & Farmhouses, 39 Station Road, Deganwy LL31 9DF **t** 0844 582 1492
**e** info@northwalesholidaycottages.co.uk
**w** northwalesholidaycottages.co.uk

Access abc

General

Unit

Payment Credit/debit cards, cash, cheques

*Level access and wide doors throughout, shower seat available, grab rails, one section of kitchen with low work surface.*

One of four properties set around the original farmyard, this modern barn conversion has two double bedrooms each with en suite facilities, one twin bedroom, wetroom and large kitchen/lounge/diner with log burner. Sauna on site. Conwy Valley location is ideal for exploring both Snowdonia and the whole of north Wales.

**open** All year
**nearest shop** 0.5 miles
**nearest pub** 1 mile

*The cottage is on an organic farm less than two miles south of Conwy town. Full details with confirmed booking.*

# Place index

If you know where you want to stay, the index by place name at the back of the guide will give you the page number listing accommodation in your chosen town, city or village. Check out the other useful indexes too.

**CONWY,** Conwy Map ref 8B1 — **SELF CATERING**

★★★★
SELF CATERING

Units **1**
Sleeps **4**
Low season per wk
**Min £260.00**
High season per wk
**Max £585.00**

ACCESS STATEMENT

## Y Bwthyn, Conwy

North Wales Holiday Cottages & Farmhouses, 39 Station Road, Deganwy LL31 9DF **t** 0844 582 1492
**e** info@northwalesholidaycottages.co.uk
**w** northwalesholidaycottages.co.uk

Access abc

General

Unit

Payment Credit/debit cards, cash, cheques

*Level access and wide doors throughout, seated shower, grab rails, one section of kitchen with low work surface.*

One of four properties set around the original farmyard, this modern barn conversion has two bedrooms (one double, one twin), wetroom, kitchen and lounge/diner with open fire. Sauna on site. This Conwy Valley location is ideal for exploring both Snowdonia and the whole of north Wales.

**open** All year
**nearest shop** 0.5 miles
**nearest pub** 1 mile

*The cottage is on an organic farm less than two miles south of Conwy town. Full details confirmed with booking.*

**CONWY,** Conwy Map ref 8B1 — **CAMPING, CARAVAN & HOLIDAY PARK**

★★★
TOURING PARK

(320) £4.85–£17.60
(25) £4.85–£17.60
(50) £4.85–£17.60
320 touring pitches

ACCESS STATEMENT

## Conwy Touring Park

Trefriw Road, Conwy LL32 8UX **t** (01492) 592856
**e** sales@conwytouringpark.co.uk **w** conwytouringpark.co.uk

Set in spectacular scenery, the perfect location for touring Snowdonia and coastal resorts. Sheltered, wooded site with splendid views. Excellent children's facilities. Special offers. Storage and servicing available.
**open** Easter to September

General

Leisure

Payment Credit/debit cards, cash, cheques

**DEESIDE,** Flintshire — **HOTEL**

★★★★
HOTEL

ACCESS STATEMENT

**De Vere St Davids Park Hotel** St Davids Park, Ewloe, Deeside CH5 3YB
**t** (01244) 520800
**e** reservations.stdavids@devere-hotels.com **w** devereonline.co.uk

**DULAS,** Ynys Mon — SELF CATERING

★★★★–★★★★★ SELF CATERING

ACCESS STATEMENT

**Minffordd Holiday Cottage** **contact** Mr H Hughes Roberts
**t** (01248) 410678
**w** minffordd-holidays.com

**DULAS,** Ynys Mon — CAMPING, CARAVAN & HOLIDAY PARK

★★★★★ HOLIDAY PARK

ACCESS STATEMENT

**Minffordd Caravan Park** Penrhos, Lligwy, Dulas LL70 9HJ
**t** (01248) 410678
**e** enq@minffordd-holidays.com **w** minffordd-holidays.com

**FISHGUARD,** Pembrokeshire — SELF CATERING

★★★–★★★★ SELF CATERING

ACCESS STATEMENT

**Gellifawr Cottages** **contact** Mr S Sheldon
**t** (01239) 820343
**e** info@gellifawr.co.uk **w** gellifawr.co.uk

**GAERWEN,** Ynys Mon — SELF CATERING

★★★★ SELF CATERING

ACCESS STATEMENT

**Garnedd Holiday Cottages** **contact** Mrs Owen
**t** (01248) 714261
**e** mail@garneddholidaycottages.co.uk **w** garneddholidaycottages.co.uk

**HOLYHEAD,** Ynys Mon — SELF CATERING

★★★★ SELF CATERING

ACCESS STATEMENT

**Trewan Sands** **contact** Mrs Karen Reay
**t** 07720 895671
**e** trewansands@virgin.net **w** trewansands.co.uk

**HOLYWELL,** Flintshire — HOTEL

★★★ HOTEL

ACCESS STATEMENT

**Springfield Hotel** A55 Expressway, Halkyn, Holywell CH8 8BD
**t** (01352) 780503
**e** admin@hotel-northwales.com **w** hotel-northwales.com

**LAMPETER,** Ceredigion — GUEST ACCOMMODATION

★★★★★ RESTAURANT WITH ROOMS

ACCESS STATEMENT

**Ty Mawr Mansion** Cilcennin, Lampeter SA48 8DB
**t** (01570) 470033
**e** info@tymawrmansion.co.uk **w** tymawrmansion.co.uk

**LAMPETER,** Ceredigion — SELF CATERING

★★★★–★★★★★ SELF CATERING

ACCESS STATEMENT

**Gaer Cottages** **contact** Mr Jeffrey Rice
**t** (01570) 470275
**e** gaer@bigfoot.com **w** selfcateringinwales.co.uk

**LAMPETER,** Ceredigion — SELF CATERING

★★★ SELF CATERING

ACCESS STATEMENT

**Ty Glyn Davis Trust** **contact** Louise Hutchins
**t** (01545) 580708
**e** tyglyndavistrust@care4free.net **w** tyglyndavistrust.co.uk

**LLANDRINDOD WELLS,** Powys — HOTEL

★★★ HOTEL

ACCESS STATEMENT

**Hotel Metropole** Temple Street, Llandrindod Wells LD1 5DY
**t** (01597) 823700
**e** info@metropole.co.uk **w** metropole.co.uk

**LLANDUDNO,** Conwy — HOTEL

★★★ HOTEL

ACCESS STATEMENT

**Cae Mor Hotel** 5/6 Penrhyn Crescent, Central Promenade, Llandudno LL30 1BA
**t** (01492) 878101
**e** info@caemorhotel.co.uk **w** caemorhotel.co.uk

**LLANDUDNO,** Conwy **HOTEL**

★★★★ HOTEL

ACCESS STATEMENT

**The Imperial** Vaughan Street, Promenade, Llandudno LL30 1AP
**t** (01492) 877466
**e** imphotel@btinternet.com **w** theimperial.co.uk

**LLANDUDNO,** Conwy **HOTEL**

★★★★ HOTEL

ACCESS STATEMENT

**St George's Hotel** The Promenade, Llandudno LL30 2LG
**t** (01492) 877544
**e** sales@stgeorgeswales.co.uk **w** stgeorgeswales.co.uk

**LLANDUDNO,** Conwy Map ref 8B1 **GUEST ACCOMMODATION**

★★★ GUEST ACCOMMODATION

HB per person per night
**£33.00–£63.00**

Awaiting NAS rating

## West Shore

West Parade, Llandudno LL30 2BB **t** (01492) 876833
**e** westshorehotel@livability.org.uk or attibble@livability.org.uk
**w** livabilityholidays.org.uk

Access abc

Rooms

General

Payment Credit/debit cards, cash, cheques, euros

*Turkey and Tinsel breaks (Nov). Taste of Wales breaks (Mar-Apr). Valentine breaks (Feb).*

Grooms Holidays property specially adapted for disabled holidaymakers. Seventeen bedrooms with roll-in shower rooms. Some equipment available including hoists, but guests needing personal help should be accompanied or arrange carer from a recommended local agency. Tail-lift bus for outings.

**open** All year
**bedrooms** 2 double, 8 twin, 7 single, 1 family
**bathrooms** All en suite

*From A55, A546 (Ffordd 6G road), roundabout exit to Gloddaeth Avenue. Right at West Parade. Collection from Llandudno station can be arranged.*

## Key to symbols

Symbols at the end of each entry help you pick out the services and facilities which are most important for your stay. A key to the symbols can be found on page 8.

**LLANFAIR CAEREINION,** Powys Map ref 8B2 **SELF CATERING**

★★★–★★★★★
SELF CATERING

Units **3**
Sleeps **2–6**
Low season per wk
£100.00–£380.00
High season per wk
£225.00–£530.00

## Madog's Wells, Llanfair Caereinion

**contact** Ann, Madog's Wells, Llanfair Caereinion, Welshpool SY21 0DE
**t** (01938) 810446 **e** info@madogswells.co.uk **w** madogswells.co.uk

Compact, cosy two-bedroom bungalow (one double, one single) and two spacious three-bedroom bungalows (one double, two twins) in beautiful secluded valley; bird-watching, walking, steam trains, lakes and mountains nearby. Access statement available.

**open** All year
**nearest shop** 3 miles
**nearest pub** 3 miles

General
Unit
Payment Cash, cheques

**LLANFAIRPWLLGWYNGYLL,** Isle of Anglesey Map ref 8A1 **SELF CATERING**

Rating Applied For
SELF CATERING

Units **1**
Sleeps **6**
Low season per wk
Min £305.00
High season per wk
Max £710.00

ACCESS STATEMENT

## Coach House Faner, Llanfairpwllgwyngyll

North Wales Holiday Cottages & Farmhouses, 39 Station Road, Deganwy LL31 9DF **t** 0844 582 1492
**e** info@northwalesholidaycottages.co.uk
**w** northwalesholidaycottages.co.uk

Access abc
General
Unit
Payment Credit/debit cards, cash, cheques

*Ramp access and wide doors throughout, wetroom with seated shower and grab rails.*

A new-build cottage designed with needs of the less mobile in mind. Three bedrooms, wetroom and large lounge/kitchen/diner in a beautiful rural setting, a little over half a mile from the Menai Straits in south-west Anglesey. A short drive to the mountains of Snowdonia or wonderful local beaches.

**open** All year
**nearest shop** 0.5 miles
**nearest pub** 0.5 miles

*The cottage is four miles from Llanfairpwllgwyngyll along a quiet lane on the edge of the village of Brynsiencyn. Full details with confirmed booking.*

**LLANFYNDD,** Carmarthenshire **SELF CATERING**

★★★★–★★★★★
SELF CATERING

ACCESS STATEMENT

**Ash Tree Lodge contact** Mrs G E Maidment
**t** (01558) 668287
**w** holidaycottagewales.com

## LLANLLYFN, Gwynedd — HOSTEL

HOSTEL

ACCESS STATEMENT

**Ozanam Centre** Tyn Y Pwll, Llanllyfni, Caernarfon LL54 6RP
**t** (01286) 881568
**e** bookings@svp-ozanamcentre.org.uk **w** ozanamcentre.org

## MOLD, Flintshire — HOTEL

★★★ HOTEL

ACCESS STATEMENT

**Beaufort Park Hotel** Alltami Road, New Brighton, Mold CH7 6RQ
**t** (01352) 758646
**e** info@beaufortparkhotel.co.uk **w** beaufortparkhotel.co.uk

## NARBERTH, Pembrokeshire — GUEST ACCOMMODATION

★★★★★ B&B

ACCESS STATEMENT

**Canaston Oaks** Canaston Bridge, Narberth SA67 8DE
**t** (01437) 541254
**e** enquiries@canastonoaks.co.uk **w** canastonoaks.co.uk

## NEWTOWN, Powys — GUEST ACCOMMODATION

★★★★★ FARMHOUSE

ACCESS STATEMENT

**Highgate Holiday Cottages** Newtown SY16 3LF
**t** (01686) 623763
**e** highgatehouse@hotmail.com **w** highgate-accommodation.co.uk

## OSWESTRY, Powys — HOTEL

★★★ HOTEL

ACCESS STATEMENT

**Lion Quays Hotel** Weston Rhyn, Oswestry SY11 3EN
**t** (01691) 684300
**e** sales@lionquays.co.uk **w** lionquays.co.uk

## PENARTH, Vale Of Glamorgan — GUEST ACCOMMODATION

★★★★★ GUEST ACCOMMODATION

ACCESS STATEMENT

**Holm House** Marine Parade, Penarth CF64 3BG
**t** (02920) 701572
**e** susan@holmhouse.co.uk **w** holmhouse.co.uk

## PENDINE, Carmarthenshire — SELF CATERING

★★–★★★ SELF CATERING

ACCESS STATEMENT

**Clyngwyn Farm Cottages** **contact** Mrs J Stuckey
**t** (01994) 453214
**e** clyngwyn@tiscali.co.uk **w** clyngwyn-farm-cottages.wales.info

## PENPARC, Ceredigion — SELF CATERING

★★★★★ SELF CATERING

ACCESS STATEMENT

**Canllefaes Ganol** **contact** Mrs L Mansfield,
**t** (01239) 613712
**e** enquiries@canllefaes.com **w** canllefaes.com

## Remember to check when booking

Please remember that all information in this guide has been supplied by the proprietors well in advance of publication. Since changes do sometimes occur it's a good idea to check details at the time of booking.

**RED ROSES,** Carmarthenshire Map ref 8A3 **SELF CATERING**

SELF CATERING

Units **6**
Sleeps **2–7**
Low season per wk
£240.00–£460.00
High season per wk
£420.00–£820.00

## Homeleigh Country Cottages, Whitland

**contact** Mrs Morfydd, Homeleigh Country Cottages, Red Roses, Whitland **t** (01834) 831765
**e** enquiries@homeleigh.org **w** homeleigh.org

Access

General

Unit

Payment Cash, cheques

*All ground floor rooms totally wheelchair accessible. Upstairs bedrooms available with second shower room.*

Small collection of six cottages, on a smallholding just four miles from the Pembrokeshire/ Carmarthenshire coast. Specifically designed for accessibility, wheelchair users in particular can appreciate the level of luxury on offer. The cottages include central heating, fully equipped kitchens, Freeview TV, wetrooms and other disabled aids.

**open** All year except Christmas
**nearest shop** 5 miles
**nearest pub** < 0.5 miles

*From Carmarthen, follow A40 St Clears. At roundabout, first exit (A477), continue for 6 miles. At Red Roses crossroads turn left, Homeleigh Country cottages 300yds on left.*

## Using map references

The map references refer to the colour maps at the front of this guide. The first figure is the map number, the letter and figure that follow indicate the grid reference on the map.

## Don't forget www.

Web addresses throughout this guide are shown without the prefix www. Please include www. in the address line of your browser. If a web address does not follow this style it is shown in full.

**ST DAVIDS,** Pembrokeshire — **GUEST ACCOMMODATION**

★★★★
GUEST ACCOMMODATION

ACCESS STATEMENT

**Ocean Haze** Haverfordwest Road,
St Davids SA62 6QN
**t** (01437) 720826

**ST DAVIDS,** Pembrokeshire — **SELF CATERING**

★★★★
SELF CATERING

ACCESS STATEMENT

**Ocean Haze contact** Mrs C Morris
**t** (01437) 720826

**SAUNDERSFOOT,** Pembrokeshire — **HOTEL**

★★★★
HOTEL

ACCESS STATEMENT

**St Brides Hotel** St Brides Hill, Saundersfoot SA69 9NH
**t** (01834) 812304
**e** reservations@stbridesspahotel.com **w** stbridesspahotel.com

**SWANSEA** — **HOTEL**

★★★
HOTEL

ACCESS STATEMENT

**Village Hotel Swansea** Langdon Road, Off Fabian Way, Swansea SA1 8QY
**t** 0844 847 2970
**e** village.swansea@village-hotels.com **w** village-hotels.co.uk/Hotels/swansea

**TENBY,** Pembrokeshire — **SELF CATERING**

★★★★★
SELF CATERING

ACCESS STATEMENT

**Tudor Lodge Cottage contact** Mr G McGivern,
**t** 07881 897730
**e** lodgecottages@btinternet.com **w** tudor-lodge-cottages.wales.info

**TYWYN,** Gwynedd — **HOTEL**

★★★
HOTEL

ACCESS STATEMENT

**Tynycornel Hotel** Talyllyn, Tywyn LL36 9AJ
**t** (01654) 782282
**e** reception@tynycornel.co.uk **w** tynycornel.co.uk

**WREXHAM** — **HOTEL**

★★★
HOTEL

ACCESS STATEMENT

**Holt Lodge Hotel** Holt Road, Wrexham LL13 9SW
**t** (01978) 661002
**w** holtlodge.co.uk

**WREXHAM** — **HOTEL**

★★★★
HOTEL

ACCESS STATEMENT

**Ramada Plaza Wrexham** Ellice Way, Wrexham LL13 7YH
**t** (01978) 291400
**e** Qamar.ahmed@qnhgroup.com **w** ramadaplazawrexham.co.uk

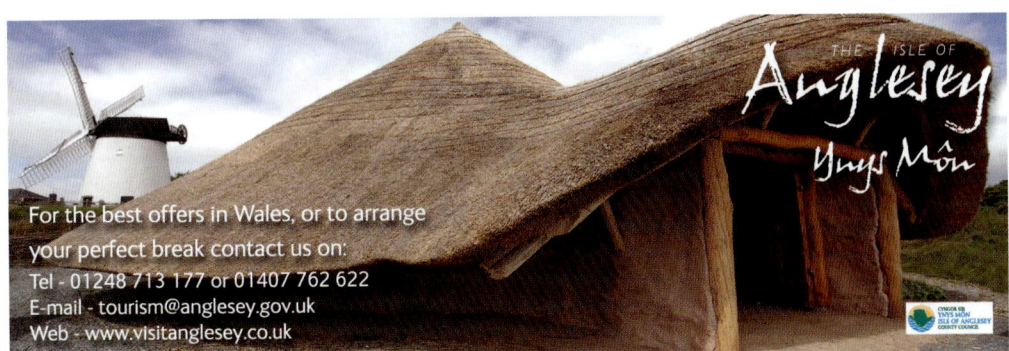



At-a-glance symbols are explained on page 8.

National Botanic Garden of Wales
Gardd Fotaneg Genedlaethol Cymru

Anglesey Sea Zoo Sŵ Môr Môn
for a splashing day out!
anglesey sea zoo
the largest aquarium in wales
over 150 british species from octopusses and seahorses to sharks and sunstars for you to get up-close and personal with!
open all year round!
includes the lobster hatchery of wales, an eerie shipwreck brimming with conger eels and a big-fish forest full of huge sea bass and sharks
daily fish feeding at 2.30pm and presentation at 12.00 noon. some days you can see a diver underwater! flexible education packages available
from kids to grown-ups, a great day out guaranteed! fully licensed bistro, gift shop, adventure play area, giant octojump bouncy castle and crazy golf
full wheelchair access throughout the site and disabled toilet. group discounts available. free coach parking
www.angleseyseazoo.co.uk
t. 01248 430411

# Northern Ireland

Clockwise: Giant's Causeway, County Antrim; Londonderry, County Londonderry; Sika deer

# Great days out

**How do you like to escape? Following wave-swept coastal drives, walking romantic mountains and lakelands, delving into Celtic mysteries or the rich heritage of cosmopolitan cities? You can do them all in Northern Ireland, be active or relax. Plus there's always plenty of time for a chat with the locals.**

## Living city history

Visit **Belfast** for a start, where Victorian streetscapes recall the city's great heydays of shipbuilding, engineering, rope works and linen. Now its industrial heritage is a major tourist attraction – come for the annual **Titanic Made in Belfast Festival Week** around Easter time, and tour the shipyard where the historic vessel was built. At the **Ulster Folk & Transport Museum** you can relive town and country life in the early 1900s. And in summer 2009 the **Ulster Museum** re-opens after major redevelopment: be among the first to view its newly presented art, history and sciences collections.

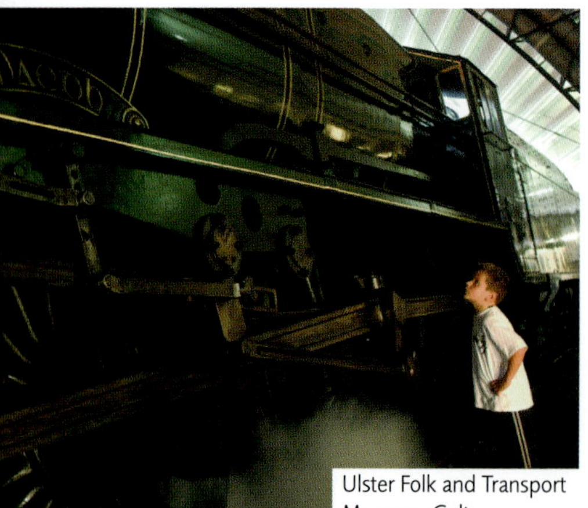

Ulster Folk and Transport Museum, Cultra

For a break from history, take the kids to **Belfast Zoo** – the rare red pandas and Barbary lions are sure-fire favourites. Then have a few peaceful hours wandering the glorious **Botanic Gardens and Queen's University**. Hungry yet? Tuck into local goodies like Champ and Irish stew, or have a gourmet treat in a top restaurant.

## Drive of your life

Up the tempo now, fasten your seat belts and set off for the drive of your life. The 80-mile **Causeway Coastal Route** from Belfast to Londonderry, also known as the Walled City of Derry, is rated as one of the world's Top Five Road Trips. Just look at the kaleidoscope of landscapes to see why: dramatic cliffs, nine green glacier-cut glens and heather-covered mountains all cascading by. Head along the north east coast to pretty villages like Cushendun and Bushmills. Discover some of the most picturesque parts of North Antrim near Ballintoy. Do you think nature or the giant Finn McCool created the amazing geometric columns of the **Giant's Causeway**? What happened on the stormy night in 1639 when part of **Dunluce Castle** (limited

Left to right: Sperrin Mountains, County Tyrone; Ulster American Folk Park, County Tyrone

**why not...** visit Tyrone Crystal and let the designers create a unique piece for you?

wheelchair access) fell into the sea? You'll still be talking about it all when you're relaxing on the beautiful beach at **Downhill**.

## Within these walls

Londonderry, also referred to as the **Walled City of Derry**, is one of the best-preserved walled cities in Europe. So where better to start exploring than with a stroll along the 400-year-old fortifications? Built to protect the new Plantation town from marauding Irish clans, they're 26 feet high in places and were never breached. Stop along the way to admire original cannons and sights like the Neo-Gothic Guildhall. Then drop into the old town to browse atmospheric streets, shops and pubs.

Learn more about the past at **The Workhouse Museum** (second floor access restricted) where exhibitions on the Great Irish Famine 1840-49 reveal the harshness of Victorian life. Or blow away the cobwebs, and learn about Derry's tumultuous history and vibrant present on a walking tour, open top bus tour, taxi tour or river cruise.

Whiterocks, Portrush, County Antrim

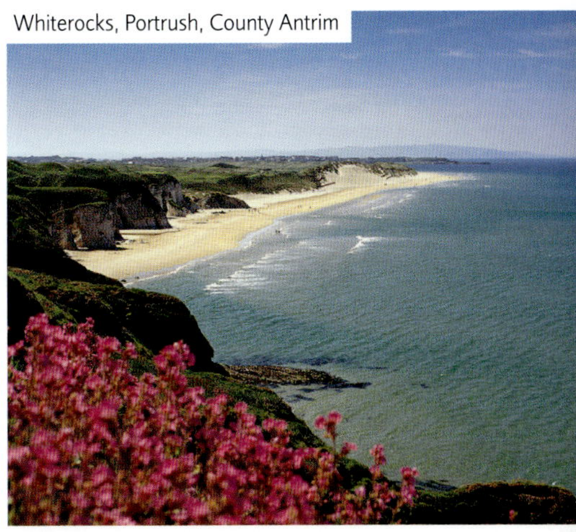

## North West adventure

Get some fresh air in the heather-coloured **Sperrin Mountains** straddling Counties Londonderry and Tyrone in the north west of the country. Follow one of the scenic driving routes available from Sperrins Tourism (download them free from sperrinstourism.com).

The **An Creagán Visitor Centre** at the mountain's foot tells the story behind the landscapes, Celtic culture and traditions. Find more outdoor fun at **Roe Valley Country Park**. Discover the park's wildlife on the specially designed accessible trail (audio guide available). Take your time, let nature set the pace.

Step indoors for a while to peruse the treasures of **The Argory**, a 19th-century Irish gentry house at Moy. There is ramped access to the ground floor only and a brochure available for those unable to visit the first floor. Climb aboard an emigrant ship at **Ulster American Folk Park** (most external exhibits are accessible), Omagh, and learn about Northern Ireland's rich links to the USA.

## Enchanted lakelands

Mystery and magnificence await you around the **Fermanagh** lakelands in the south west. Sense the spirits of the Celtic tribe that settled these shores as you view the enigmatic pagan stone idols of **Boa Island**. Wander the twin lakes of Lough Erne and catch the ferry from Trory to **Devenish Island** to be inspired by the monastic site originally founded by St Molaise in the sixth century (paths on the island are quite

Clockwise: Devenish Island, County Fermanagh; Belleek Pottery, County Fermanagh; Florence Court, County Fermanagh

steep). Go bat watching at the **Crom Estate**, one of Northern Ireland's most important conservation areas – the grounds are partly accessible by wheelchair and there is a courtesy PMV available (booking essential). Compare the man-made magnificence of stately homes – 18th-century **Florence Court** and **Tully Castle**, or take your own treasures home, from **Belleek Pottery**.

## St Patrick's country

Follow in the steps of Ireland's patron saint. Patrick is most closely associated with the lovely countryside around **Armagh** and **Downpatrick** in the south east.

**did you know...** it's claimed the Mourne Mountains inspired CS Lewis's Kingdom of Narnia?

He founded Armagh, Ireland's ecclesiastical capital – find out more about his life in the fascinating interactive *Armagh Story* at the **Saint Patrick's Trian Visitor Complex**. Trace his living heritage in the city's two cathedrals and, before you leave, visit **Armagh Planetarium** for a gaze into the heavens. Then make a pilgrimage to St Patrick's Grave at **Down Cathedral**. If you can, come in March and experience countrywide **St Patrick's Day Celebrations**.

Patrick seldom ventured into the **Mountains of Mourne**, but you should to enjoy one of Ireland's most scenic areas. **Mount Stewart House** is another must, with its famous gardens flourishing in the sub-tropical micro-climate.

# Useful national contacts

**Northern Ireland Tourist Board**
**t** (028) 9024 6609
**w** discovernorthernireland.com

**Belfast Visitor and Convention Bureau**
**t** (028) 9024 6609
**e** welcomecentre@belfastvisitor.com
**w** gotobelfast.com

**Causeway Coast and Glens Tourism Partnership**
**t** (028) 7032 7720
**e** mail@causewaycoastandglens.com
**w** causewaycoastandglens.com

**Derry Visitor and Convention Bureau**
**t** (028) 7126 7284
**e** info@derryvisitor.com
**w** derryvisitor.com

**Sperrin Tourism Limited**
**t** (028) 8674 7700
**e** info@sperrinstourism.com
**w** sperrinstourism.com

**Fermanagh Lakelands Tourism**
**t** (028) 6632 3110
**e** info@fermanaghlakelands.com
**w** fermanaghlakelands.com

**Armagh and Down Tourism Partnership**
**t** (028) 9182 2881
**e** info@armaghanddown.com
**w** armaghanddown.com

## Publications

### Northern Ireland Tourist Board

A range of free guides are available to order online from discovernorthernireland.com or by calling (028) 9023 1221, including the Northern Ireland Visitor Guide and Uniquely Northern Ireland.

## Information

### Disability Action

**t** (028) 9029 7880
**t** (028) 9029 7882 (textphone)
**e** hq@disabilityaction.org
**w** disabilityaction.org

### Disability Sports NI

**t** (028) 9050 8255
**w** dsni.co.uk
Fishing, horseriding, water-skiing and lots more from Disability Sports NI.

### Share Holiday Village

**t** (028) 6772 2122
**w** sharevillage.org
A holiday village for disabled visitors, friends and family.

### ADAPT

**t** (028) 9023 1211
**t** (028) 9023 4391 (textphone)
**e** info@adaptni.org
**w** adaptni.org
Aim is to promote improved access to arts, community, heritage and leisure venues in Northern Ireland, check on the link 'Access 400' for a list of accessible venues.

# Tourist Information Centres

## Belfast

| | | | |
|---|---|---|---|
| **Belfast Welcome Centre (Belfast and Northern Ireland)** | 47 Donegall Place | (028) 9024 6609 | welcomecentre@belfastvisitor.com |
| **Belfast International Airport** | Arrivals Hall | (028) 9448 4677 | welcomecentre@belfastvisitor.com |
| **George Best Belfast City Airport** | Sydenham Bypass | (028) 9093 5372 | welcomecentre@belfastvisitor.com |

## Elsewhere in Northern Ireland

| | | | |
|---|---|---|---|
| **Antrim** | 16 High Street | (028) 9442 8331 | info@antrim.gov.uk |
| **Armagh** | 40 English Street | (028) 3752 1800 | tic@armagh.gov.uk |
| **Ballycastle** | 7 Mary Street | (028) 2076 2024 | tourism@moyle-council.org |
| **Ballymena** | 1-29 Bridge Street | (028) 2563 5900 | tourist.information@ballymena.gov.uk |
| **Ballymoney** | 1 Townhead Street | (028) 2766 0230 | touristinfo@ballymoney.gov.uk |
| **Banbridge** | The Outlet, Bridgewater Park | (028) 4062 3322/ (028) 4062 9054 | tic@banbridge.gov.uk |
| **Bangor** | Tower House, Quay St | (028) 9127 0069 | tic@northdown.gov.uk |
| **Carrickfergus** | 11 Antrim Street | (028) 9335 8049 | touristinfo@carrickfergus.org |
| **Coleraine** | Railway Road | (028) 7034 4723 | info@northcoastni.com |
| **Cookstown** | The Burnavon, Burn Rd | (028) 8676 9949 | tic@cookstown.gov.uk |
| **Downpatrick** | The Saint Patrick Centre | (028) 4461 2233 | downpatrick.tic@downdc.gov.uk |
| **Enniskillen** | Wellington Road | (028) 6632 3110 | tic@fermanagh.gov.uk |
| **Giant's Causeway** | 44 Causeway Road | (028) 2073 1855 | info@giantscausewaycentre.com |
| **Hillsborough** | The Courthouse | (028) 9268 9717 | tic.hillsborough@lisburn.gov.uk |
| **Kilkeel** | The Nautilus Centre | (028) 4176 2525 | kdakilkeel@hotmail.com |
| **Killymaddy** | 190 Ballygawley Road | (028) 8776 7259 | killymaddy.reception@dungannon.gov.uk |
| **Larne** | Narrow Gauge Road | (028) 2826 0088 | larnetourism@btconnect.com |
| **Limavady** | 7 Connell Street | (028) 7776 0307 | tourism@limavady.gov.uk |
| **Lisburn** | 15 Lisburn Square | (028) 9266 0038 | tic.lisburn@lisburn.gov.uk |
| **Londonderry** | 44 Foyle Street | (028) 7126 7284 | info@derryvisitor.com |
| **Magherafelt** | The Bridewell | (028) 7963 1510 | thebridewell@magherafelt.gov.uk |
| **Newcastle** | 10-14 Central Promenade | (028) 4372 2222 | newcastle.tic@downdc.gov.uk |
| **Newry** | Bagenal's Castle | (028) 3031 3170 | newrytic@newryandmourne.gov.uk |
| **Newtownards** | 31 Regent Street | (028) 9182 6846 | tourism@ards-council.gov.uk |
| **Omagh** | Strule Arts Centre | (028) 8224 7831 | info@omagh.gov.uk |
| **Portaferry*** | The Stables, Castle Street | (028) 4272 9882 | tourism.portaferry@ards-council.gov.uk |
| **Portrush*** | Dunluce Centre, Sandhill Drive | (028) 7082 3333 | portrushtic@btconnect.com |
| **Strabane** | Alley Arts & Conference Centre | (028) 7138 4444 | tic@strabanedc.com |

*seasonal opening

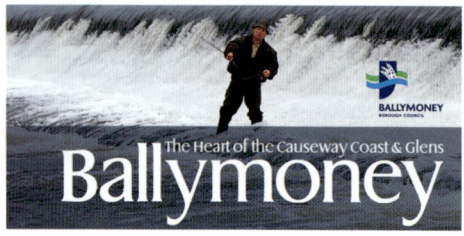

Mount Stewart House, County Down

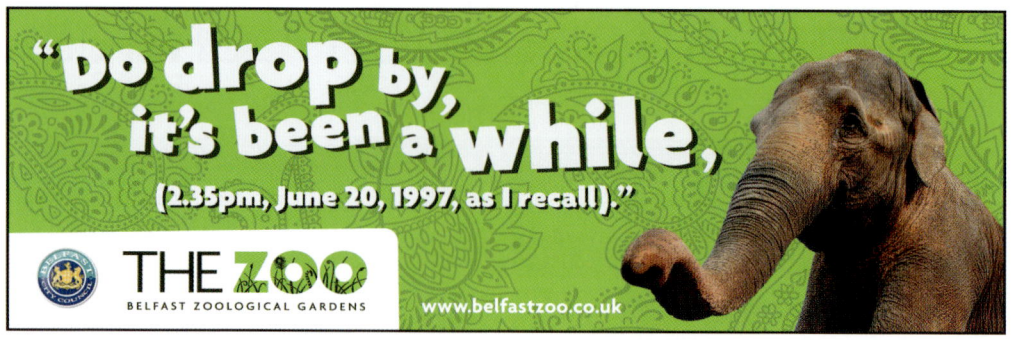

## Accessibility in Northern Ireland

We do not feature accommodation in this section because the Northern Ireland Tourist Board does not currently operate an accessible scheme under which to assess accommodation and attractions. However, most Northern Ireland museums and visitor centres have first-class access.

# Further information

Clockwise from above: Big Ben, London; Eilean Donan Castle, Scotland; Caernarfon Castle, Wales

# National organisations

## National tourism organisations

### Caravanable

43 Playfield Road, Kennington, Oxford, OX1 5RS
**t** (01865) 739653
**e** info@caravanable.co.uk
**w** caravanable.co.uk

The website provides details of caravan sites in the UK which have the minimum requirements for disabled people of a shower, basin and toilet with ramped access, or more. The sites have all been recommended by other campers and caravan users. It is advisable to contact the park owners before making your booking. There is also a section on accessible beaches in the UK.

### Disabled Holiday Information

PO Box 186, Oswestry, Shropshire SY10 1AF
**e** info@disabledholidayinfo.org.uk
**w** disabledholidayinfo.org.uk

An organisation providing holiday information for people with disabilities including wheelchair accessible visitor attractions, activities and accommodation.

### Disabled Ramblers

c/o 14 Belmont Park Road, Maidenhead, Berkshire SL6 6HT
**t** (01628) 621414
**e** chairman@disabledramblers.co.uk
**w** disabledrambers.co.uk

An organisation with a programme of one- and two-day supported rambles in a variety of settings mainly for users of mobility vehicles including wheelchairs, scooters and buggies.

### English Heritage

Customer Services Department, PO Box 570, Swindon, Wiltshire SN2 2YP
**t** 0870 333 1181
**t** 0800 015 0516 (textphone)
**e** customers@english-heritage.org.uk
**w** english-heritage.org.uk

English Heritage manage sites of historical interest, including around 400 properties that are open to visitors. It produces an *Access Guide* giving information on access, parking and available services, such as audio tours, tactile exhibitions and sensory gardens. The guide is available online, or from customer services in different formats.

For information on Historic Scotland, see page 307. For information on Cadw: Welsh Historic Monuments, see page 354.

## Holidays for All

Tourism for All c/o Vistalise
Shap Road Industrial Estate, Shap Road
Kendal, Cumbria LA9 6NZ
**t** 0845 124 9971
**e** info@tourismforall.org.uk
**w** holidaysforall.org.uk

Holidays for All is a consortium of disability organisations offering accommodation and holidays for people with disabilities. For a brochure, contact Tourism for All (see page 20).

## National Caravan Council

Catherine House, Victoria Road,
Aldershot GU11 1SS
**e** info@nationalcaravan.co.uk
**w** nationalcaravan.co.uk

The representative trade body for the UK caravan industry. You can search their website of caravan sites for 'disabled access'.

## National Federation of Shopmobility UK

PO Box 6641, Christchurch BH23 9DQ
**t** 0845 644 2446
**e** info@shopmobilityuk.org
**w** shopmobilityuk.org

NFSUK is the national body for UK-wide Shopmobility schemes which hire out manual and powered wheelchairs and scooters to people with mobility impairments for shopping and visits to leisure and commercial facilities. Some schemes are free and some make a charge; all welcome donations. You do not have to be registered disabled to use a scheme and, with advance notice, many schemes can arrange an escort around their locality. Ask for a copy of the NFSUK Directory or check the website for the online version.

## National Trust

The National Trust, PO Box 39,
Warrington WA5 7WD
**t** 0844 800 1895
**t** 0844 800 4410 (textphone)
**e** enquiries@thenationaltrust.org.uk
**w** nationaltrust.org.uk

For Admit One card, links pass and access enquiries contact:
The National Trust Access for All Office, Heelis, Kemble Drive,
Swindon SN2 2NA
**t** (01793) 817400
**e** accessforall@nationaltrust.org.uk

The National Trust welcomes all visitors to its properties. It produces a free booklet *The National Trust Access Guide* which contains details of access to properties throughout the country. The booklet is also available online.

For information on the National Trust for Scotland, see page 307.

# National voluntary organisations offering assistance

## British Red Cross

44 Moorfields, London EC2Y 9AL
**t** 0844 412 2804
**e** information@redcross.org.uk
**w** redcross.org.uk

Some county branches will advise on, or even help arrange, holidays, and have members willing to accompany you on holiday. Look in the phone book for your local Red Cross branch or visit the website.

## Carers Information

Carers Association Southern Staffordshire, The Carers Centre, Austin Friars, Stafford ST17 4AP
**t** 01785 606675
**e** info@carersinformation.org.uk
**w** carersinformation.org.uk

A website providing up to date information and resources on caring for people at home, to help both informal carers and professionals who work with them.

## Carers UK

20-25 Glasshouse Yard, London EC1A 4JT
**t** 0808 808 7777 (CarersLine freephone, Weds and Thurs 10am-12pm and 2-4pm)
**e** info@ukcarers.org
**w** carersuk.org

A campaigning organisation with a free advice line for carers, staffed by welfare rights, community care and benefit advisers. It has a UK-wide network of offices, branches and individuals offering support to carers.

## DIAL UK

St Catherine's, Tickhill Road, Doncaster DN4 8QN
**t** (01302) 310123
**e** informationenquiries@dialuk.org.uk
**w** dialuk.info

A national network of approximately 120 local disability advice services run by and for disabled people. For local branch contact details, visit the website.

## Disabled Living Foundation

380-384 Harrow Road, London, W9 2HU
**t** (020) 7289 6111
**t** 0845 130 9177 (helpline)
**t** (020) 7432 8009 (textphone)
**e** advice@dlf.org.uk
**w** dlf.org.uk

A national charity providing impartial information and advice on disability equipment and suppliers. It provides free fact sheets on a variety of equipment and related topics. You can visit the equipment demonstration centre by appointment.

## Help With ME

**t** (0131) 556 8144
**w** helpwithme.com
Help With ME is a support site which supplies adaptive technology products to help people with Myalgic Encephalomyelitis/Chronic Fatigue Syndrome (ME/CFS).

## Jubilee Sailing Trust

Hazel Road, Woolston, Southampton SO19 7GB
**t** (023) 8044 9108
**e** info@jst.org.uk
**w** jst.org.uk

A charity enabling both able-bodied and disabled people to sail on two tall ships, Lord Nelson and Tenacious.

## MENCAP

Mencap National Centre, 123 Golden Lane, London EC1Y 0RT
**t** (020) 7454 0454
**t** 0808 808 1111 (helpline)
**e** help@mencap.org.uk
**w** mencap.org.uk

The society provides support to people with a learning disability and their carers and families through its national network. Contact the helpline for a copy of their holiday grant and holiday information factsheet.

### New Jumbulance Travel Trust

Delaport Coach House, Lamer Lane, Wheathampstead, St Albans AL4 8RQ
**t** (01582) 831 4444
**e** njtt@clara.co.uk
**w** jumbulance.org.uk
Jumbulance have a fleet of adapted coaches enabling severely disabled, sick and dependent elderly people to travel on holiday and take day trips.

### RADAR

12 City Forum, 250 City Road, London EC1V 8AF
**t** (020) 7250 3222
**t** (020) 7250 4119 (minicom)
**e** radar@radar.org.uk
**w** radar.org.uk

A national organisation working with and for disabled people. It produces a number of publications, including *Holidays in Britain and Ireland*.

### Royal National Institute for the Blind (RNIB)

105 Judd Street, London WC1H 9NE
**t** (020) 7388 1266
**t** 0845 766 9999 (helpline)
**t** 0845 702 3153 (Customer Services)
**e** helpline@rnib.org.uk
**w** rnib.org.uk

The RNIB promotes equal opportunities in leisure for people with visual impairments. It produces information sheets on the arts and heritage, sport and recreation, music, broadcasting and holidays. Their customer services offer products, advice and publications, including a guide to hotels recommended by blind or visually impaired people.

### Royal Society for the Protection of Birds UK (RSPB)

The Lodge, Potton Road,
Sandy, Bedfordshire
SG19 2DL
**t** (01767) 680551
**w** rspb.org.uk

The RSPB produces leaflets for visitors with disabilities or visit their website for information on accessible reserves and facilities.

### SCOPE

Scope Response, PO Box 833, Milton Keynes MK12 5NY
**t** 0808 800 3333
**t** 18001 0808 800 3333 (textphone)
**e** response@scope.org.
**w** scope.org.uk

Scope is a national disability charity focussing on cerebral palsy. It provides in-depth information and advice on all aspects of cerebral palsy and disability issues. The Helpline is open from 9am-7pm weekdays and 10am-2pm on Saturday.

# Getting around Britain

To help you on your way contact the organisations listed below and refer to the sections on travelling by rail, car, coach and air.

For comprehensive advice on all forms of travel in the UK see the Department of Transport's Door to Door website **dptac.gov.uk/door-to-door**.

### The Automobile Association (AA)

Member Administration Contact Centre, Lambert House Stockport Road, Cheadle SK8 2DY
**t** 0870 600 0371
**t** 0800 262 050 (disability helpline)
**t** 0800 328 2810 (textphone)
**w** theaa.com

The AA's disability helpline provides advice to members on mobility issues, including home touring and route requests, motorway service area facilities, wheelchair maintenance and driving schools. Written information also available.

### Directenquiries

Direct Enquiries Ltd, Amber House, Market Street, Bracknell, Berkshire RG12 1JB
**t** (01344) 360101
**e** customerservices@directenquiries.com
**w** directenquiries.com

Directenquiries has online information on a range of businesses with accessible facilities, and includes detailed information on the London Underground and on the National Key Scheme for accessible toilets.

### The Disabled Motorcyclists Association

Ada House, 77 Thompson Street, Manchester M4 5FY
**t** (0161) 833 8817
**w** thedma.org.uk

The Disabled Motorcyclists Association supports disabled people who wish to try motorcycling, or return to it, by offering discounts, member services, a magazine and guidance.

### Eurotunnel

UK Passenger Terminal, Ashford Road, Folkestone Kent CT18 8XX
**t** 0870 535 3535 (call centre)
**t** 0800 096 9992 (information line)
**w** eurotunnel.com

Eurotunnel operates the Channel tunnel car shuttle. Book via telephone or online. Terminals in the UK and France are accessible. Eurotunnel now has a special lane for disabled passengers checking in. Passengers with disabilities are requested to alert check-in staff to ensure assistance if an evacuation is necessary.

## Forum of Mobility Centres

Providence Chapel, Warehorne, Ashford, Kent TN26 2JX

**t** 0800 5593636

**e** mobility@rcht.cornwall.nhs.uk

**w** mobility-centres.org.uk

A UK-wide network of 17 independent organisations offering car adaptation information, advice and assessment.

## Gatwick Travel-Care

Room 3014B Village Level, South Terminal, Gatwick Airport, Gatwick RH6 0NP

**t** (01293) 504283

**e** travel.care@btconnect.com

Gatwick Travel-Care offer information, advice and practical help. The office is open weekdays from 9am-5pm.

## Green Flag Group

Green Flag Motoring Assistance, 2 Eldridge Road, Croydon, Surrey CR9 1AG

**t** 0845 246 1557

**t** 0800 800 610 (textphone)

**w** greenflag.com

Green Flag can recover specially modified road vehicles and disabled drivers, from anywhere in the UK.

## Heathrow Travel-Care

Room 1308 Queens Building, Heathrow Airport, Hounslow, Middlesex TW6 1B6

**t** (020) 8745 7495

**t** (020) 8745 7565 (minicom)

**e** heathrow_travel_care@baa.com

Provides 24-hour information, advice and counselling for people using facilities at Heathrow. There is a meet and assist service for passengers with special needs available via the office (9am-5pm Monday to Friday), Heathrow information desks, or by phoning (020) 8745 6011.

## Mobilise

Mobilise Organisation, National Headquarters, Ashwellthorpe, Norwich NR16 1EX

**t** (01508) 489449

**e** enquiries@mobilise.info

**w** mobilise.info

Offers transport information to its members on a number of travel services including ferries, RAC membership and parking.

## Newick Packers

Unit 7, Gatwick Metro Centre, Balcombe Road, Horley RH6 9GA

**t** (01293) 772473

**e** enquiries@newickpackers.com

**w** http://homepage.ntlworld.com/paul.neilson/newick

Provides a service for packing fully-sealed electric wheelchair batteries for transport by air. Rates vary depending on size, weight and type of battery.

## Transport Direct

**w** transportdirect.info

An online journey planning service for travel by car, train, coach or air. Features also include car park locations, a day trip planner and live travel information.

# Britain at a glance

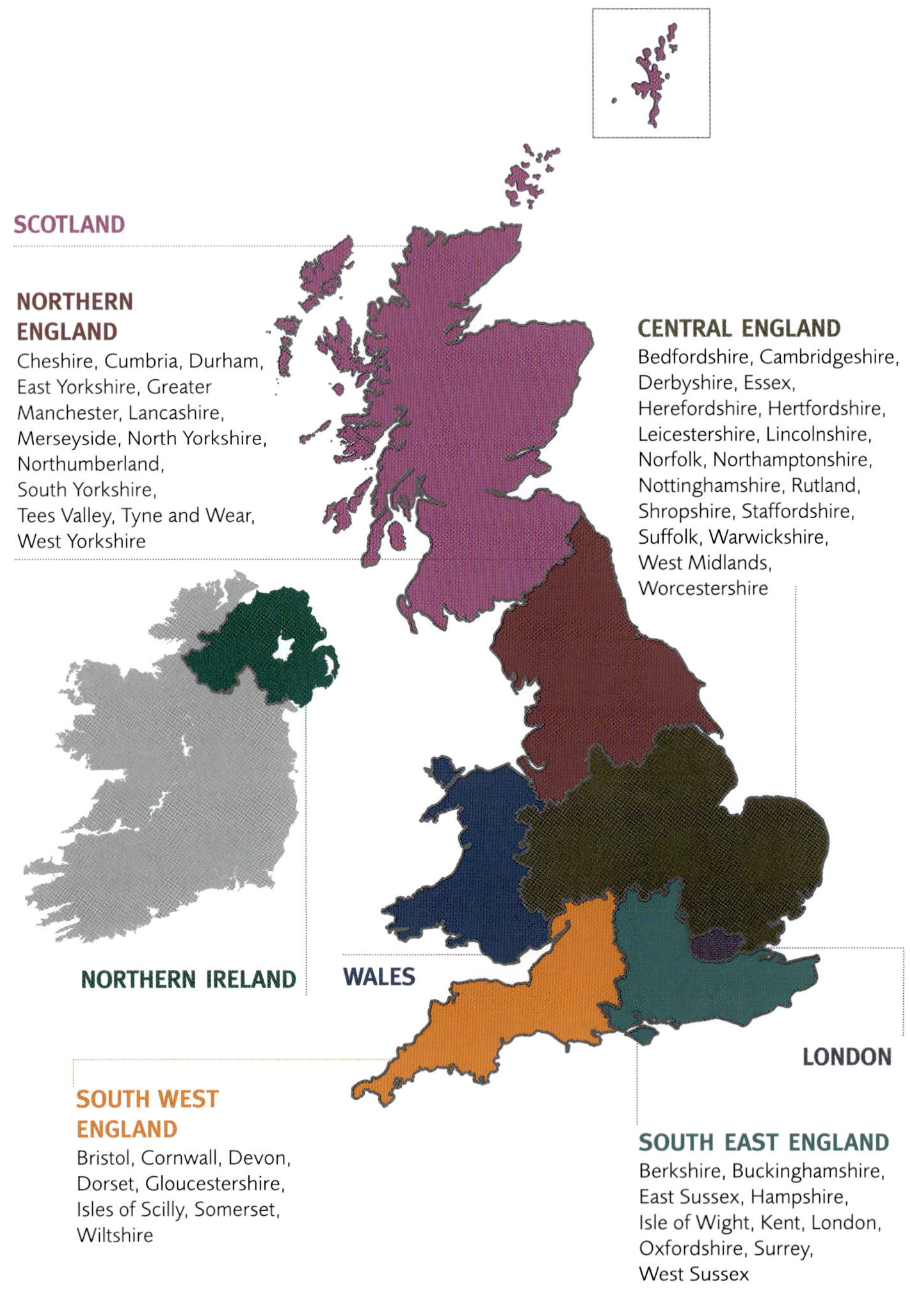
SCOTLAND
NORTHERN ENGLAND
Cheshire, Cumbria, Durham, East Yorkshire, Greater Manchester, Lancashire, Merseyside, North Yorkshire, Northumberland, South Yorkshire, Tees Valley, Tyne and Wear, West Yorkshire
CENTRAL ENGLAND
Bedfordshire, Cambridgeshire, Derbyshire, Essex, Herefordshire, Hertfordshire, Leicestershire, Lincolnshire, Norfolk, Northamptonshire, Nottinghamshire, Rutland, Shropshire, Staffordshire, Suffolk, Warwickshire, West Midlands, Worcestershire
NORTHERN IRELAND
WALES
LONDON
SOUTH WEST ENGLAND
Bristol, Cornwall, Devon, Dorset, Gloucestershire, Isles of Scilly, Somerset, Wiltshire
SOUTH EAST ENGLAND
Berkshire, Buckinghamshire, East Sussex, Hampshire, Isle of Wight, Kent, London, Oxfordshire, Surrey, West Sussex

# A guide to English counties

If you know what English county you wish to visit you'll find it in the regional section shown below.

| County | Region |
|---|---|
| Bedfordshire | Central England |
| Berkshire | South East England |
| Bristol | South West England |
| Buckinghamshire | South East England |
| Cambridgeshire | Central England |
| Cheshire | Northern England |
| Cornwall | South West England |
| Cumbria | Northern England |
| Derbyshire | Central England |
| Devon | South West England |
| Dorset | South West England |
| Durham | Northern England |
| East Yorkshire | Northern England |
| East Sussex | South East England |
| Essex | Central England |
| Gloucestershire | South West England |
| Greater Manchester | Northern England |
| Hampshire | South East England |
| Herefordshire | Central England |
| Hertfordshire | Central England |
| Isle of Wight | South East England |
| Isles of Scilly | South West England |
| Kent | South East England |
| Lancashire | Northern England |

| County | Region |
|---|---|
| Leicestershire | Central England |
| Lincolnshire | Central England |
| Merseyside | Northern England |
| Norfolk | Central England |
| North Yorkshire | Northern England |
| Northamptonshire | Central England |
| Northumberland | Northern England |
| Nottinghamshire | Central England |
| Oxfordshire | South East England |
| Rutland | Central England |
| Shropshire | Central England |
| Somerset | South West England |
| South Yorkshire | Northern England |
| Staffordshire | Central England |
| Suffolk | Central England |
| Surrey | South East England |
| Tees Valley | Northern England |
| Tyne and Wear | Northern England |
| Warwickshire | Central England |
| West Midlands | Central England |
| West Sussex | South East England |
| West Yorkshire | Northern England |
| Wiltshire | South West England |
| Worcestershire | Central England |

To help readers we do not refer to unitary authorities in this guide.

# Travel by rail

National Rail (the train companies) produce *Rail Travel for Disabled Passengers*, a booklet giving details of the minimum level of service that you can expect throughout Britain's rail network and how to request assistance with a rail journey. The booklet is available from most staffed railway station ticket offices, Citizen's Advice Bureaux, some libraries and, in case of difficulty, a copy can be requested from the Disabled Persons Railcard Office address, below.

UK residents with disabilities are entitled to purchase a Disabled Persons Railcard, which allows you to buy discounted rail tickets (generally one third off) with the same discount for an accompanying carer. For qualifying and application details visit the website at disabledpersons-railcard.co.uk, call the application helpline on 0845 605 0525 or textphone 0845 601 0132, or write to Disabled Persons Railcard Office, PO Box 163, Newcastle-Upon-Tyne NE12 8WX.

For advice on planning your journey, or for contact details of your local train company, please telephone National Rail Enquiries on 08457 48 49 50 (textphone 0845 60 50 600) for assistance.

## Assistance on trains

Most of train operators publish guides for disabled passengers, giving details about their route and the facilities available at the stations they use. Assistance can be arranged for you at your departure, destination and connecting stations should you need to change trains.

## Useful tips

To ensure the best service, it is essential that you communicate your travel requirements at least 24 hours before you travel. If you are unable to give adequate notice, staff will help you as much as possible but they cannot guarantee to provide the normal level of service.

- So that you can be met by station staff, inform the train operator how you will travel to and from the mainline stations.
- Check whether you need to change train during your journey. If you do, ensure that station staff have been notified so that you can be assisted from one train to the other.
- Let the station know if you will need to borrow a wheelchair.
- Tell staff whether you are travelling alone or with a companion.

- If you have booked your journey in advance, train companies will help if your journey is disrupted, or if you have any other problems. If you do not book in advance, they will still help where possible. Train companies will give a refund if they cannot provide the arrangements you booked in advance.

## Britrail Pass

If you live abroad and plan to visit Britain, the BritRail Pass gives the freedom to travel on all National Rail services. Ask for details from your travel agent before leaving. BritRail Passes can normally be bought from travel agents outside Britain or by visiting the BritRail website, britrail.com.

## Useful contacts

| | | | |
|---|---|---|---|
| **National Rail Enquiries** | nationalrail.co.uk | 0845 748 4950<br>0845 605 0600 | <br>(textphone) |
| **Train operating companies** | rail.co.uk | | |
| **The Trainline** | trainline.co.uk | | |
| **Arriva Trains** | arrivatrainswales.co.uk | 0845 606 1660<br>0845 300 3005<br>0845 605 0600 | <br>(assisted travel)<br>(textphone) |
| **c2c** | c2c-online.co.uk | 0845 601 4873<br>(01702) 357640<br>0845 712 5988 | <br>(assisted travel)<br>(textphone) |
| **Chiltern Railways** | chilternrailways.co.uk | 0845 600 5165<br>0845 707 8051 | <br>(textphone) |
| **CrossCountry** | crosscountrytrains.co.uk | 0870 010 0084<br>0844 811 0125<br>0844 811 0126 | <br>(assisted travel)<br>(textphone) |
| **East Midlands Trains** | eastmidlandstrains.co.uk | 0845 712 5678<br>18001 0845 712 5678 | <br>(textphone) |
| **Eurostar** | eurostar.com | 0870 518 6186* | |
| **First Capital Connect** | firstcapitalconnect.co.uk | 0845 026 4700<br>0800 058 2844<br>0800 975 1052 | <br>(assisted travel)<br>(textphone) |
| **First Great Western** | firstgreatwestern.co.uk | 0845 700 0125<br>0800 197 1329<br>0800 294 9209 | <br>(assisted travel)<br>(textphone) |
| **First ScotRail** | firstgroup.com/scotrail | 0845 601 5929<br>0800 912 2901<br>0800 912 2899 | <br>(assisted travel)<br>(textphone) |
| **Gatwick Express** | gatwickexpress.co.uk | 0845 850 1530 | |
| **Heathrow Connect** | heathrowconnect.com | 0845 678 6975 | |
| **Heathrow Express** | heathrowexpress.com | 0845 600 1515 | |

*Phone numbers listed are for general enquiries unless otherwise stated.*
**Booking line only.*

| | | | |
|---|---|---|---|
| **Hull Trains** | hulltrains.co.uk | 0845 071 0222 | |
| **Island Line** | island-line.co.uk | 0845 600 0650 | |
| | | 0800 692 0792 | (textphone) |
| **London Midland** | londonmidland.com | 0844 811 0133 | |
| | | 0800 092 4260 | (assisted travel) |
| | | 0845 707 8051 | (textphone) |
| **Merseyrail** | merseyrail.org | 0151 702 2534 | |
| | | (0151) 702 2071 | (textphone available) |
| **National Express East Anglia** | nationalexpress eastanglia.com | 0845 600 7245 | |
| **National Express East Coast** | nationalexpress eastcoast.com | 0845 722 5333 | |
| | | 0845 722 5225 | (assisted travel) |
| | | 0845 120 2067 | (textphone) |
| **Northern Rail** | northernrail.org | 0845 000 0125 | |
| | | 0845 600 8008 | (assisted travel) |
| | | 0845 604 5608 | (textphone) |
| **South Eastern Trains** | southeasternrailway.co.uk | 0845 000 2222 | |
| | | 0800 783 4524 | (assisted travel) |
| | | 0800 783 4548 | (textphone) |
| **South West Trains** | southwesttrains.co.uk | 0845 600 0650 | |
| | | 0800 528 2100 | (assisted travel) |
| | | 0800 692 0792 | (textphone) |
| **Southern** | southernrailway.com | 0845 127 2920 | |
| | | 0800 138 1016 | (assisted travel) |
| | | 0800 138 1018 | (textphone) |
| **Stansted Express** | stanstedexpress.com | 0845 600 7245 | |
| **Translink** | nirailways.co.uk | (028) 9066 6630 | |
| | | 18001 028 9038 7505 | (textphone) |
| **Transpennine Express** | tpexpress.co.uk | 0845 600 1671 | |
| | | 0800 107 2149 | (assisted travel) |
| | | 0845 600 1673 | (textphone) |
| **Virgin Trains** | virgintrains.co.uk | 0845 722 2333* | |
| | | 0845 744 3366 | (assisted travel) |
| | | 0845 744 3367 | (textphone) |

*Phone numbers listed are for general enquiries unless otherwise stated.*
**Booking line only.*

# Travel by car

For information on driving, visit dptac.gov.uk/door-to-door/04/02.htm.

## Parking

The Blue Badge scheme provides a range of parking benefits for disabled people who travel either as drivers or as passengers. The scheme operates throughout the UK. There are Blue Badge parking bays in 64 towns and cities across the UK. For information visit parkingforbluebadges.com.

Some Central London boroughs, including City of London, Westminster, Kensington, Chelsea and Camden, are regulated differently. They generally issue a special parking permit, which restricts mobility around the capital. For more information, contact the Association of Local Government Transport, New Zealand House, 80 Haymarket, London SW1Y 4TG or telephone (020) 7747 4767.

If you are travelling from abroad and are a member of a disabled badge scheme, check whether your badge is valid in the UK with the issuing authority. Although there are no reciprocal arrangements between Britain and the USA, most places (with the exception of Central London) will honour the US sticker, providing the car is safely parked.

## Essential documents

If you are travelling from abroad ask the Automobile Association (AA) what documents you will need. Call their disability helpline on 0800 262 050.

## Breakdown assistance

The Green Flag Group offers a recovery service for modified vehicles and disabled drivers. See page 385 for contact details.

| Car hire companies | | |
|---|---|---|
| **Alamo** | alamo.co.uk | 0870 400 4562* |
| **Avis** | avis.co.uk | 0844 581 0147* |
| **Budget** | budget.co.uk | 0844 581 9998 |
| **Easycar** | easycar.com | 0906 333 3333 |
| **Enterprise** | enterprise.co.uk | 0870 350 3000* |
| **Hertz** | hertz.co.uk | 0870 844 8844* |
| **National** | nationalcar.co.uk | 0870 400 4581 |
| **Wheelchair Travel** | wheelchair-travel.co.uk | (01483) 233640 |

*Cars with special features are not common and need to be requested well in advance.*
**Booking line only.*

# Travel by coach

## National Express customer support

Disabled Persons Travel Helpline, P.O. Box 9854, Birmingham B16 8XN

**t** 0871 781 8179 (assisted travel helpline is option 3)
**t** (0121) 455 0086 (textphone)
**e** DPTH@nationalexpress.com
**w** nationalexpress.com

It is advisable to contact National Express at least 24 hours in advance of travel to discuss available assistance. Lightweight wheelchairs (weighing less than 20kg) are accepted, but heavier wheelchairs, powered wheelchairs and scooters cannot be carried. Service dogs are accepted and travellers requiring oxygen may carry supplies in hand held bottles. Contact the Disabled Persons Travel Helpline for a copy of their information leaflet (also available in large print or audio format).

## Sixt Rent a Car (Sixt Kenning Ltd)

Durrant House, 47 Holywell Street, Chesterfield S41 7SJ

**t** (01246) 220111
**w** sixt.co.uk

Sixt has wheelchair-accessible minibuses available nationally at over 80 of their branches with short- and long-term rates.

## Victoria Coach Station

164 Buckingham Palace Road, London SW1 9TP

**t** (020) 7824 0000
**w** tfl.gov.uk/gettingaround/1210.aspx

Operates a mobility assistance service 10am-6pm which can be booked 24 hours in advance by telephone or online. The station is fully accessible including the toilets. There is a help point in the station.

## Wheelchair Travel

1 Johnston Green, Guildford, Surrey GU2 9XS

**t** (01483) 233640
**e** info@wheelchair-travel.co.uk
**w** wheelchair-travel.co.uk

Hires out accessible mini-vans and hand controlled cars throughout the country and can provide airport transfers, city tours, wheelchair-accessible taxis, chauffeurs and guides.

# Travel by air

If you have special travel requirements, it is important to notify the airline when you book, and advisable to re-check that these have been noted a day or so before travel.

Display your Blue Badge at airport car parks, for a discounted rate at both short- and long-stay car parks. If you are a non-European visitor, you will not be eligible for discounted parking rates and may sometimes be required to pay a long-stay fee regardless of the length of your stay. We recommend you check at the airport before travelling.

For further advice, see the Door to Door website at dptac.gov.uk/door-to-door/06/index.htm. Alternatively, ask DPTAC (Disabled Persons Transport Advisory Committee) for a copy of their Access to Air Travel guidance by calling (020) 7944 8011 or textphone (020) 7944 3277.

The consumer body, Air Transport Users Council, also offers advice. Contact them at Room K705, CAA House, 45-59 Kingsway, London WC2B 6TB, telephone (020) 7240 6061 or visit caa.co.uk/auc.

## Useful contacts

| | | |
|---|---|---|
| **Air Southwest** | airsouthwest.com | 0870 043 4553 |
| **Blue Islands** (Channel Islands) | blueislands.com | 0845 620 2122 |
| **BMI** | flybmi.com | 0870 607 0555 |
| **BMI Baby** | bmibaby.com | 0871 224 0224 |
| **British Airways** | britishairways.com | 0844 493 0787*<br>0845 700 7706 (textphone) |
| **British International**<br>(Isles of Scilly to Penzance) | islesofscillyhelicopter.com | (01736) 363871* |
| **Eastern Airways** | easternairways.com | 0870 366 9100 * |
| **Easyjet** | easyjet.com | 0871 244 2366 |
| **Flybe** | flybe.com | 0871 700 2000* |
| **Jet2.com** | jet2.com | 0871 226 1737* |
| **Ryanair** | ryanair.com | 0871 246 0000 |
| **Skybus** (Isles of Scilly) | islesofscilly-travel.co.uk | 0845 710 5555 |
| **VLM** | flyvlm.com | 0871 666 5050 |

**Booking line only.*

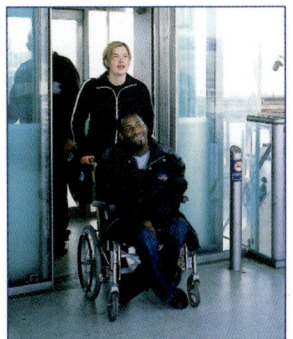

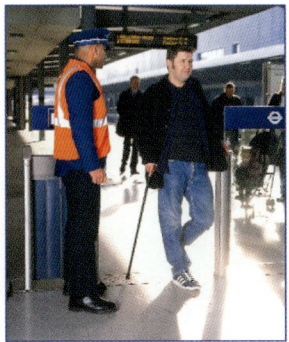

# Quality assessment schemes

When you're looking for a place to stay, you need a rating system you can trust. Quality ratings are your clear guide to what to expect, in an easy-to-understand form.

National tourist board professional assessors pay unannounced visits to establishments that are new to the rating scheme and stay overnight where appropriate. Once in the scheme establishments receive an annual pre-arranged day visit, with an overnight stay generally every other year for hotel and bed and breakfast accommodation. On these occasions the assessors book in anonymously, and test all the facilities and services.

Based on internationally recognised star ratings, the system puts great emphasis on quality, and reflects exactly what consumers are looking for. Ratings are awarded from one to five stars – the more stars, the higher the quality and the greater the range of facilities and services provided – and are the sign of quality assurance, giving you the confidence to book the accommodation that meets your expectations.

Look out, too, for Enjoy England Gold and Silver Awards, which are awarded to hotels and bed and breakfast accommodation in England achieving the highest levels of quality within their star rating. While the overall rating is based on a combination of facilities and quality, the Gold and Silver Awards are based solely on quality.

## Hotels

All hotels that are awarded a star rating will meet the minimum standards – so you can be confident that you will find the basic services, such as:

- All bedrooms with an en suite or private bathroom
- A designated reception facility and staff members who will be available during the day and evening (24hrs in case of an emergency)
- A licence to serve alcohol (unless a temperance hotel)
- Access to the hotel at all times for registered guests
- Dinner available at least five days a week (with the exception of a Town House Hotel or Metro Hotel)
- All statutory obligations will be met.

Hotels have to provide certain additional facilities and services at the higher star levels, some of which may be important to you:

### TWO-STAR hotels must provide:

- Dinner seven nights a week.

### THREE-STAR hotels must provide:

- All en suite bedrooms (ie no private bathrooms)

- Direct dial phones in all rooms
- Room service during core hours
- A permanently staffed reception.

### FOUR-STAR hotels must provide:

- 24-hour room service
- 50% of all en suites with bath **and** shower.

### FIVE-STAR hotels must provide:

- Some permanent suites
- Enhanced services, such as concierge.

Sometimes a hotel with a lower star rating has exceptional bedrooms and bathrooms and offers its guests a very special welcome, but cannot achieve a higher rating because, for example, it does not offer dinner every evening (two star), room service (three star) or does not have the minimum 50% of bathrooms with bath and shower (four star).

## Bed and breakfast accommodation

All bed and breakfast accommodation that is awarded a star rating will meet the minimum standards – so you can be confident that you will find the basic services that you would expect, such as:

- A clear explanation of booking charges, services offered and cancellation terms
- A full cooked breakfast or substantial continental breakfast
- At least one bathroom or shower room for every six guests
- For a stay of more than one night, rooms cleaned and beds made daily
- Printed advice on how to summon emergency assistance at night
- All statutory obligations will be met.

Proprietors of bed and breakfast accommodation have to provide certain additional facilities and services at the higher star levels, some of which may be important to you:

### THREE-STAR accommodation must provide:

- Private bathroom/shower room (cannot be shared with the owners)
- Bedrooms must have a washbasin if not en suite.

### FOUR-STAR accommodation must provide:

- 50% of bedrooms en suite or with private bathroom.

### FIVE-STAR accommodation must provide:

- All bedrooms with en suite or private bathroom.

Sometimes a bed and breakfast establishment has exceptional bedrooms and bathrooms and offers guests a very special welcome, but cannot achieve a higher star rating because, for example, there are no en suite bedrooms, or it is difficult to put washbasins in the bedrooms (three star). This is sometimes the case with period properties.

## Quality in hotels and bed and breakfast accommodation

The availability of additional services and facilities alone is not enough for an establishment to achieve a higher star rating. Hotels and bed and breakfast accommodation have to meet exacting standards for quality in critical areas. Consumer research has shown the critical areas to be: cleanliness, bedrooms, bathrooms, hospitality and services, and food.

## Self-catering accommodation

All self-catering accommodation that is awarded a star rating will meet the minimum standards – so you can be confident that you will find the basic services that you would expect, such as:

- Clear information prior to booking on all aspects of the accommodation including location, facilities, prices, deposit, policies on smoking, children etc
- No shared facilities, with the exception of a laundry room in multi-unit sites
- All appliances and furnishings will meet product safety standards for self-catering accommodation, particularly regarding fire safety
- At least one smoke alarm in the unit and a fire blanket in the kitchen
- Clear information on emergency procedures, including who to contact
- Contact details for the local doctor, dentist etc
- All statutory obligations will be met including an annual gas check and public liability insurance.

Certain additional facilities and services are required at the higher star levels, some of which may be important to you:

### TWO-STAR accommodation must provide:

- Single beds which are a minimum of 3ft wide and double beds a minimum of 4ft 6in.

### THREE-STAR accommodation must provide:

- Bed linen (with or without additional charge).

### FOUR-STAR accommodation must provide:

- All advertised sleeping space in bedrooms (unless a studio)
- Bed linen included in the hire charge and beds are made up for arrival.

### FIVE-STAR accommodation must provide:

- Full-size beds, including those for children
- At least two of the following items: tumble-dryer, telephone, Hi-Fi, video, DVD.

Some self-catering establishments offer a choice of units that may have different ratings. In this case, the entry shows the range available.

## Quality in self-catering accommodation

The availability of additional facilities, such as a dishwasher or DVD, is not enough to achieve a higher star rating – the quality of the furnishings, equipment and decoration must be of a high standard. Self-catering accommodation with a lower star rating may offer some or all of the above, but to achieve the higher star ratings, the overall quality score has to be reached and exacting standards have to be met in critical areas. Consumer research has shown these to be: cleanliness, bedrooms, bathrooms, kitchens and public areas.

## Holiday, touring and camping parks

Holiday, touring and camping parks are assessed under the British Graded Holiday Parks Scheme. Operated jointly by the national tourist boards for England, Scotland, Wales and Northern Ireland, it was devised in association with the British Holiday and Home Parks Association and the National Caravan Council. It gives you a clear guide of what to expect in an easy-to-understand form.

The process to arrive at a star rating is very thorough to ensure that when you make a booking you can be confident it will meet your expectations. Professional assessors visit parks annually and take into account over 50 separate aspects, from landscaping and layout to maintenance, customer care and, most importantly, cleanliness.

Strict guidelines are in place to ensure that every park is assessed to the same criteria. A random check is made of a sample of accommodation provided for hire (caravans, chalets etc) **but the quality of the accommodation itself is not included in the grading assessment**.

In addition to The British Graded Holiday Parks Scheme, VisitBritain operates a rating scheme for Holiday Villages. The assessor stays on the site overnight and grades the overall quality of the visitor experience, including accommodation, facilities, cleanliness, service and food.

Parks are required to meet progressively higher standards of quality as they move up the scale from one to five stars:

### ONE STAR Acceptable

To achieve this grade, the park must be clean with good standards of maintenance and customer care.

### TWO STAR Good

All the above points plus an improved level of landscaping, lighting, refuse disposal and maintenance. May be less expensive than more highly rated parks.

### THREE STAR Very good

Most parks fall within this category; three stars represent the industry standard. The range of facilities provided may vary from park to park, but they will be of a very good standard and will be well maintained.

### FOUR STAR Excellent

You can expect careful attention to detail in the provision of all services and facilities. Four star parks rank among the industry's best.

### FIVE STAR Exceptional

Highest levels of customer care will be provided. All facilities will be maintained in pristine condition in attractive surroundings.

## Holiday villages

Holiday Villages are assessed under a separate rating scheme and are awarded one to five stars based on both the quality of facilities and the range of services provided. The option to include breakfast and dinner is normally available. A variety of accommodation if offered, mostly in chalets.

★ Simple, practical, no frills
★★ Well presented and well run
★★★ Good level of quality and comfort
★★★★ Very good standard throughout
★★★★★ Excellent facilities and services

# Accommodation advice and information

## Making a booking

When enquiring about accommodation, make sure you check prices, the quality rating and other important details. You will also need to state your requirements clearly and precisely, for example:

- Arrival and departure dates, with acceptable alternatives if appropriate
- Accessible requirements
- The type of accommodation you need – for example, room with twin beds, en suite bathroom
- The terms you want – for example, room only, bed and breakfast
- The age of any children with you, whether you want them to share your room or be next door, and any other special requirements, such as a cot
- Any particular requirements you may have, such as a special diet, ground-floor room.

## Confirmation

Misunderstandings can easily happen over the telephone, so do request a written confirmation, together with details of any terms and conditions.

## Deposits

If you make a hotel or bed and breakfast reservation weeks or months in advance, you will probably be asked for a deposit, which will then be deducted from the final bill when you leave. The amount will vary from establishment to establishment and could be payment in full at peak times.

Proprietors of self-catering accommodation will normally ask you to pay a deposit immediately, and then to pay the full balance before your holiday date. This safeguards the proprietor in case you decide to cancel at a late stage or simply do not turn up. He or she may have turned down other bookings on the strength of yours and may find it hard to re-let if you cancel.

In the case of caravan, camping and touring parks, and holiday villages the full charge often has to be paid in advance. This may be in two instalments – a deposit at the time of booking and the balance by, say, two weeks before the start of the booked period.

## Payment on arrival

Some establishments, especially large hotels in big towns, ask you to pay for your room on arrival if you have not booked it in advance. This is especially likely to happen if you arrive late and have little or no luggage.

If you are asked to pay on arrival, it is a good idea to see your room first, to make sure it meets your requirements.

## Cancellations

### Legal contract

When you accept accommodation that is offered to you, by telephone or in writing, you enter a legally binding contract with the proprietor. This means that if you cancel your booking, fail to take up the accommodation or leave early, the proprietor may be entitled to compensation if he or she cannot re-let for all or a good part of the booked period. You will probably forfeit any deposit you have paid, and may well be asked for an additional payment.

At the time of booking you should be advised of what charges would be made in the event of cancelling the accommodation or leaving early. If this is not mentioned you should ask so that future disputes can be avoided. The proprietor cannot make a claim until after the booked period, and during that time he or she should make every effort to re-let the accommodation. If there is a dispute it is sensible for both sides to seek legal advice on the matter. If you do have to change your travel plans, it is in your own interests to let the proprietor know in writing as soon as possible, to give them a chance to re-let your accommodation.

And remember, if you book by telephone and are asked for your credit card number, you should check whether the proprietor intends charging your credit card account should you later cancel your reservation. A proprietor should not be able to charge your credit card account with a cancellation fee unless he or she has made this clear at the time of your booking and you have agreed. However, to avoid later disputes, we suggest you check whether this is the intention.

## Insurance

A travel or holiday insurance policy will safeguard you if you have to cancel or change your holiday plans. You can arrange a policy quite cheaply through your insurance company or travel agent. Some hotels also offer their own insurance schemes and many self-catering agencies insist their customers take out a policy when they book their holidays.

## Arrival time

If you know you will be arriving late in the evening, it is a good idea to say so when you book. If you are delayed on your way, a telephone call to say that you will be late would be appreciated.

It is particularily important to liaise with the owner of self-catering accommodation about key collection as he or she will not necessarily be on site.

## Service charges and tipping

These days many places levy service charges automatically. If they do, they must clearly say so in their offer of accommodation, at the time of booking. The service charge then becomes part of the legal contract when you accept the offer of accommodation.

If a service charge is levied automatically, there is no need to tip the staff, unless they provide some exceptional service. The usual tip for meals is 10% of the total bill.

## Telephone charges

Establishments can set their own charges for telephone calls made through their switchboard or from direct-dial telephones in bedrooms. These charges are often much higher than telephone companies' standard charges (to defray the cost of providing the service).

## Comparing costs

It is a condition of the quality assessment schemes that an establishment's unit charges are on display by the telephones or with the room information. It is not always easy to compare these charges with standard rates, so before using a telephone for long-distance calls, you may decide to ask how the charges compare.

## Security of valuables

You can deposit your valuables with the proprietor or manager during your stay, and we recommend you do this as a sensible precaution. Make sure you obtain a receipt for them. Some places do not accept articles for safe custody, and in that case it is wisest to keep your valuables with you.

## Disclaimer

Some proprietors put up a notice that disclaims liability for property brought on to their premises by a guest. In fact, they can only restrict their liability. By law, a proprietor is liable for the value of the loss or damage to any property (except a car or its contents) of a guest who has engaged overnight accommodation, but if the proprietor has the notice on display, liability is limited to £50 for one article and a total of £100 for any one guest. The notice must be prominently displayed in the reception area or main entrance. These limits do not apply to valuables you have deposited with the proprietor for safekeeping, or to property lost through the default, neglect or wilful act of the proprietor or his staff.

## Finding a camping or touring park

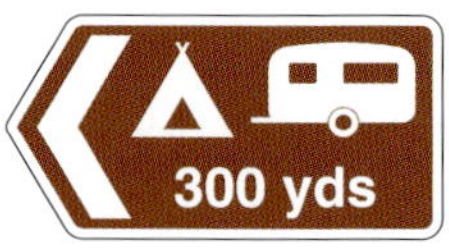


Tourist signs similar to the one shown here are designed to help visitors find their park. They clearly show whether the park is for tents or caravans or both.

Tourist information centres throughout Britain are able to give campers and caravanners information about parks in their areas. Some tourist information centres have camping and caravanning advisory services that provide details of park availability and often assist with park booking.

## Electric hook-up points

Most parks now have electric hook-up points for caravans and tents. Voltage is generally 240v AC, 50 cycles. Parks may charge extra for this facility, and it is advisable to check rates when making a booking.

## Travelling with pets

Dogs, cats, ferrets and some other pet mammals can be brought into the UK from certain countries without having to undertake six months' quarantine on arrival provided they meet all the rules of the Pet Travel Scheme (PETS).

For full details, visit the PETS website at
**w** defra.gov.uk/animalh/quarantine/index.htm or contact the PETS Helpline
**t** +44 (0) 870 241 1710
**e** quarantine@animalhealth.gsi.gov.uk

Ask for fact sheets which cover dogs and cats, ferrets or domestic rabbits and rodents.

## What to expect

### Hotels, guest and self-catering accommodation, holiday villages

The proprietor/management is required to undertake the following:

- To maintain standards of guest care, cleanliness and service appropriate to the type of establishment;
- To describe accurately in any advertisement, brochure or other printed or electronic media, the facilities and services provided;
- To make clear to visitors exactly what is included in all prices quoted for accommodation, including taxes, and any other surcharges. Details of charges for additional services/facilities should also be made clear;
- To give a clear statement of the policy on cancellations to guests at the time of booking ie by telephone, fax, email, as well as information given in a printed format;
- To adhere to and not to exceed prices quoted at the time of booking for accommodation and other services;
- To advise visitors at the time of booking, and subsequently if any change, if the accommodation offered is in an unconnected annexe or similar and to indicate the location of such accommodation and any difference in comfort and/or amenities from accommodation in the establishment;
- To register all guests on arrival (except self-catering accommodation);
- To give each visitor on request details of payments due and a receipt, if required;
- To deal promptly and courteously with all enquiries, requests, bookings and correspondence from visitors;
- To ensure complaint handling procedures are in place and that complaints received are investigated promptly and courteously and that the outcome is communicated to the visitor;
- To give due consideration to the requirements of visitors with disabilities and visitors with special needs, and to make suitable provision where applicable;
- To provide public liability insurance or comparable arrangements and to comply with all applicable planning, safety and other statutory requirements;
- To allow a quality ratings assessor reasonable access to the establishment on request, to confirm the Code of Conduct is being observed.

## What to expect

### Holiday, touring and camping parks

In addition to fulfilling its statutory obligations, including having applied for a certificate under the Fire Precautions Act 1971 (if applicable) and holding public liability insurance, and ensuring that all caravan holiday homes/chalets for hire and the park and all buildings and facilities thereon, the fixtures, furnishings, fittings and decor are maintained in sound and clean condition and are fit for the purposes intended, the management is required to undertake the following:

- To ensure high standards of courtesy, cleanliness, catering and service appropriate to the type of park;

- To describe to all visitors and prospective visitors the amenities, facilities and services provided by the park and/or caravan holiday homes/chalets whether by advertisement, brochure, word of mouth or other means;
- To allow visitors to see the park or caravan holiday homes/chalets for hire, if requested, before booking;
- To present grading awards and/or any other national tourist board awards unambiguously;
- To make clear to visitors exactly what is included in prices quoted for the park or caravan holiday homes/chalets, meals and refreshments, including service charge, taxes and other surcharges. Details of charges, if any, for heating or for additional services or facilities available should also be made clear;
- To adhere to, and not to exceed, prices current at time of occupation for caravan holiday homes/chalets or other services;
- To advise visitors at the time of booking, and subsequently if any change, if the caravan holiday home/chalet or pitch offered is in a different location or on another park, and to indicate the location of this and any difference in comfort and amenities;
- To give each visitor, on request, details of payments due and a receipt if required;
- To advise visitors at the time of booking of the charges that might be incurred if the booking is subsequently cancelled;
- To register all guests on arrival;
- To deal promptly and courteously with all visitors and prospective visitors, including enquiries, requests, reservations, correspondence and complaints;
- To allow a national tourist board representative reasonable access to the park and/or caravan holiday homes/chalet whether by prior appointment or on an unannounced assessment, to confirm that the VisitBritain Code of Conduct is being observed and that the appropriate quality standard is being maintained;
- The operator must comply with the provision of the caravan industry Codes of Practice.

## Comments and complaints

### The law

Places that offer accommodation have legal and statutory responsibilities to their customers, such as providing information about prices, providing adequate fire precautions and safeguarding valuables. They must also describe their accommodation and facilities accurately. All the places featured in this guide have declared that they do fulfil all applicable statutory obligations.

### Information

The proprietors themselves supply the descriptions of their establishments and other information for the entries, (except national tourist board ratings and awards). The publishers cannot guarantee the accuracy of information in this guide, and accept no responsibility for any error or misrepresentation.

All liability for loss, disappointment, negligence or other damage caused by reliance on the information contained in this guide, or in the event of bankruptcy or liquidation or cessation of trade of any company, individual or firm mentioned, is hereby excluded. We strongly recommend that you carefully check prices and other details when you book your accommodation.

### Quality signage

All establishments displaying a quality sign have to hold current membership of a quality assessment scheme. When an establishment is sold the new owner has to reapply and be reassessed. In some areas the rating may be carried forward in the interim.

### Problems

Of course, we hope you will not have cause for complaint, but problems do occur from time to time.
If you are dissatisfied with anything, make your complaint to the management immediately. Then the management can take action at once to investigate the matter and put things right. The longer you leave a complaint, the harder it is to deal with it effectively.

In certain circumstances, the national tourist boards may look into complaints. However they have no statutory control over establishments or their methods of operating and cannot become involved in legal or contractual matters, nor can they get involved in seeking financial recompense.

If you do have problems that have not been resolved by the proprietor and which you would like to bring to our attention, please write to:

**England**
Quality in Tourism, Farncombe House, Broadway, Worcestershire WR12 7LJ

**London**
Visitor Services Advisor, Visit London, 6th Floor, 2 More London Riverside, London SE1 2RR
**e** listen@visitlondon.com

**Scotland**
Customer Feedback Department, VisitScotland, Quality and Standards, Cowan House, Inverness Retail and Business Park, Inverness
IV2 7GF

**Wales**
VisitWales, Ty Glyndwr, Treowain Enterprise Park, Machynlleth, Powys SY20 8WW

# About the accommodation entries

## Entries

All the establishments and parks featured in this guide have been assessed or have applied for assessment under a quality assessment scheme.

Proprietors with either a standard entry (includes description, facilities and prices) or enhanced entry (photograph and extended details) have paid to have their establishment featured.

## Locations

Places to stay are generally listed under the town, city or village where they are located. If a place is in a small village, you may find it listed under a nearby town (providing it is within a seven-mile radius).

Place names are listed alphabetically within each regional section of the guide, along with the name of the ceremonial county they are in and their map reference.

Complete addresses for self-catering properties are not given and the town(s) listed may be a distance from the actual establishment. Please check the precise location at the time of booking.

## Map references

These refer to the colour location maps at the front of the guide. The first figure shown is the map number, the following letter and figure indicate the grid reference on the map. Some entries were included just before the guide went to press, so they do not appear on the maps.

## Addresses

County names, which appear in the place headings, are not repeated in the entries. When you are writing, you should of course make sure you use the full address and postcode.

## Telephone numbers

Telephone numbers, listed below the accommodation address for each entry. Area codes are shown in brackets.

## Prices

The prices shown are only a general guide; they were supplied to us by proprietors in summer 2008. Remember, changes may occur after the guide goes to press, so we strongly advise you to check prices when you book your accommodation.

Prices are shown in pounds sterling and include VAT where applicable. Some places also include a service charge in their standard tariff, so check this when you book.

**Bed and breakfast**: the prices shown are per room for overnight accommodation with breakfast. The double room price is for two people. (If a double room is occupied by one person there is sometimes a reduction in price.)

**Half board**: the prices shown are per person per night for room, evening meal and breakfast. These prices are usually based on two people sharing a room.

**Evening meal**: the prices shown are per person per night.

Some places only provide a continental breakfast in the set price, and you may have to pay extra if you want a full cooked breakfast.

According to the law, establishments with at least four bedrooms or eight beds must display their overnight accommodation charges in the reception area or entrance. In your own interests, do make sure you check prices and what they include.

**Self catering**: prices shown are per unit per week and include VAT.

**Touring pitches:** prices are based on the minimum and maximum charges for one night for two persons, car and either caravan or tent. (Some parks may charge separately for car, caravan or tent, and for each person and there may be an extra charge for caravan awnings.)

**Caravan holiday homes:** minimum and maximum prices are given per week.

### Children's rates

You will find that many places charge a reduced rate for children, especially if they share a room with their parents. Some places charge the full rate, however, when a child occupies a room which might otherwise have been let to an adult. The upper age limit for reductions for children varies from one establishment to another, so check this when you book.

### Seasonal packages and special promotions

Prices often vary through the year and may be significantly lower outside peak holiday weeks. Many places offer special package rates – fully inclusive weekend breaks, for example – in the autumn, winter and spring. A number of establishments taking an enhanced entry have included any special offers, themed breaks etc that are available.

You can get details of other bargain packages that may be available from the establishments themselves, regional tourism organisations or your local Tourist Information Centre (TIC). Your local travel agent may also have information and can help you make reservations.

## Bathrooms

### (hotels and bed and breakfast)

Each accommodation entry shows you the number of en suite and private bathrooms available. En suite bathroom means the bath or shower and wc are contained behind the main door of the bedroom. Private bathroom means a bath or shower and wc solely for the occupants of one bedroom, on the same floor, reasonably close and with a key provided. If the availability of a bath, rather than a shower, is important to you, remember to check when you book.

## Meals

### (hotels and bed and breakfast)

It is advisable to check availability of meals and set times when making your reservation. Some smaller places may ask you at breakfast whether you want an evening meal. The prices shown in each entry are for bed and breakfast or half board, but many places also offer lunch.

## Opening period

If an entry does not indicate an opening period, please check directly with the establishment.

## Symbols

The at-a-glance symbols included at the end of each entry show many of the services and facilities available at each establishment. You will find the key to these symbols on page 8.

## Smoking

In the UK, it is illegal to smoke in enclosed public spaces and places of work. This means that smoking is banned in the public and communal areas of hotels, guesthouses and B&Bs, and in restaurants, bars and pubs.

Some hotels, guesthouses and B&Bs may choose to provide designated smoking bedrooms, and B&Bs and guest houses may allow smoking in private areas that are not used by any staff. Smoking may also be allowed in self-contained short-term rental accommodation, such as holiday cottages, flats or caravans, if the owner chooses to allow it.

If you wish to smoke, it is advisable to check whether it is allowed when you book.

## Alcoholic drinks

All hotels (except temperance hotels) hold an alcohol licence. Some bed and breakfast accommodation may also be licensed, however, the licence may be restricted – to diners only, for example. If a bar is available this is shown by the 🍷 symbol.

## Pets

Many places accept guests with dogs, but we do advise that you check this when you book, and ask if there are any extra charges or rules about exactly where your pet is allowed. The acceptance of dogs is not always extended to cats and it is strongly advised that cat owners contact the establishment well in advance. Some establishments do not accept pets at all. Pets are welcome by arrangement where you see this symbol 🐕.

The quarantine laws have changed, and dogs, cats and ferrets are able to come into the UK and the Channel Islands from certain countries. For details of the Pet Travel Scheme (PETS) please turn to page 404.

## Payment accepted

The types of payment accepted by an establishment are listed in the payment accepted section. If you plan to pay by card, check that the establishment will take your particular card before you book. Some proprietors will charge you a higher rate if you pay by credit card rather than cash or cheque. The difference is to cover the percentage paid by the proprietor to the credit card company. When you book by telephone, you may be asked for your credit card number as confirmation. But remember, the proprietor may then charge your credit card account if you cancel your booking. See under Cancellations on page 403.

## Rating Applied For

At the time of going to press some establishments featured in this guide had not yet been assessed and so their new rating could not be included. Rating Applied For indicates this.

# Accessible Scheme index

Establishments participating in accessible schemes are listed below. At the front of the guide you can find information about the different schemes. Establishments listed have a detailed entry in this guide.

## England

### Mobility level 1

## Mobility level 1 continued



## Mobility level 2

## Mobility level 2 continued

| | | |
|---|---|---|
| *Malvern* Central England | **Hidelow House Cottages ★★★★–★★★★★** | 153 |
| *Manningtree* Central England | **Curlews ★★★★** SILVER | 154 |
| *Nayland* Central England | **Gladwins Farm ★★★★★** | 155 |
| *Redditch* Central England | **White Hart Inn ★★★** | 157 |
| *Ross-on-Wye* Central England | **Portland House Guest House ★★★★** | 157 |
| *St Owens Cross* Central England | **Trevase Granary ★★★★★** | 158 |
| *Wisbech* Central England | **Common Right Barns ★★★★** | 161 |
| *Lewes* South East England | **Heath Farm ★★★★** | 198 |
| *Witney* South East England | **Swallows Nest ★★★★** | 201 |
| *Alton Pancras* South West England | **Bookham Court ★★★★–★★★★★** | 256 |
| *Bath* South West England | **The Carfax ★★★★★** | 257 |
| *Beaminster* South West England | **Stable Cottage ★★★★** | 258 |
| *Bratton* South West England | **Woodcombe Lodges ★★★★** | 259 |
| *Langton Herring* South West England | **Character Farm Cottages ★★★★** | 264 |
| *Lydney* South West England | **2 Danby Cottages ★★★** | 266 |
| *Minehead* South West England | **The Promenade** | 282 |
| *Portreath* South West England | **Higher Laity Farm ★★★★★** | 269 |
| *St Austell* South West England | **Owls Reach ★★★★** | 270 |
| *St Just-in-Penwith* South West England | **Swallow's End ★★★★** | 271 |
| *Torquay* South West England | **Atlantis Holiday Apartments ★★★–★★★★** | 274 |
| *Veryan* South West England | **Trenona Farm Holidays ★★★★** | 275 |
| *Wells* South West England | **Double-Gate Farm ★★★★** GOLD | 276 |
| *Wells* South West England | **Swallow Barn ★★★★** | 277 |
| *Yelverton* South West England | **Overcombe House ★★★★** | 280 |

## Mobility level 3 Independent

| | | |
|---|---|---|
| *Henley* Central England | **Damerons Farm Holidays ★★★★** | 148 |
| *Malvern* Central England | **Hidelow House Cottages ★★★★–★★★★★** | 153 |
| *Wigsthorpe* Central England | **Nene Valley Cottages ★★★★★** | 160 |
| *Corfe Castle* South West England | **Mortons House Hotel ★★★** GOLD | 262 |
| *Torquay* South West England | **Crown Lodge ★★★★** | 273 |
| *Wells* South West England | **Double-Gate Farm ★★★★** GOLD | 276 |
| *Wells* South West England | **Swallow Barn ★★★★** | 277 |
| *West Bexington* South West England | **Tamarisk Farm Cottages ★★★–★★★★** | 277 |
| *Weston-super-Mare* South West England | **Royal Hotel ★★★** | 278 |

## Mobility level 3 Assisted

| | | |
|---|---|---|
| *Cockfield* Northern England | **Stonecroft and Swallows Nest ★★★★** | 89 |
| *Cornriggs* Northern England | **Cornriggs Cottages ★★★★★** | 90 |
| *Riccall* Northern England | **South Newlands Farm Self Catering ★★★★** | 103 |
| *Diss* Central England | **Norfolk Cottages – Malthouse Farm ★★★★** | 144 |
| *Norton* South East England | **The Savoy ★★★★** | 199 |
| *Looe* South West England | **Bocaddon Holiday Cottages ★★★★** | 265 |
| *Lostwithiel* South West England | **Brean Park ★★★★★** | 266 |
| *Minehead* South West England | **The Promenade** | 282 |
| *Wells* South West England | **Double-Gate Farm ★★★★** GOLD | 276 |
| *Wells* South West England | **Swallow Barn ★★★★** | 277 |

## Access Exceptional Assisted

| | | |
|---|---|---|
| *Bowness-on-Windermere* Northern England | **Lake District Disabled Holidays ★★★★** | 87 |
| *King's Lynn* Central England | **Park House Hotel ★★** SILVER | 150 |

Establishments listed here have a detailed entry in this guide.

## Hearing impairment level 1



## Visual impairment level 1



# Scotland

## Category 1



## Category 2



## Category 3



# Wales

## Mobility level 1



## Mobility level 2



## Access Statement

# Quick reference index

If you're looking for a specific facility use this index to see at-a-glance detailed accommodation entries that match your requirements.

## Induction loop system at reception



## Level entry shower



Establishments listed here have a detailed entry in this guide.

## Level entry shower continued

## Level entry shower continued



## Hoist available



## Adapted kitchen

## Adapted kitchen continued



## Facilities for service dogs

## Facilities for service dogs continued

Gold and Silver Awards
VisitBritain's unique Gold and Silver Awards recognise exceptional quality in serviced accommodation.
Enjoy England assessors make recommendations for Gold and Silver Awards during assessments in recognition of levels of quality over and above that expected of a particular rating.
Look for the Gold and Silver Awards in the regional sections.
enjoyEngland.com
Gold AWARD
enjoyEngland.com
Silver AWARD

# Index to display advertisers

**All display advertisers are listed below.**

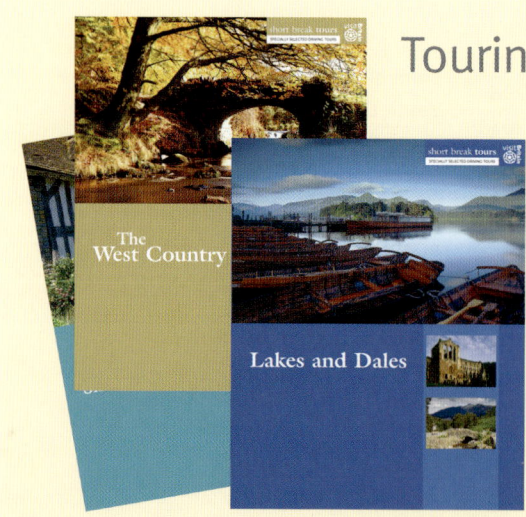

# Index by place name

The following places all have detailed accommodation entries in this guide. If the place where you wish to stay is not shown, the location maps (starting on page 22) will help you find somewhere to stay in the area.

# Index by property name

All accommodation with a detailed entry in this guide is listed below.



Establishments listed here have a detailed entry in this guide.

# Bank holiday dates

| holiday | 2009 | 2010 |
|---|---|---|
| **New Year's Day** | 1 January | 1 January |
| **January Bank Holiday** (Scotland) | 2 January | 4 January |
| **St Patrick's Day** (Northern Ireland) | 17 March | 17 March |
| **Good Friday** | 10 April | 2 April |
| **Easter Monday** (not Scotland) | 13 April | 5 April |
| **Early May Bank Holiday** | 4 May | 3 May |
| **Spring Bank Holiday** | 25 May | 31 May |
| **Battle of the Boyne Orangemen's Day** (Northern Ireland) | 13 July | 12 July |
| **Summer Bank Holiday** (Scotland) | 3 August | 2 August |
| **Summer Bank Holiday** (not Scotland) | 31 August | 30 August |
| **St Andrews Day*** (Scotland) | 30 November | 30 November |
| **Christmas Day Holiday** | 25 December | 27 December |
| **Boxing Day Holiday** | 28 December | 28 December |

*(a voluntary public holiday)

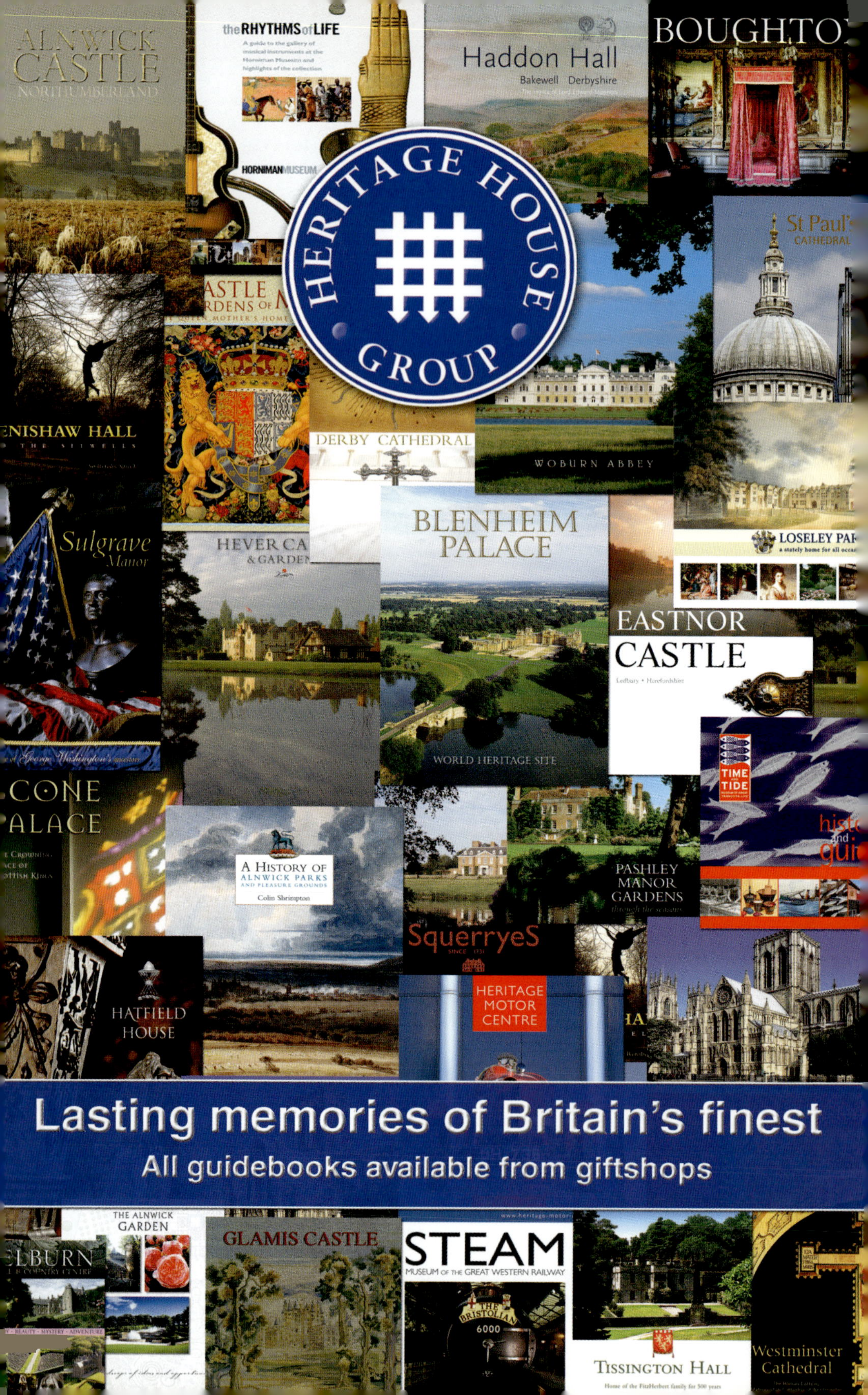
ALNWICK CASTLE
NORTHUMBERLAND
the RHYTHMS of LIFE
HORNIMAN MUSEUM
Haddon Hall
Bakewell Derbyshire
BOUGHTO
HERITAGE HOUSE GROUP
St Paul's
CATHEDRAL
RENISHAW HALL
DERBY CATHEDRAL
WOBURN ABBEY
Sulgrave
Manor
HEVER CA
& GARDEN
BLENHEIM
PALACE
WORLD HERITAGE SITE
LOSELEY PA
EASTNOR
CASTLE
Ledbury • Herefordshire
TIME and TIDE
A HISTORY OF
ALNWICK PARKS
AND PLEASURE GROUNDS
Colin Shrimpton
PASHLEY
MANOR
GARDENS
SquerryeS
HATFIELD
HOUSE
HERITAGE
MOTOR
CENTRE
Lasting memories of Britain's finest
All guidebooks available from giftshops
THE ALNWICK
GARDEN
GLAMIS CASTLE
STEAM
MUSEUM OF THE GREAT WESTERN RAILWAY
THE BRISTOLIAN
6000
TISSINGTON HALL
Westminster
Cathedral

**Published by:** Tourism for All UK, c/o Vitalise, Shap Road Industrial Estate, Kendal LA9 6NT and VisitBritain, Thames Tower, Blacks Road, London W6 9EL in partnership with Britain's tourism industry visitbritain.com
Publishing Manager: Jenifer Littman
Production Manager: Iris Buckley
Compilation, design, copywriting, production and advertisement sales: Jackson Lowe, 3 St Andrews Place, Southover Road, Lewes, East Sussex BN7 1UP
t (01273) 487487 jacksonlowe.com
Cover design: Jamieson Eley and Nick McCann
Typesetting: Marlinzo Services, Somerset and Jackson Lowe
Maps: Based on digital map data © ESR Cartography, 2008
Printing and binding: 1010 Printing International Ltd, China

**Front cover:** Lulworth Cove, Dorset; Ellwood Cottages, Woolland, Dorset (britainonview/Pawel Libera)
**Back cover (from top):** Double-gate Farm, Wells, Somerset; Ellwood Cottages, Woolland, Dorset (britainonview/Pawel Libera)

**Photography credits:** © Crown copyright (2008) Visit Wales; britainonview/David Angel/Daniel Bosworth/Martin Brent/Caravan Club/East Midlands Tourism/Rod Edwards/ Klaus Hagmeier/Adrian Houston/Pawel Libera/McCormick-McAdam/Eric Nathan/David Noton/Tony Pleavin/Grant Pritchard/Olivier Roques-Ro/Jon Spaull/Thanet District Council/Juliet White/Jennie Woodcock/Worcestershire County Council; Iris Buckley; The Deep; Denbies Wine Estate; Len Grant; Northern Ireland Tourist Board; One NorthEast Tourism; RAF Cosford; P Tomkins/VisitScotland/Scottishviewpoint; visitlondonimages/britainonview; VisitScotland/Scottishviewpoint


ISBN 978-0-7095-8455-1

**A VisitBritain Publishing guide**